RISE OF THE BLACK PANTHER

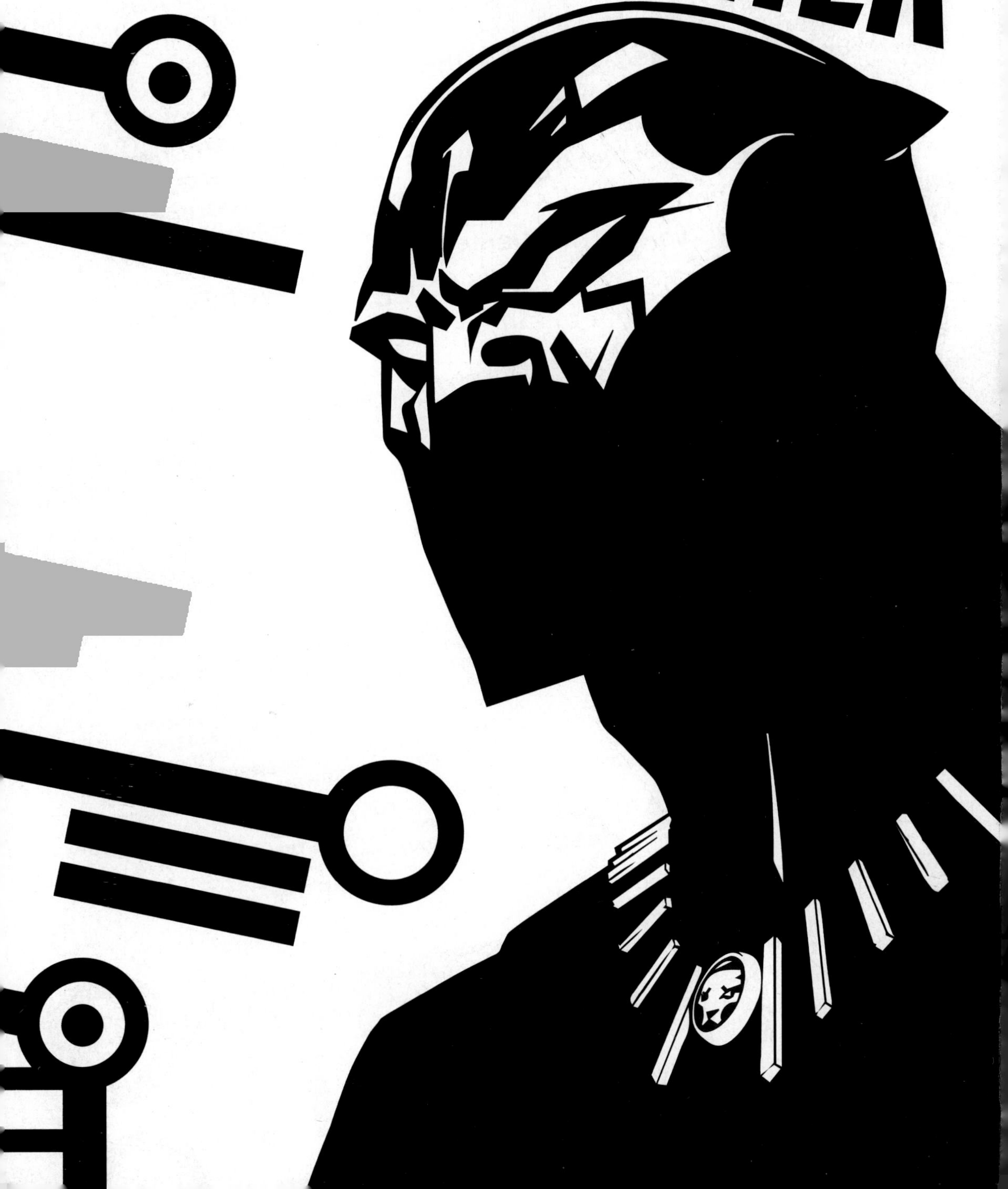

Since time immemorial, a lineage of fierce warrior kings have protected the African country of Wakanda. Theirs was the title of Black Panther, a mantle of spiritual and political leadership handed down for generations.

Thanks to the Black Panthers, the country has remained hidden, uncolonized and unconquered for untold centuries. Wakanda is home to secret technological advancements and contains the Great Sacred Mound of Vibranium, a source of a rare, ultra-durable metal that absorbs energy and vibration.

Many have sought to conquer Wakanda. All have failed. No king has ever died at the hands of outsiders...

BLACK PANTHER CREATED BY **STAN LEE** & **JACK KIRBY**

COLLECTION EDITOR/**JENNIFER GRÜNWALD**
ASSISTANT EDITOR/**CAITLIN O'CONNELL**
ASSOCIATE MANAGING EDITOR/**KATERI WOODY**
EDITOR, SPECIAL PROJECTS/**MARK D. BEAZLEY**
VP PRODUCTION & SPECIAL PROJECTS/**JEFF YOUNGQUIST**
SVP PRINT, SALES & MARKETING/**DAVID GABRIEL**
BOOK DESIGNERS/**JAY BOWEN** & **MANNY MEDEROS**

EDITOR IN CHIEF/**C.B. CEBULSKI**
CHIEF CREATIVE OFFICER/**JOE QUESADA**
PRESIDENT/**DAN BUCKLEY**
EXECUTIVE PRODUCER/**ALAN FINE**

RISE OF THE BLACK PANTHER

Writer/**Evan Narcisse**

Consultant/**Ta-Nehisi Coates**

Artists/**Paul Renaud** (#1, #3)
& Javier Pina (#2, #4-6)
with **Edgar Salazar & Keith Champagne** (#5)

Color Artist/**Stéphane Paitreau**
with **Morry Hollowell** (#6)

Cover Art/**Brian Stelfreeze**

Letterer/**VC's Joe Sabino**

Logo/**Rian Hughes**

Associate Editor/**Sarah Brunstad**

Editor/**Wil Moss**

RISE OF THE BLACK PANTHER. Contains material originally published in magazine form as RISE OF THE BLACK PANTHER #1-6. First printing 2018. ISBN 978-1-302-90884-3. Published by MARVEL WORLDWIDE, INC., a subsidiary of MARVEL ENTERTAINMENT, LLC. OFFICE OF PUBLICATION: 135 West 50th Street, New York, NY 10020. Copyright © 2018 MARVEL. No similarity between any of the names, characters, persons, and/or institutions in this magazine with those of any living or dead person or institution is intended, and any such similarity which may exist is purely coincidental. **Printed in Canada.** DAN BUCKLEY, President, Marvel Entertainment; JOHN NEE, Publisher; JOE QUESADA, Chief Creative Officer; TOM BREVOORT, SVP of Publishing; DAVID BOGART, SVP of Business Affairs & Operations, Publishing & Partnership; DAVID GABRIEL, SVP of Sales & Marketing, Publishing; JEFF YOUNGQUIST, VP of Production & Special Projects; DAN CARR, Executive Director of Publishing Technology; ALEX MORALES, Director of Publishing Operations; DAN EDINGTON, Managing Editor; SUSAN CRESPI, Production Manager; STAN LEE, Chairman Emeritus. For information regarding advertising in Marvel Comics or on Marvel.com, please contact Vit DeBellis, Custom Solutions & Integrated Advertising Manager, at vdebellis@marvel.com. For Marvel subscription inquiries, please call 888-511-5480. **Manufactured between 6/8/2018 and 7/10/2018 by SOLISCO PRINTERS, SCOTT, QC, CANADA.**

10 9 8 7 6 5 4 3 2 1

FOREWORD

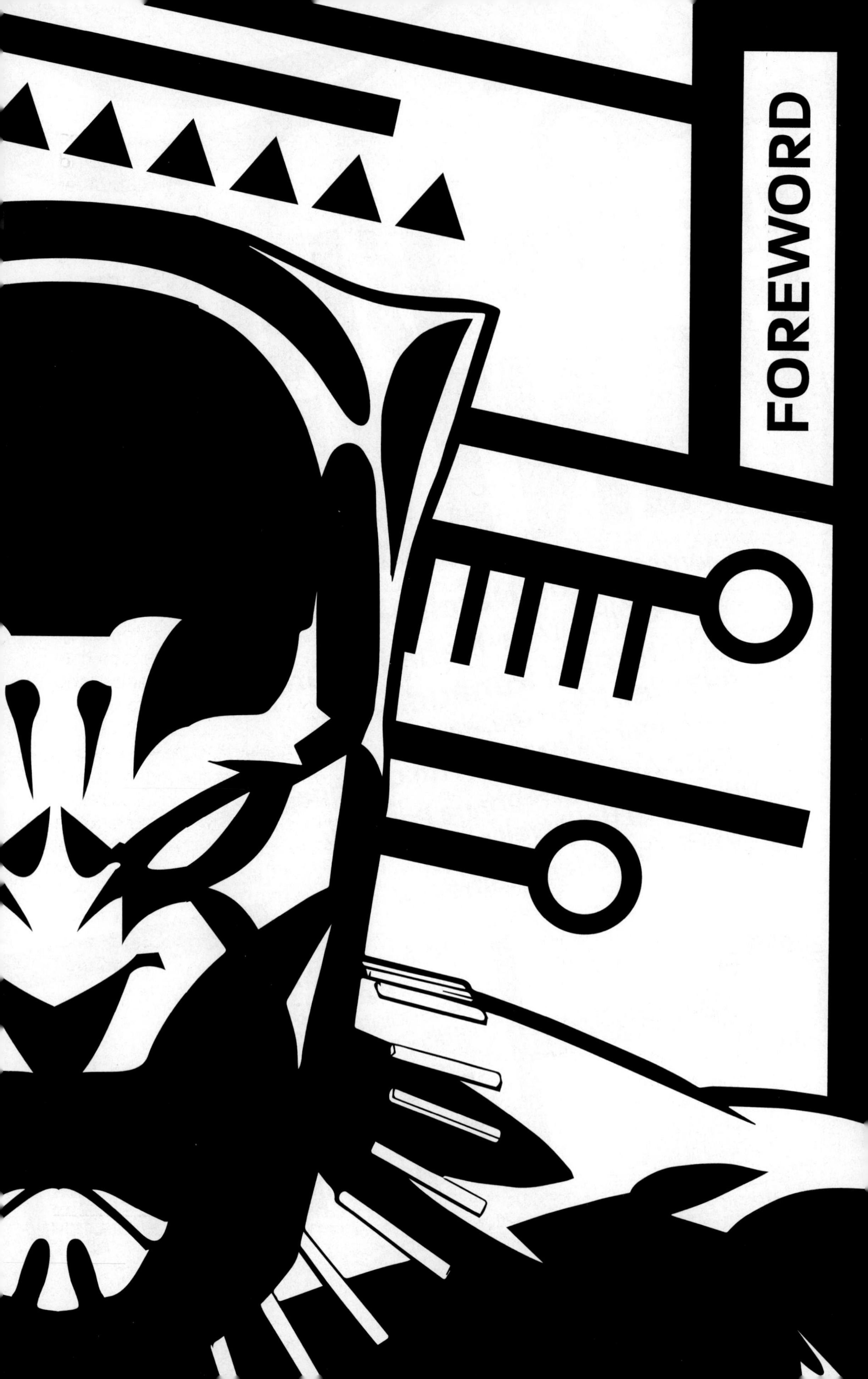

It started, fittingly, with Christopher Priest.

The seed for what became *Rise of the Black Panther* came, in part, from a thought I had while reading his legendary tenure on the 1998 Black Panther title. A scene during Priest's run showed the Wakanda Design Group tanking on the New York Stock Exchange as a result of intricate, labyrinthine machinations. Those shares became a chess piece in Black Panther and Iron Man's tense rivalry during the "Enemy of the State II" storyline, and the presence of a Wakandan business was being publicly traded stood out to me.

I wondered when the Design Group started being listed on the NYSE and when Wakanda as a whole began engaging with the outside world. This was a civilization that chose to stay zealously hidden for centuries. What kind of thinking would lead a king to pull the Unconquered Realm out of secrecy? Having been a Panther fan all of my life and a comics journalist and critic for about half of it, I knew the story of Wakanda's glasnost moment hadn't been told.

More importantly, I knew how it could be told. Syncretism is the act of combining already extant cultural traditions into a new whole. As a child of Haitian immigrants, I'd grown up experiencing those new wholes all my life, and I wanted the idea of syncretism to inform my first-ever comics work. So, the goal was to weave together the threads of previous creators and stories with new elements to ask and answer questions about the Black Panther. How would Jakarra — the wildly colorful stepbrother created by Jack Kirby — impact the ice-cold realpolitik that characterized Priest's T'Challa? Who would the world's shadiest black ops outfit send to steal from the most secretive nation in the Marvel Universe? Where did the son of a warrior-king get his genius-level scientific aptitude from?

I had the perfect creative partners to help me answer these questions. Paul Renaud, Javier Pina, Edgar Salazar, Stéphane Paitreau and Joe Sabino drew fashion and technology that made Wakanda feel like a place with its own unique Afrofuturistic culture and glory. They created colors that danced across the page, emotions that you could feel pass from one member of the Panther family to another, and drama-filled action that showed why T'Challa belongs among the elite class of Marvel characters.

Rise of the Black Panther is a story about creating trust in a world filled with reasons that make it feel impossible to do so. It's also a story with love at its core: love between parents and children, brothers and sisters, kings and countries. It's my hope that we've told a tale that makes you fall in love with T'Chaka, N'Yami, Ramonda, T'Challa, Shuri and, yes, even Hunter. Wakanda is wonder; here's how the world found out.

— Evan Narcisse

EVAN NARCISSE IS A JOURNALIST AND CRITIC WHO WRITES ABOUT VIDEO GAMES, COMIC BOOKS, MOVIES AND TV, OFTEN FOCUSING ON THE INTERSECTION OF BLACKNESS AND POP CULTURE. HE IS A SENIOR STAFF WRITER AT IO9, HAVING PREVIOUSLY WRITTEN FOR *THE ATLANTIC*, *TIME MAGAZINE* AND KOTAKU. HE'S TAUGHT A COURSE ON VIDEO GAME JOURNALISM AT NEW YORK UNIVERSITY AND APPEARED AS AN EXPERT GUEST ON CNN AND NPR. HE'S CURRENTLY WRITING THE *RISE OF THE BLACK PANTHER* MINISERIES FOR MARVEL COMICS. A NATIVE NEW YORKER, HE NOW LIVES IN AUSTIN, TEXAS.

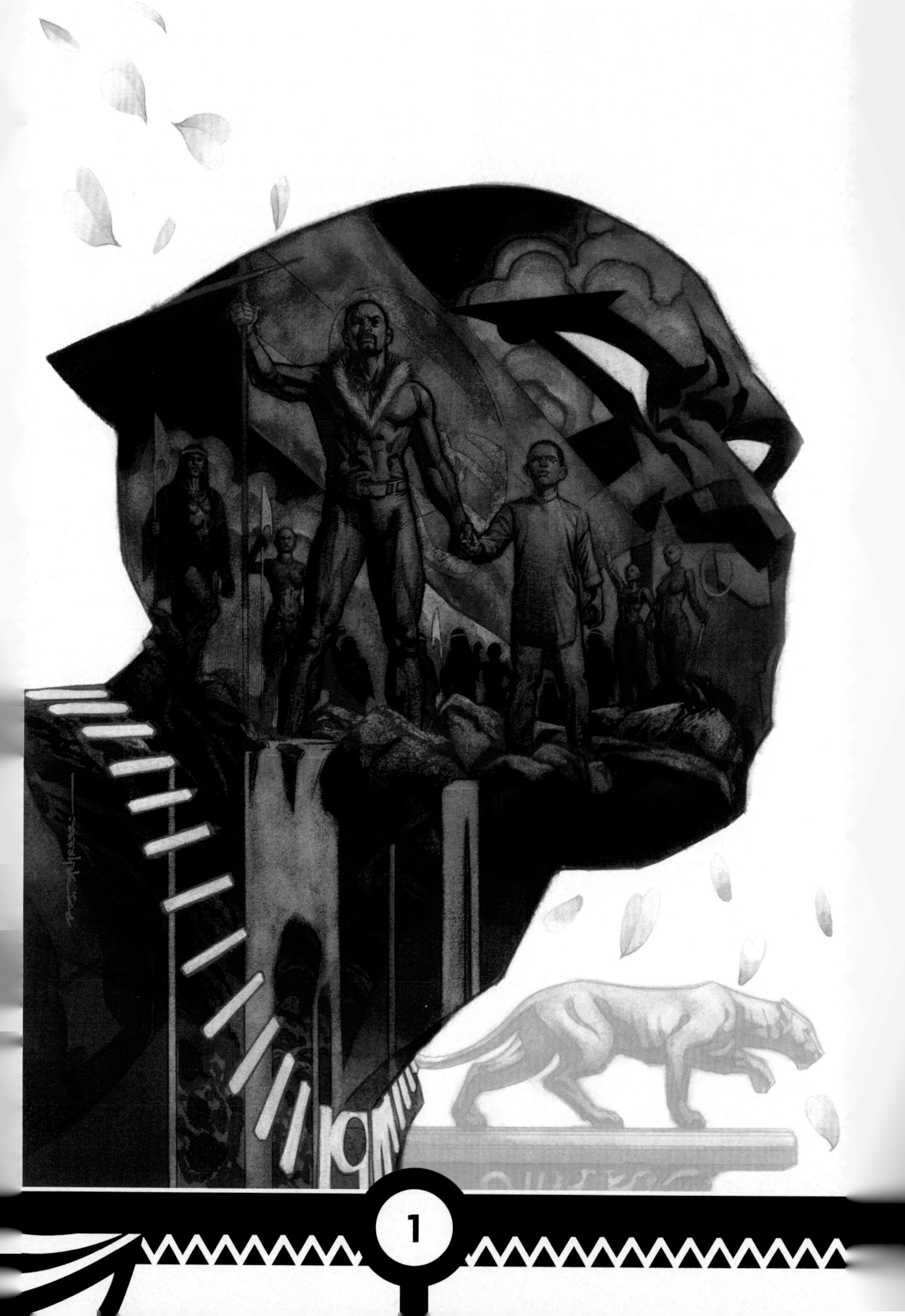

1

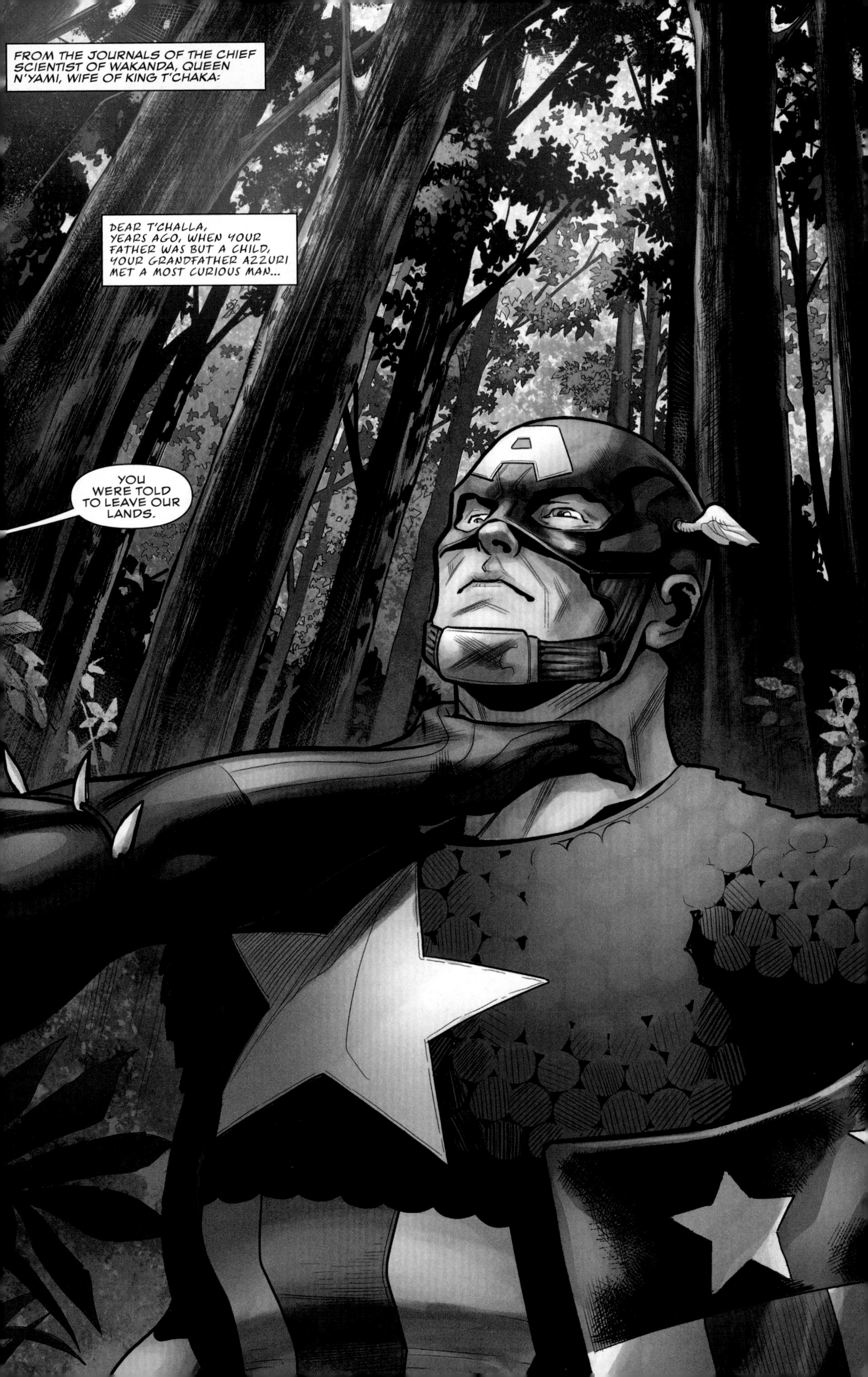
FROM THE JOURNALS OF THE CHIEF SCIENTIST OF WAKANDA, QUEEN N'YAMI, WIFE OF KING T'CHAKA:
DEAR T'CHALLA, YEARS AGO, WHEN YOUR FATHER WAS BUT A CHILD, YOUR GRANDFATHER AZZURI MET A MOST CURIOUS MAN...
YOU WERE TOLD TO LEAVE OUR LANDS.

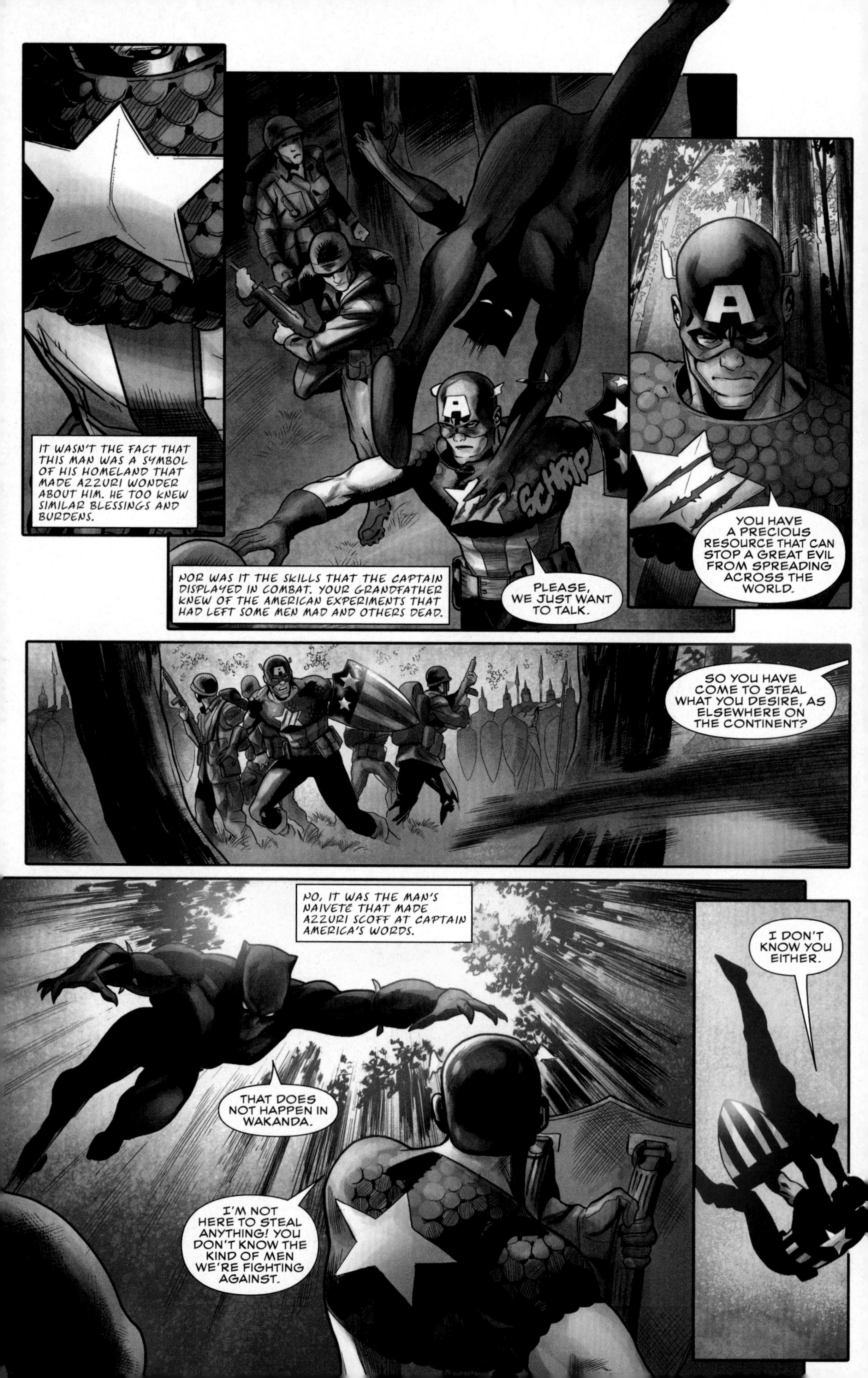
IT WASN'T THE FACT THAT THIS MAN WAS A SYMBOL OF HIS HOMELAND THAT MADE AZZURI WONDER ABOUT HIM. HE TOO KNEW SIMILAR BLESSINGS AND BURDENS.
NOR WAS IT THE SKILLS THAT THE CAPTAIN DISPLAYED IN COMBAT. YOUR GRANDFATHER KNEW OF THE AMERICAN EXPERIMENTS THAT HAD LEFT SOME MEN MAD AND OTHERS DEAD.
SCHRIP
PLEASE, WE JUST WANT TO TALK.
YOU HAVE A PRECIOUS RESOURCE THAT CAN STOP A GREAT EVIL FROM SPREADING ACROSS THE WORLD.
SO YOU HAVE COME TO STEAL WHAT YOU DESIRE, AS ELSEWHERE ON THE CONTINENT?
NO, IT WAS THE MAN'S NAIVETÉ THAT MADE AZZURI SCOFF AT CAPTAIN AMERICA'S WORDS.
THAT DOES NOT HAPPEN IN WAKANDA.
I'M NOT HERE TO STEAL ANYTHING! YOU DON'T KNOW THE KIND OF MEN WE'RE FIGHTING AGAINST.
I DON'T KNOW YOU EITHER.

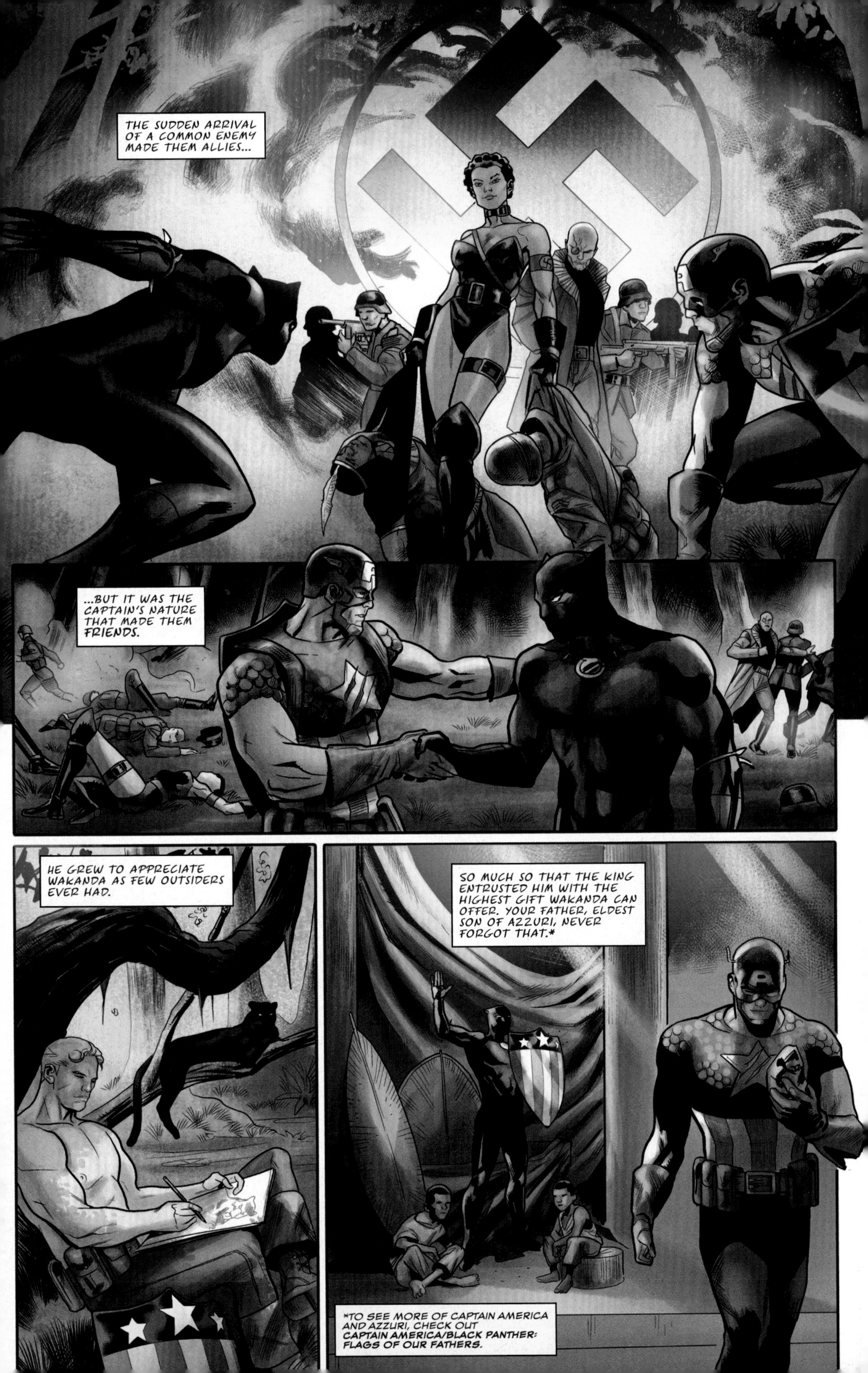
THE SUDDEN ARRIVAL OF A COMMON ENEMY MADE THEM ALLIES...
...BUT IT WAS THE CAPTAIN'S NATURE THAT MADE THEM FRIENDS.
HE GREW TO APPRECIATE WAKANDA AS FEW OUTSIDERS EVER HAD.
SO MUCH SO THAT THE KING ENTRUSTED HIM WITH THE HIGHEST GIFT WAKANDA CAN OFFER. YOUR FATHER, ELDEST SON OF AZZURI, NEVER FORGOT THAT.*
*TO SEE MORE OF CAPTAIN AMERICA AND AZZURI, CHECK OUT CAPTAIN AMERICA/BLACK PANTHER: FLAGS OF OUR FATHERS.

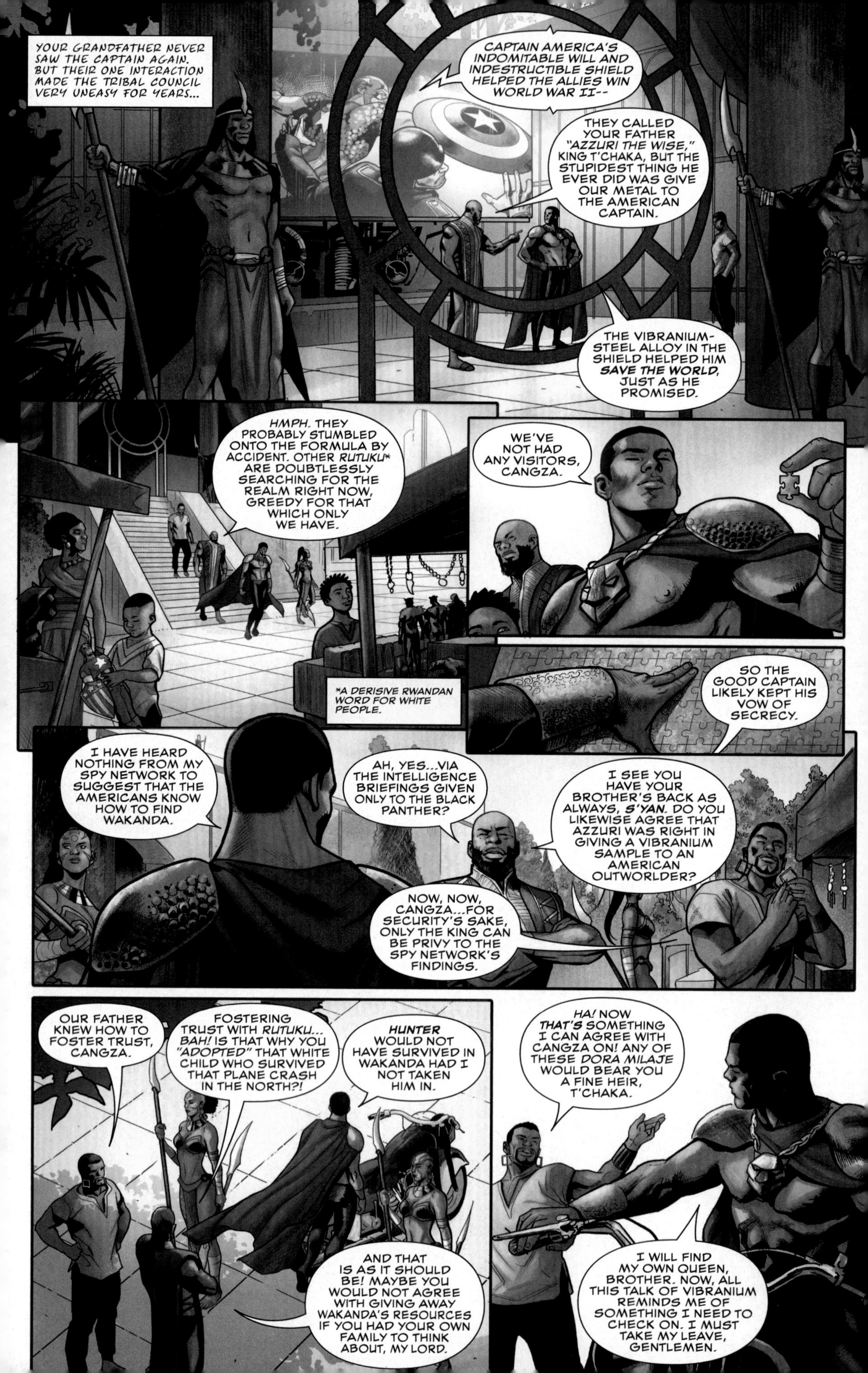
YOUR GRANDFATHER NEVER SAW THE CAPTAIN AGAIN. BUT THEIR ONE INTERACTION MADE THE TRIBAL COUNCIL VERY UNEASY FOR YEARS...
CAPTAIN AMERICA'S INDOMITABLE WILL AND INDESTRUCTIBLE SHIELD HELPED THE ALLIES WIN WORLD WAR II--
THEY CALLED YOUR FATHER "AZZURI THE WISE," KING T'CHAKA, BUT THE STUPIDEST THING HE EVER DID WAS GIVE OUR METAL TO THE AMERICAN CAPTAIN.
THE VIBRANIUM-STEEL ALLOY IN THE SHIELD HELPED HIM SAVE THE WORLD, JUST AS HE PROMISED.
HMPH. THEY PROBABLY STUMBLED ONTO THE FORMULA BY ACCIDENT. OTHER RUTUKU* ARE DOUBTLESSLY SEARCHING FOR THE REALM RIGHT NOW, GREEDY FOR THAT WHICH ONLY WE HAVE.
*A DERISIVE RWANDAN WORD FOR WHITE PEOPLE.
WE'VE NOT HAD ANY VISITORS, CANGZA.
SO THE GOOD CAPTAIN LIKELY KEPT HIS VOW OF SECRECY.
I HAVE HEARD NOTHING FROM MY SPY NETWORK TO SUGGEST THAT THE AMERICANS KNOW HOW TO FIND WAKANDA.
AH, YES...VIA THE INTELLIGENCE BRIEFINGS GIVEN ONLY TO THE BLACK PANTHER?
I SEE YOU HAVE YOUR BROTHER'S BACK AS ALWAYS, S'YAN. DO YOU LIKEWISE AGREE THAT AZZURI WAS RIGHT IN GIVING A VIBRANIUM SAMPLE TO AN AMERICAN OUTWORLDER?
NOW, NOW, CANGZA...FOR SECURITY'S SAKE, ONLY THE KING CAN BE PRIVY TO THE SPY NETWORK'S FINDINGS.
OUR FATHER KNEW HOW TO FOSTER TRUST, CANGZA.
FOSTERING TRUST WITH RUTUKU... BAH! IS THAT WHY YOU "ADOPTED" THAT WHITE CHILD WHO SURVIVED THAT PLANE CRASH IN THE NORTH?!
HUNTER WOULD NOT HAVE SURVIVED IN WAKANDA HAD I NOT TAKEN HIM IN.
AND THAT IS AS IT SHOULD BE! MAYBE YOU WOULD NOT AGREE WITH GIVING AWAY WAKANDA'S RESOURCES IF YOU HAD YOUR OWN FAMILY TO THINK ABOUT, MY LORD.
HA! NOW THAT'S SOMETHING I CAN AGREE WITH CANGZA ON! ANY OF THESE DORA MILAJE WOULD BEAR YOU A FINE HEIR, T'CHAKA.
I WILL FIND MY OWN QUEEN, BROTHER. NOW, ALL THIS TALK OF VIBRANIUM REMINDS ME OF SOMETHING I NEED TO CHECK ON. I MUST TAKE MY LEAVE, GENTLEMEN.

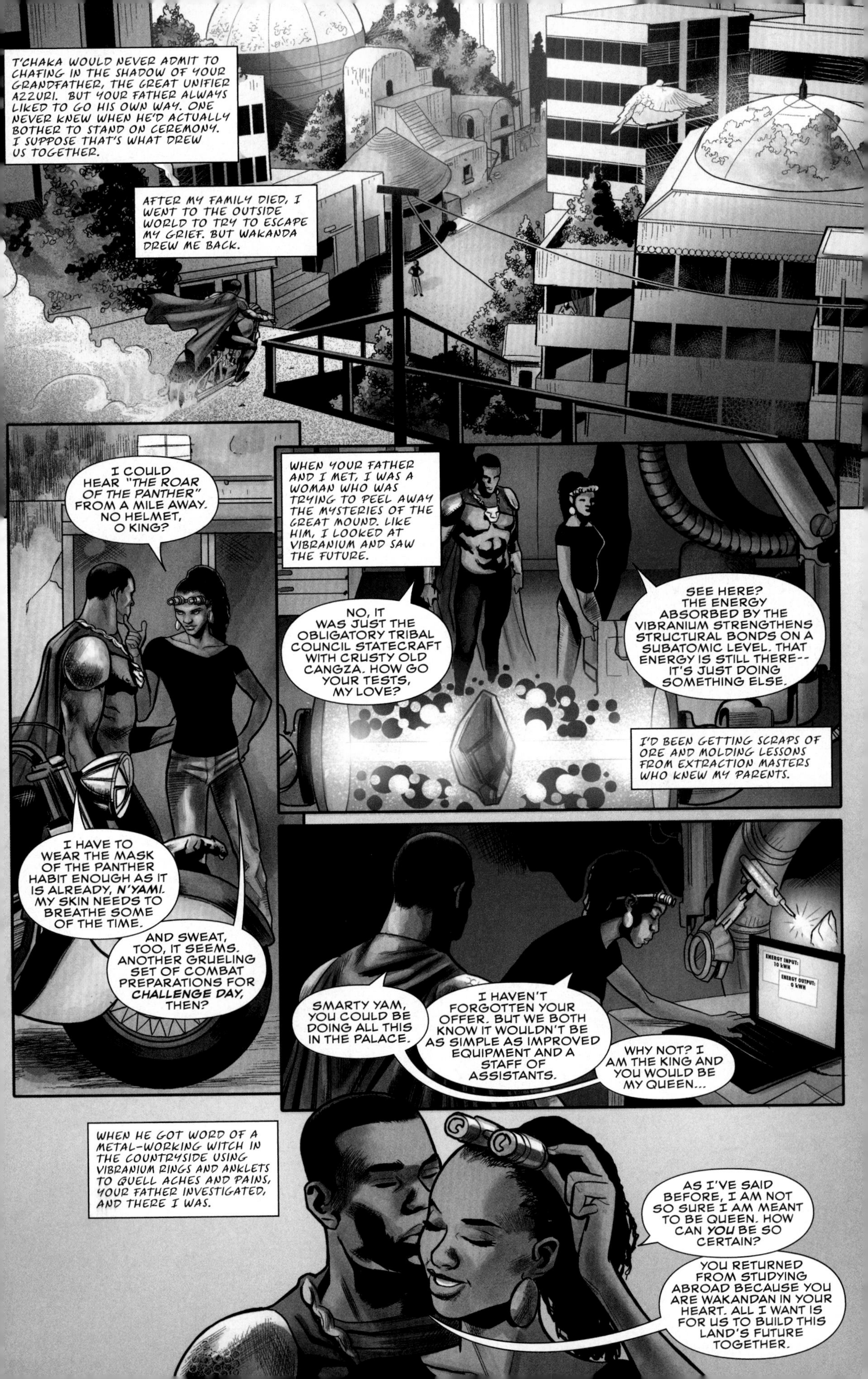
T'CHAKA WOULD NEVER ADMIT TO CHAFING IN THE SHADOW OF YOUR GRANDFATHER, THE GREAT UNIFIER AZZURI. BUT YOUR FATHER ALWAYS LIKED TO GO HIS OWN WAY. ONE NEVER KNEW WHEN HE'D ACTUALLY BOTHER TO STAND ON CEREMONY. I SUPPOSE THAT'S WHAT DREW US TOGETHER.
AFTER MY FAMILY DIED, I WENT TO THE OUTSIDE WORLD TO TRY TO ESCAPE MY GRIEF. BUT WAKANDA DREW ME BACK.
I COULD HEAR "THE ROAR OF THE PANTHER" FROM A MILE AWAY. NO HELMET, O KING?
I HAVE TO WEAR THE MASK OF THE PANTHER HABIT ENOUGH AS IT IS ALREADY, N'YAMI. MY SKIN NEEDS TO BREATHE SOME OF THE TIME.
AND SWEAT, TOO, IT SEEMS. ANOTHER GRUELING SET OF COMBAT PREPARATIONS FOR CHALLENGE DAY, THEN?
WHEN YOUR FATHER AND I MET, I WAS A WOMAN WHO WAS TRYING TO PEEL AWAY THE MYSTERIES OF THE GREAT MOUND. LIKE HIM, I LOOKED AT VIBRANIUM AND SAW THE FUTURE.
NO, IT WAS JUST THE OBLIGATORY TRIBAL COUNCIL STATECRAFT WITH CRUSTY OLD CANGZA. HOW GO YOUR TESTS, MY LOVE?
SEE HERE? THE ENERGY ABSORBED BY THE VIBRANIUM STRENGTHENS STRUCTURAL BONDS ON A SUBATOMIC LEVEL. THAT ENERGY IS STILL THERE-- IT'S JUST DOING SOMETHING ELSE.
I'D BEEN GETTING SCRAPS OF ORE AND MOLDING LESSONS FROM EXTRACTION MASTERS WHO KNEW MY PARENTS.
ENERGY INPUT: 10 kWH
ENERGY OUTPUT: 0 kWH
SMARTY YAM, YOU COULD BE DOING ALL THIS IN THE PALACE.
I HAVEN'T FORGOTTEN YOUR OFFER. BUT WE BOTH KNOW IT WOULDN'T BE AS SIMPLE AS IMPROVED EQUIPMENT AND A STAFF OF ASSISTANTS.
WHY NOT? I AM THE KING AND YOU WOULD BE MY QUEEN...
WHEN HE GOT WORD OF A METAL-WORKING WITCH IN THE COUNTRYSIDE USING VIBRANIUM RINGS AND ANKLETS TO QUELL ACHES AND PAINS, YOUR FATHER INVESTIGATED, AND THERE I WAS.
AS I'VE SAID BEFORE, I AM NOT SO SURE I AM MEANT TO BE QUEEN. HOW CAN YOU BE SO CERTAIN?
YOU RETURNED FROM STUDYING ABROAD BECAUSE YOU ARE WAKANDAN IN YOUR HEART. ALL I WANT IS FOR US TO BUILD THIS LAND'S FUTURE TOGETHER.

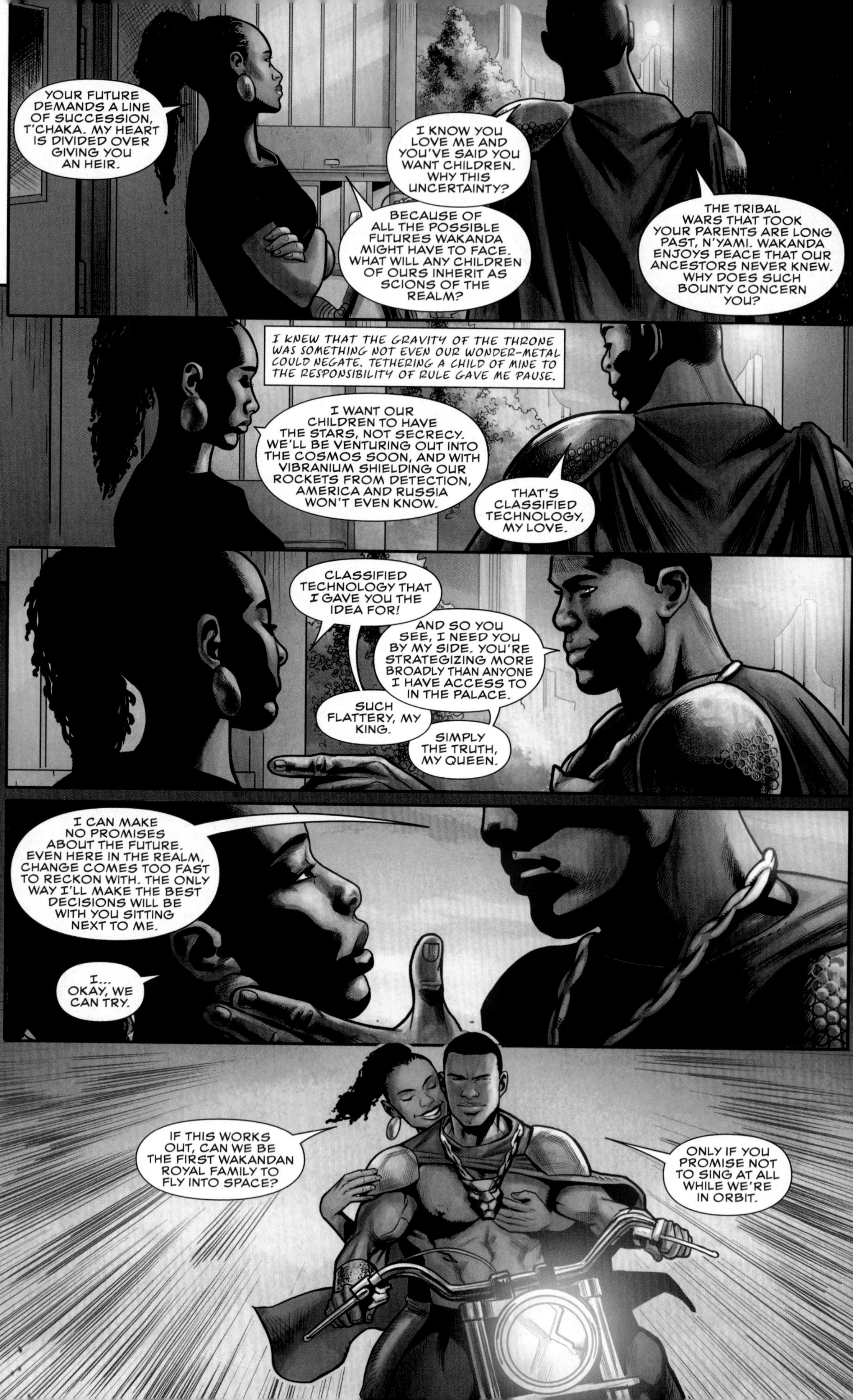
YOUR FUTURE DEMANDS A LINE OF SUCCESSION, T'CHAKA. MY HEART IS DIVIDED OVER GIVING YOU AN HEIR.
I KNOW YOU LOVE ME AND YOU'VE SAID YOU WANT CHILDREN. WHY THIS UNCERTAINTY?
BECAUSE OF ALL THE POSSIBLE FUTURES WAKANDA MIGHT HAVE TO FACE. WHAT WILL ANY CHILDREN OF OURS INHERIT AS SCIONS OF THE REALM?
THE TRIBAL WARS THAT TOOK YOUR PARENTS ARE LONG PAST, N'YAMI. WAKANDA ENJOYS PEACE THAT OUR ANCESTORS NEVER KNEW. WHY DOES SUCH BOUNTY CONCERN YOU?
I KNEW THAT THE GRAVITY OF THE THRONE WAS SOMETHING NOT EVEN OUR WONDER-METAL COULD NEGATE. TETHERING A CHILD OF MINE TO THE RESPONSIBILITY OF RULE GAVE ME PAUSE.
I WANT OUR CHILDREN TO HAVE THE STARS, NOT SECRECY. WE'LL BE VENTURING OUT INTO THE COSMOS SOON, AND WITH VIBRANIUM SHIELDING OUR ROCKETS FROM DETECTION, AMERICA AND RUSSIA WON'T EVEN KNOW.
THAT'S CLASSIFIED TECHNOLOGY, MY LOVE.
CLASSIFIED TECHNOLOGY THAT I GAVE YOU THE IDEA FOR!
AND SO YOU SEE, I NEED YOU BY MY SIDE. YOU'RE STRATEGIZING MORE BROADLY THAN ANYONE I HAVE ACCESS TO IN THE PALACE.
SUCH FLATTERY, MY KING.
SIMPLY THE TRUTH, MY QUEEN.
I CAN MAKE NO PROMISES ABOUT THE FUTURE. EVEN HERE IN THE REALM, CHANGE COMES TOO FAST TO RECKON WITH. THE ONLY WAY I'LL MAKE THE BEST DECISIONS WILL BE WITH YOU SITTING NEXT TO ME.
I... OKAY, WE CAN TRY.
IF THIS WORKS OUT, CAN WE BE THE FIRST WAKANDAN ROYAL FAMILY TO FLY INTO SPACE?
ONLY IF YOU PROMISE NOT TO SING AT ALL WHILE WE'RE IN ORBIT.

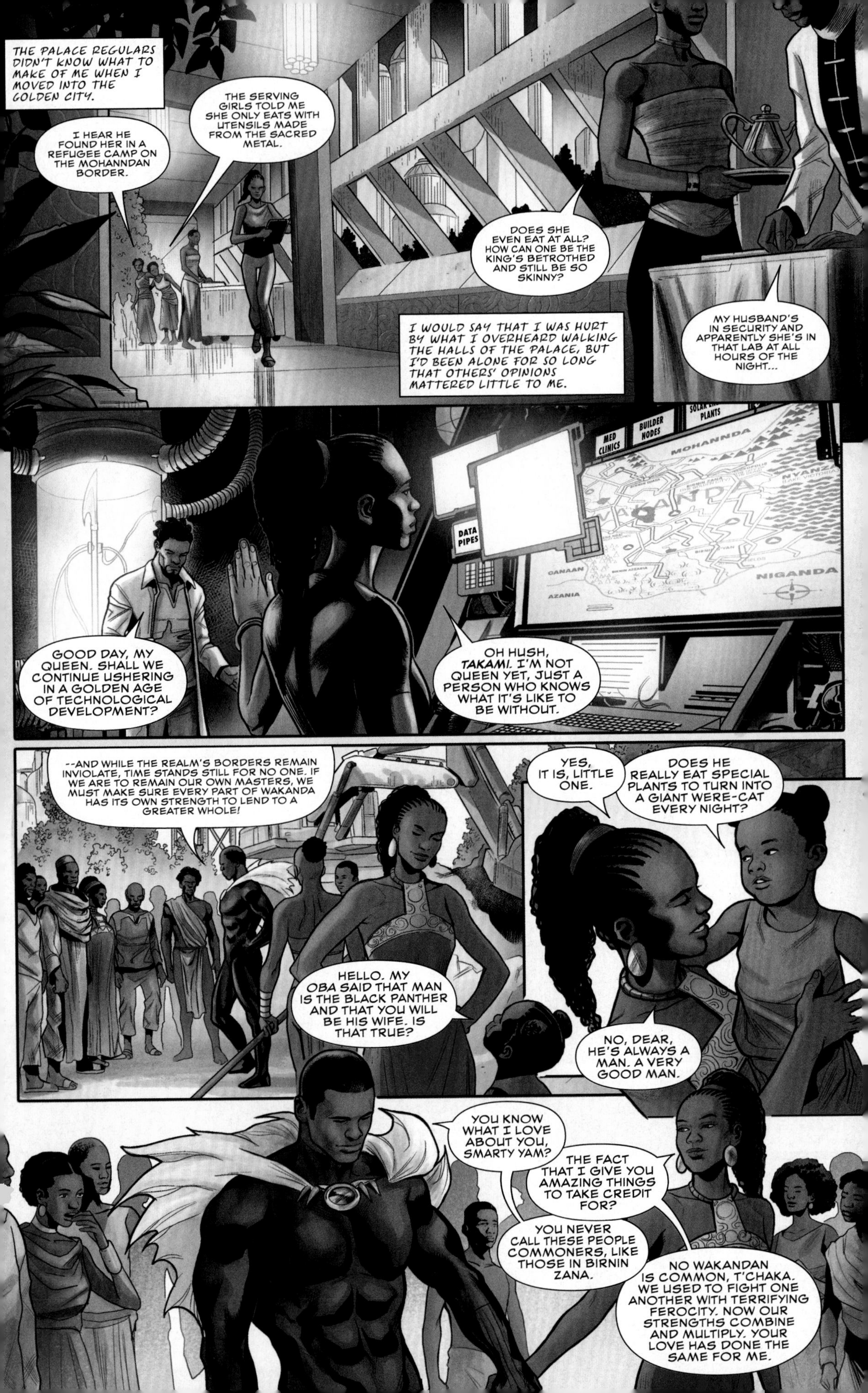
THE PALACE REGULARS DIDN'T KNOW WHAT TO MAKE OF ME WHEN I MOVED INTO THE GOLDEN CITY.
I HEAR HE FOUND HER IN A REFUGEE CAMP ON THE MOHANNDAN BORDER.
THE SERVING GIRLS TOLD ME SHE ONLY EATS WITH UTENSILS MADE FROM THE SACRED METAL.
DOES SHE EVEN EAT AT ALL? HOW CAN ONE BE THE KING'S BETROTHED AND STILL BE SO SKINNY?
I WOULD SAY THAT I WAS HURT BY WHAT I OVERHEARD WALKING THE HALLS OF THE PALACE, BUT I'D BEEN ALONE FOR SO LONG THAT OTHERS' OPINIONS MATTERED LITTLE TO ME.
MY HUSBAND'S IN SECURITY AND APPARENTLY SHE'S IN THAT LAB AT ALL HOURS OF THE NIGHT...
MED CLINICS
BUILDER NODES
PLANTS
DATA PIPES
MOHANNDA
NIGANDA
CANAAN
AZANIA
GOOD DAY, MY QUEEN. SHALL WE CONTINUE USHERING IN A GOLDEN AGE OF TECHNOLOGICAL DEVELOPMENT?
OH HUSH, TAKAMI. I'M NOT QUEEN YET, JUST A PERSON WHO KNOWS WHAT IT'S LIKE TO BE WITHOUT.
--AND WHILE THE REALM'S BORDERS REMAIN INVIOLATE, TIME STANDS STILL FOR NO ONE. IF WE ARE TO REMAIN OUR OWN MASTERS, WE MUST MAKE SURE EVERY PART OF WAKANDA HAS ITS OWN STRENGTH TO LEND TO A GREATER WHOLE!
HELLO. MY OBA SAID THAT MAN IS THE BLACK PANTHER AND THAT YOU WILL BE HIS WIFE. IS THAT TRUE?
YES, IT IS, LITTLE ONE.
DOES HE REALLY EAT SPECIAL PLANTS TO TURN INTO A GIANT WERE-CAT EVERY NIGHT?
NO, DEAR, HE'S ALWAYS A MAN. A VERY GOOD MAN.
YOU KNOW WHAT I LOVE ABOUT YOU, SMARTY YAM?
THE FACT THAT I GIVE YOU AMAZING THINGS TO TAKE CREDIT FOR?
YOU NEVER CALL THESE PEOPLE COMMONERS, LIKE THOSE IN BIRNIN ZANA.
NO WAKANDAN IS COMMON, T'CHAKA. WE USED TO FIGHT ONE ANOTHER WITH TERRIFYING FEROCITY. NOW OUR STRENGTHS COMBINE AND MULTIPLY. YOUR LOVE HAS DONE THE SAME FOR ME.

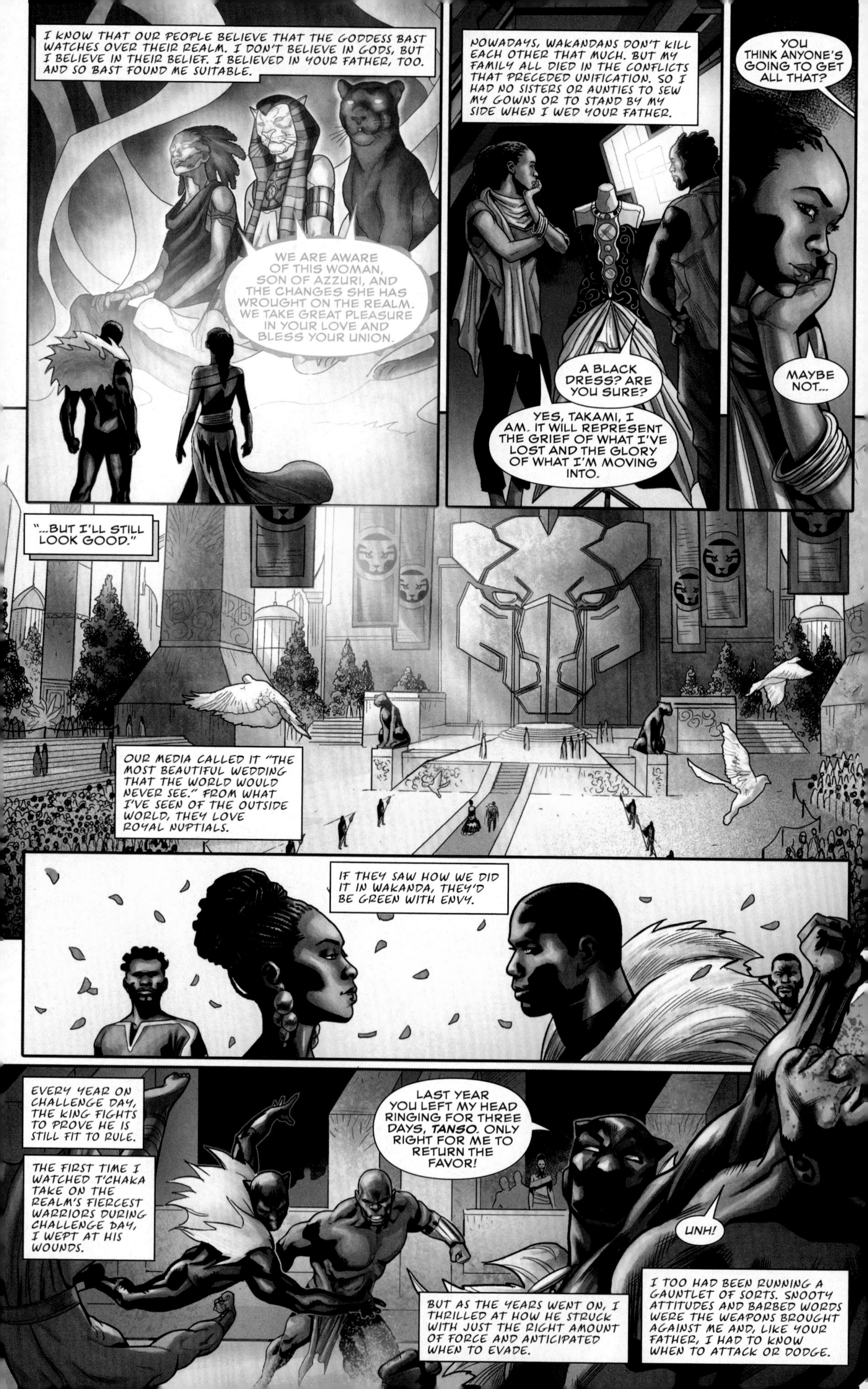
I KNOW THAT OUR PEOPLE BELIEVE THAT THE GODDESS BAST WATCHES OVER THEIR REALM. I DON'T BELIEVE IN GODS, BUT I BELIEVE IN THEIR BELIEF. I BELIEVED IN YOUR FATHER, TOO. AND SO BAST FOUND ME SUITABLE.
WE ARE AWARE OF THIS WOMAN, SON OF AZZURI, AND THE CHANGES SHE HAS WROUGHT ON THE REALM. WE TAKE GREAT PLEASURE IN YOUR LOVE AND BLESS YOUR UNION.
NOWADAYS, WAKANDANS DON'T KILL EACH OTHER THAT MUCH. BUT MY FAMILY ALL DIED IN THE CONFLICTS THAT PRECEDED UNIFICATION. SO I HAD NO SISTERS OR AUNTIES TO SEW MY GOWNS OR TO STAND BY MY SIDE WHEN I WED YOUR FATHER.
A BLACK DRESS? ARE YOU SURE?
YES, TAKAMI, I AM. IT WILL REPRESENT THE GRIEF OF WHAT I'VE LOST AND THE GLORY OF WHAT I'M MOVING INTO.
YOU THINK ANYONE'S GOING TO GET ALL THAT?
MAYBE NOT...
"...BUT I'LL STILL LOOK GOOD."
OUR MEDIA CALLED IT "THE MOST BEAUTIFUL WEDDING THAT THE WORLD WOULD NEVER SEE." FROM WHAT I'VE SEEN OF THE OUTSIDE WORLD, THEY LOVE ROYAL NUPTIALS.
IF THEY SAW HOW WE DID IT IN WAKANDA, THEY'D BE GREEN WITH ENVY.
EVERY YEAR ON CHALLENGE DAY, THE KING FIGHTS TO PROVE HE IS STILL FIT TO RULE.
THE FIRST TIME I WATCHED T'CHAKA TAKE ON THE REALM'S FIERCEST WARRIORS DURING CHALLENGE DAY, I WEPT AT HIS WOUNDS.
LAST YEAR YOU LEFT MY HEAD RINGING FOR THREE DAYS, TANSO. ONLY RIGHT FOR ME TO RETURN THE FAVOR!
UNH!
BUT AS THE YEARS WENT ON, I THRILLED AT HOW HE STRUCK WITH JUST THE RIGHT AMOUNT OF FORCE AND ANTICIPATED WHEN TO EVADE.
I TOO HAD BEEN RUNNING A GAUNTLET OF SORTS. SNOOTY ATTITUDES AND BARBED WORDS WERE THE WEAPONS BROUGHT AGAINST ME AND, LIKE YOUR FATHER, I HAD TO KNOW WHEN TO ATTACK OR DODGE.

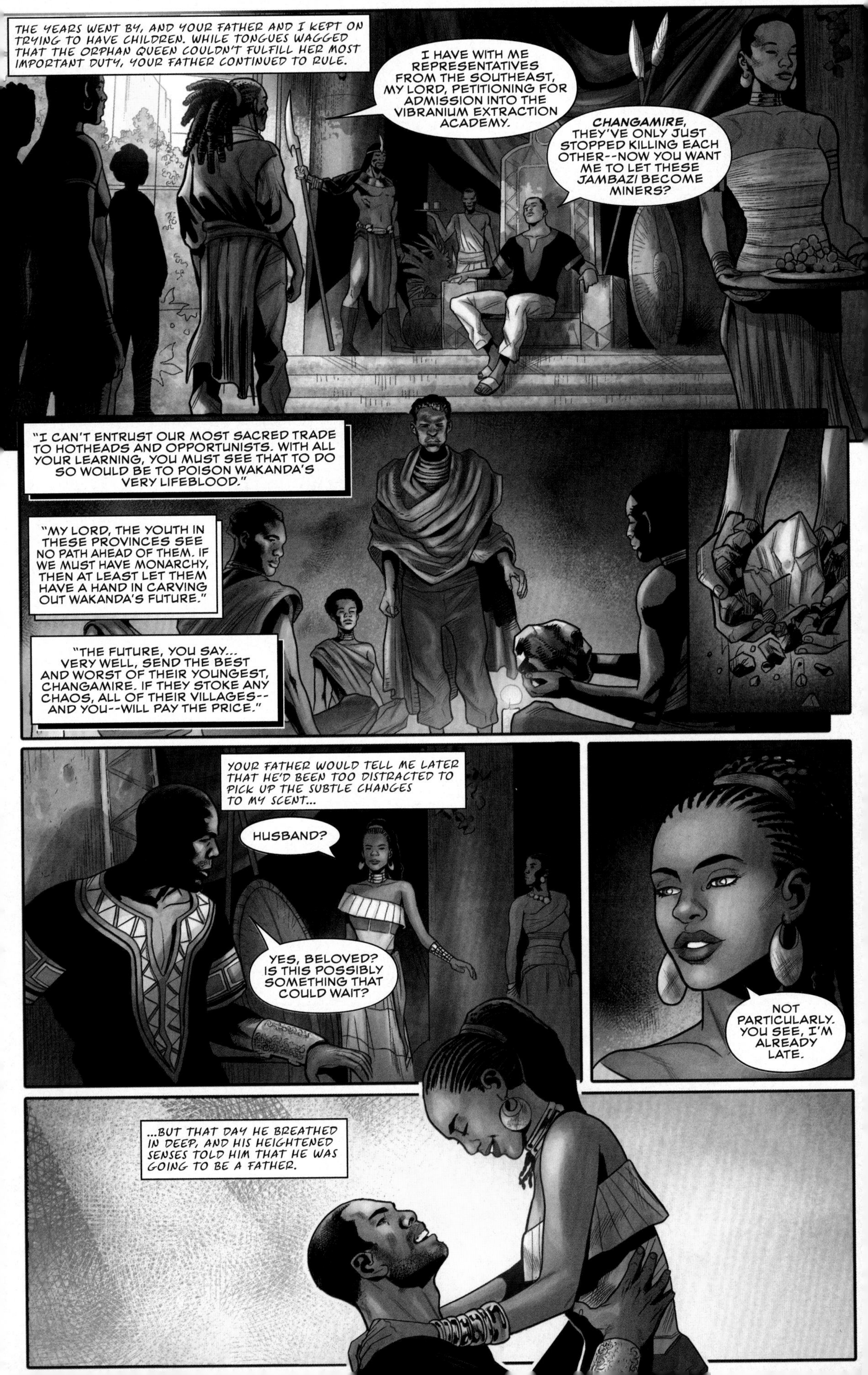
THE YEARS WENT BY, AND YOUR FATHER AND I KEPT ON TRYING TO HAVE CHILDREN. WHILE TONGUES WAGGED THAT THE ORPHAN QUEEN COULDN'T FULFILL HER MOST IMPORTANT DUTY, YOUR FATHER CONTINUED TO RULE.
I HAVE WITH ME REPRESENTATIVES FROM THE SOUTHEAST, MY LORD, PETITIONING FOR ADMISSION INTO THE VIBRANIUM EXTRACTION ACADEMY.
CHANGAMIRE, THEY'VE ONLY JUST STOPPED KILLING EACH OTHER--NOW YOU WANT ME TO LET THESE JAMBAZI BECOME MINERS?
"I CAN'T ENTRUST OUR MOST SACRED TRADE TO HOTHEADS AND OPPORTUNISTS. WITH ALL YOUR LEARNING, YOU MUST SEE THAT TO DO SO WOULD BE TO POISON WAKANDA'S VERY LIFEBLOOD."
"MY LORD, THE YOUTH IN THESE PROVINCES SEE NO PATH AHEAD OF THEM. IF WE MUST HAVE MONARCHY, THEN AT LEAST LET THEM HAVE A HAND IN CARVING OUT WAKANDA'S FUTURE."
"THE FUTURE, YOU SAY... VERY WELL, SEND THE BEST AND WORST OF THEIR YOUNGEST, CHANGAMIRE. IF THEY STOKE ANY CHAOS, ALL OF THEIR VILLAGES--AND YOU--WILL PAY THE PRICE."
YOUR FATHER WOULD TELL ME LATER THAT HE'D BEEN TOO DISTRACTED TO PICK UP THE SUBTLE CHANGES TO MY SCENT...
HUSBAND?
YES, BELOVED? IS THIS POSSIBLY SOMETHING THAT COULD WAIT?
NOT PARTICULARLY. YOU SEE, I'M ALREADY LATE.
...BUT THAT DAY HE BREATHED IN DEEP, AND HIS HEIGHTENED SENSES TOLD HIM THAT HE WAS GOING TO BE A FATHER.

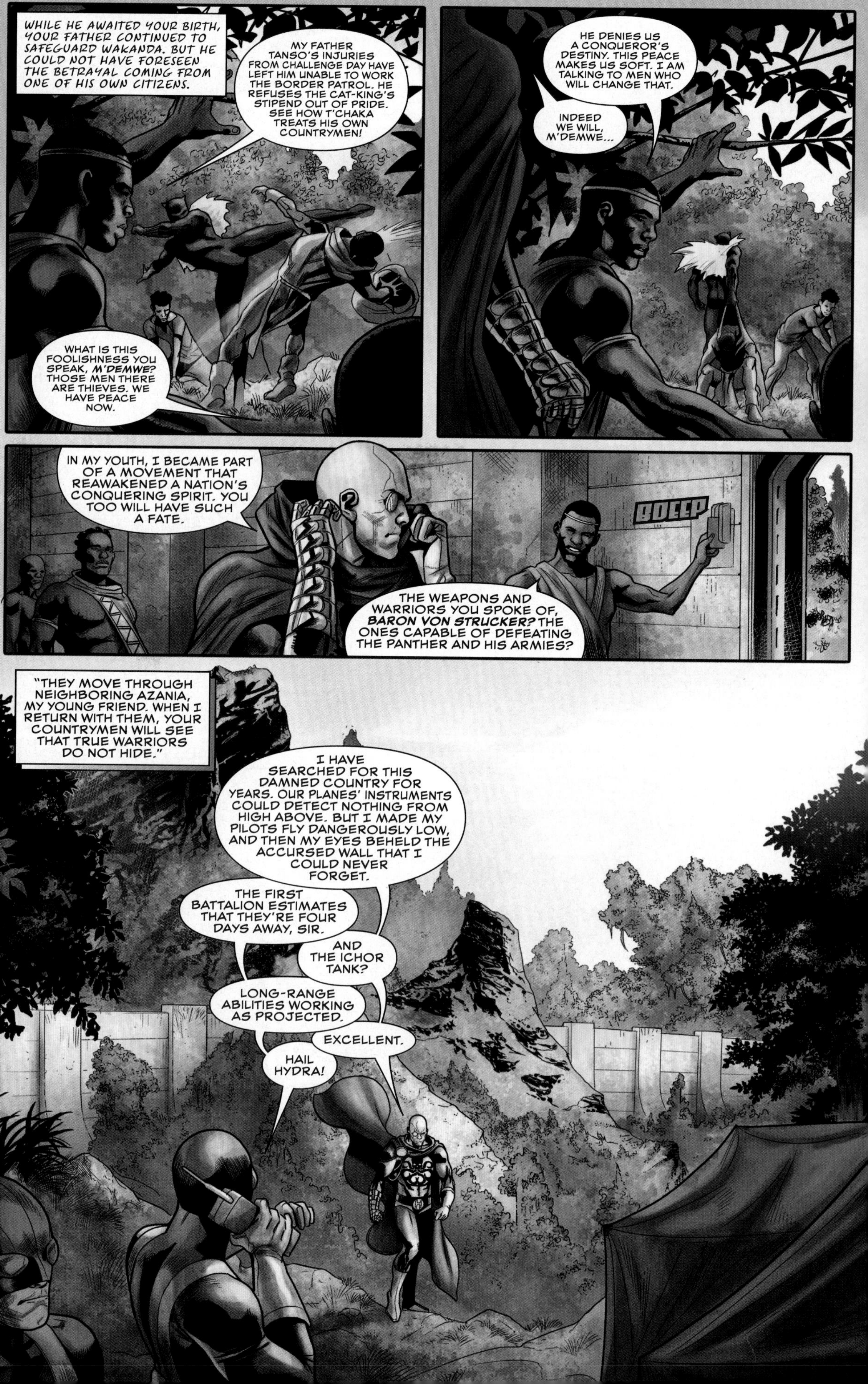
WHILE HE AWAITED YOUR BIRTH, YOUR FATHER CONTINUED TO SAFEGUARD WAKANDA. BUT HE COULD NOT HAVE FORESEEN THE BETRAYAL COMING FROM ONE OF HIS OWN CITIZENS.
MY FATHER TANSO'S INJURIES FROM CHALLENGE DAY HAVE LEFT HIM UNABLE TO WORK THE BORDER PATROL. HE REFUSES THE CAT-KING'S STIPEND OUT OF PRIDE. SEE HOW T'CHAKA TREATS HIS OWN COUNTRYMEN!
WHAT IS THIS FOOLISHNESS YOU SPEAK, M'DEMWE? THOSE MEN THERE ARE THIEVES. WE HAVE PEACE NOW.
HE DENIES US A CONQUEROR'S DESTINY. THIS PEACE MAKES US SOFT. I AM TALKING TO MEN WHO WILL CHANGE THAT.
INDEED WE WILL, M'DEMWE...
IN MY YOUTH, I BECAME PART OF A MOVEMENT THAT REAWAKENED A NATION'S CONQUERING SPIRIT. YOU TOO WILL HAVE SUCH A FATE.
BDEEP
THE WEAPONS AND WARRIORS YOU SPOKE OF, BARON VON STRUCKER? THE ONES CAPABLE OF DEFEATING THE PANTHER AND HIS ARMIES?
"THEY MOVE THROUGH NEIGHBORING AZANIA, MY YOUNG FRIEND. WHEN I RETURN WITH THEM, YOUR COUNTRYMEN WILL SEE THAT TRUE WARRIORS DO NOT HIDE."
I HAVE SEARCHED FOR THIS DAMNED COUNTRY FOR YEARS. OUR PLANES' INSTRUMENTS COULD DETECT NOTHING FROM HIGH ABOVE. BUT I MADE MY PILOTS FLY DANGEROUSLY LOW, AND THEN MY EYES BEHELD THE ACCURSED WALL THAT I COULD NEVER FORGET.
THE FIRST BATTALION ESTIMATES THAT THEY'RE FOUR DAYS AWAY, SIR.
AND THE ICHOR TANK?
LONG-RANGE ABILITIES WORKING AS PROJECTED.
EXCELLENT.
HAIL HYDRA!

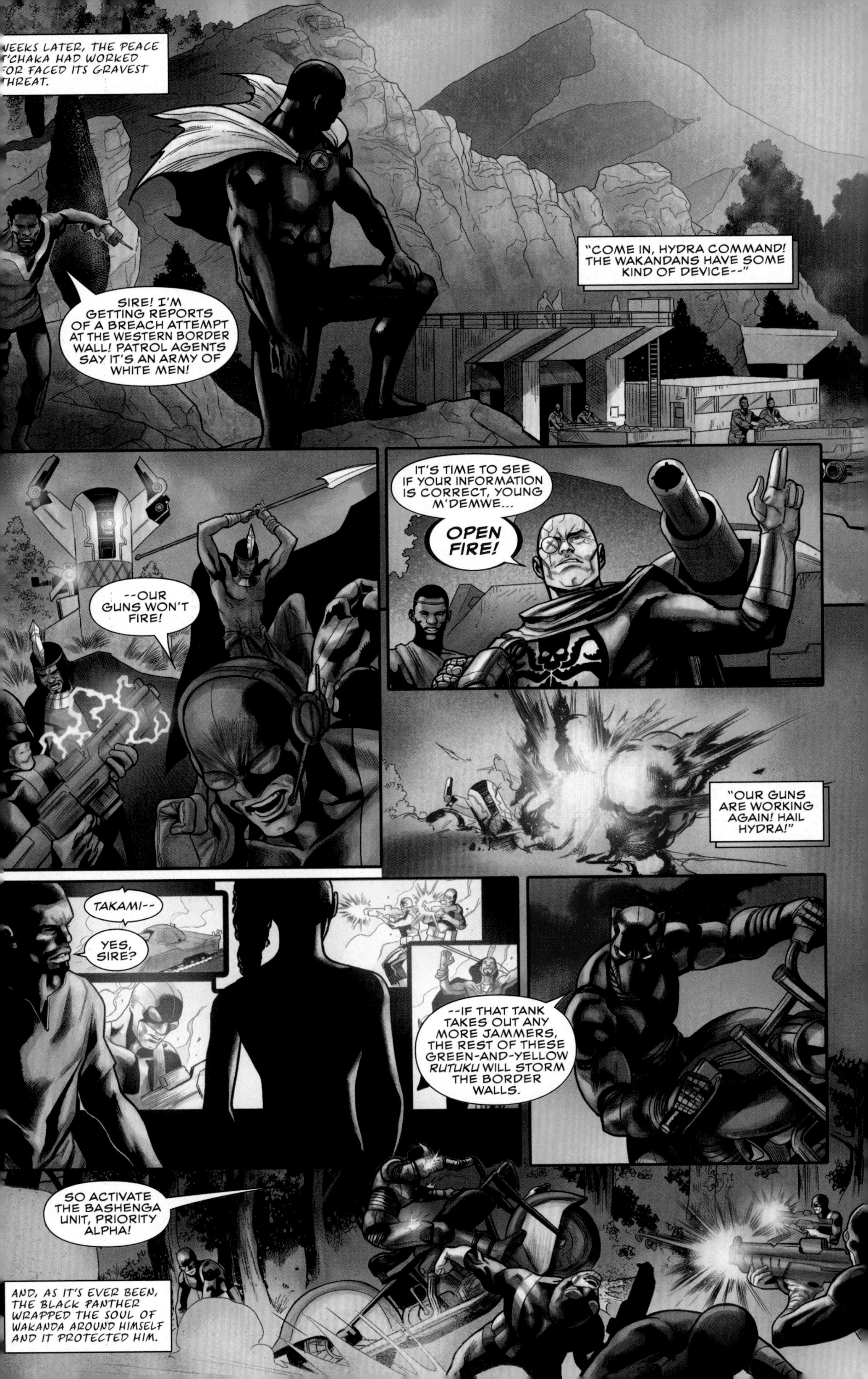
WEEKS LATER, THE PEACE T'CHAKA HAD WORKED FOR FACED ITS GRAVEST THREAT.
SIRE! I'M GETTING REPORTS OF A BREACH ATTEMPT AT THE WESTERN BORDER WALL! PATROL AGENTS SAY IT'S AN ARMY OF WHITE MEN!
"COME IN, HYDRA COMMAND! THE WAKANDANS HAVE SOME KIND OF DEVICE--"
--OUR GUNS WON'T FIRE!
IT'S TIME TO SEE IF YOUR INFORMATION IS CORRECT, YOUNG M'DEMWE...
OPEN FIRE!
"OUR GUNS ARE WORKING AGAIN! HAIL HYDRA!"
TAKAMI--
YES, SIRE?
--IF THAT TANK TAKES OUT ANY MORE JAMMERS, THE REST OF THESE GREEN-AND-YELLOW RUTUKU WILL STORM THE BORDER WALLS.
SO ACTIVATE THE BASHENGA UNIT, PRIORITY ALPHA!
AND, AS IT'S EVER BEEN, THE BLACK PANTHER WRAPPED THE SOUL OF WAKANDA AROUND HIMSELF AND IT PROTECTED HIM.

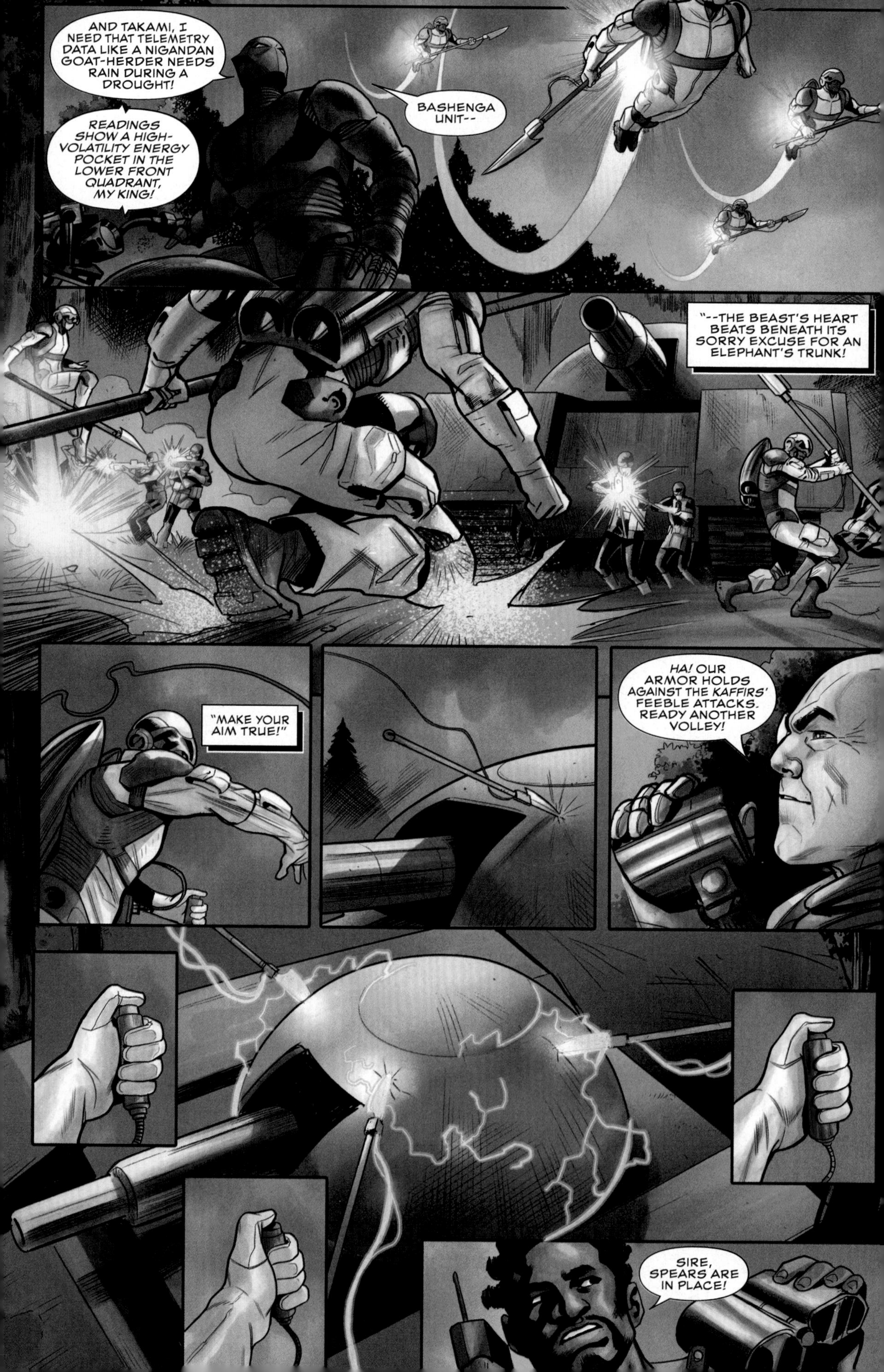
AND TAKAMI, I NEED THAT TELEMETRY DATA LIKE A NIGANDAN GOAT-HERDER NEEDS RAIN DURING A DROUGHT!
READINGS SHOW A HIGH-VOLATILITY ENERGY POCKET IN THE LOWER FRONT QUADRANT, MY KING!
BASHENGA UNIT--
"--THE BEAST'S HEART BEATS BENEATH ITS SORRY EXCUSE FOR AN ELEPHANT'S TRUNK!
"MAKE YOUR AIM TRUE!"
HA! OUR ARMOR HOLDS AGAINST THE KAFFIRS' FEEBLE ATTACKS. READY ANOTHER VOLLEY!
SIRE, SPEARS ARE IN PLACE!

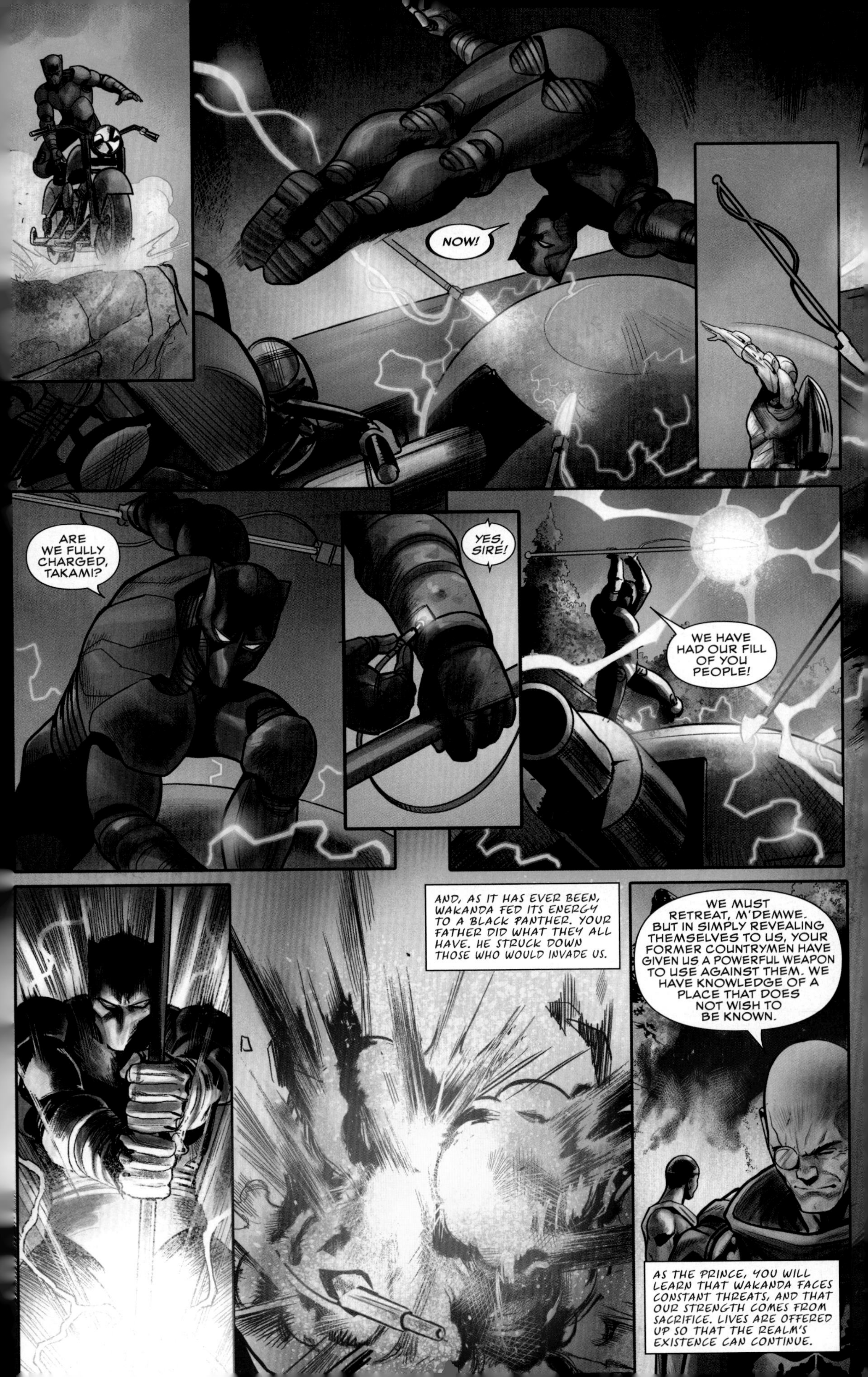
NOW!
ARE WE FULLY CHARGED, TAKAMI?
YES, SIRE!
WE HAVE HAD OUR FILL OF YOU PEOPLE!
AND, AS IT HAS EVER BEEN, WAKANDA FED ITS ENERGY TO A BLACK PANTHER. YOUR FATHER DID WHAT THEY ALL HAVE. HE STRUCK DOWN THOSE WHO WOULD INVADE US.
WE MUST RETREAT, M'DEMWE. BUT IN SIMPLY REVEALING THEMSELVES TO US, YOUR FORMER COUNTRYMEN HAVE GIVEN US A POWERFUL WEAPON TO USE AGAINST THEM. WE HAVE KNOWLEDGE OF A PLACE THAT DOES NOT WISH TO BE KNOWN.
AS THE PRINCE, YOU WILL LEARN THAT WAKANDA FACES CONSTANT THREATS, AND THAT OUR STRENGTH COMES FROM SACRIFICE. LIVES ARE OFFERED UP SO THAT THE REALM'S EXISTENCE CAN CONTINUE.

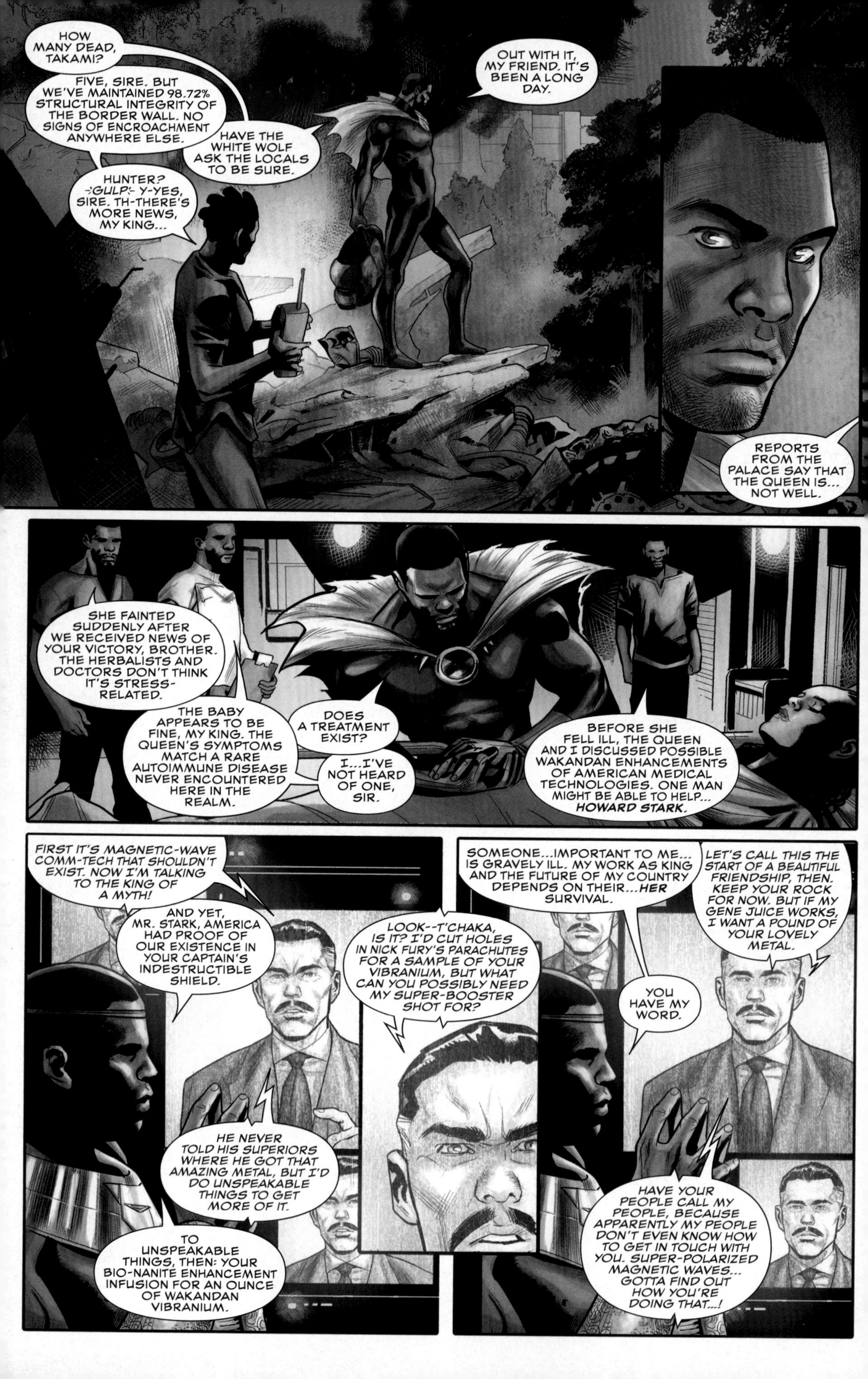
HOW MANY DEAD, TAKAMI?
FIVE, SIRE. BUT WE'VE MAINTAINED 98.72% STRUCTURAL INTEGRITY OF THE BORDER WALL. NO SIGNS OF ENCROACHMENT ANYWHERE ELSE.
HAVE THE WHITE WOLF ASK THE LOCALS TO BE SURE.
HUNTER? -GULP- Y-YES, SIRE. TH-THERE'S MORE NEWS, MY KING...
OUT WITH IT, MY FRIEND. IT'S BEEN A LONG DAY.
REPORTS FROM THE PALACE SAY THAT THE QUEEN IS... NOT WELL.
SHE FAINTED SUDDENLY AFTER WE RECEIVED NEWS OF YOUR VICTORY, BROTHER. THE HERBALISTS AND DOCTORS DON'T THINK IT'S STRESS-RELATED.
THE BABY APPEARS TO BE FINE, MY KING. THE QUEEN'S SYMPTOMS MATCH A RARE AUTOIMMUNE DISEASE NEVER ENCOUNTERED HERE IN THE REALM.
DOES A TREATMENT EXIST?
I...I'VE NOT HEARD OF ONE, SIR.
BEFORE SHE FELL ILL, THE QUEEN AND I DISCUSSED POSSIBLE WAKANDAN ENHANCEMENTS OF AMERICAN MEDICAL TECHNOLOGIES. ONE MAN MIGHT BE ABLE TO HELP... HOWARD STARK.
FIRST IT'S MAGNETIC-WAVE COMM-TECH THAT SHOULDN'T EXIST. NOW I'M TALKING TO THE KING OF A MYTH!
AND YET, MR. STARK, AMERICA HAD PROOF OF OUR EXISTENCE IN YOUR CAPTAIN'S INDESTRUCTIBLE SHIELD.
HE NEVER TOLD HIS SUPERIORS WHERE HE GOT THAT AMAZING METAL, BUT I'D DO UNSPEAKABLE THINGS TO GET MORE OF IT.
TO UNSPEAKABLE THINGS, THEN: YOUR BIO-NANITE ENHANCEMENT INFUSION FOR AN OUNCE OF WAKANDAN VIBRANIUM.
LOOK--T'CHAKA, IS IT? I'D CUT HOLES IN NICK FURY'S PARACHUTES FOR A SAMPLE OF YOUR VIBRANIUM, BUT WHAT CAN YOU POSSIBLY NEED MY SUPER-BOOSTER SHOT FOR?
SOMEONE...IMPORTANT TO ME... IS GRAVELY ILL. MY WORK AS KING AND THE FUTURE OF MY COUNTRY DEPENDS ON THEIR...HER SURVIVAL.
LET'S CALL THIS THE START OF A BEAUTIFUL FRIENDSHIP, THEN. KEEP YOUR ROCK FOR NOW. BUT IF MY GENE JUICE WORKS, I WANT A POUND OF YOUR LOVELY METAL.
YOU HAVE MY WORD.
HAVE YOUR PEOPLE CALL MY PEOPLE, BECAUSE APPARENTLY MY PEOPLE DON'T EVEN KNOW HOW TO GET IN TOUCH WITH YOU. SUPER-POLARIZED MAGNETIC WAVES... GOTTA FIND OUT HOW YOU'RE DOING THAT...!

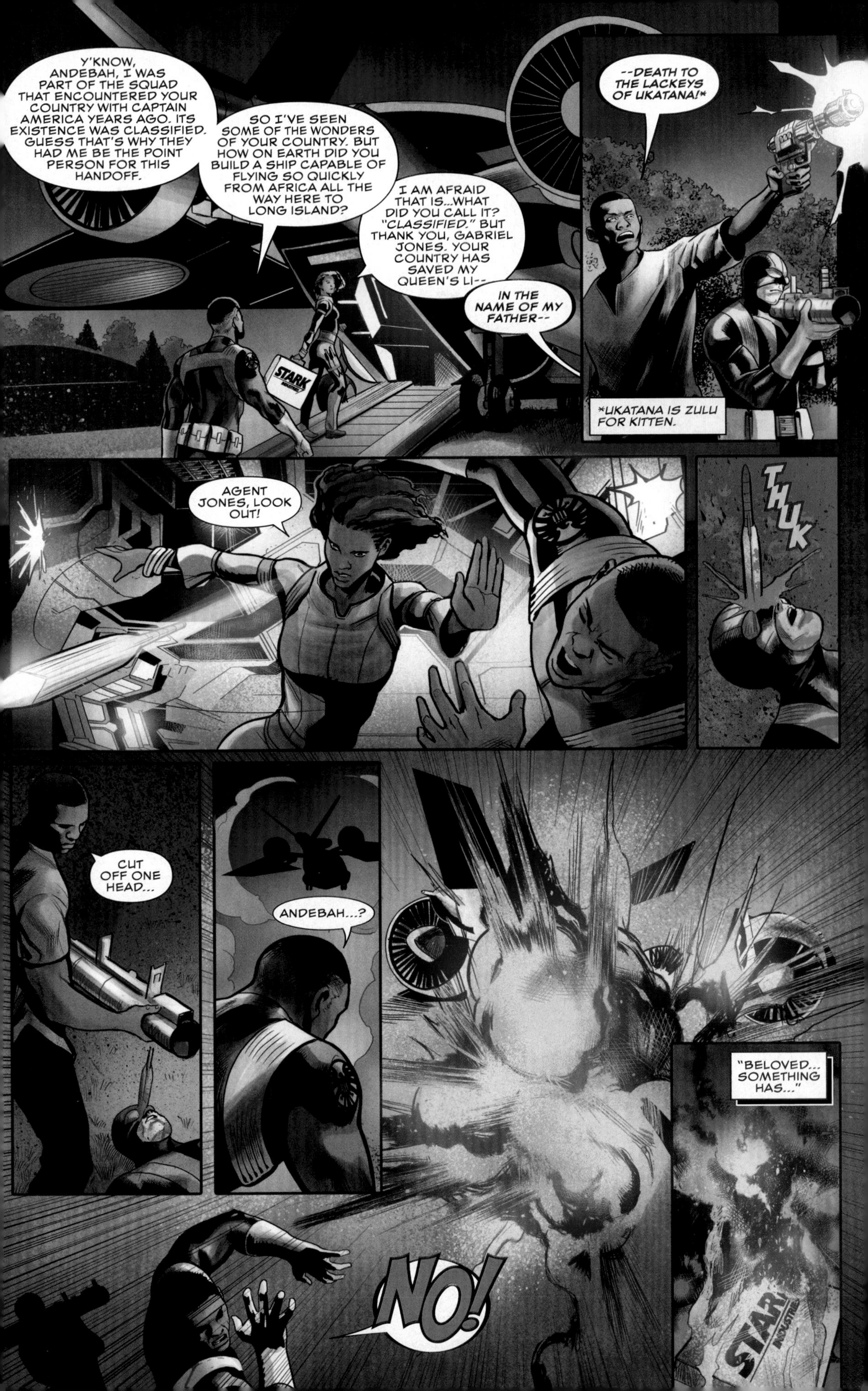
Y'KNOW, ANDEBAH, I WAS PART OF THE SQUAD THAT ENCOUNTERED YOUR COUNTRY WITH CAPTAIN AMERICA YEARS AGO. ITS EXISTENCE WAS CLASSIFIED. GUESS THAT'S WHY THEY HAD ME BE THE POINT PERSON FOR THIS HANDOFF.
SO I'VE SEEN SOME OF THE WONDERS OF YOUR COUNTRY. BUT HOW ON EARTH DID YOU BUILD A SHIP CAPABLE OF FLYING SO QUICKLY FROM AFRICA ALL THE WAY HERE TO LONG ISLAND?
I AM AFRAID THAT IS...WHAT DID YOU CALL IT? "CLASSIFIED." BUT THANK YOU, GABRIEL JONES. YOUR COUNTRY HAS SAVED MY QUEEN'S LI--
STARK
IN THE NAME OF MY FATHER--
--DEATH TO THE LACKEYS OF UKATANA!*
*UKATANA IS ZULU FOR KITTEN.
AGENT JONES, LOOK OUT!
THUK
CUT OFF ONE HEAD...
ANDEBAH...?
"BELOVED... SOMETHING HAS..."
NO!
STARK INDUSTRIES

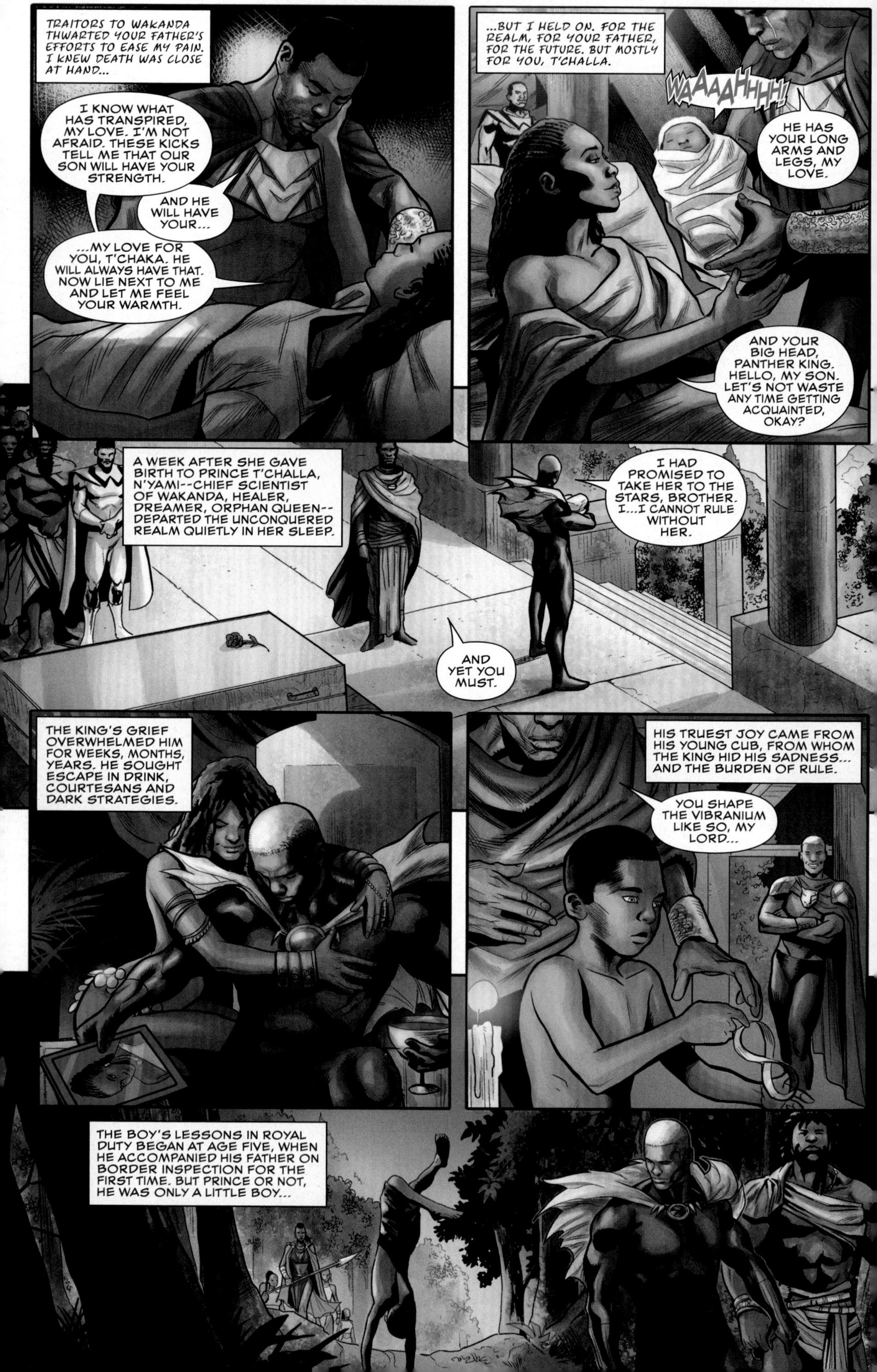
TRAITORS TO WAKANDA THWARTED YOUR FATHER'S EFFORTS TO EASE MY PAIN. I KNEW DEATH WAS CLOSE AT HAND...
I KNOW WHAT HAS TRANSPIRED, MY LOVE. I'M NOT AFRAID. THESE KICKS TELL ME THAT OUR SON WILL HAVE YOUR STRENGTH.
AND HE WILL HAVE YOUR...
...MY LOVE FOR YOU, T'CHAKA. HE WILL ALWAYS HAVE THAT. NOW LIE NEXT TO ME AND LET ME FEEL YOUR WARMTH.
...BUT I HELD ON. FOR THE REALM, FOR YOUR FATHER, FOR THE FUTURE. BUT MOSTLY FOR YOU, T'CHALLA.
WAAAAHHHH!
HE HAS YOUR LONG ARMS AND LEGS, MY LOVE.
AND YOUR BIG HEAD, PANTHER KING. HELLO, MY SON. LET'S NOT WASTE ANY TIME GETTING ACQUAINTED, OKAY?
A WEEK AFTER SHE GAVE BIRTH TO PRINCE T'CHALLA, N'YAMI--CHIEF SCIENTIST OF WAKANDA, HEALER, DREAMER, ORPHAN QUEEN--DEPARTED THE UNCONQUERED REALM QUIETLY IN HER SLEEP.
I HAD PROMISED TO TAKE HER TO THE STARS, BROTHER. I...I CANNOT RULE WITHOUT HER.
AND YET YOU MUST.
THE KING'S GRIEF OVERWHELMED HIM FOR WEEKS, MONTHS, YEARS. HE SOUGHT ESCAPE IN DRINK, COURTESANS AND DARK STRATEGIES.
HIS TRUEST JOY CAME FROM HIS YOUNG CUB, FROM WHOM THE KING HID HIS SADNESS... AND THE BURDEN OF RULE.
YOU SHAPE THE VIBRANIUM LIKE SO, MY LORD...
THE BOY'S LESSONS IN ROYAL DUTY BEGAN AT AGE FIVE, WHEN HE ACCOMPANIED HIS FATHER ON BORDER INSPECTION FOR THE FIRST TIME. BUT PRINCE OR NOT, HE WAS ONLY A LITTLE BOY...

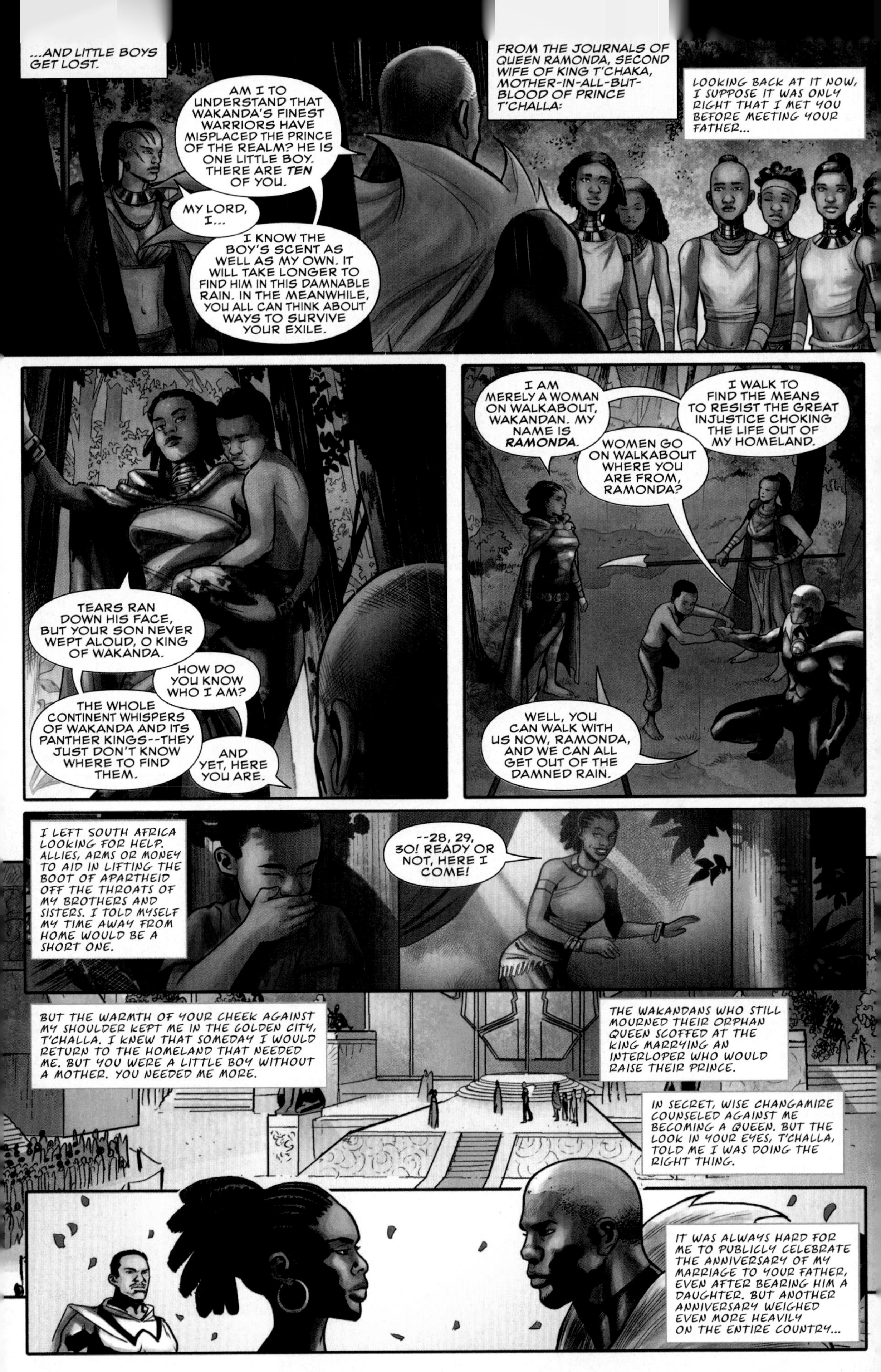
...AND LITTLE BOYS GET LOST.
AM I TO UNDERSTAND THAT WAKANDA'S FINEST WARRIORS HAVE MISPLACED THE PRINCE OF THE REALM? HE IS ONE LITTLE BOY. THERE ARE TEN OF YOU.
MY LORD, I...
I KNOW THE BOY'S SCENT AS WELL AS MY OWN. IT WILL TAKE LONGER TO FIND HIM IN THIS DAMNABLE RAIN. IN THE MEANWHILE, YOU ALL CAN THINK ABOUT WAYS TO SURVIVE YOUR EXILE.
FROM THE JOURNALS OF QUEEN RAMONDA, SECOND WIFE OF KING T'CHAKA, MOTHER-IN-ALL-BUT-BLOOD OF PRINCE T'CHALLA:
LOOKING BACK AT IT NOW, I SUPPOSE IT WAS ONLY RIGHT THAT I MET YOU BEFORE MEETING YOUR FATHER...
TEARS RAN DOWN HIS FACE, BUT YOUR SON NEVER WEPT ALOUD, O KING OF WAKANDA.
HOW DO YOU KNOW WHO I AM?
THE WHOLE CONTINENT WHISPERS OF WAKANDA AND ITS PANTHER KINGS--THEY JUST DON'T KNOW WHERE TO FIND THEM.
AND YET, HERE YOU ARE.
I AM MERELY A WOMAN ON WALKABOUT, WAKANDAN. MY NAME IS RAMONDA.
I WALK TO FIND THE MEANS TO RESIST THE GREAT INJUSTICE CHOKING THE LIFE OUT OF MY HOMELAND.
WOMEN GO ON WALKABOUT WHERE YOU ARE FROM, RAMONDA?
WELL, YOU CAN WALK WITH US NOW, RAMONDA, AND WE CAN ALL GET OUT OF THE DAMNED RAIN.
I LEFT SOUTH AFRICA LOOKING FOR HELP. ALLIES, ARMS OR MONEY TO AID IN LIFTING THE BOOT OF APARTHEID OFF THE THROATS OF MY BROTHERS AND SISTERS. I TOLD MYSELF MY TIME AWAY FROM HOME WOULD BE A SHORT ONE.
--28, 29, 30! READY OR NOT, HERE I COME!
BUT THE WARMTH OF YOUR CHEEK AGAINST MY SHOULDER KEPT ME IN THE GOLDEN CITY, T'CHALLA. I KNEW THAT SOMEDAY I WOULD RETURN TO THE HOMELAND THAT NEEDED ME. BUT YOU WERE A LITTLE BOY WITHOUT A MOTHER. YOU NEEDED ME MORE.
THE WAKANDANS WHO STILL MOURNED THEIR ORPHAN QUEEN SCOFFED AT THE KING MARRYING AN INTERLOPER WHO WOULD RAISE THEIR PRINCE.
IN SECRET, WISE CHANGAMIRE COUNSELED AGAINST ME BECOMING A QUEEN. BUT THE LOOK IN YOUR EYES, T'CHALLA, TOLD ME I WAS DOING THE RIGHT THING.
IT WAS ALWAYS HARD FOR ME TO PUBLICLY CELEBRATE THE ANNIVERSARY OF MY MARRIAGE TO YOUR FATHER, EVEN AFTER BEARING HIM A DAUGHTER. BUT ANOTHER ANNIVERSARY WEIGHED EVEN MORE HEAVILY ON THE ENTIRE COUNTRY...

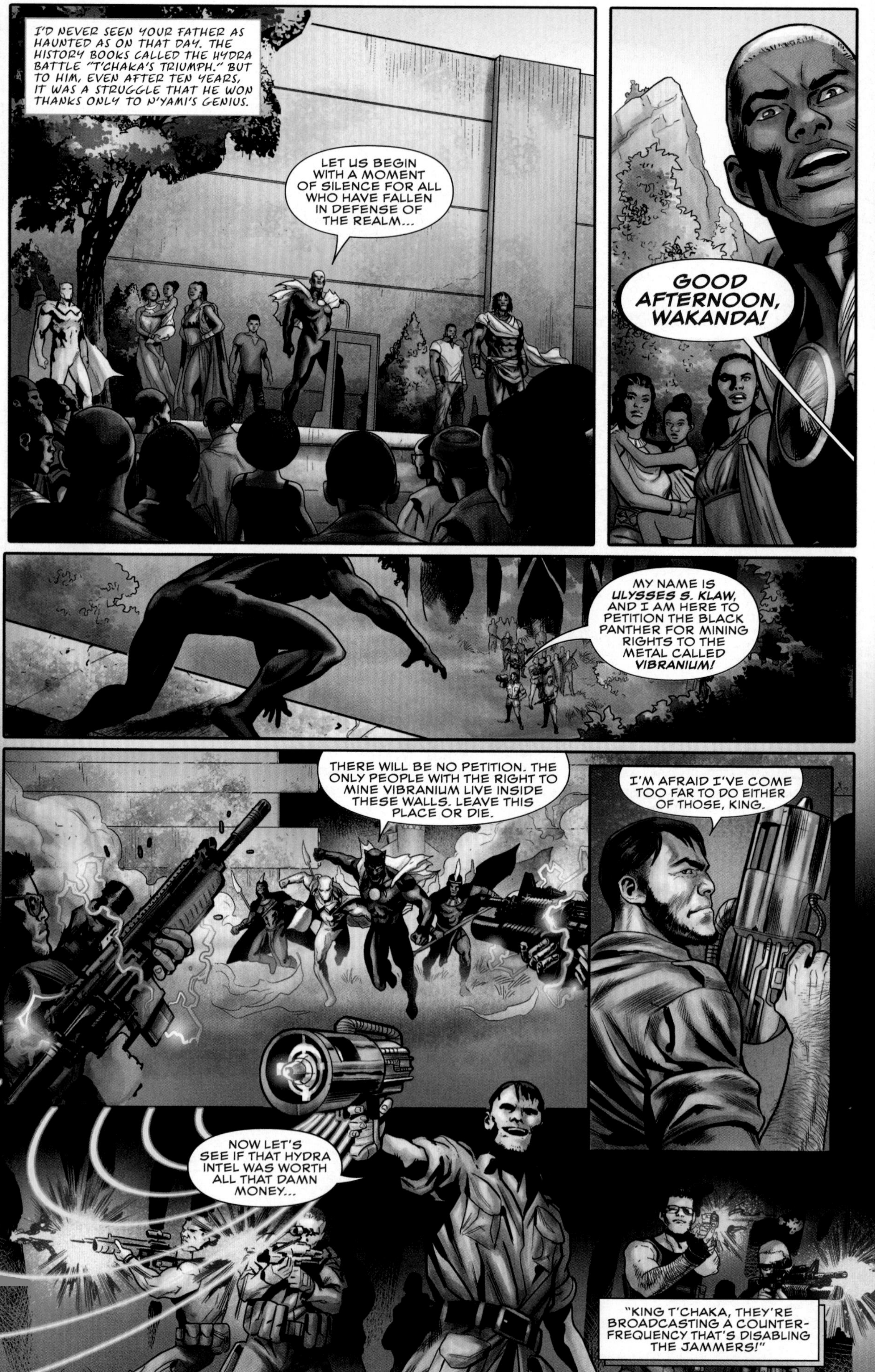
I'D NEVER SEEN YOUR FATHER AS HAUNTED AS ON THAT DAY. THE HISTORY BOOKS CALLED THE HYDRA BATTLE "T'CHAKA'S TRIUMPH." BUT TO HIM, EVEN AFTER TEN YEARS, IT WAS A STRUGGLE THAT HE WON THANKS ONLY TO N'YAMI'S GENIUS.
LET US BEGIN WITH A MOMENT OF SILENCE FOR ALL WHO HAVE FALLEN IN DEFENSE OF THE REALM...
GOOD AFTERNOON, WAKANDA!
MY NAME IS ULYSSES S. KLAW, AND I AM HERE TO PETITION THE BLACK PANTHER FOR MINING RIGHTS TO THE METAL CALLED VIBRANIUM!
THERE WILL BE NO PETITION. THE ONLY PEOPLE WITH THE RIGHT TO MINE VIBRANIUM LIVE INSIDE THESE WALLS. LEAVE THIS PLACE OR DIE.
I'M AFRAID I'VE COME TOO FAR TO DO EITHER OF THOSE, KING.
NOW LET'S SEE IF THAT HYDRA INTEL WAS WORTH ALL THAT DAMN MONEY...
"KING T'CHAKA, THEY'RE BROADCASTING A COUNTER-FREQUENCY THAT'S DISABLING THE JAMMERS!"

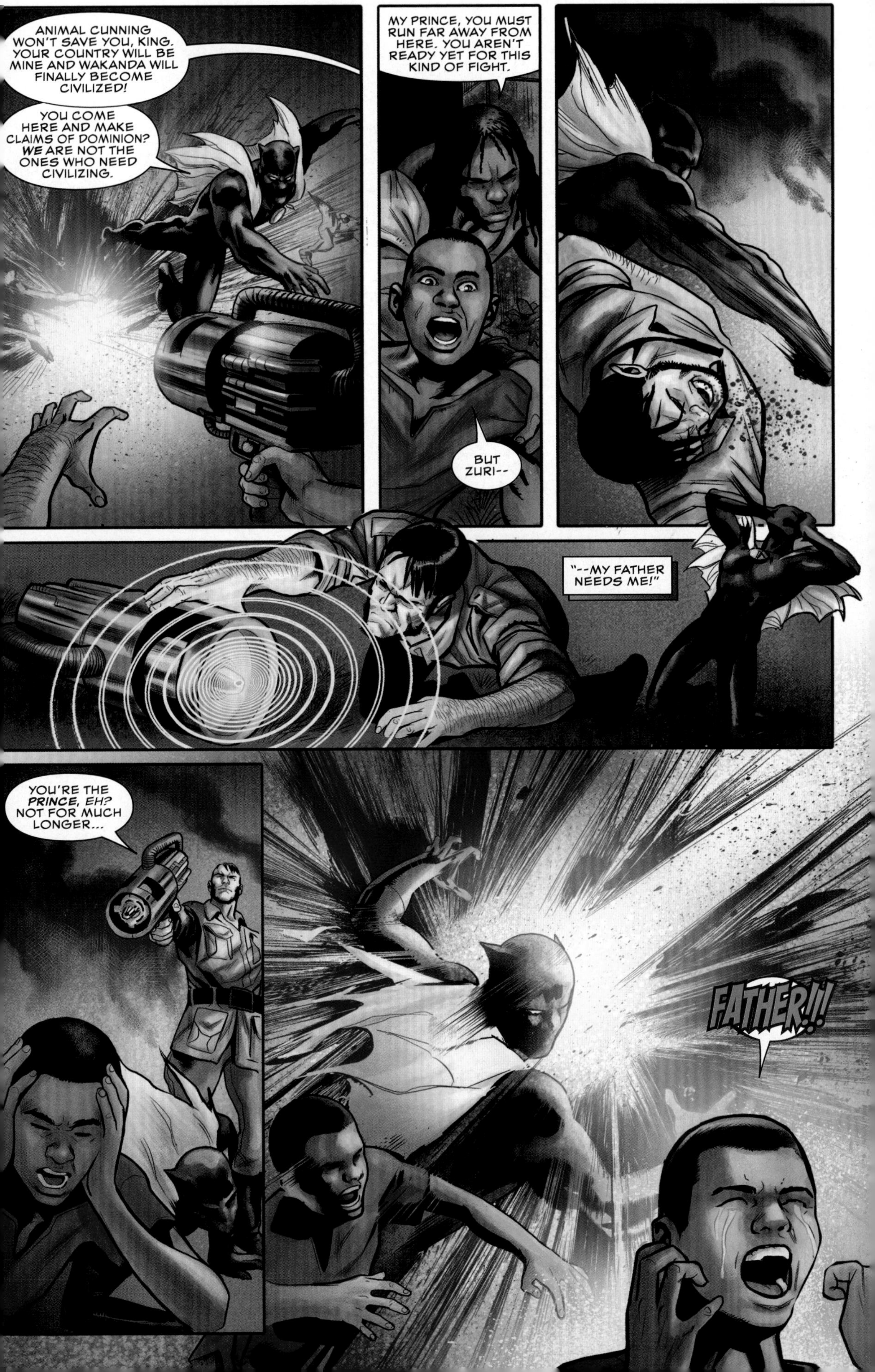
ANIMAL CUNNING WON'T SAVE YOU, KING. YOUR COUNTRY WILL BE MINE AND WAKANDA WILL FINALLY BECOME CIVILIZED!
YOU COME HERE AND MAKE CLAIMS OF DOMINION? WE ARE NOT THE ONES WHO NEED CIVILIZING.
MY PRINCE, YOU MUST RUN FAR AWAY FROM HERE. YOU AREN'T READY YET FOR THIS KIND OF FIGHT.
BUT ZURI--
"--MY FATHER NEEDS ME!"
YOU'RE THE PRINCE, EH? NOT FOR MUCH LONGER...
FATHER!!!

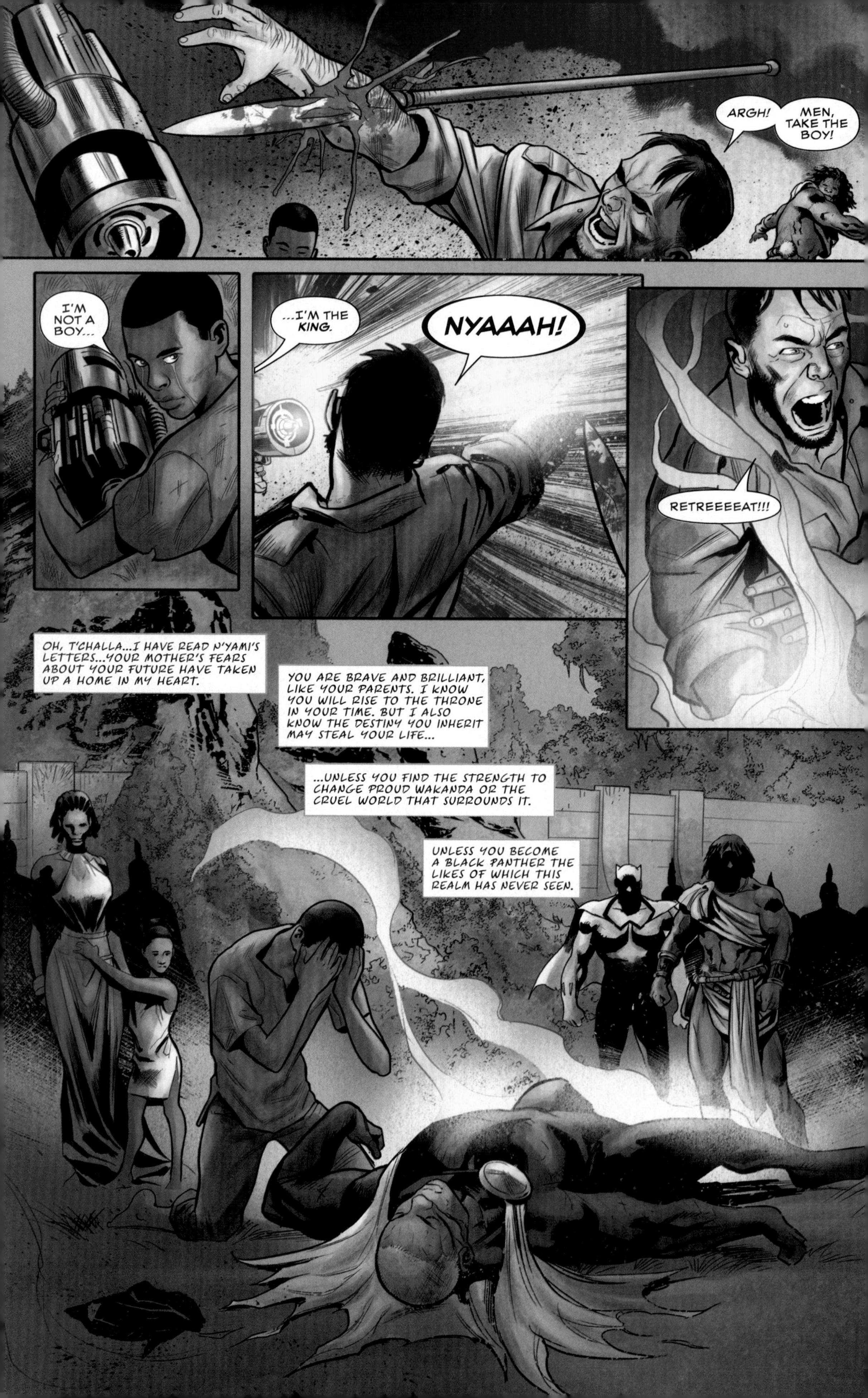
ARGH!
MEN, TAKE THE BOY!
I'M NOT A BOY...
...I'M THE KING.
NYAAAH!
RETREEEEAT!!!
OH, T'CHALLA...I HAVE READ N'YAMI'S LETTERS...YOUR MOTHER'S FEARS ABOUT YOUR FUTURE HAVE TAKEN UP A HOME IN MY HEART.
YOU ARE BRAVE AND BRILLIANT, LIKE YOUR PARENTS. I KNOW YOU WILL RISE TO THE THRONE IN YOUR TIME. BUT I ALSO KNOW THE DESTINY YOU INHERIT MAY STEAL YOUR LIFE...
...UNLESS YOU FIND THE STRENGTH TO CHANGE PROUD WAKANDA OR THE CRUEL WORLD THAT SURROUNDS IT.
UNLESS YOU BECOME A BLACK PANTHER THE LIKES OF WHICH THIS REALM HAS NEVER SEEN.

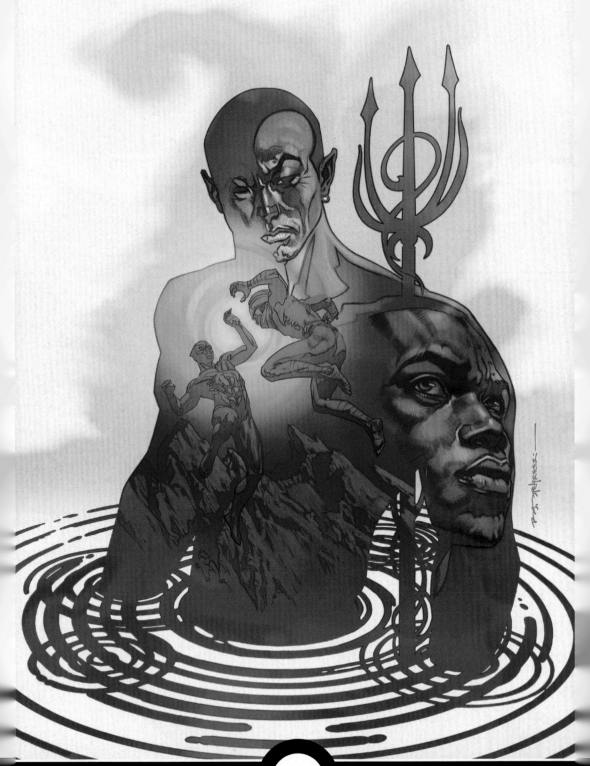

2

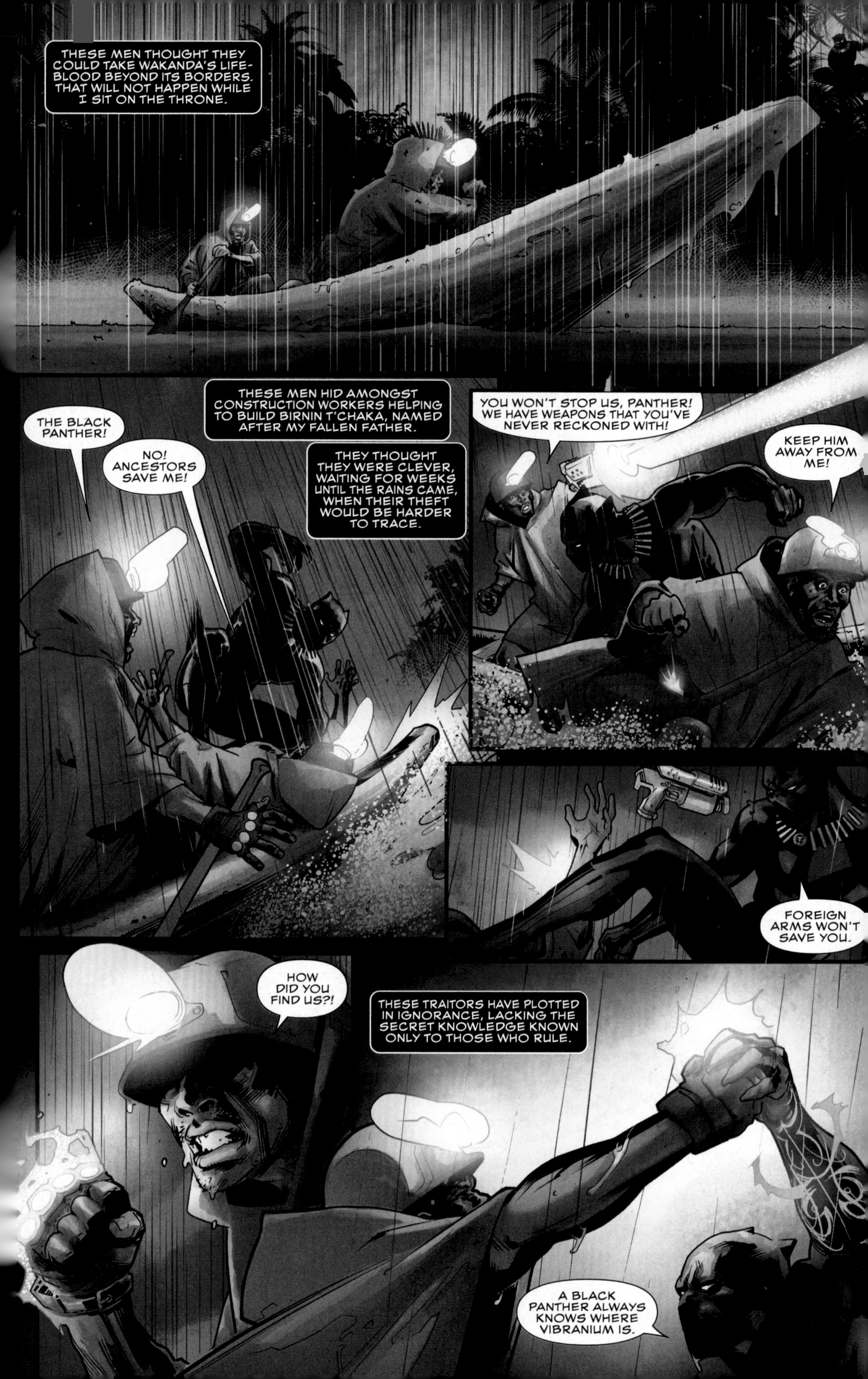
THESE MEN THOUGHT THEY COULD TAKE WAKANDA'S LIFE-BLOOD BEYOND ITS BORDERS. THAT WILL NOT HAPPEN WHILE I SIT ON THE THRONE.
THESE MEN HID AMONGST CONSTRUCTION WORKERS HELPING TO BUILD BIRNIN T'CHAKA, NAMED AFTER MY FALLEN FATHER.
THE BLACK PANTHER!
NO! ANCESTORS SAVE ME!
THEY THOUGHT THEY WERE CLEVER, WAITING FOR WEEKS UNTIL THE RAINS CAME, WHEN THEIR THEFT WOULD BE HARDER TO TRACE.
YOU WON'T STOP US, PANTHER! WE HAVE WEAPONS THAT YOU'VE NEVER RECKONED WITH!
KEEP HIM AWAY FROM ME!
FOREIGN ARMS WON'T SAVE YOU.
HOW DID YOU FIND US?!
THESE TRAITORS HAVE PLOTTED IN IGNORANCE, LACKING THE SECRET KNOWLEDGE KNOWN ONLY TO THOSE WHO RULE.
A BLACK PANTHER ALWAYS KNOWS WHERE VIBRANIUM IS.

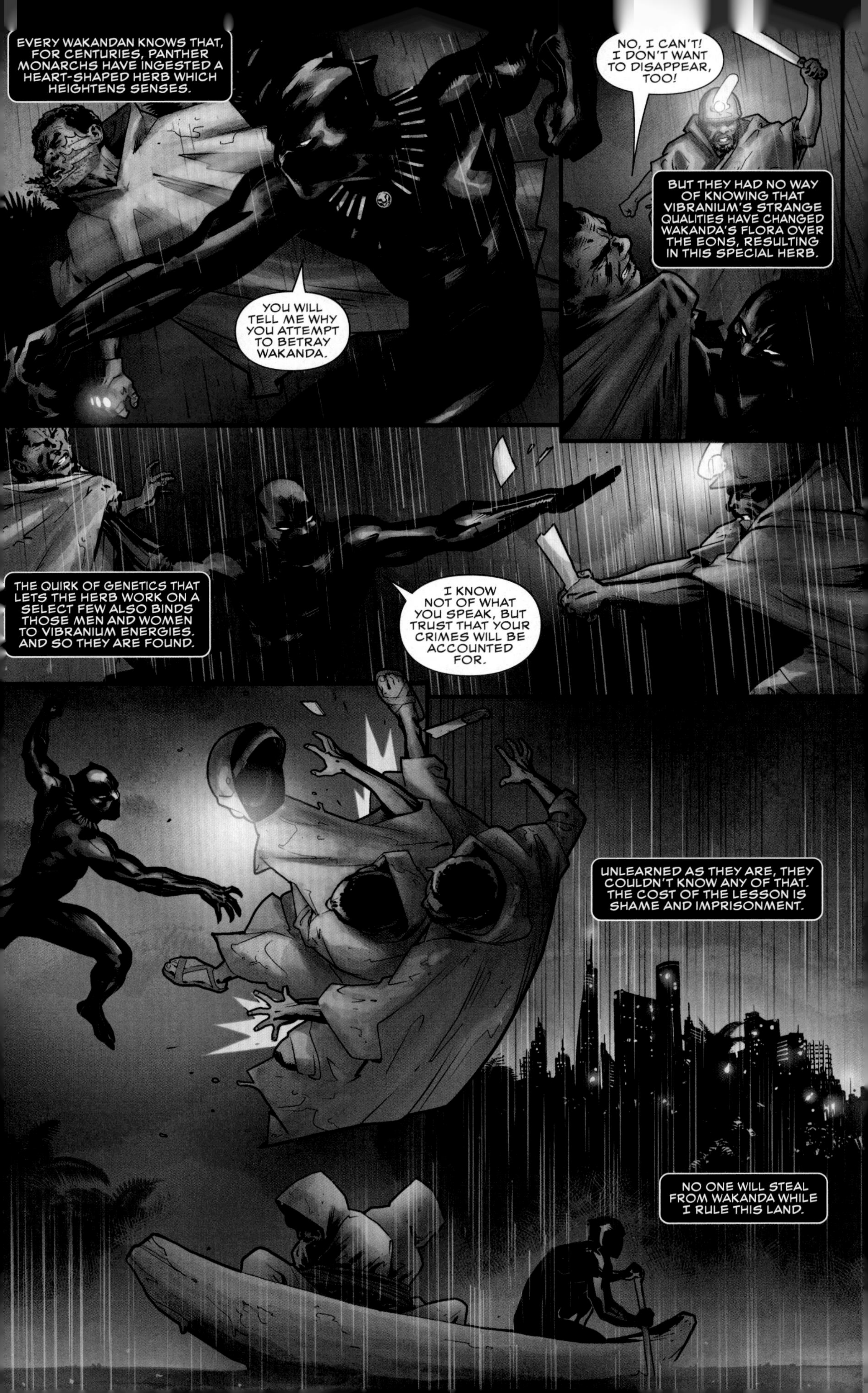
EVERY WAKANDAN KNOWS THAT, FOR CENTURIES, PANTHER MONARCHS HAVE INGESTED A HEART-SHAPED HERB WHICH HEIGHTENS SENSES.
YOU WILL TELL ME WHY YOU ATTEMPT TO BETRAY WAKANDA.
NO, I CAN'T! I DON'T WANT TO DISAPPEAR, TOO!
BUT THEY HAD NO WAY OF KNOWING THAT VIBRANIUM'S STRANGE QUALITIES HAVE CHANGED WAKANDA'S FLORA OVER THE EONS, RESULTING IN THIS SPECIAL HERB.
THE QUIRK OF GENETICS THAT LETS THE HERB WORK ON A SELECT FEW ALSO BINDS THOSE MEN AND WOMEN TO VIBRANIUM ENERGIES. AND SO THEY ARE FOUND.
I KNOW NOT OF WHAT YOU SPEAK, BUT TRUST THAT YOUR CRIMES WILL BE ACCOUNTED FOR.
UNLEARNED AS THEY ARE, THEY COULDN'T KNOW ANY OF THAT. THE COST OF THE LESSON IS SHAME AND IMPRISONMENT.
NO ONE WILL STEAL FROM WAKANDA WHILE I RULE THIS LAND.

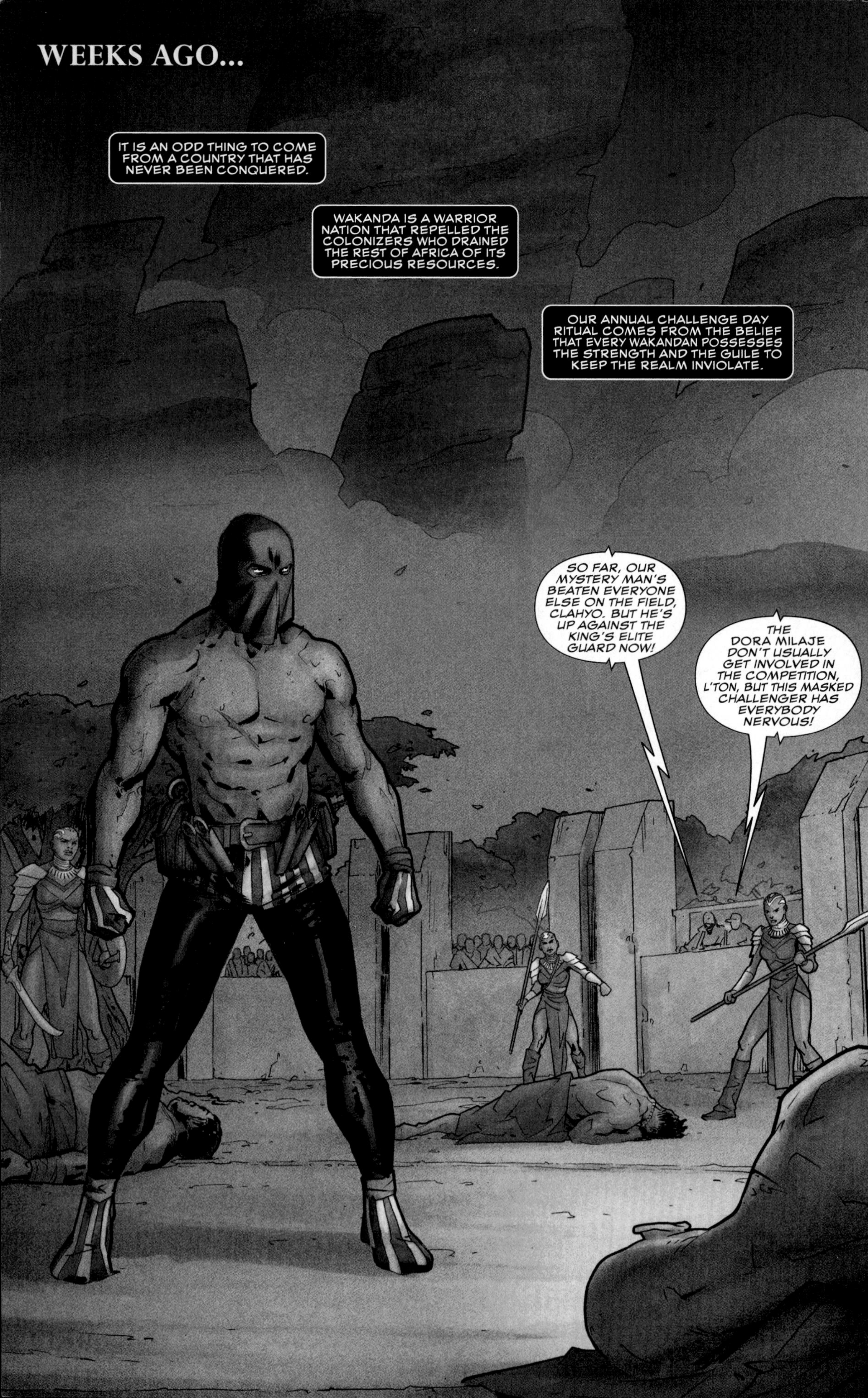
WEEKS AGO...
IT IS AN ODD THING TO COME FROM A COUNTRY THAT HAS NEVER BEEN CONQUERED.
WAKANDA IS A WARRIOR NATION THAT REPELLED THE COLONIZERS WHO DRAINED THE REST OF AFRICA OF ITS PRECIOUS RESOURCES.
OUR ANNUAL CHALLENGE DAY RITUAL COMES FROM THE BELIEF THAT EVERY WAKANDAN POSSESSES THE STRENGTH AND THE GUILE TO KEEP THE REALM INVIOLATE.
SO FAR, OUR MYSTERY MAN'S BEATEN EVERYONE ELSE ON THE FIELD, CLAHYO. BUT HE'S UP AGAINST THE KING'S ELITE GUARD NOW!
THE DORA MILAJE DON'T USUALLY GET INVOLVED IN THE COMPETITION, L'TON, BUT THIS MASKED CHALLENGER HAS EVERYBODY NERVOUS!

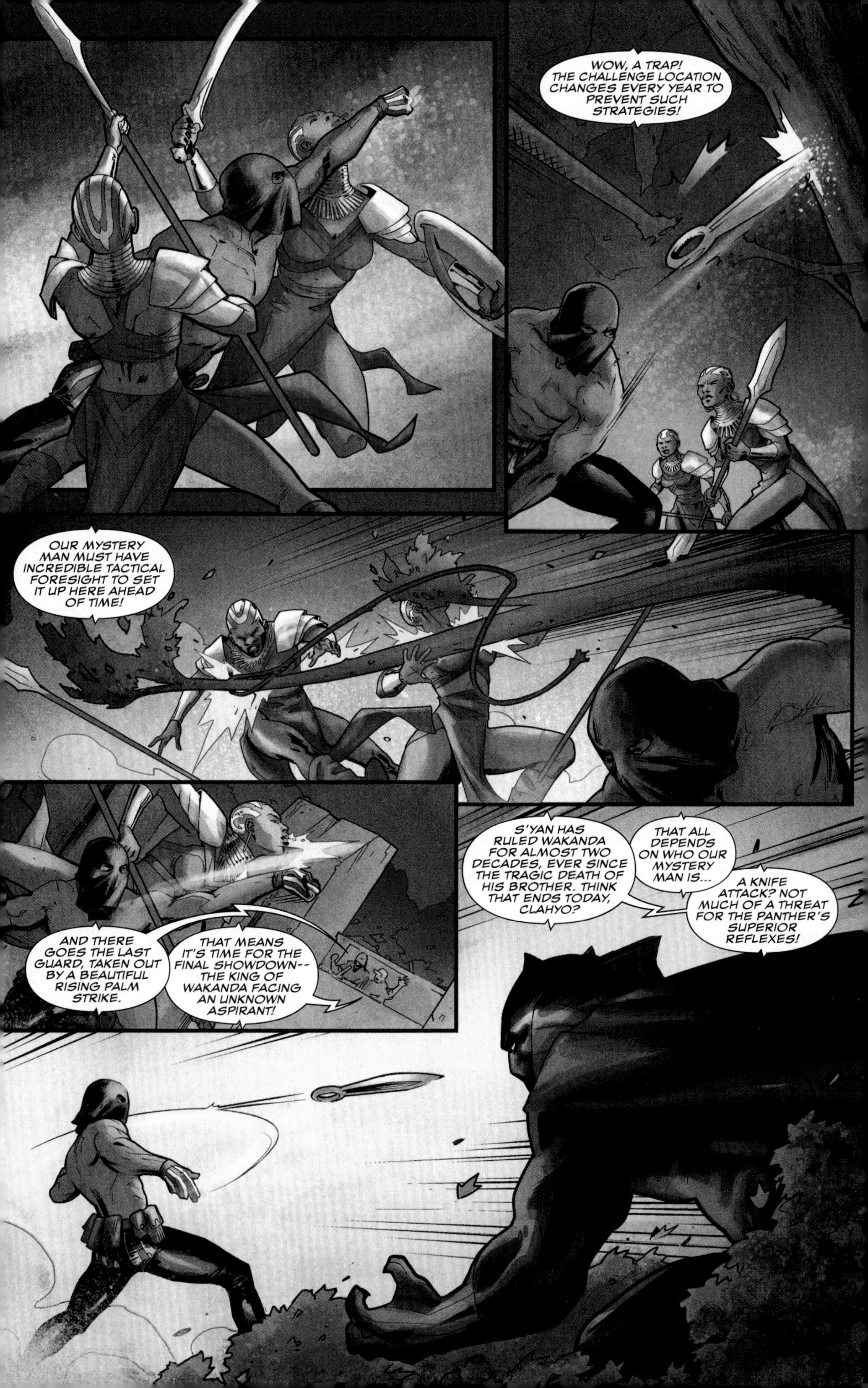
WOW, A TRAP! THE CHALLENGE LOCATION CHANGES EVERY YEAR TO PREVENT SUCH STRATEGIES!
OUR MYSTERY MAN MUST HAVE INCREDIBLE TACTICAL FORESIGHT TO SET IT UP HERE AHEAD OF TIME!
AND THERE GOES THE LAST GUARD, TAKEN OUT BY A BEAUTIFUL RISING PALM STRIKE.
THAT MEANS IT'S TIME FOR THE FINAL SHOWDOWN-- THE KING OF WAKANDA FACING AN UNKNOWN ASPIRANT!
S'YAN HAS RULED WAKANDA FOR ALMOST TWO DECADES, EVER SINCE THE TRAGIC DEATH OF HIS BROTHER. THINK THAT ENDS TODAY, CLAHYO?
THAT ALL DEPENDS ON WHO OUR MYSTERY MAN IS...
A KNIFE ATTACK? NOT MUCH OF A THREAT FOR THE PANTHER'S SUPERIOR REFLEXES!

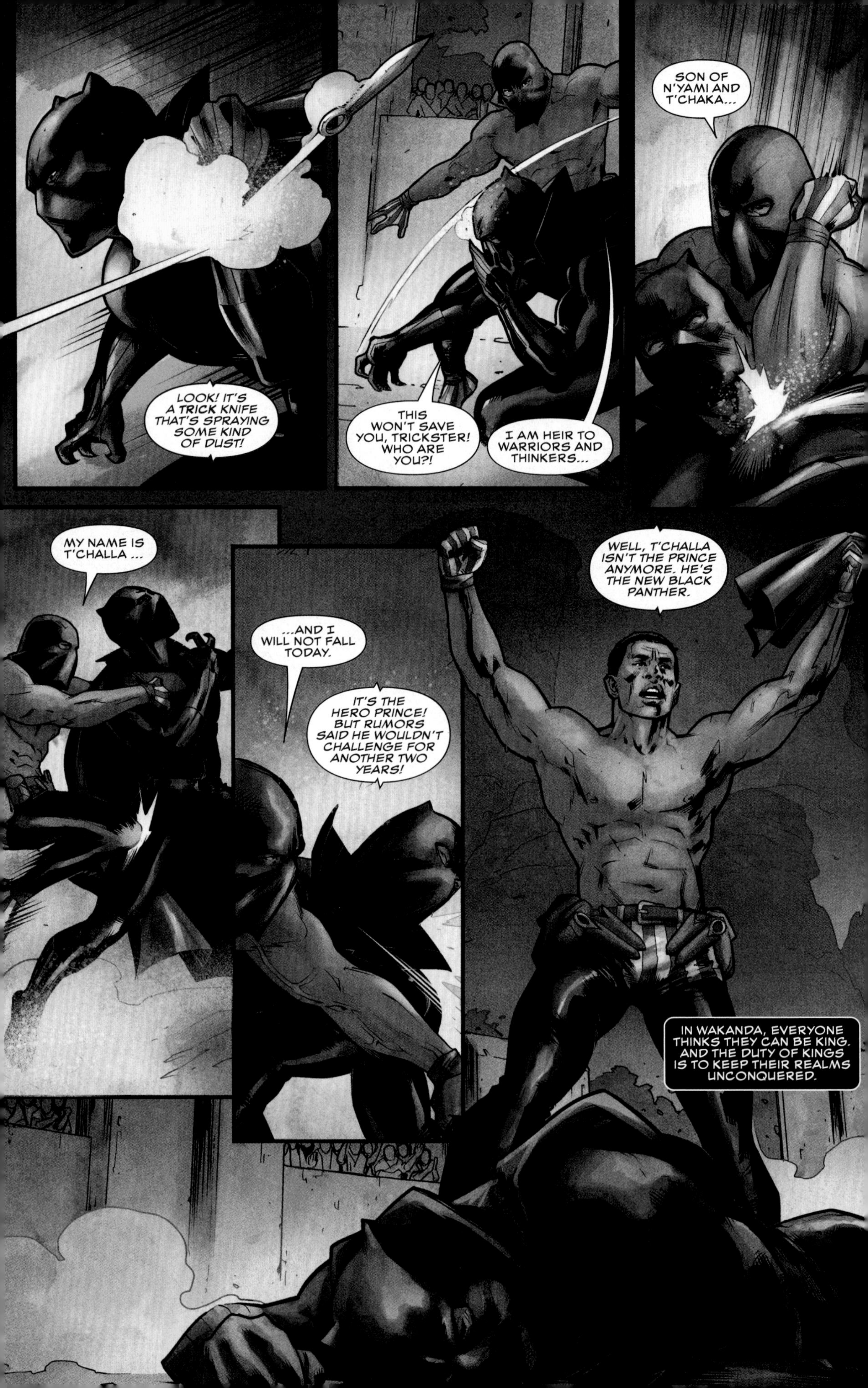
LOOK! IT'S A TRICK KNIFE THAT'S SPRAYING SOME KIND OF DUST!
THIS WON'T SAVE YOU, TRICKSTER! WHO ARE YOU?!
I AM HEIR TO WARRIORS AND THINKERS...
SON OF N'YAMI AND T'CHAKA...
MY NAME IS T'CHALLA ...
...AND I WILL NOT FALL TODAY.
IT'S THE HERO PRINCE! BUT RUMORS SAID HE WOULDN'T CHALLENGE FOR ANOTHER TWO YEARS!
WELL, T'CHALLA ISN'T THE PRINCE ANYMORE. HE'S THE NEW BLACK PANTHER.
IN WAKANDA, EVERYONE THINKS THEY CAN BE KING. AND THE DUTY OF KINGS IS TO KEEP THEIR REALMS UNCONQUERED.

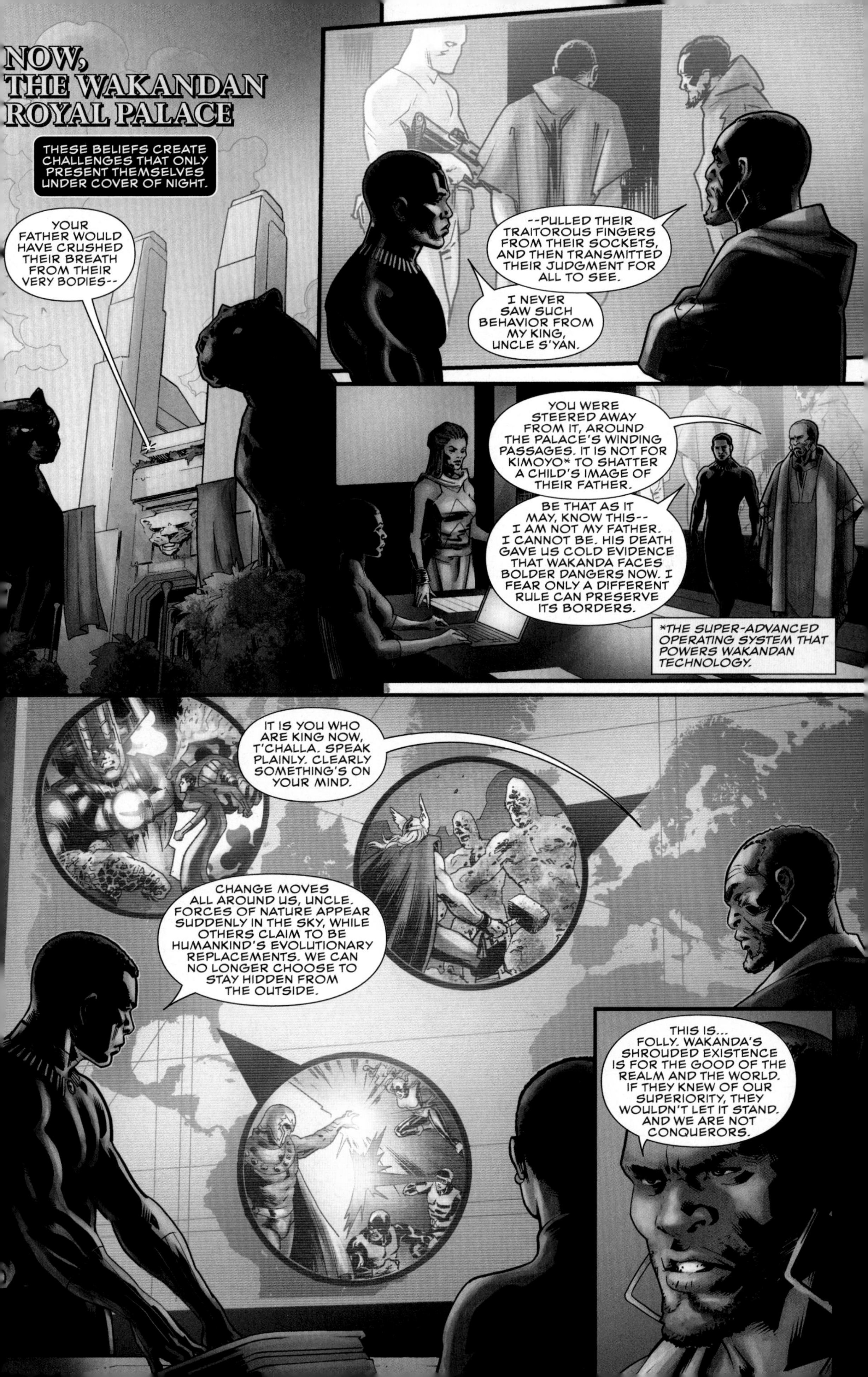
NOW, THE WAKANDAN ROYAL PALACE
THESE BELIEFS CREATE CHALLENGES THAT ONLY PRESENT THEMSELVES UNDER COVER OF NIGHT.
YOUR FATHER WOULD HAVE CRUSHED THEIR BREATH FROM THEIR VERY BODIES--
--PULLED THEIR TRAITOROUS FINGERS FROM THEIR SOCKETS, AND THEN TRANSMITTED THEIR JUDGMENT FOR ALL TO SEE.
I NEVER SAW SUCH BEHAVIOR FROM MY KING, UNCLE S'YAN.
YOU WERE STEERED AWAY FROM IT, AROUND THE PALACE'S WINDING PASSAGES. IT IS NOT FOR KIMOYO* TO SHATTER A CHILD'S IMAGE OF THEIR FATHER.
BE THAT AS IT MAY, KNOW THIS-- I AM NOT MY FATHER. I CANNOT BE. HIS DEATH GAVE US COLD EVIDENCE THAT WAKANDA FACES BOLDER DANGERS NOW. I FEAR ONLY A DIFFERENT RULE CAN PRESERVE ITS BORDERS.
*THE SUPER-ADVANCED OPERATING SYSTEM THAT POWERS WAKANDAN TECHNOLOGY.
IT IS YOU WHO ARE KING NOW, T'CHALLA. SPEAK PLAINLY. CLEARLY SOMETHING'S ON YOUR MIND.
CHANGE MOVES ALL AROUND US, UNCLE. FORCES OF NATURE APPEAR SUDDENLY IN THE SKY, WHILE OTHERS CLAIM TO BE HUMANKIND'S EVOLUTIONARY REPLACEMENTS. WE CAN NO LONGER CHOOSE TO STAY HIDDEN FROM THE OUTSIDE.
THIS IS... FOLLY. WAKANDA'S SHROUDED EXISTENCE IS FOR THE GOOD OF THE REALM AND THE WORLD. IF THEY KNEW OF OUR SUPERIORITY, THEY WOULDN'T LET IT STAND. AND WE ARE NOT CONQUERORS.

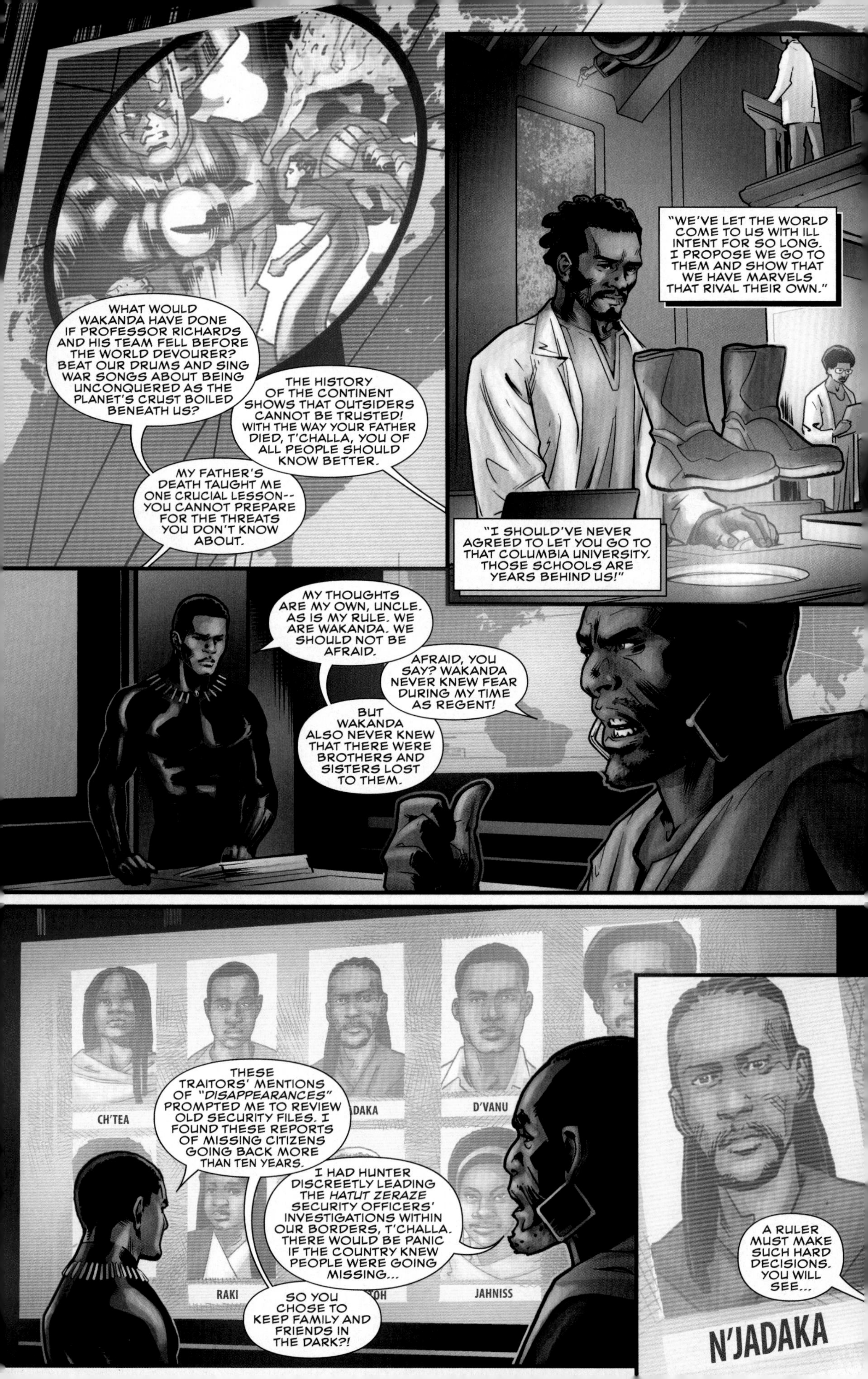
WHAT WOULD WAKANDA HAVE DONE IF PROFESSOR RICHARDS AND HIS TEAM FELL BEFORE THE WORLD DEVOURER? BEAT OUR DRUMS AND SING WAR SONGS ABOUT BEING UNCONQUERED AS THE PLANET'S CRUST BOILED BENEATH US?
THE HISTORY OF THE CONTINENT SHOWS THAT OUTSIDERS CANNOT BE TRUSTED! WITH THE WAY YOUR FATHER DIED, T'CHALLA, YOU OF ALL PEOPLE SHOULD KNOW BETTER.
MY FATHER'S DEATH TAUGHT ME ONE CRUCIAL LESSON-- YOU CANNOT PREPARE FOR THE THREATS YOU DON'T KNOW ABOUT.
"WE'VE LET THE WORLD COME TO US WITH ILL INTENT FOR SO LONG. I PROPOSE WE GO TO THEM AND SHOW THAT WE HAVE MARVELS THAT RIVAL THEIR OWN."
"I SHOULD'VE NEVER AGREED TO LET YOU GO TO THAT COLUMBIA UNIVERSITY. THOSE SCHOOLS ARE YEARS BEHIND US!"
MY THOUGHTS ARE MY OWN, UNCLE. AS IS MY RULE. WE ARE WAKANDA. WE SHOULD NOT BE AFRAID.
AFRAID, YOU SAY? WAKANDA NEVER KNEW FEAR DURING MY TIME AS REGENT!
BUT WAKANDA ALSO NEVER KNEW THAT THERE WERE BROTHERS AND SISTERS LOST TO THEM.
CH'TEA
D'VANU
RAKI
JAHNISS
THESE TRAITORS' MENTIONS OF *"DISAPPEARANCES"* PROMPTED ME TO REVIEW OLD SECURITY FILES. I FOUND THESE REPORTS OF MISSING CITIZENS GOING BACK MORE THAN TEN YEARS.
I HAD HUNTER DISCREETLY LEADING THE *HATUT ZERAZE* SECURITY OFFICERS' INVESTIGATIONS WITHIN OUR BORDERS, T'CHALLA. THERE WOULD BE PANIC IF THE COUNTRY KNEW PEOPLE WERE GOING MISSING...
SO YOU CHOSE TO KEEP FAMILY AND FRIENDS IN THE DARK?!
A RULER MUST MAKE SUCH HARD DECISIONS. YOU WILL SEE...
N'JADAKA

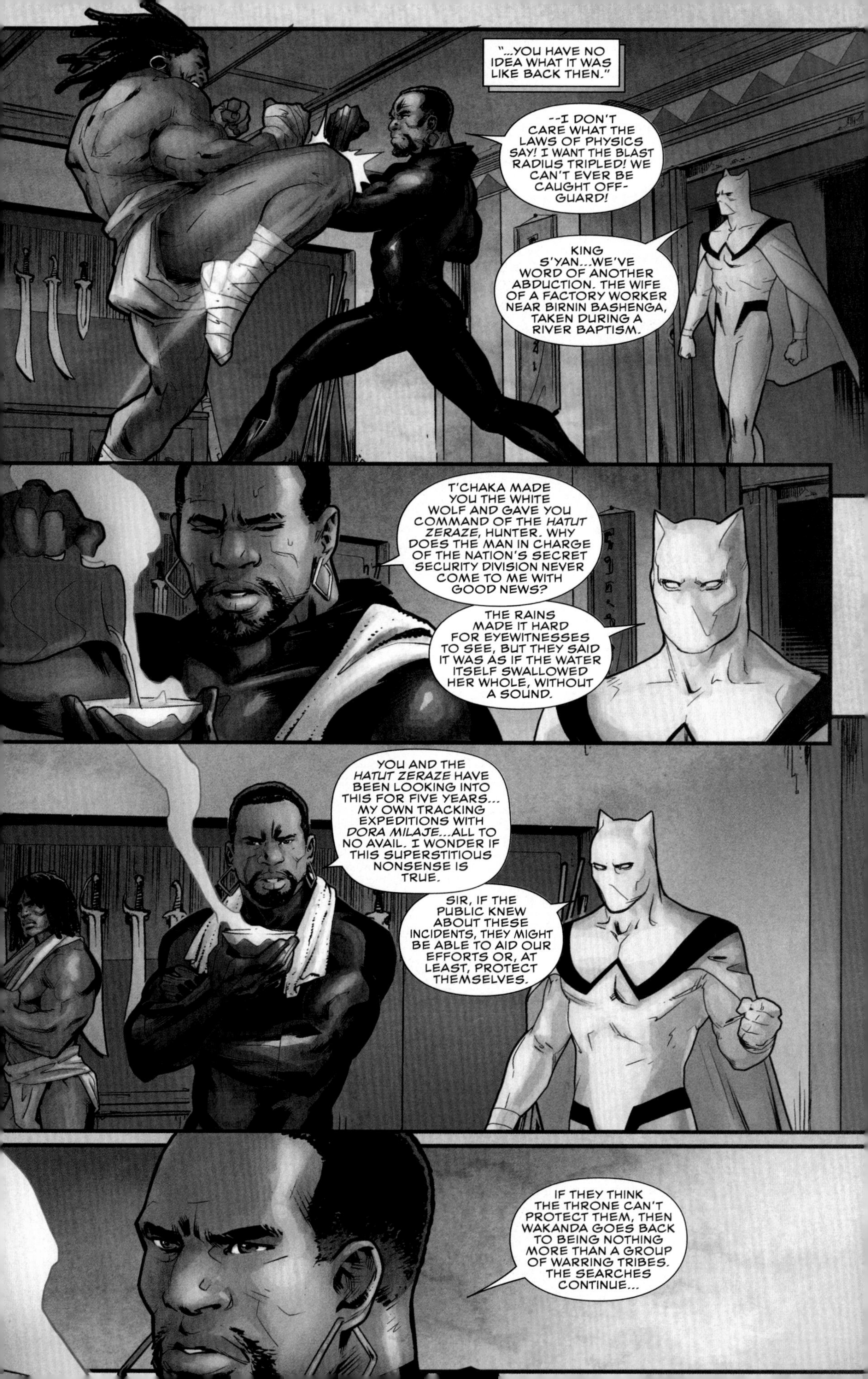
"...YOU HAVE NO IDEA WHAT IT WAS LIKE BACK THEN."
--I DON'T CARE WHAT THE LAWS OF PHYSICS SAY! I WANT THE BLAST RADIUS TRIPLED! WE CAN'T EVER BE CAUGHT OFF-GUARD!
KING S'YAN...WE'VE WORD OF ANOTHER ABDUCTION. THE WIFE OF A FACTORY WORKER NEAR BIRNIN BASHENGA, TAKEN DURING A RIVER BAPTISM.
T'CHAKA MADE YOU THE WHITE WOLF AND GAVE YOU COMMAND OF THE *HATUT ZERAZE*, HUNTER. WHY DOES THE MAN IN CHARGE OF THE NATION'S SECRET SECURITY DIVISION NEVER COME TO ME WITH GOOD NEWS?
THE RAINS MADE IT HARD FOR EYEWITNESSES TO SEE, BUT THEY SAID IT WAS AS IF THE WATER ITSELF SWALLOWED HER WHOLE, WITHOUT A SOUND.
YOU AND THE *HATUT ZERAZE* HAVE BEEN LOOKING INTO THIS FOR FIVE YEARS... MY OWN TRACKING EXPEDITIONS WITH *DORA MILAJE*...ALL TO NO AVAIL. I WONDER IF THIS SUPERSTITIOUS NONSENSE IS TRUE.
SIR, IF THE PUBLIC KNEW ABOUT THESE INCIDENTS, THEY MIGHT BE ABLE TO AID OUR EFFORTS OR, AT LEAST, PROTECT THEMSELVES.
IF THEY THINK THE THRONE CAN'T PROTECT THEM, THEN WAKANDA GOES BACK TO BEING NOTHING MORE THAN A GROUP OF WARRING TRIBES. THE SEARCHES CONTINUE...

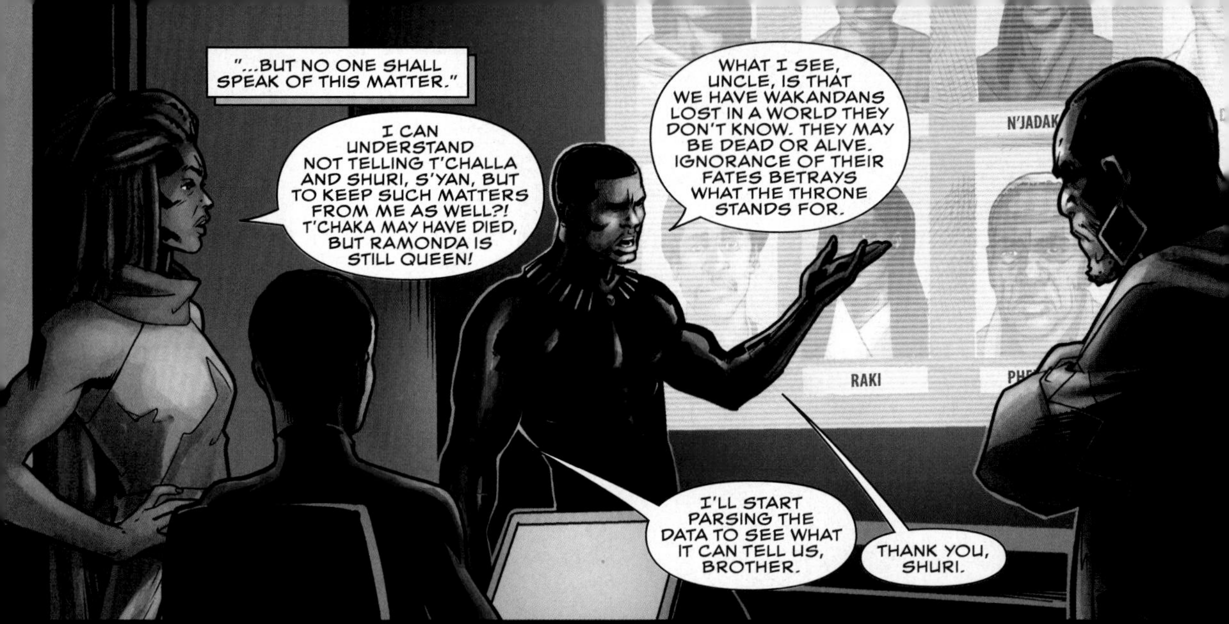
"...BUT NO ONE SHALL SPEAK OF THIS MATTER."
I CAN UNDERSTAND NOT TELLING T'CHALLA AND SHURI, S'YAN, BUT TO KEEP SUCH MATTERS FROM ME AS WELL?! T'CHAKA MAY HAVE DIED, BUT RAMONDA IS STILL QUEEN!
WHAT I SEE, UNCLE, IS THAT WE HAVE WAKANDANS LOST IN A WORLD THEY DON'T KNOW. THEY MAY BE DEAD OR ALIVE. IGNORANCE OF THEIR FATES BETRAYS WHAT THE THRONE STANDS FOR.
N'JADAK
RAKI
I'LL START PARSING THE DATA TO SEE WHAT IT CAN TELL US, BROTHER.
THANK YOU, SHURI.

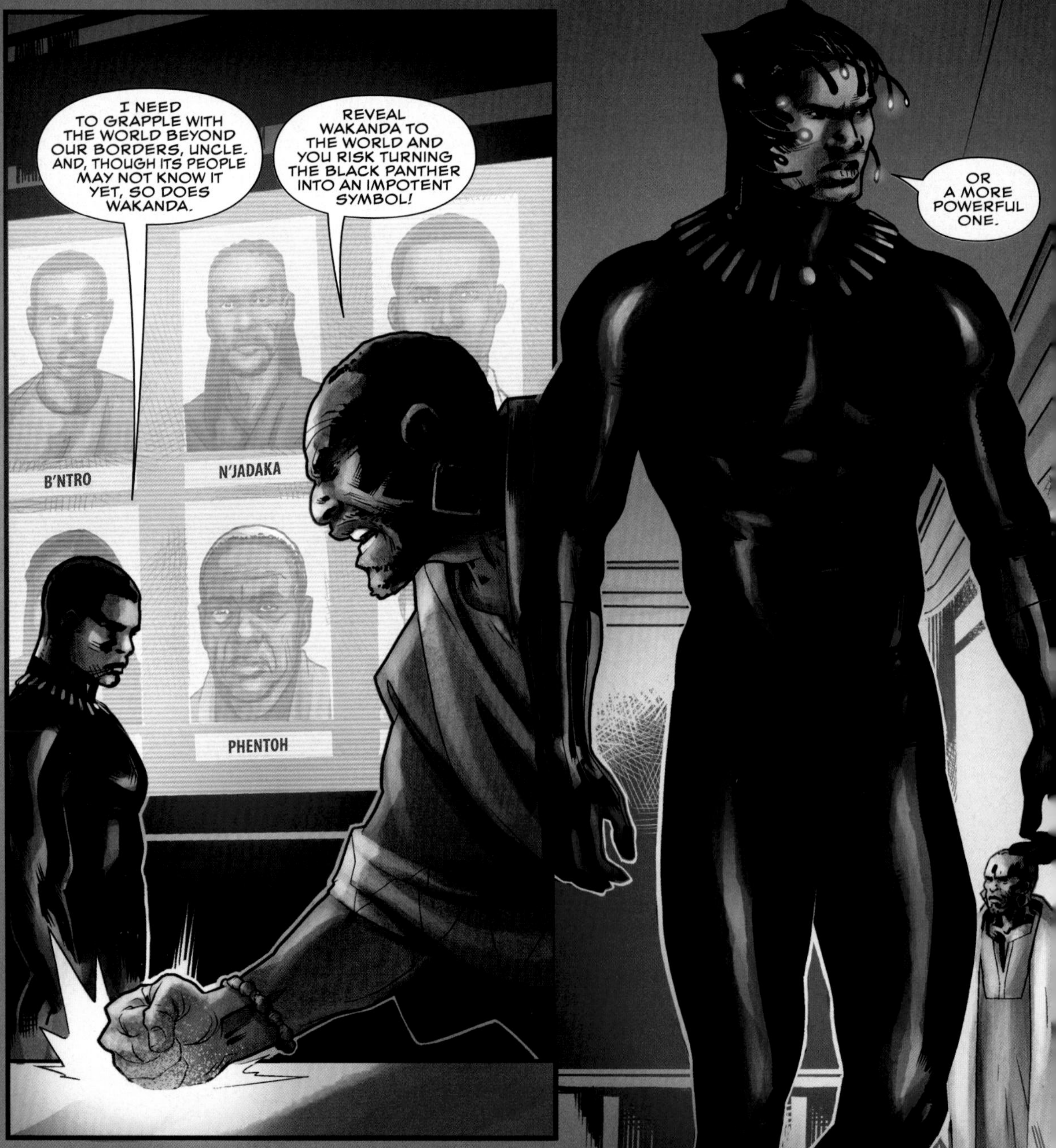
I NEED TO GRAPPLE WITH THE WORLD BEYOND OUR BORDERS, UNCLE. AND, THOUGH ITS PEOPLE MAY NOT KNOW IT YET, SO DOES WAKANDA.
REVEAL WAKANDA TO THE WORLD AND YOU RISK TURNING THE BLACK PANTHER INTO AN IMPOTENT SYMBOL!
OR A MORE POWERFUL ONE.
B'NTRO
N'JADAKA
PHENTOH

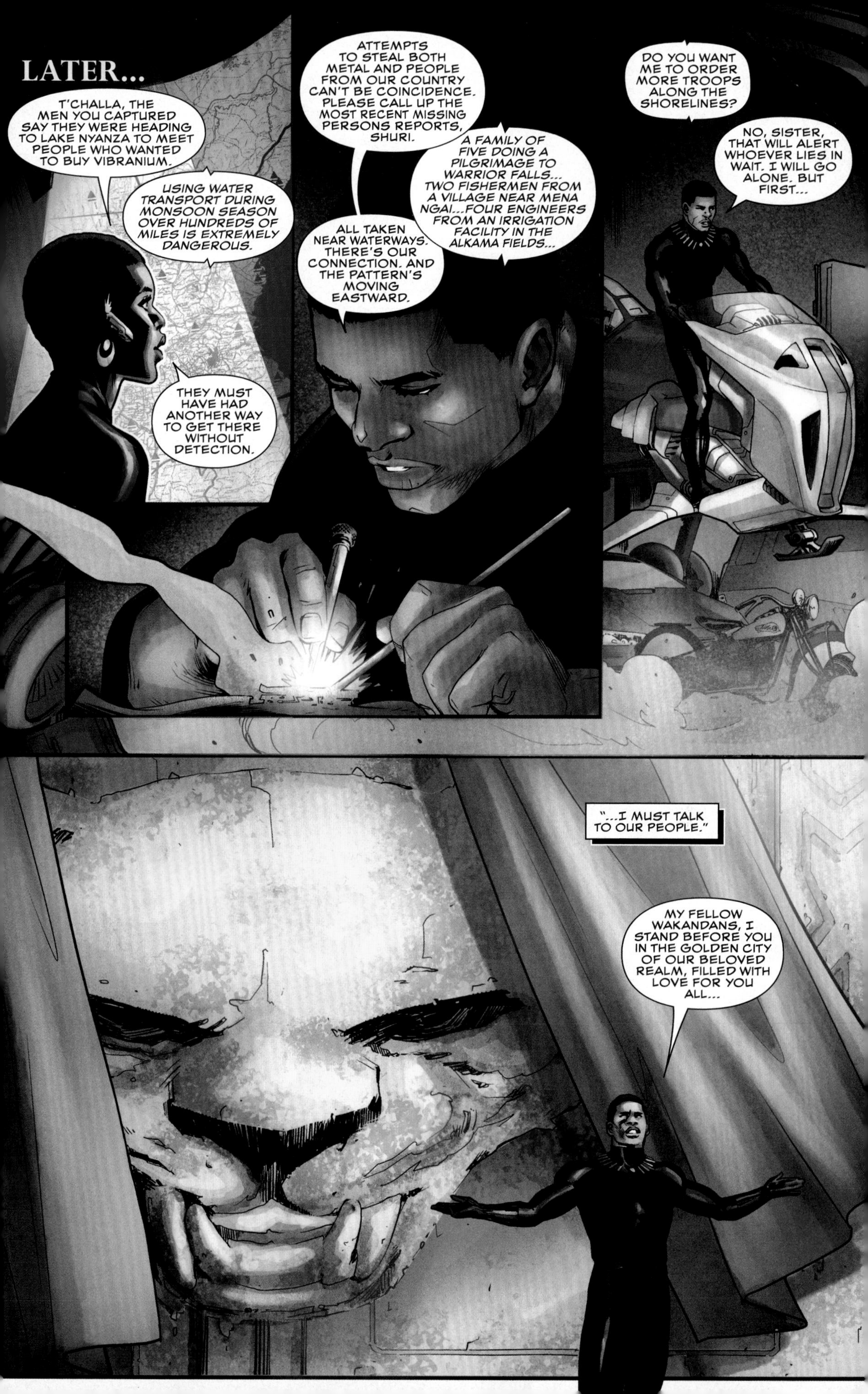
LATER...
T'CHALLA, THE MEN YOU CAPTURED SAY THEY WERE HEADING TO LAKE NYANZA TO MEET PEOPLE WHO WANTED TO BUY VIBRANIUM.
USING WATER TRANSPORT DURING MONSOON SEASON OVER HUNDREDS OF MILES IS EXTREMELY DANGEROUS.
THEY MUST HAVE HAD ANOTHER WAY TO GET THERE WITHOUT DETECTION.
ATTEMPTS TO STEAL BOTH METAL AND PEOPLE FROM OUR COUNTRY CAN'T BE COINCIDENCE. PLEASE CALL UP THE MOST RECENT MISSING PERSONS REPORTS, SHURI.
A FAMILY OF FIVE DOING A PILGRIMAGE TO WARRIOR FALLS... TWO FISHERMEN FROM A VILLAGE NEAR MENA NGAI...FOUR ENGINEERS FROM AN IRRIGATION FACILITY IN THE ALKAMA FIELDS...
ALL TAKEN NEAR WATERWAYS. THERE'S OUR CONNECTION. AND THE PATTERN'S MOVING EASTWARD.
DO YOU WANT ME TO ORDER MORE TROOPS ALONG THE SHORELINES?
NO, SISTER, THAT WILL ALERT WHOEVER LIES IN WAIT. I WILL GO ALONE. BUT FIRST...
"...I MUST TALK TO OUR PEOPLE."
MY FELLOW WAKANDANS, I STAND BEFORE YOU IN THE GOLDEN CITY OF OUR BELOVED REALM, FILLED WITH LOVE FOR YOU ALL...

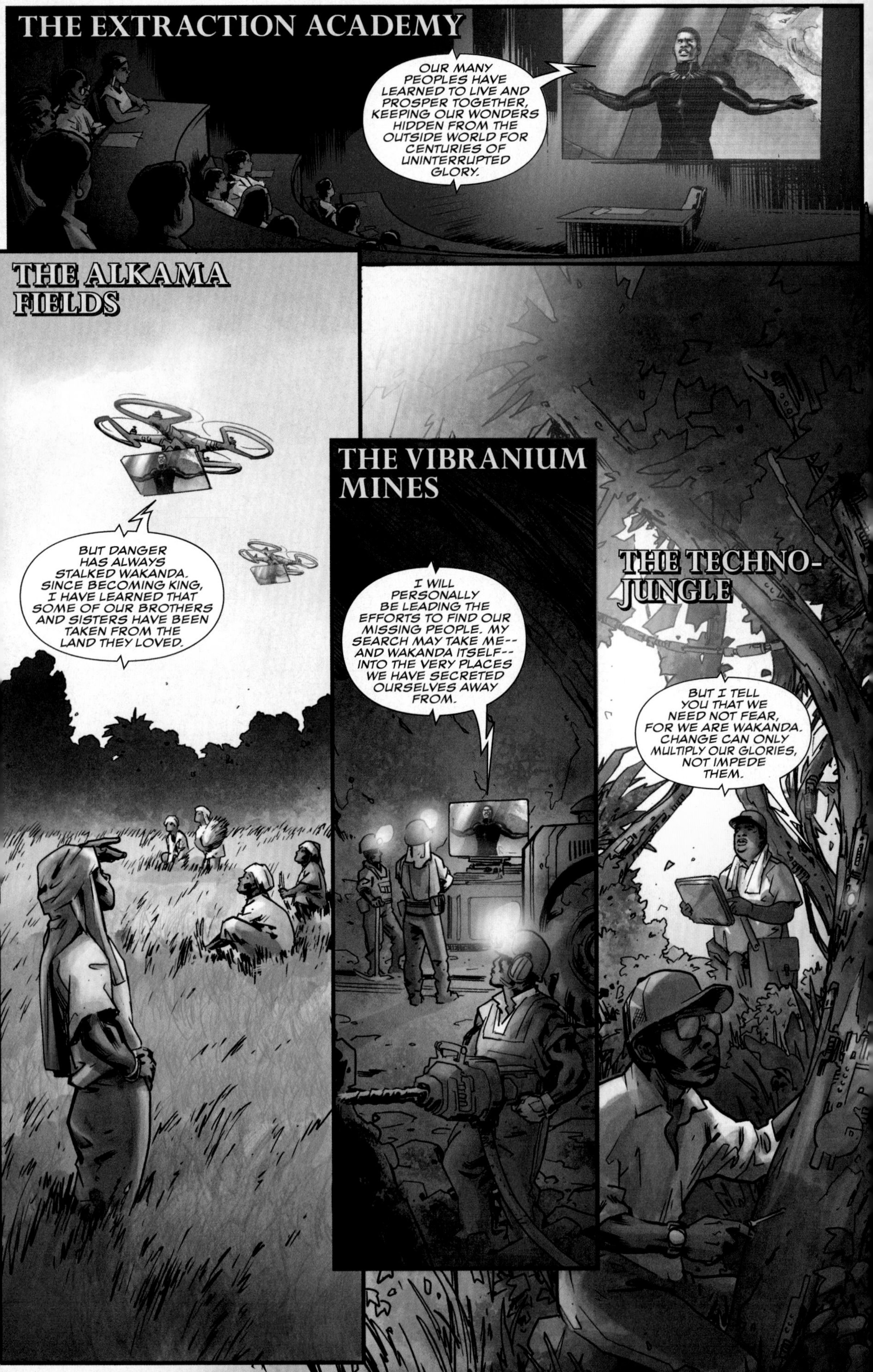
THE EXTRACTION ACADEMY
OUR MANY PEOPLES HAVE LEARNED TO LIVE AND PROSPER TOGETHER, KEEPING OUR WONDERS HIDDEN FROM THE OUTSIDE WORLD FOR CENTURIES OF UNINTERRUPTED GLORY.
THE ALKAMA FIELDS
BUT DANGER HAS ALWAYS STALKED WAKANDA. SINCE BECOMING KING, I HAVE LEARNED THAT SOME OF OUR BROTHERS AND SISTERS HAVE BEEN TAKEN FROM THE LAND THEY LOVED.
THE VIBRANIUM MINES
I WILL PERSONALLY BE LEADING THE EFFORTS TO FIND OUR MISSING PEOPLE. MY SEARCH MAY TAKE ME--AND WAKANDA ITSELF--INTO THE VERY PLACES WE HAVE SECRETED OURSELVES AWAY FROM.
THE TECHNO-JUNGLE
BUT I TELL YOU THAT WE NEED NOT FEAR, FOR WE ARE WAKANDA. CHANGE CAN ONLY MULTIPLY OUR GLORIES, NOT IMPEDE THEM.

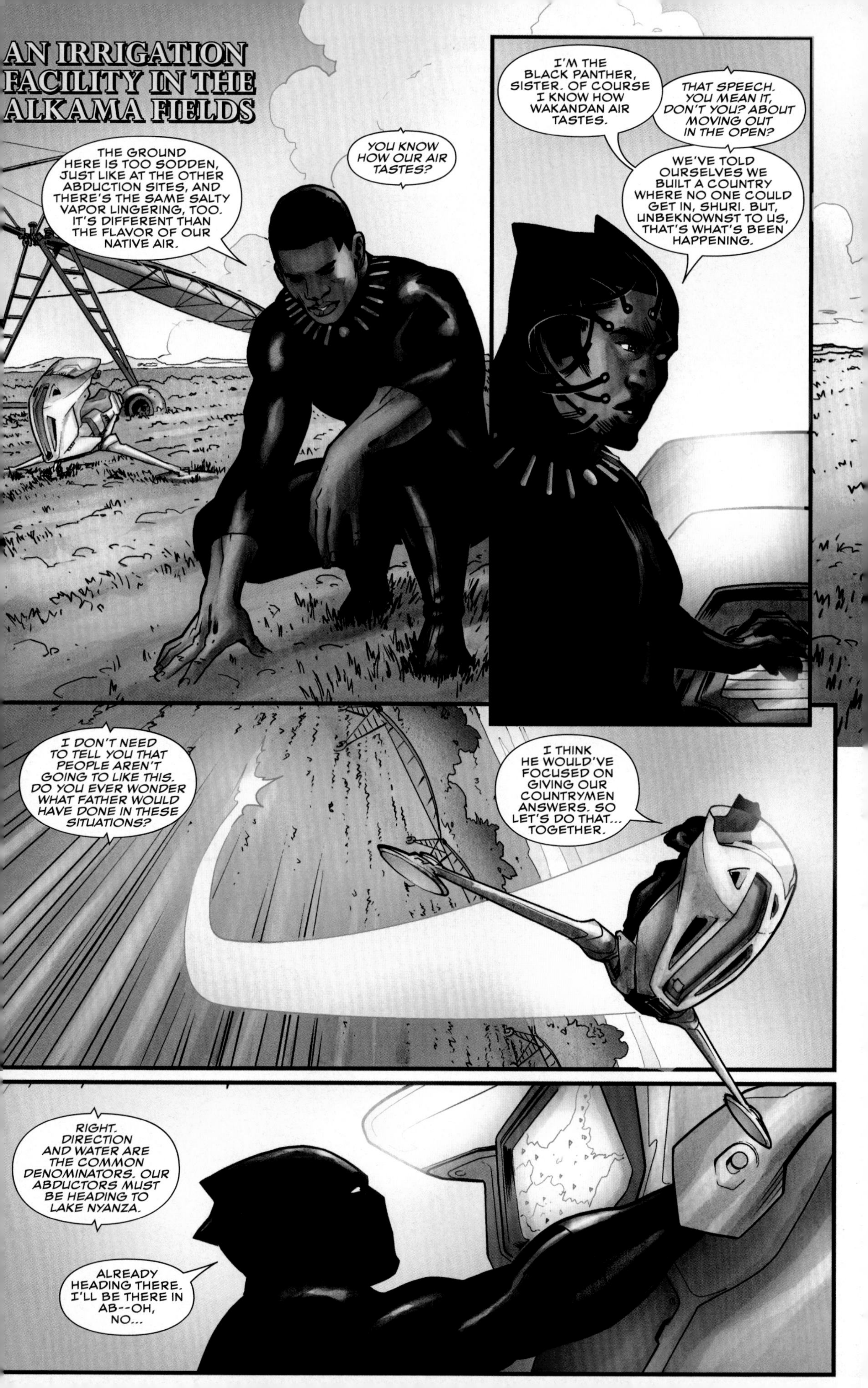
AN IRRIGATION FACILITY IN THE ALKAMA FIELDS
THE GROUND HERE IS TOO SODDEN, JUST LIKE AT THE OTHER ABDUCTION SITES, AND THERE'S THE SAME SALTY VAPOR LINGERING, TOO. IT'S DIFFERENT THAN THE FLAVOR OF OUR NATIVE AIR.
YOU KNOW HOW OUR AIR TASTES?
I'M THE BLACK PANTHER, SISTER. OF COURSE I KNOW HOW WAKANDAN AIR TASTES.
THAT SPEECH. YOU MEAN IT, DON'T YOU? ABOUT MOVING OUT IN THE OPEN?
WE'VE TOLD OURSELVES WE BUILT A COUNTRY WHERE NO ONE COULD GET IN, SHURI. BUT, UNBEKNOWNST TO US, THAT'S WHAT'S BEEN HAPPENING.
I DON'T NEED TO TELL YOU THAT PEOPLE AREN'T GOING TO LIKE THIS. DO YOU EVER WONDER WHAT FATHER WOULD HAVE DONE IN THESE SITUATIONS?
I THINK HE WOULD'VE FOCUSED ON GIVING OUR COUNTRYMEN ANSWERS. SO LET'S DO THAT... TOGETHER.
RIGHT. DIRECTION AND WATER ARE THE COMMON DENOMINATORS. OUR ABDUCTORS MUST BE HEADING TO LAKE NYANZA.
ALREADY HEADING THERE. I'LL BE THERE IN AB--OH, NO...

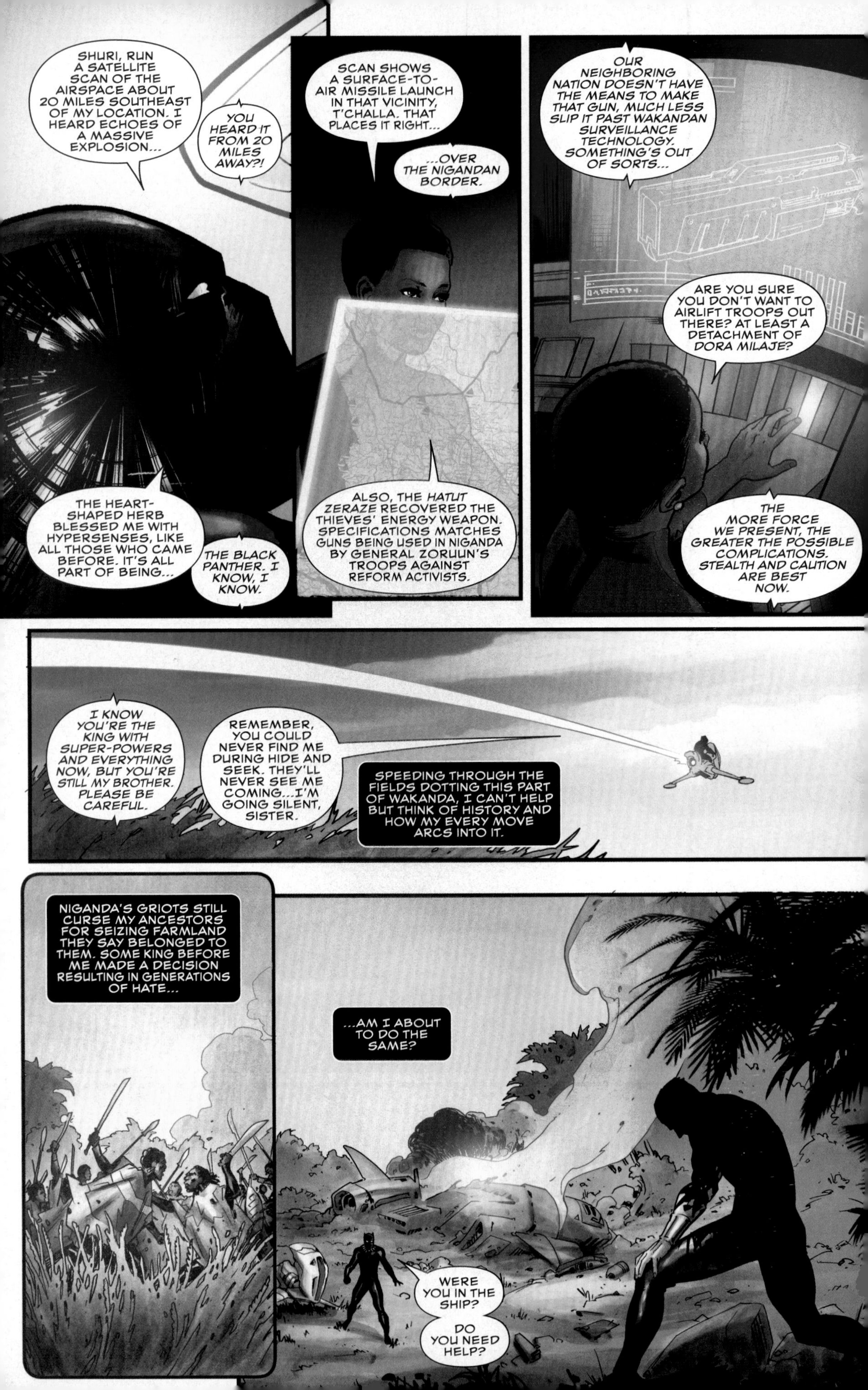

SHURI, RUN A SATELLITE SCAN OF THE AIRSPACE ABOUT 20 MILES SOUTHEAST OF MY LOCATION. I HEARD ECHOES OF A MASSIVE EXPLOSION...
YOU HEARD IT FROM 20 MILES AWAY?!
THE HEART-SHAPED HERB BLESSED ME WITH HYPERSENSES, LIKE ALL THOSE WHO CAME BEFORE. IT'S ALL PART OF BEING...
THE BLACK PANTHER. I KNOW, I KNOW.
SCAN SHOWS A SURFACE-TO-AIR MISSILE LAUNCH IN THAT VICINITY, T'CHALLA. THAT PLACES IT RIGHT...
...OVER THE NIGANDAN BORDER.
ALSO, THE HATUT ZERAZE RECOVERED THE THIEVES' ENERGY WEAPON. SPECIFICATIONS MATCHES GUNS BEING USED IN NIGANDA BY GENERAL ZORUUN'S TROOPS AGAINST REFORM ACTIVISTS.
OUR NEIGHBORING NATION DOESN'T HAVE THE MEANS TO MAKE THAT GUN, MUCH LESS SLIP IT PAST WAKANDAN SURVEILLANCE TECHNOLOGY. SOMETHING'S OUT OF SORTS...
ARE YOU SURE YOU DON'T WANT TO AIRLIFT TROOPS OUT THERE? AT LEAST A DETACHMENT OF DORA MILAJE?
THE MORE FORCE WE PRESENT, THE GREATER THE POSSIBLE COMPLICATIONS. STEALTH AND CAUTION ARE BEST NOW.
I KNOW YOU'RE THE KING WITH SUPER-POWERS AND EVERYTHING NOW, BUT YOU'RE STILL MY BROTHER. PLEASE BE CAREFUL.
REMEMBER, YOU COULD NEVER FIND ME DURING HIDE AND SEEK. THEY'LL NEVER SEE ME COMING...I'M GOING SILENT, SISTER.
SPEEDING THROUGH THE FIELDS DOTTING THIS PART OF WAKANDA, I CAN'T HELP BUT THINK OF HISTORY AND HOW MY EVERY MOVE ARCS INTO IT.
NIGANDA'S GRIOTS STILL CURSE MY ANCESTORS FOR SEIZING FARMLAND THEY SAY BELONGED TO THEM. SOME KING BEFORE ME MADE A DECISION RESULTING IN GENERATIONS OF HATE...
...AM I ABOUT TO DO THE SAME?
WERE YOU IN THE SHIP?
DO YOU NEED HELP?

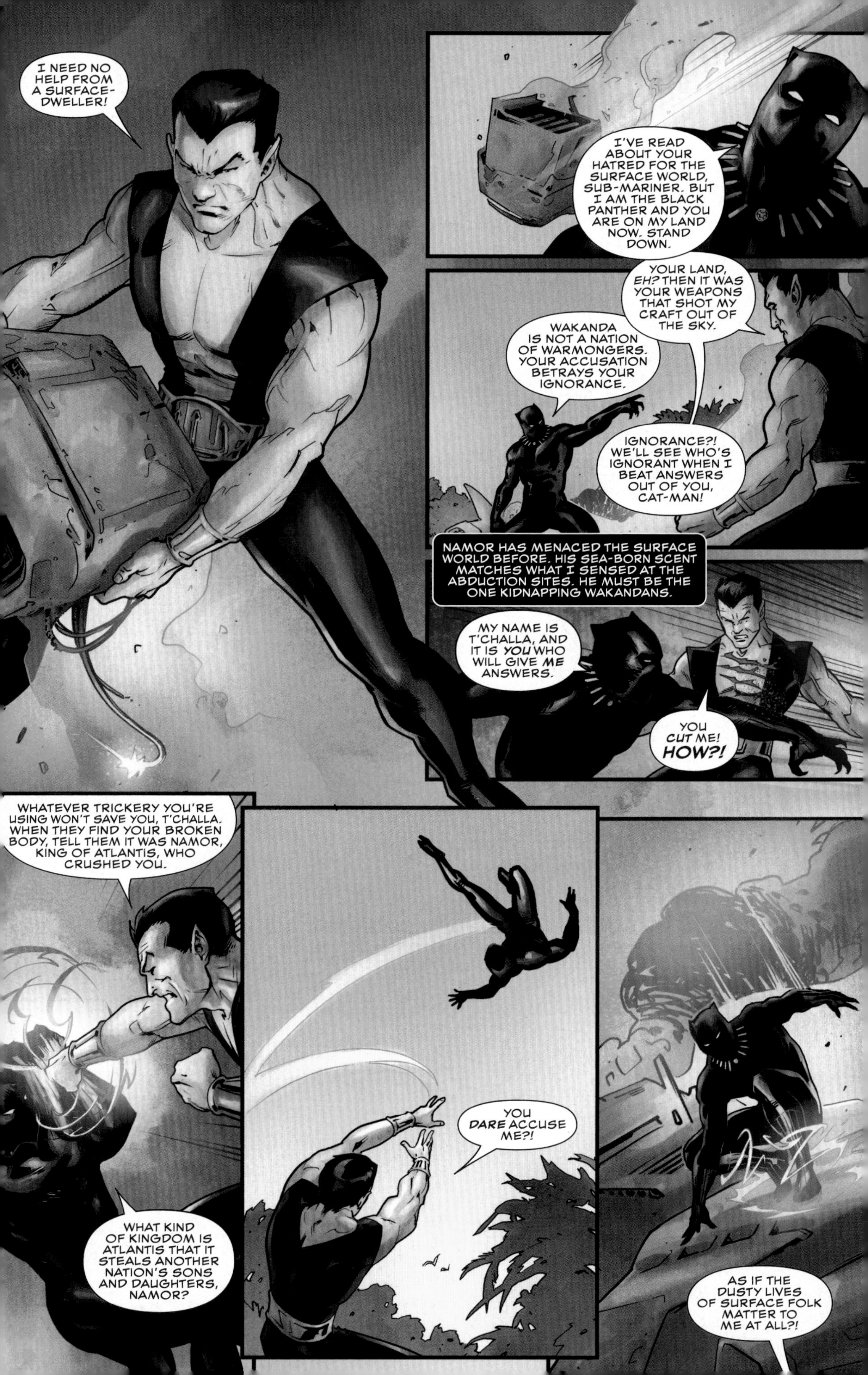
I NEED NO HELP FROM A SURFACE-DWELLER!
I'VE READ ABOUT YOUR HATRED FOR THE SURFACE WORLD, SUB-MARINER. BUT I AM THE BLACK PANTHER AND YOU ARE ON MY LAND NOW. STAND DOWN.
YOUR LAND, EH? THEN IT WAS YOUR WEAPONS THAT SHOT MY CRAFT OUT OF THE SKY.
WAKANDA IS NOT A NATION OF WARMONGERS. YOUR ACCUSATION BETRAYS YOUR IGNORANCE.
IGNORANCE?! WE'LL SEE WHO'S IGNORANT WHEN I BEAT ANSWERS OUT OF YOU, CAT-MAN!
NAMOR HAS MENACED THE SURFACE WORLD BEFORE. HIS SEA-BORN SCENT MATCHES WHAT I SENSED AT THE ABDUCTION SITES. HE MUST BE THE ONE KIDNAPPING WAKANDANS.
MY NAME IS T'CHALLA, AND IT IS YOU WHO WILL GIVE ME ANSWERS.
YOU CUT ME! HOW?!
WHATEVER TRICKERY YOU'RE USING WON'T SAVE YOU, T'CHALLA. WHEN THEY FIND YOUR BROKEN BODY, TELL THEM IT WAS NAMOR, KING OF ATLANTIS, WHO CRUSHED YOU.
WHAT KIND OF KINGDOM IS ATLANTIS THAT IT STEALS ANOTHER NATION'S SONS AND DAUGHTERS, NAMOR?
YOU DARE ACCUSE ME?!
AS IF THE DUSTY LIVES OF SURFACE FOLK MATTER TO ME AT ALL?!

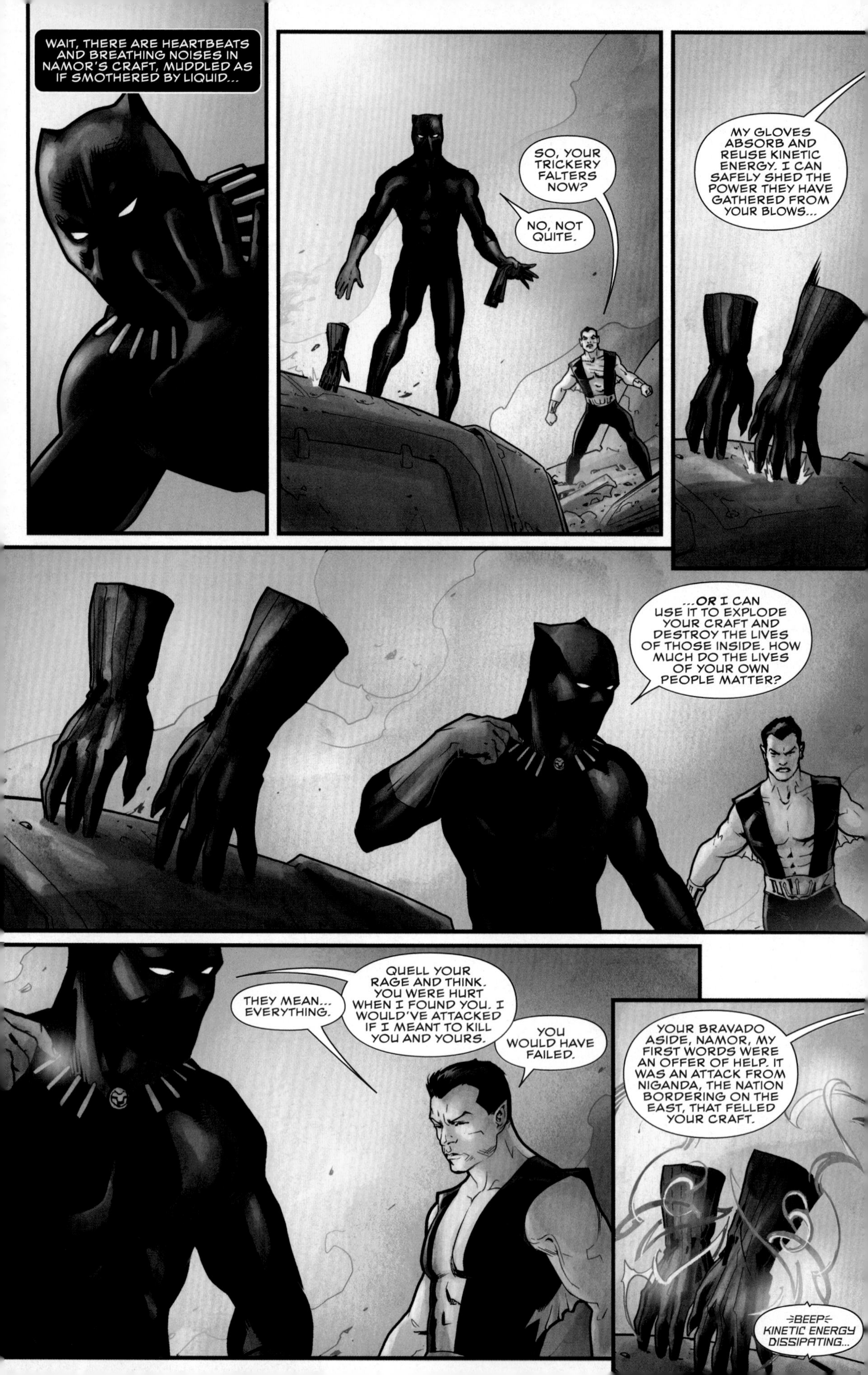
WAIT, THERE ARE HEARTBEATS AND BREATHING NOISES IN NAMOR'S CRAFT, MUDDLED AS IF SMOTHERED BY LIQUID...
SO, YOUR TRICKERY FALTERS NOW?
NO, NOT QUITE.
MY GLOVES ABSORB AND REUSE KINETIC ENERGY. I CAN SAFELY SHED THE POWER THEY HAVE GATHERED FROM YOUR BLOWS...
...OR I CAN USE IT TO EXPLODE YOUR CRAFT AND DESTROY THE LIVES OF THOSE INSIDE. HOW MUCH DO THE LIVES OF YOUR OWN PEOPLE MATTER?
THEY MEAN... EVERYTHING.
QUELL YOUR RAGE AND THINK. YOU WERE HURT WHEN I FOUND YOU. I WOULD'VE ATTACKED IF I MEANT TO KILL YOU AND YOURS.
YOU WOULD HAVE FAILED.
YOUR BRAVADO ASIDE, NAMOR, MY FIRST WORDS WERE AN OFFER OF HELP. IT WAS AN ATTACK FROM NIGANDA, THE NATION BORDERING ON THE EAST, THAT FELLED YOUR CRAFT.
BEEP
KINETIC ENERGY DISSIPATING...

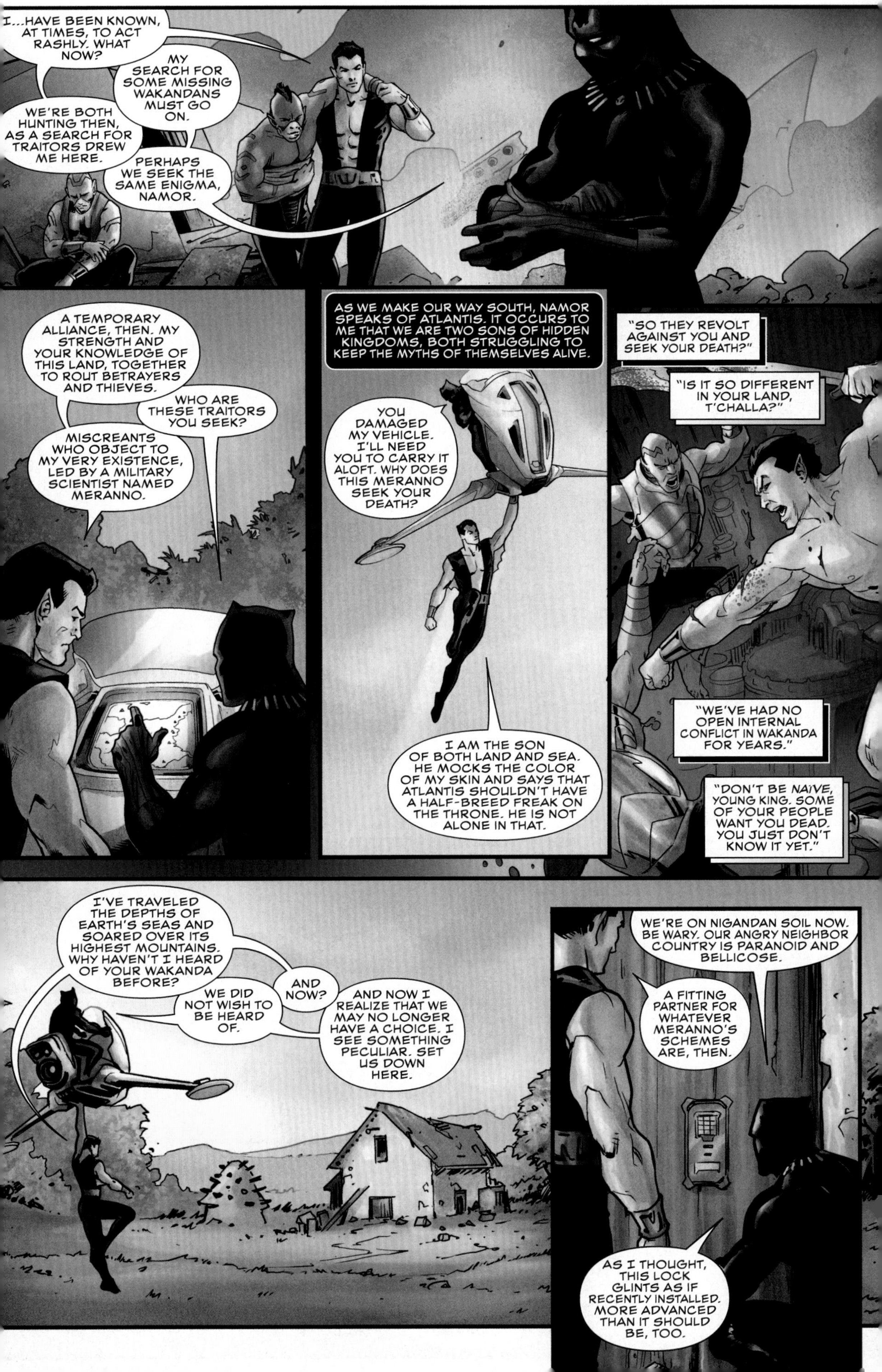
I...HAVE BEEN KNOWN, AT TIMES, TO ACT RASHLY. WHAT NOW?
MY SEARCH FOR SOME MISSING WAKANDANS MUST GO ON.
WE'RE BOTH HUNTING THEN, AS A SEARCH FOR TRAITORS DREW ME HERE.
PERHAPS WE SEEK THE SAME ENIGMA, NAMOR.
A TEMPORARY ALLIANCE, THEN. MY STRENGTH AND YOUR KNOWLEDGE OF THIS LAND, TOGETHER TO ROUT BETRAYERS AND THIEVES.
WHO ARE THESE TRAITORS YOU SEEK?
MISCREANTS WHO OBJECT TO MY VERY EXISTENCE, LED BY A MILITARY SCIENTIST NAMED MERANNO.
AS WE MAKE OUR WAY SOUTH, NAMOR SPEAKS OF ATLANTIS. IT OCCURS TO ME THAT WE ARE TWO SONS OF HIDDEN KINGDOMS, BOTH STRUGGLING TO KEEP THE MYTHS OF THEMSELVES ALIVE.
YOU DAMAGED MY VEHICLE. I'LL NEED YOU TO CARRY IT ALOFT. WHY DOES THIS MERANNO SEEK YOUR DEATH?
I AM THE SON OF BOTH LAND AND SEA. HE MOCKS THE COLOR OF MY SKIN AND SAYS THAT ATLANTIS SHOULDN'T HAVE A HALF-BREED FREAK ON THE THRONE. HE IS NOT ALONE IN THAT.
"SO THEY REVOLT AGAINST YOU AND SEEK YOUR DEATH?"
"IS IT SO DIFFERENT IN YOUR LAND, T'CHALLA?"
"WE'VE HAD NO OPEN INTERNAL CONFLICT IN WAKANDA FOR YEARS."
"DON'T BE *NAÏVE*, YOUNG KING. SOME OF YOUR PEOPLE WANT YOU DEAD. YOU JUST DON'T KNOW IT YET."
I'VE TRAVELED THE DEPTHS OF EARTH'S SEAS AND SOARED OVER ITS HIGHEST MOUNTAINS. WHY HAVEN'T I HEARD OF YOUR WAKANDA BEFORE?
WE DID NOT WISH TO BE HEARD OF.
AND NOW?
AND NOW I REALIZE THAT WE MAY NO LONGER HAVE A CHOICE. I SEE SOMETHING PECULIAR. SET US DOWN HERE.
WE'RE ON NIGANDAN SOIL NOW. BE WARY. OUR ANGRY NEIGHBOR COUNTRY IS PARANOID AND BELLICOSE.
A FITTING PARTNER FOR WHATEVER MERANNO'S SCHEMES ARE, THEN.
AS I THOUGHT, THIS LOCK GLINTS AS IF RECENTLY INSTALLED. MORE ADVANCED THAN IT SHOULD BE, TOO.

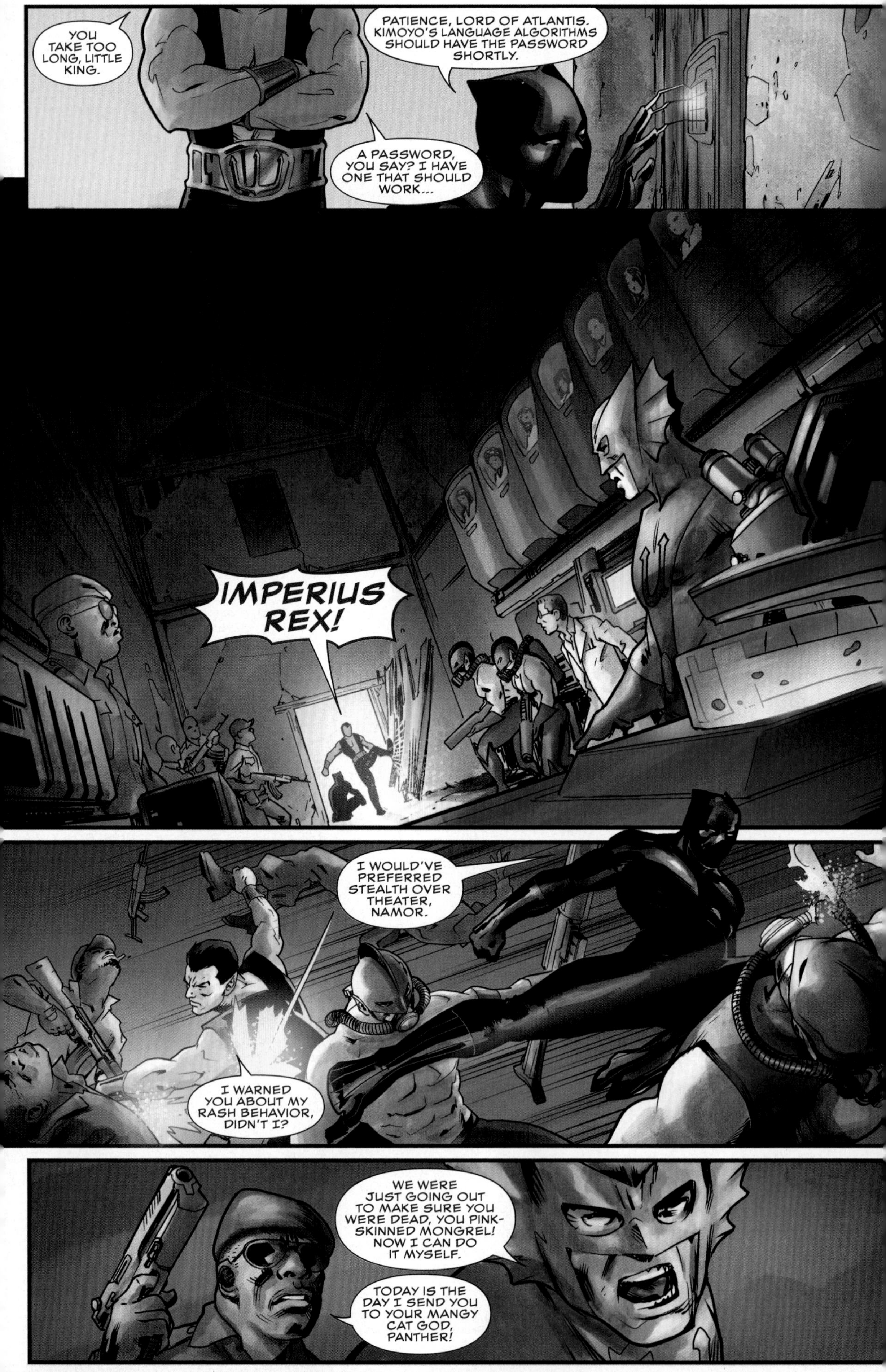
YOU TAKE TOO LONG, LITTLE KING.
PATIENCE, LORD OF ATLANTIS. KIMOYO'S LANGUAGE ALGORITHMS SHOULD HAVE THE PASSWORD SHORTLY.
A PASSWORD, YOU SAY? I HAVE ONE THAT SHOULD WORK...
IMPERIUS REX!
I WOULD'VE PREFERRED STEALTH OVER THEATER, NAMOR.
I WARNED YOU ABOUT MY RASH BEHAVIOR, DIDN'T I?
WE WERE JUST GOING OUT TO MAKE SURE YOU WERE DEAD, YOU PINK-SKINNED MONGREL! NOW I CAN DO IT MYSELF.
TODAY IS THE DAY I SEND YOU TO YOUR MANGY CAT GOD, PANTHER!

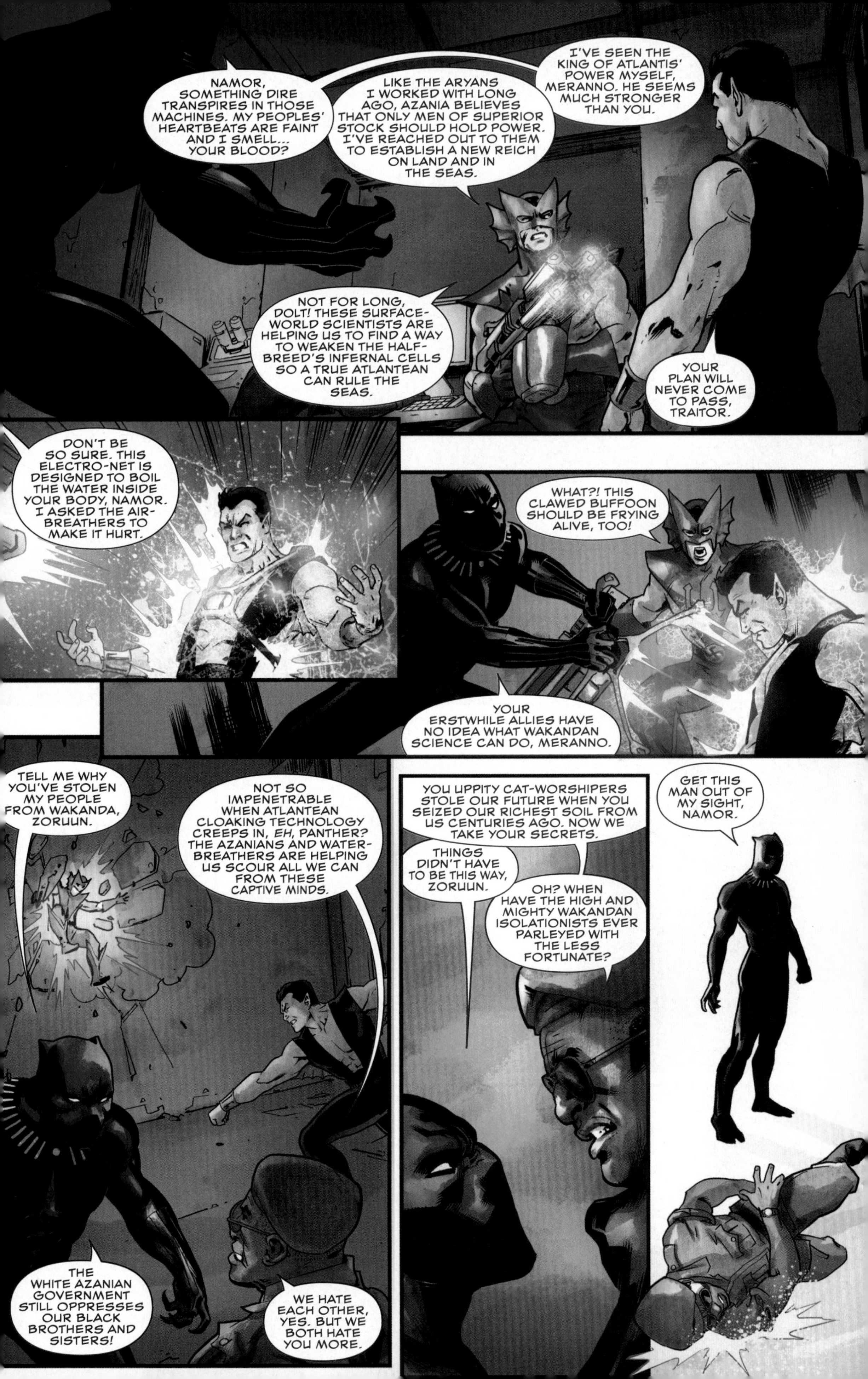
NAMOR, SOMETHING DIRE TRANSPIRES IN THOSE MACHINES. MY PEOPLES' HEARTBEATS ARE FAINT AND I SMELL... YOUR BLOOD?
LIKE THE ARYANS I WORKED WITH LONG AGO, AZANIA BELIEVES THAT ONLY MEN OF SUPERIOR STOCK SHOULD HOLD POWER. I'VE REACHED OUT TO THEM TO ESTABLISH A NEW REICH ON LAND AND IN THE SEAS.
I'VE SEEN THE KING OF ATLANTIS' POWER MYSELF, MERANNO. HE SEEMS MUCH STRONGER THAN YOU.
NOT FOR LONG, DOLT! THESE SURFACE-WORLD SCIENTISTS ARE HELPING US TO FIND A WAY TO WEAKEN THE HALF-BREED'S INFERNAL CELLS SO A TRUE ATLANTEAN CAN RULE THE SEAS.
YOUR PLAN WILL NEVER COME TO PASS, TRAITOR.
DON'T BE SO SURE. THIS ELECTRO-NET IS DESIGNED TO BOIL THE WATER INSIDE YOUR BODY, NAMOR. I ASKED THE AIR-BREATHERS TO MAKE IT HURT.
WHAT?! THIS CLAWED BUFFOON SHOULD BE FRYING ALIVE, TOO!
YOUR ERSTWHILE ALLIES HAVE NO IDEA WHAT WAKANDAN SCIENCE CAN DO, MERANNO.
TELL ME WHY YOU'VE STOLEN MY PEOPLE FROM WAKANDA, ZORUUN.
NOT SO IMPENETRABLE WHEN ATLANTEAN CLOAKING TECHNOLOGY CREEPS IN, *EH*, PANTHER? THE AZANIANS AND WATER-BREATHERS ARE HELPING US SCOUR ALL WE CAN FROM THESE CAPTIVE MINDS.
THE WHITE AZANIAN GOVERNMENT STILL OPPRESSES OUR BLACK BROTHERS AND SISTERS!
WE HATE EACH OTHER, YES. BUT WE BOTH HATE YOU MORE.
YOU UPPITY CAT-WORSHIPERS STOLE OUR FUTURE WHEN YOU SEIZED OUR RICHEST SOIL FROM US CENTURIES AGO. NOW WE TAKE YOUR SECRETS.
THINGS DIDN'T HAVE TO BE THIS WAY, ZORUUN.
OH? WHEN HAVE THE HIGH AND MIGHTY WAKANDAN ISOLATIONISTS EVER PARLEYED WITH THE LESS FORTUNATE?
GET THIS MAN OUT OF MY SIGHT, NAMOR.

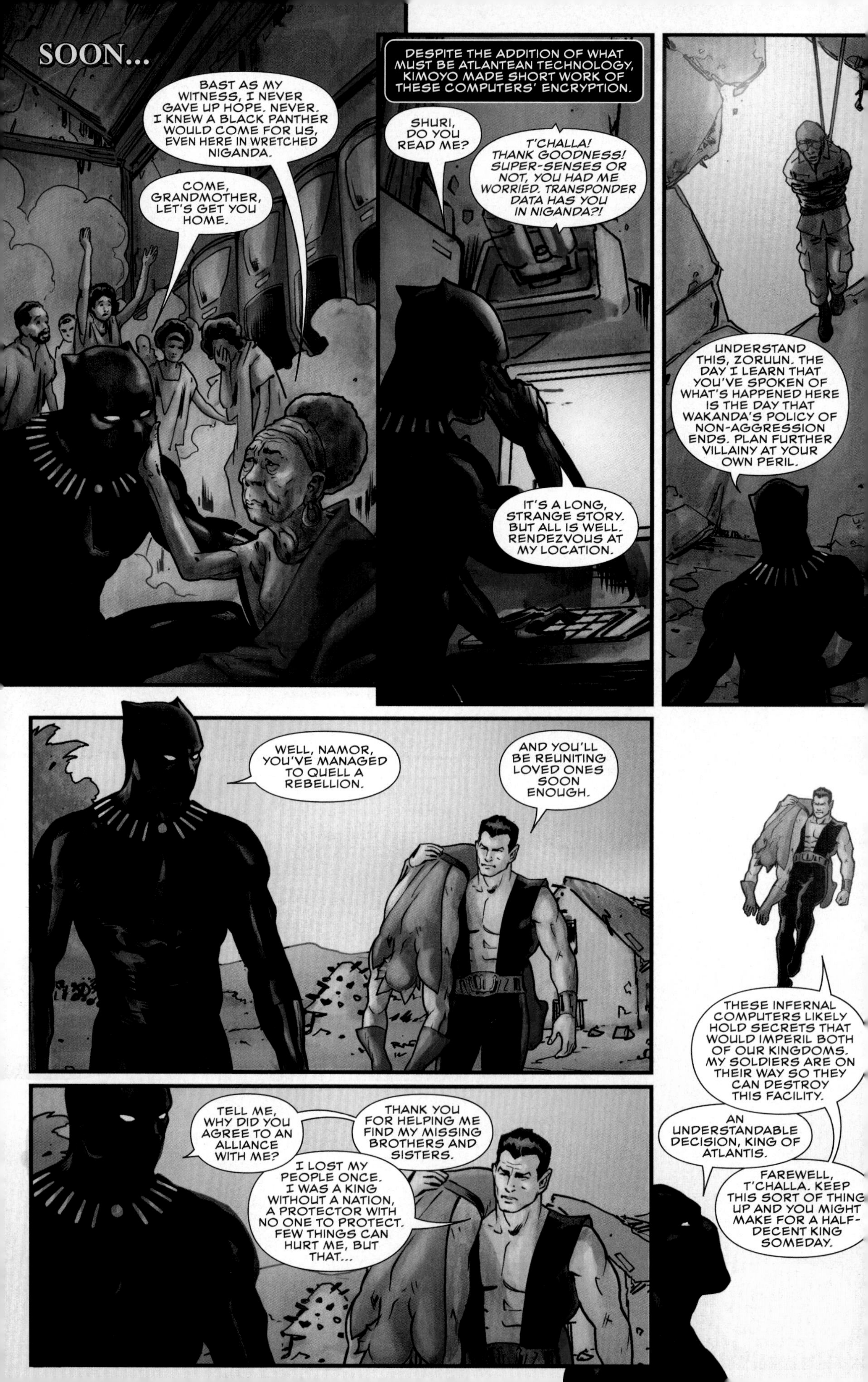
SOON...
BAST AS MY WITNESS, I NEVER GAVE UP HOPE. NEVER. I KNEW A BLACK PANTHER WOULD COME FOR US, EVEN HERE IN WRETCHED NIGANDA.
COME, GRANDMOTHER, LET'S GET YOU HOME.
DESPITE THE ADDITION OF WHAT MUST BE ATLANTEAN TECHNOLOGY, KIMOYO MADE SHORT WORK OF THESE COMPUTERS' ENCRYPTION.
SHURI, DO YOU READ ME?
T'CHALLA! THANK GOODNESS! SUPER-SENSES OR NOT, YOU HAD ME WORRIED. TRANSPONDER DATA HAS YOU IN NIGANDA?!
IT'S A LONG, STRANGE STORY. BUT ALL IS WELL. RENDEZVOUS AT MY LOCATION.
UNDERSTAND THIS, ZORUUN. THE DAY I LEARN THAT YOU'VE SPOKEN OF WHAT'S HAPPENED HERE IS THE DAY THAT WAKANDA'S POLICY OF NON-AGGRESSION ENDS. PLAN FURTHER VILLAINY AT YOUR OWN PERIL.
WELL, NAMOR, YOU'VE MANAGED TO QUELL A REBELLION.
AND YOU'LL BE REUNITING LOVED ONES SOON ENOUGH.
TELL ME, WHY DID YOU AGREE TO AN ALLIANCE WITH ME?
THANK YOU FOR HELPING ME FIND MY MISSING BROTHERS AND SISTERS.
I LOST MY PEOPLE ONCE. I WAS A KING WITHOUT A NATION, A PROTECTOR WITH NO ONE TO PROTECT. FEW THINGS CAN HURT ME, BUT THAT...
THESE INFERNAL COMPUTERS LIKELY HOLD SECRETS THAT WOULD IMPERIL BOTH OF OUR KINGDOMS. MY SOLDIERS ARE ON THEIR WAY SO THEY CAN DESTROY THIS FACILITY.
AN UNDERSTANDABLE DECISION, KING OF ATLANTIS.
FAREWELL, T'CHALLA. KEEP THIS SORT OF THING UP AND YOU MIGHT MAKE FOR A HALF-DECENT KING SOMEDAY.

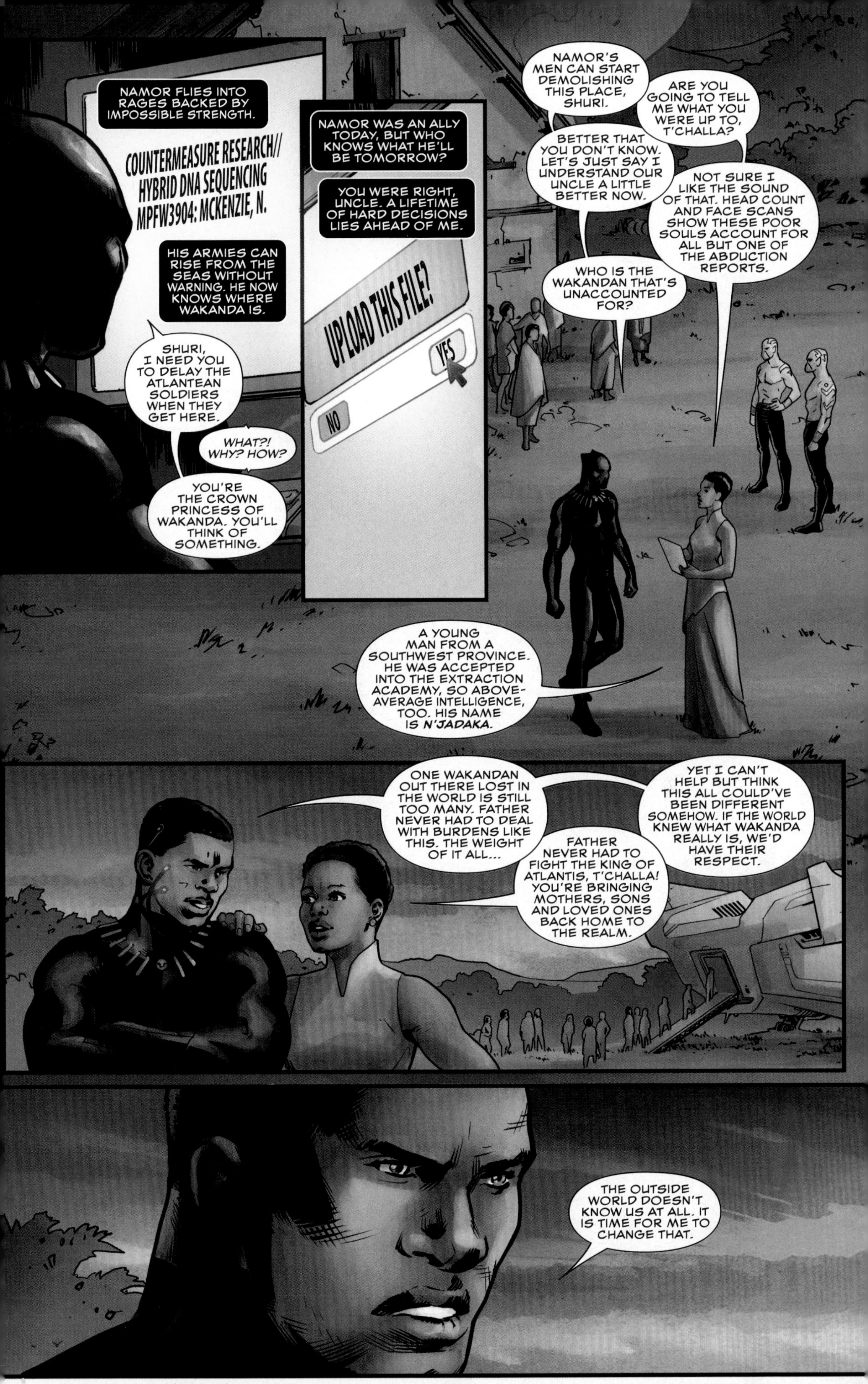
NAMOR FLIES INTO RAGES BACKED BY IMPOSSIBLE STRENGTH.
COUNTERMEASURE RESEARCH// HYBRID DNA SEQUENCING MPFW3904: MCKENZIE, N.
HIS ARMIES CAN RISE FROM THE SEAS WITHOUT WARNING. HE NOW KNOWS WHERE WAKANDA IS.
SHURI, I NEED YOU TO DELAY THE ATLANTEAN SOLDIERS WHEN THEY GET HERE.
WHAT?! WHY? HOW?
YOU'RE THE CROWN PRINCESS OF WAKANDA. YOU'LL THINK OF SOMETHING.
NAMOR WAS AN ALLY TODAY, BUT WHO KNOWS WHAT HE'LL BE TOMORROW?
YOU WERE RIGHT, UNCLE. A LIFETIME OF HARD DECISIONS LIES AHEAD OF ME.
UPLOAD THIS FILE?
YES
NO
NAMOR'S MEN CAN START DEMOLISHING THIS PLACE, SHURI.
ARE YOU GOING TO TELL ME WHAT YOU WERE UP TO, T'CHALLA?
BETTER THAT YOU DON'T KNOW. LET'S JUST SAY I UNDERSTAND OUR UNCLE A LITTLE BETTER NOW.
NOT SURE I LIKE THE SOUND OF THAT. HEAD COUNT AND FACE SCANS SHOW THESE POOR SOULS ACCOUNT FOR ALL BUT ONE OF THE ABDUCTION REPORTS.
WHO IS THE WAKANDAN THAT'S UNACCOUNTED FOR?
A YOUNG MAN FROM A SOUTHWEST PROVINCE. HE WAS ACCEPTED INTO THE EXTRACTION ACADEMY, SO ABOVE-AVERAGE INTELLIGENCE, TOO. HIS NAME IS N'JADAKA.
ONE WAKANDAN OUT THERE LOST IN THE WORLD IS STILL TOO MANY. FATHER NEVER HAD TO DEAL WITH BURDENS LIKE THIS. THE WEIGHT OF IT ALL...
FATHER NEVER HAD TO FIGHT THE KING OF ATLANTIS, T'CHALLA! YOU'RE BRINGING MOTHERS, SONS AND LOVED ONES BACK HOME TO THE REALM.
YET I CAN'T HELP BUT THINK THIS ALL COULD'VE BEEN DIFFERENT SOMEHOW. IF THE WORLD KNEW WHAT WAKANDA REALLY IS, WE'D HAVE THEIR RESPECT.
THE OUTSIDE WORLD DOESN'T KNOW US AT ALL. IT IS TIME FOR ME TO CHANGE THAT.

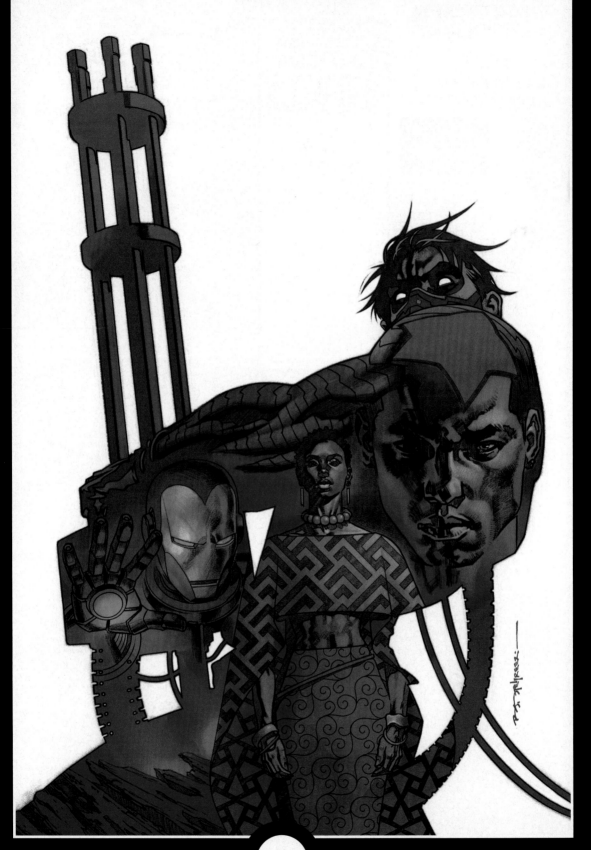

3

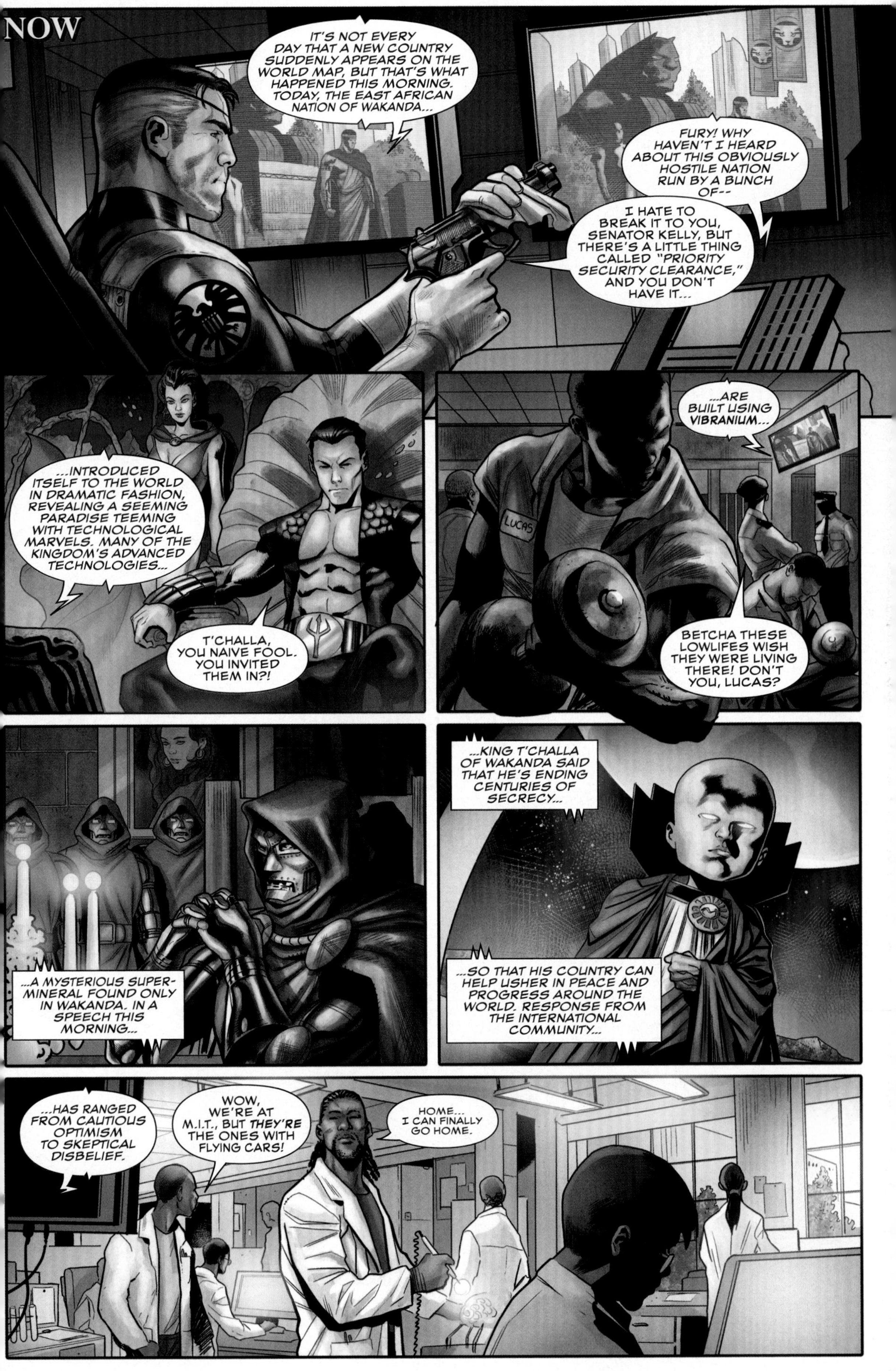
NOW
IT'S NOT EVERY DAY THAT A NEW COUNTRY SUDDENLY APPEARS ON THE WORLD MAP, BUT THAT'S WHAT HAPPENED THIS MORNING. TODAY, THE EAST AFRICAN NATION OF WAKANDA...
FURY! WHY HAVEN'T I HEARD ABOUT THIS OBVIOUSLY HOSTILE NATION RUN BY A BUNCH OF--
I HATE TO BREAK IT TO YOU, SENATOR KELLY, BUT THERE'S A LITTLE THING CALLED "PRIORITY SECURITY CLEARANCE," AND YOU DON'T HAVE IT...
...INTRODUCED ITSELF TO THE WORLD IN DRAMATIC FASHION, REVEALING A SEEMING PARADISE TEEMING WITH TECHNOLOGICAL MARVELS. MANY OF THE KINGDOM'S ADVANCED TECHNOLOGIES...
T'CHALLA, YOU NAIVE FOOL. YOU INVITED THEM IN?!
...ARE BUILT USING VIBRANIUM...
LUCAS
BETCHA THESE LOWLIFES WISH THEY WERE LIVING THERE! DON'T YOU, LUCAS?
...A MYSTERIOUS SUPER-MINERAL FOUND ONLY IN WAKANDA. IN A SPEECH THIS MORNING...
...KING T'CHALLA OF WAKANDA SAID THAT HE'S ENDING CENTURIES OF SECRECY...
...SO THAT HIS COUNTRY CAN HELP USHER IN PEACE AND PROGRESS AROUND THE WORLD. RESPONSE FROM THE INTERNATIONAL COMMUNITY...
...HAS RANGED FROM CAUTIOUS OPTIMISM TO SKEPTICAL DISBELIEF.
WOW, WE'RE AT M.I.T., BUT THEY'RE THE ONES WITH FLYING CARS!
HOME... I CAN FINALLY GO HOME.

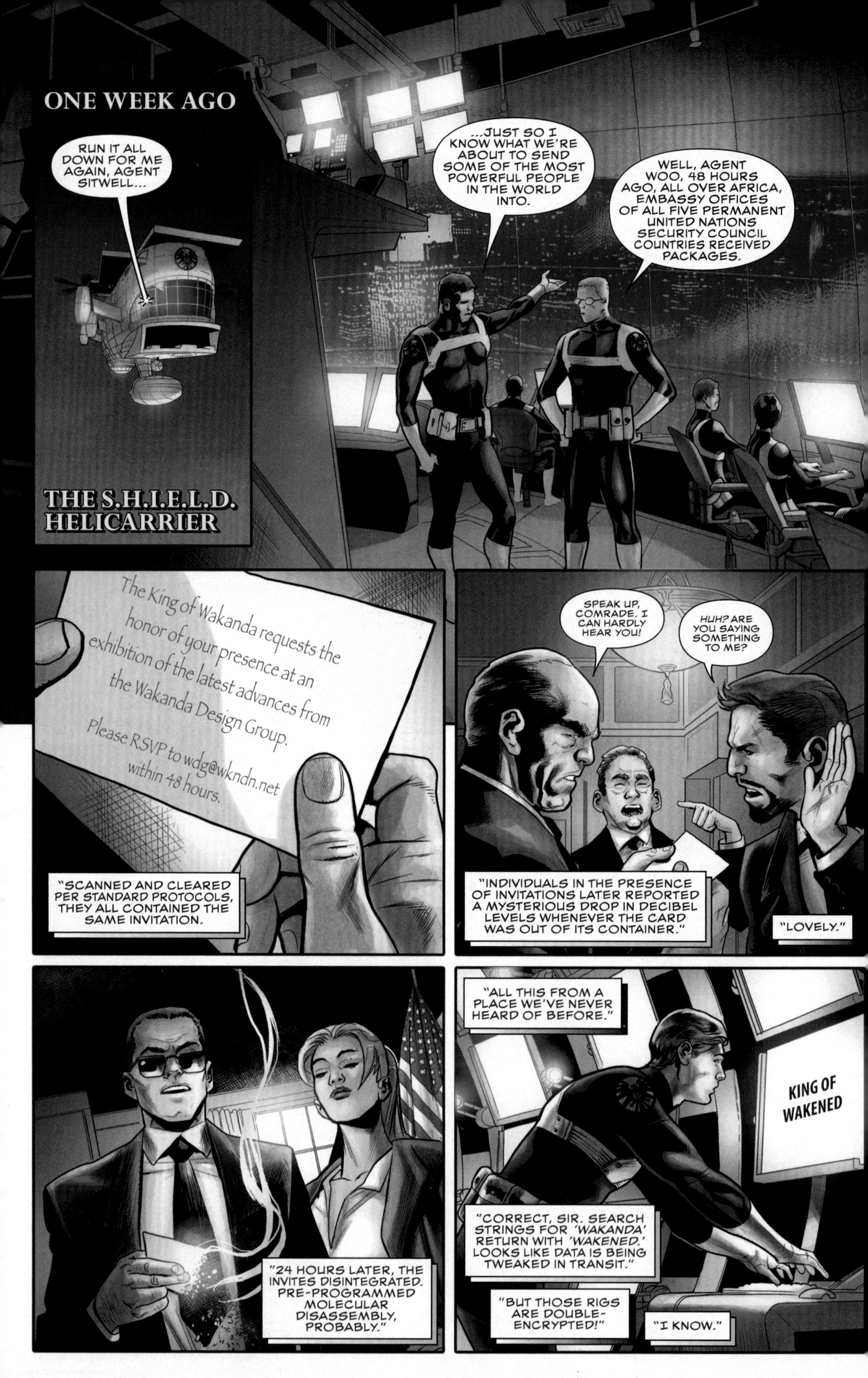
ONE WEEK AGO
RUN IT ALL DOWN FOR ME AGAIN, AGENT SITWELL...
...JUST SO I KNOW WHAT WE'RE ABOUT TO SEND SOME OF THE MOST POWERFUL PEOPLE IN THE WORLD INTO.
WELL, AGENT WOO, 48 HOURS AGO, ALL OVER AFRICA, EMBASSY OFFICES OF ALL FIVE PERMANENT UNITED NATIONS SECURITY COUNCIL COUNTRIES RECEIVED PACKAGES.
THE S.H.I.E.L.D. HELICARRIER
The King of Wakanda requests the honor of your presence at an exhibition of the latest advances from the Wakanda Design Group.
Please RSVP to wdg@wkndn.net within 48 hours.
"SCANNED AND CLEARED PER STANDARD PROTOCOLS, THEY ALL CONTAINED THE SAME INVITATION.
SPEAK UP, COMRADE. I CAN HARDLY HEAR YOU!
HUH? ARE YOU SAYING SOMETHING TO ME?
"INDIVIDUALS IN THE PRESENCE OF INVITATIONS LATER REPORTED A MYSTERIOUS DROP IN DECIBEL LEVELS WHENEVER THE CARD WAS OUT OF ITS CONTAINER."
"LOVELY."
"24 HOURS LATER, THE INVITES DISINTEGRATED. PRE-PROGRAMMED MOLECULAR DISASSEMBLY, PROBABLY."
"ALL THIS FROM A PLACE WE'VE NEVER HEARD OF BEFORE."
KING OF WAKENED
"CORRECT, SIR. SEARCH STRINGS FOR 'WAKANDA' RETURN WITH 'WAKENED.' LOOKS LIKE DATA IS BEING TWEAKED IN TRANSIT."
"BUT THOSE RIGS ARE DOUBLE-ENCRYPTED!"
"I KNOW."

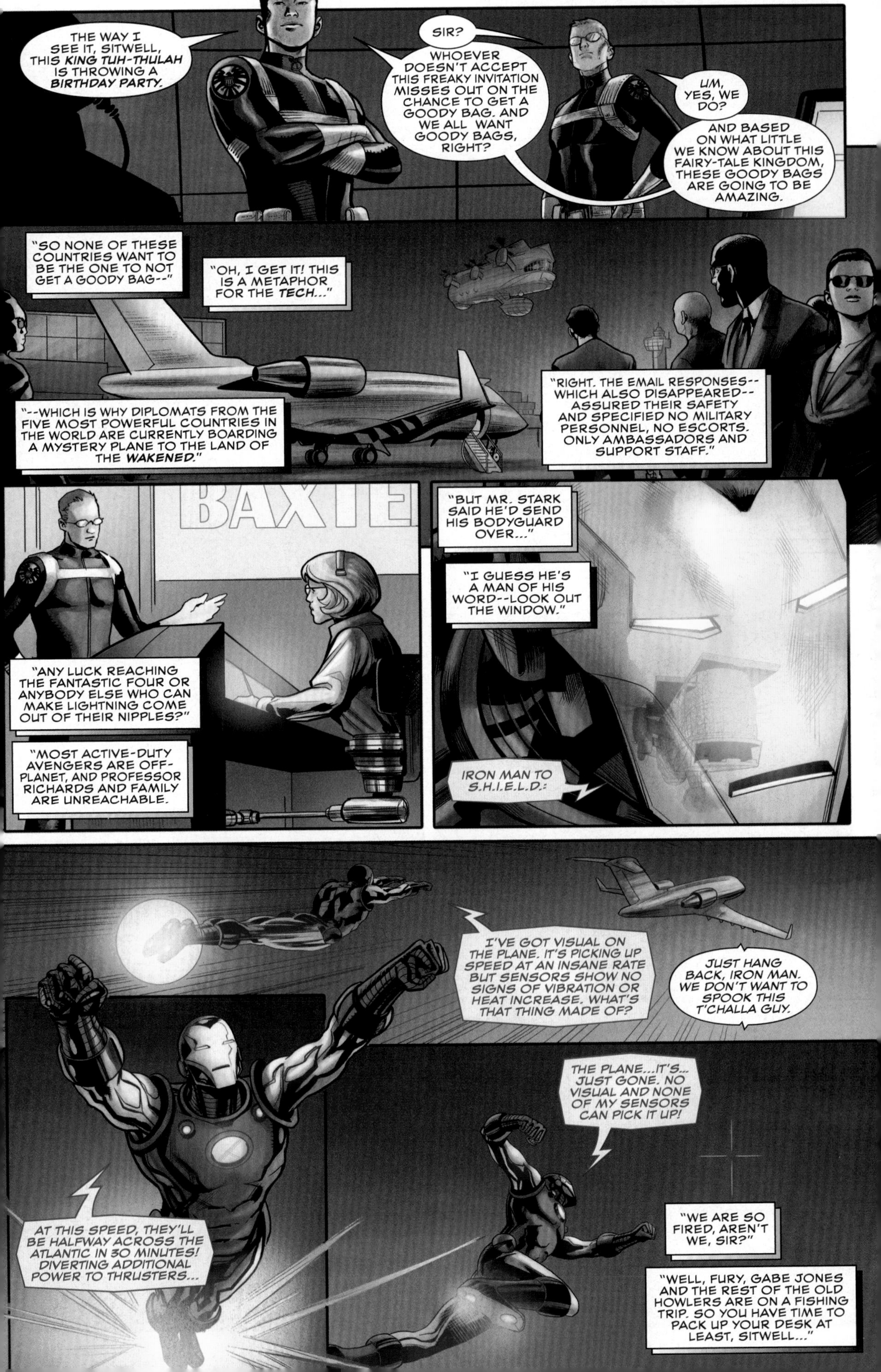
THE WAY I SEE IT, SITWELL, THIS KING TUH-THULAH IS THROWING A BIRTHDAY PARTY.
SIR?
WHOEVER DOESN'T ACCEPT THIS FREAKY INVITATION MISSES OUT ON THE CHANCE TO GET A GOODY BAG. AND WE ALL WANT GOODY BAGS, RIGHT?
UM, YES, WE DO?
AND BASED ON WHAT LITTLE WE KNOW ABOUT THIS FAIRY-TALE KINGDOM, THESE GOODY BAGS ARE GOING TO BE AMAZING.
"SO NONE OF THESE COUNTRIES WANT TO BE THE ONE TO NOT GET A GOODY BAG--"
"OH, I GET IT! THIS IS A METAPHOR FOR THE TECH..."
"--WHICH IS WHY DIPLOMATS FROM THE FIVE MOST POWERFUL COUNTRIES IN THE WORLD ARE CURRENTLY BOARDING A MYSTERY PLANE TO THE LAND OF THE WAKENED."
"RIGHT. THE EMAIL RESPONSES--WHICH ALSO DISAPPEARED--ASSURED THEIR SAFETY AND SPECIFIED NO MILITARY PERSONNEL, NO ESCORTS. ONLY AMBASSADORS AND SUPPORT STAFF."
BAXTE
"ANY LUCK REACHING THE FANTASTIC FOUR OR ANYBODY ELSE WHO CAN MAKE LIGHTNING COME OUT OF THEIR NIPPLES?"
"MOST ACTIVE-DUTY AVENGERS ARE OFF-PLANET, AND PROFESSOR RICHARDS AND FAMILY ARE UNREACHABLE."
"BUT MR. STARK SAID HE'D SEND HIS BODYGUARD OVER..."
"I GUESS HE'S A MAN OF HIS WORD--LOOK OUT THE WINDOW."
IRON MAN TO S.H.I.E.L.D.:
I'VE GOT VISUAL ON THE PLANE. IT'S PICKING UP SPEED AT AN INSANE RATE BUT SENSORS SHOW NO SIGNS OF VIBRATION OR HEAT INCREASE. WHAT'S THAT THING MADE OF?
JUST HANG BACK, IRON MAN. WE DON'T WANT TO SPOOK THIS T'CHALLA GUY.
AT THIS SPEED, THEY'LL BE HALFWAY ACROSS THE ATLANTIC IN 30 MINUTES! DIVERTING ADDITIONAL POWER TO THRUSTERS...
THE PLANE...IT'S... JUST GONE. NO VISUAL AND NONE OF MY SENSORS CAN PICK IT UP!
"WE ARE SO FIRED, AREN'T WE, SIR?"
"WELL, FURY, GABE JONES AND THE REST OF THE OLD HOWLERS ARE ON A FISHING TRIP. SO YOU HAVE TIME TO PACK UP YOUR DESK AT LEAST, SITWELL..."

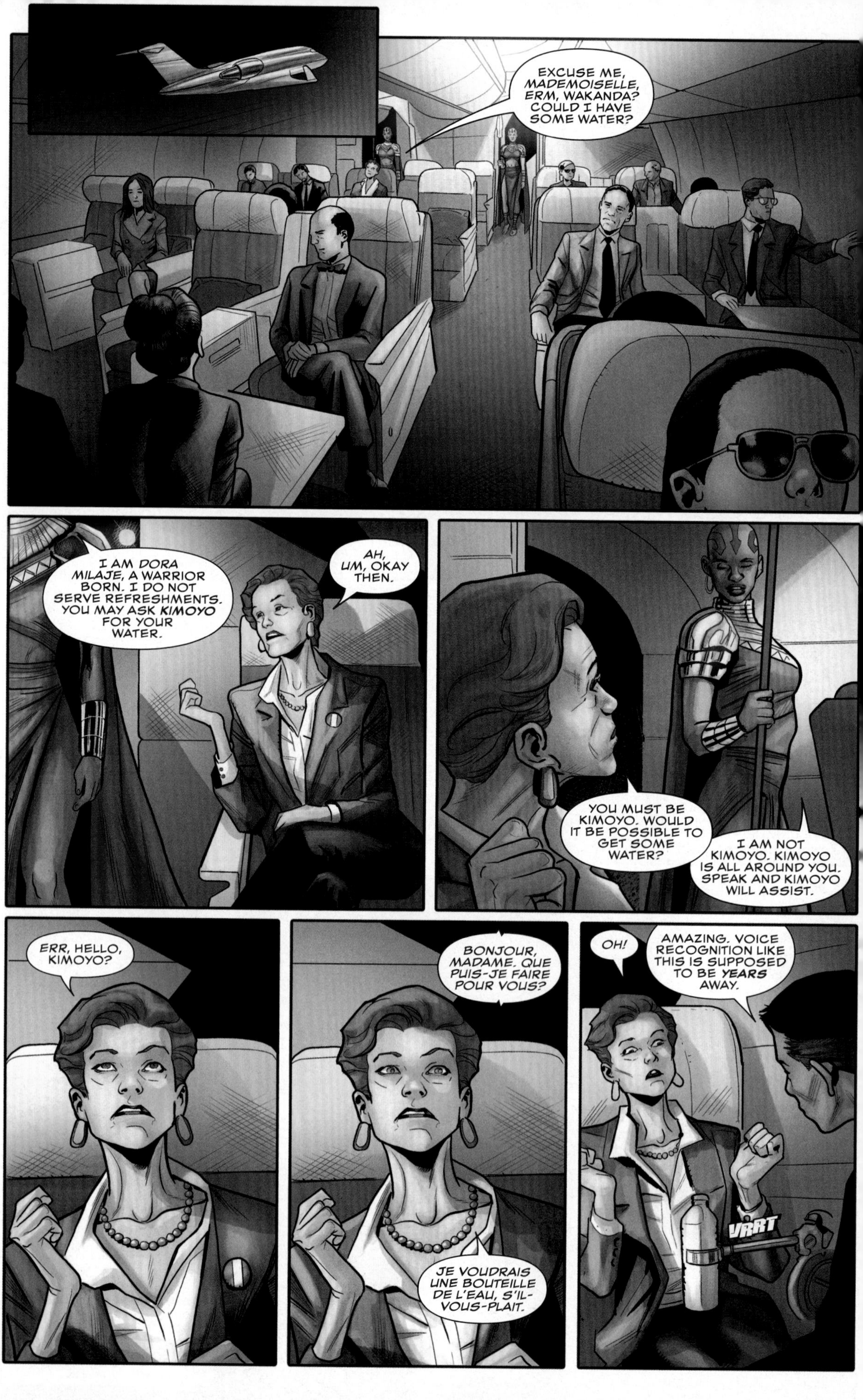
EXCUSE ME, MADEMOISELLE, ERM, WAKANDA? COULD I HAVE SOME WATER?
I AM DORA MILAJE, A WARRIOR BORN. I DO NOT SERVE REFRESHMENTS. YOU MAY ASK KIMOYO FOR YOUR WATER.
AH, UM, OKAY THEN.
YOU MUST BE KIMOYO. WOULD IT BE POSSIBLE TO GET SOME WATER?
I AM NOT KIMOYO. KIMOYO IS ALL AROUND YOU. SPEAK AND KIMOYO WILL ASSIST.
ERR, HELLO, KIMOYO?
BONJOUR, MADAME. QUE PUIS-JE FAIRE POUR VOUS?
JE VOUDRAIS UNE BOUTEILLE DE L'EAU, S'IL-VOUS-PLAIT.
OH!
AMAZING. VOICE RECOGNITION LIKE THIS IS SUPPOSED TO BE YEARS AWAY.
VRRT

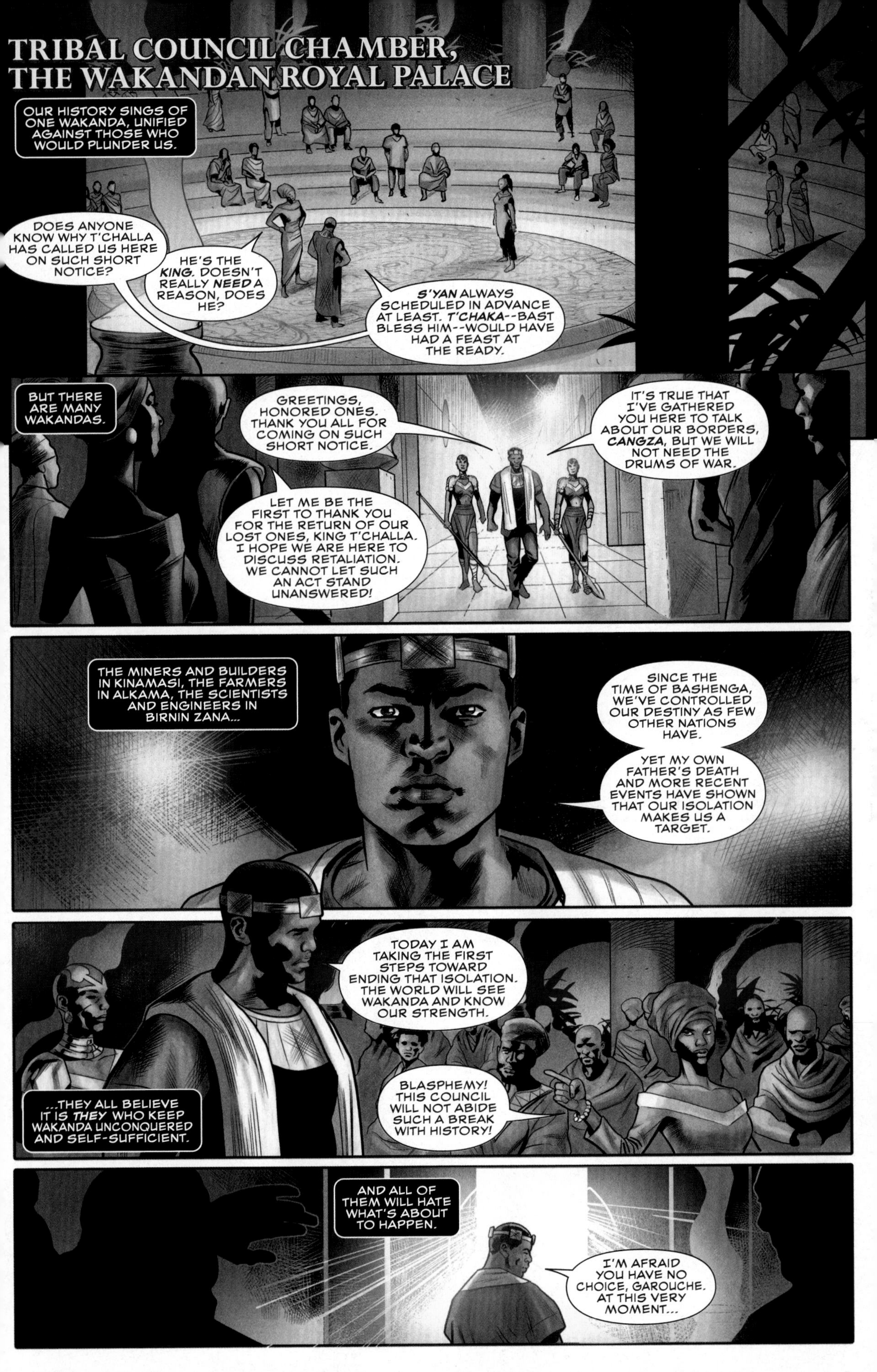
TRIBAL COUNCIL CHAMBER, THE WAKANDAN ROYAL PALACE
OUR HISTORY SINGS OF ONE WAKANDA, UNIFIED AGAINST THOSE WHO WOULD PLUNDER US.
DOES ANYONE KNOW WHY T'CHALLA HAS CALLED US HERE ON SUCH SHORT NOTICE?
HE'S THE KING. DOESN'T REALLY NEED A REASON, DOES HE?
S'YAN ALWAYS SCHEDULED IN ADVANCE AT LEAST. T'CHAKA--BAST BLESS HIM--WOULD HAVE HAD A FEAST AT THE READY.
BUT THERE ARE MANY WAKANDAS.
GREETINGS, HONORED ONES. THANK YOU ALL FOR COMING ON SUCH SHORT NOTICE.
LET ME BE THE FIRST TO THANK YOU FOR THE RETURN OF OUR LOST ONES, KING T'CHALLA. I HOPE WE ARE HERE TO DISCUSS RETALIATION. WE CANNOT LET SUCH AN ACT STAND UNANSWERED!
IT'S TRUE THAT I'VE GATHERED YOU HERE TO TALK ABOUT OUR BORDERS, CANGZA, BUT WE WILL NOT NEED THE DRUMS OF WAR.
THE MINERS AND BUILDERS IN KINAMASI, THE FARMERS IN ALKAMA, THE SCIENTISTS AND ENGINEERS IN BIRNIN ZANA...
SINCE THE TIME OF BASHENGA, WE'VE CONTROLLED OUR DESTINY AS FEW OTHER NATIONS HAVE.
YET MY OWN FATHER'S DEATH AND MORE RECENT EVENTS HAVE SHOWN THAT OUR ISOLATION MAKES US A TARGET.
TODAY I AM TAKING THE FIRST STEPS TOWARD ENDING THAT ISOLATION. THE WORLD WILL SEE WAKANDA AND KNOW OUR STRENGTH.
...THEY ALL BELIEVE IT IS THEY WHO KEEP WAKANDA UNCONQUERED AND SELF-SUFFICIENT.
BLASPHEMY! THIS COUNCIL WILL NOT ABIDE SUCH A BREAK WITH HISTORY!
AND ALL OF THEM WILL HATE WHAT'S ABOUT TO HAPPEN.
I'M AFRAID YOU HAVE NO CHOICE, GAROUCHE. AT THIS VERY MOMENT...

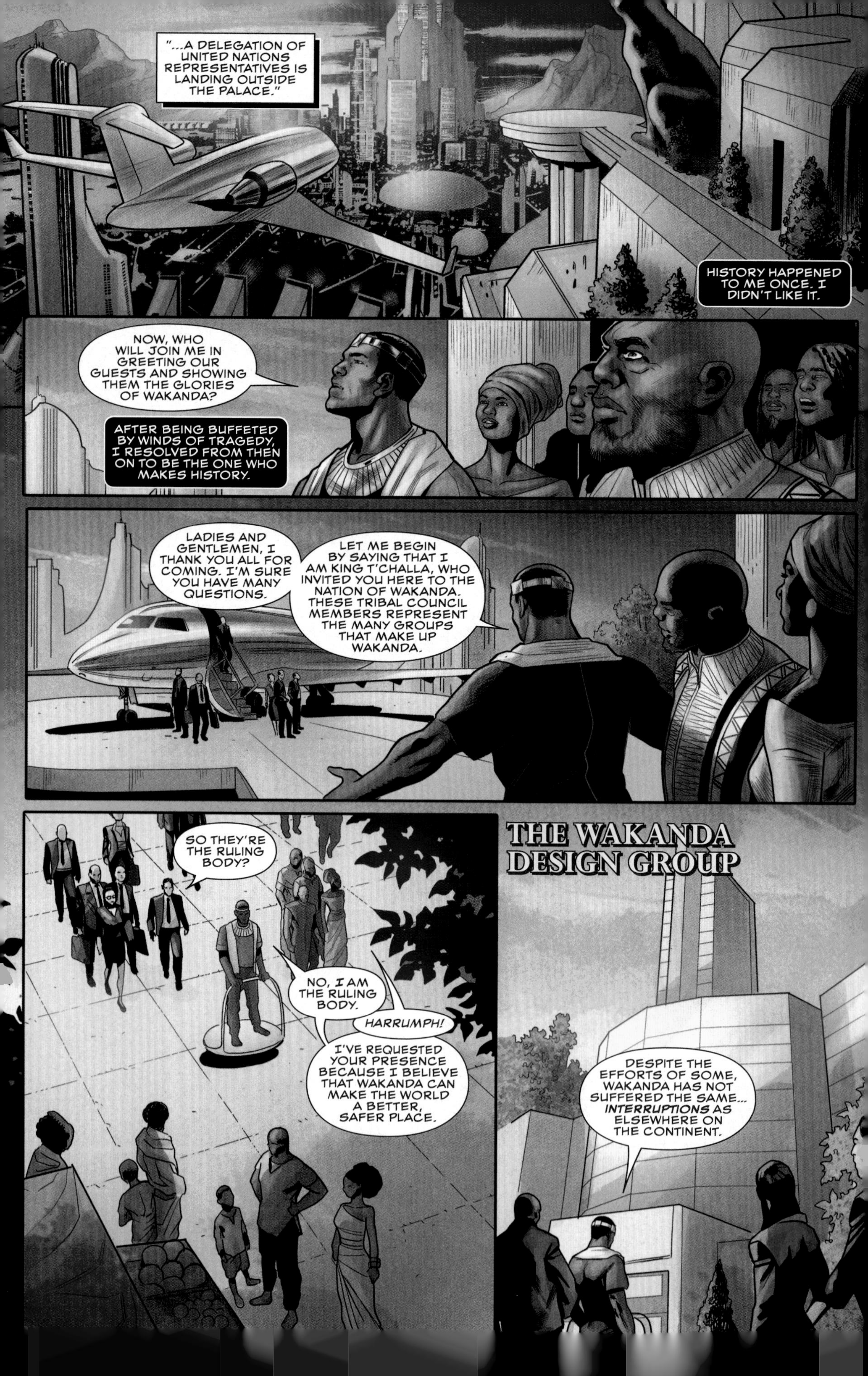
"...A DELEGATION OF UNITED NATIONS REPRESENTATIVES IS LANDING OUTSIDE THE PALACE."
HISTORY HAPPENED TO ME ONCE. I DIDN'T LIKE IT.
NOW, WHO WILL JOIN ME IN GREETING OUR GUESTS AND SHOWING THEM THE GLORIES OF WAKANDA?
AFTER BEING BUFFETED BY WINDS OF TRAGEDY, I RESOLVED FROM THEN ON TO BE THE ONE WHO MAKES HISTORY.
LADIES AND GENTLEMEN, I THANK YOU ALL FOR COMING. I'M SURE YOU HAVE MANY QUESTIONS.
LET ME BEGIN BY SAYING THAT I AM KING T'CHALLA, WHO INVITED YOU HERE TO THE NATION OF WAKANDA. THESE TRIBAL COUNCIL MEMBERS REPRESENT THE MANY GROUPS THAT MAKE UP WAKANDA.
SO THEY'RE THE RULING BODY?
NO, I AM THE RULING BODY.
HARRUMPH!
I'VE REQUESTED YOUR PRESENCE BECAUSE I BELIEVE THAT WAKANDA CAN MAKE THE WORLD A BETTER, SAFER PLACE.
THE WAKANDA DESIGN GROUP
DESPITE THE EFFORTS OF SOME, WAKANDA HAS NOT SUFFERED THE SAME... INTERRUPTIONS AS ELSEWHERE ON THE CONTINENT.

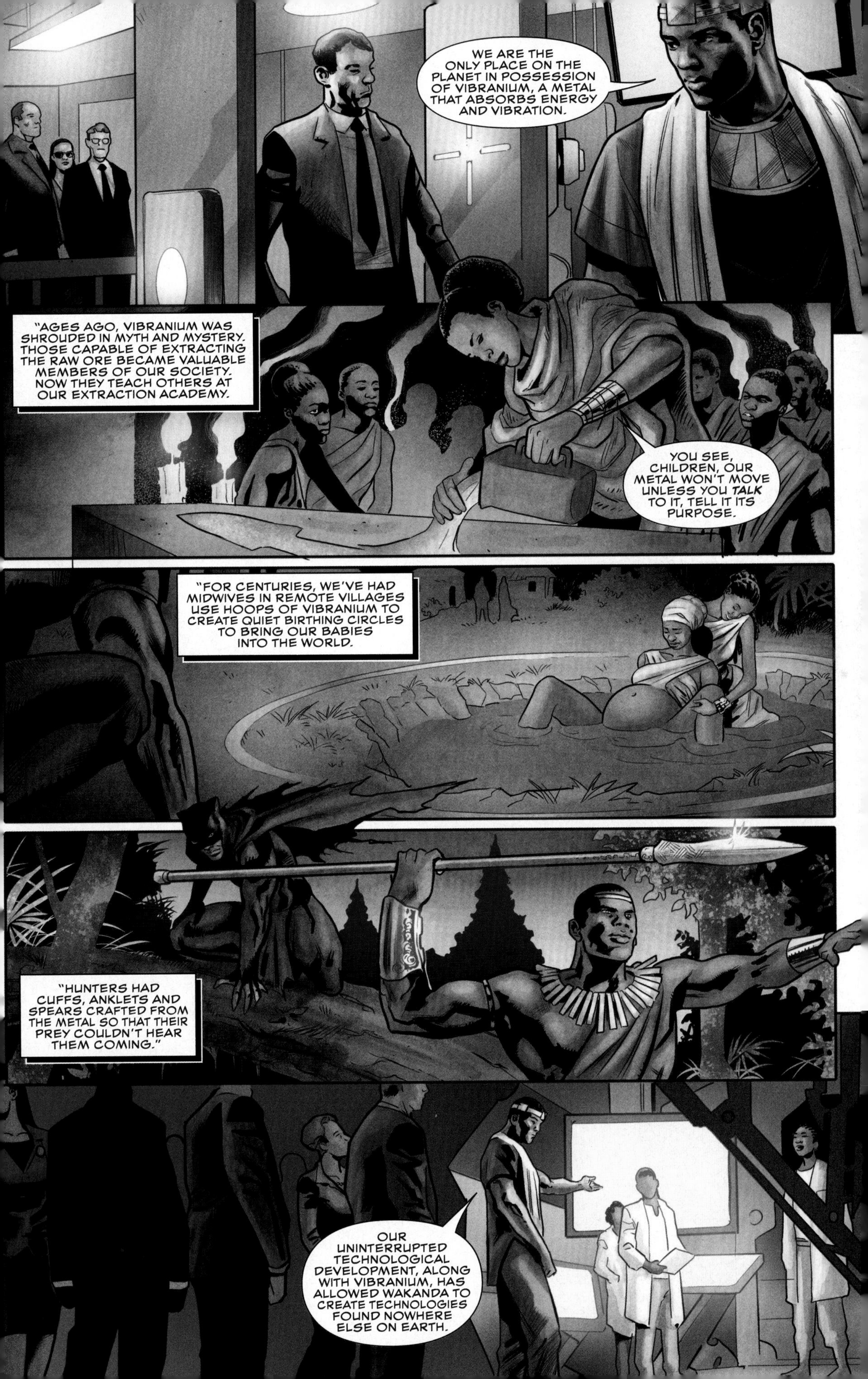
WE ARE THE ONLY PLACE ON THE PLANET IN POSSESSION OF VIBRANIUM, A METAL THAT ABSORBS ENERGY AND VIBRATION.
"AGES AGO, VIBRANIUM WAS SHROUDED IN MYTH AND MYSTERY. THOSE CAPABLE OF EXTRACTING THE RAW ORE BECAME VALUABLE MEMBERS OF OUR SOCIETY. NOW THEY TEACH OTHERS AT OUR EXTRACTION ACADEMY.
YOU SEE, CHILDREN, OUR METAL WON'T MOVE UNLESS YOU *TALK* TO IT, TELL IT ITS PURPOSE.
"FOR CENTURIES, WE'VE HAD MIDWIVES IN REMOTE VILLAGES USE HOOPS OF VIBRANIUM TO CREATE QUIET BIRTHING CIRCLES TO BRING OUR BABIES INTO THE WORLD.
"HUNTERS HAD CUFFS, ANKLETS AND SPEARS CRAFTED FROM THE METAL SO THAT THEIR PREY COULDN'T HEAR THEM COMING."
OUR UNINTERRUPTED TECHNOLOGICAL DEVELOPMENT, ALONG WITH VIBRANIUM, HAS ALLOWED WAKANDA TO CREATE TECHNOLOGIES FOUND NOWHERE ELSE ON EARTH.

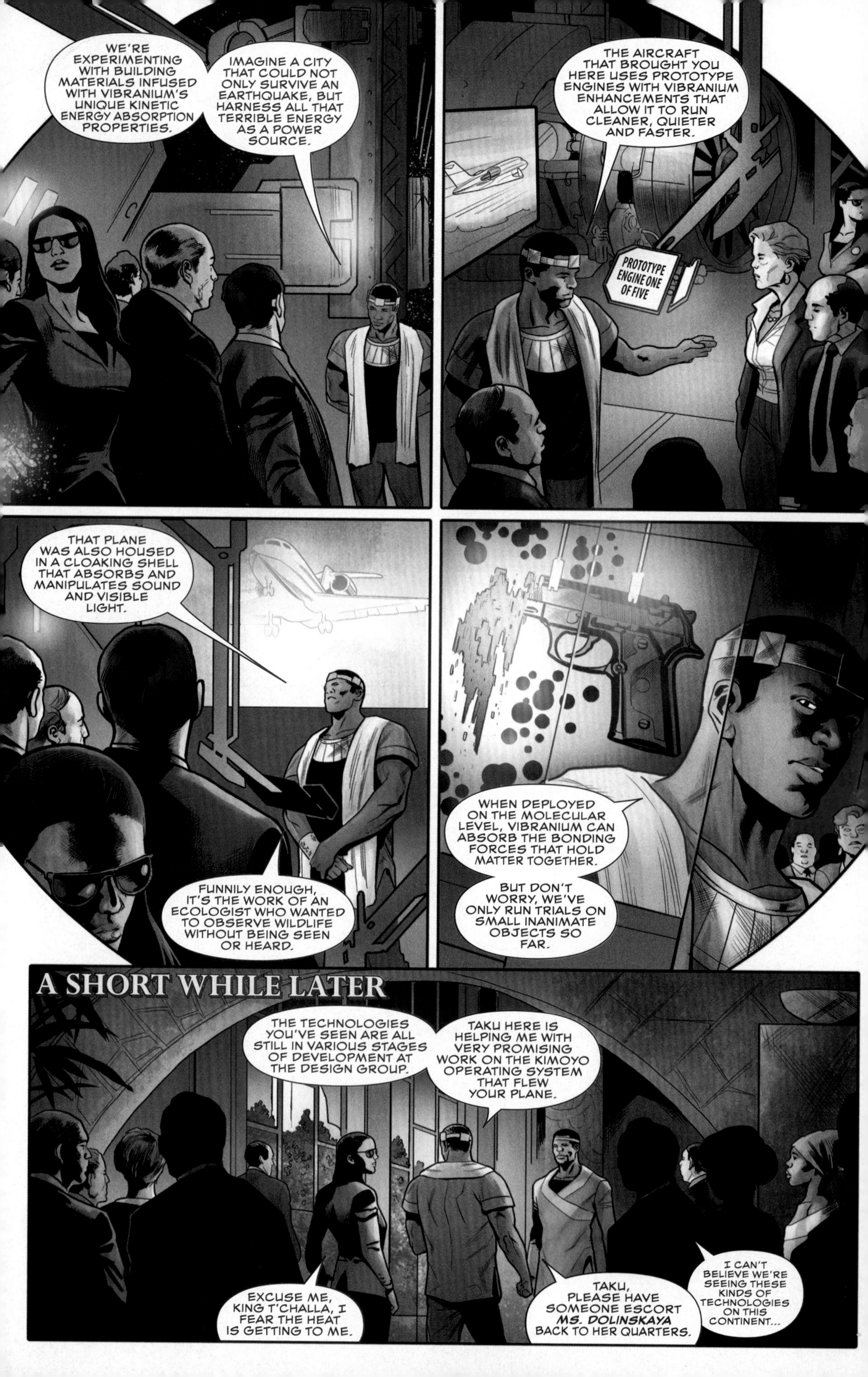
WE'RE EXPERIMENTING WITH BUILDING MATERIALS INFUSED WITH VIBRANIUM'S UNIQUE KINETIC ENERGY ABSORPTION PROPERTIES.
IMAGINE A CITY THAT COULD NOT ONLY SURVIVE AN EARTHQUAKE, BUT HARNESS ALL THAT TERRIBLE ENERGY AS A POWER SOURCE.
THE AIRCRAFT THAT BROUGHT YOU HERE USES PROTOTYPE ENGINES WITH VIBRANIUM ENHANCEMENTS THAT ALLOW IT TO RUN CLEANER, QUIETER AND FASTER.
PROTOTYPE ENGINE ONE OF FIVE
THAT PLANE WAS ALSO HOUSED IN A CLOAKING SHELL THAT ABSORBS AND MANIPULATES SOUND AND VISIBLE LIGHT.
FUNNILY ENOUGH, IT'S THE WORK OF AN ECOLOGIST WHO WANTED TO OBSERVE WILDLIFE WITHOUT BEING SEEN OR HEARD.
WHEN DEPLOYED ON THE MOLECULAR LEVEL, VIBRANIUM CAN ABSORB THE BONDING FORCES THAT HOLD MATTER TOGETHER.
BUT DON'T WORRY, WE'VE ONLY RUN TRIALS ON SMALL INANIMATE OBJECTS SO FAR.
A SHORT WHILE LATER
THE TECHNOLOGIES YOU'VE SEEN ARE ALL STILL IN VARIOUS STAGES OF DEVELOPMENT AT THE DESIGN GROUP.
TAKU HERE IS HELPING ME WITH VERY PROMISING WORK ON THE KIMOYO OPERATING SYSTEM THAT FLEW YOUR PLANE.
EXCUSE ME, KING T'CHALLA, I FEAR THE HEAT IS GETTING TO ME.
TAKU, PLEASE HAVE SOMEONE ESCORT *MS. DOLINSKAYA* BACK TO HER QUARTERS.
I CAN'T BELIEVE WE'RE SEEING THESE KINDS OF TECHNOLOGIES ON THIS CONTINENT...

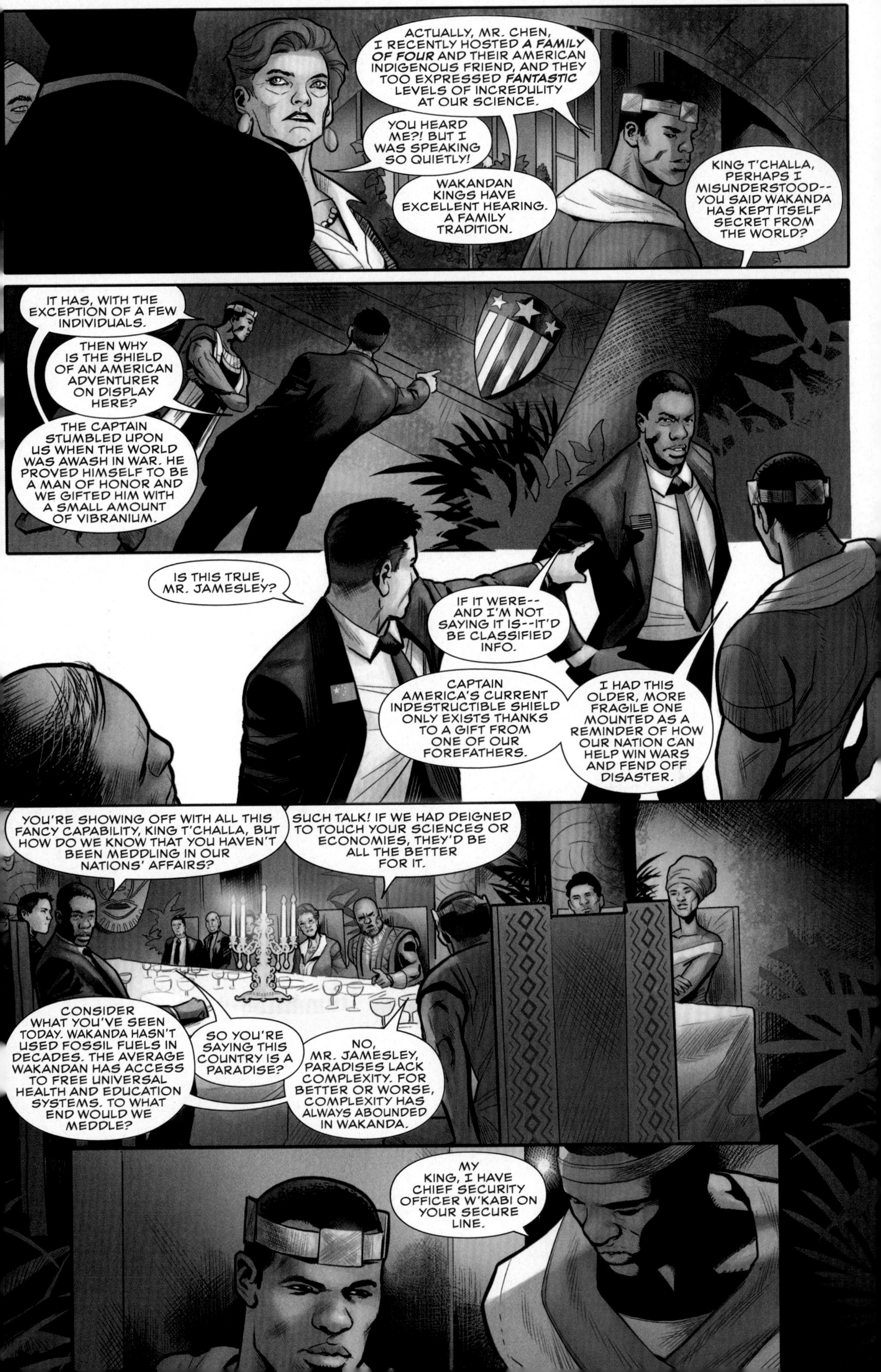
ACTUALLY, MR. CHEN, I RECENTLY HOSTED A FAMILY OF FOUR AND THEIR AMERICAN INDIGENOUS FRIEND, AND THEY TOO EXPRESSED FANTASTIC LEVELS OF INCREDULITY AT OUR SCIENCE.
YOU HEARD ME?! BUT I WAS SPEAKING SO QUIETLY!
WAKANDAN KINGS HAVE EXCELLENT HEARING. A FAMILY TRADITION.
KING T'CHALLA, PERHAPS I MISUNDERSTOOD--YOU SAID WAKANDA HAS KEPT ITSELF SECRET FROM THE WORLD?
IT HAS, WITH THE EXCEPTION OF A FEW INDIVIDUALS.
THEN WHY IS THE SHIELD OF AN AMERICAN ADVENTURER ON DISPLAY HERE?
THE CAPTAIN STUMBLED UPON US WHEN THE WORLD WAS AWASH IN WAR. HE PROVED HIMSELF TO BE A MAN OF HONOR AND WE GIFTED HIM WITH A SMALL AMOUNT OF VIBRANIUM.
IS THIS TRUE, MR. JAMESLEY?
IF IT WERE--AND I'M NOT SAYING IT IS--IT'D BE CLASSIFIED INFO.
CAPTAIN AMERICA'S CURRENT INDESTRUCTIBLE SHIELD ONLY EXISTS THANKS TO A GIFT FROM ONE OF OUR FOREFATHERS.
I HAD THIS OLDER, MORE FRAGILE ONE MOUNTED AS A REMINDER OF HOW OUR NATION CAN HELP WIN WARS AND FEND OFF DISASTER.
YOU'RE SHOWING OFF WITH ALL THIS FANCY CAPABILITY, KING T'CHALLA, BUT HOW DO WE KNOW THAT YOU HAVEN'T BEEN MEDDLING IN OUR NATIONS' AFFAIRS?
SUCH TALK! IF WE HAD DEIGNED TO TOUCH YOUR SCIENCES OR ECONOMIES, THEY'D BE ALL THE BETTER FOR IT.
CONSIDER WHAT YOU'VE SEEN TODAY. WAKANDA HASN'T USED FOSSIL FUELS IN DECADES. THE AVERAGE WAKANDAN HAS ACCESS TO FREE UNIVERSAL HEALTH AND EDUCATION SYSTEMS. TO WHAT END WOULD WE MEDDLE?
SO YOU'RE SAYING THIS COUNTRY IS A PARADISE?
NO, MR. JAMESLEY, PARADISES LACK COMPLEXITY. FOR BETTER OR WORSE, COMPLEXITY HAS ALWAYS ABOUNDED IN WAKANDA.
MY KING, I HAVE CHIEF SECURITY OFFICER W'KABI ON YOUR SECURE LINE.

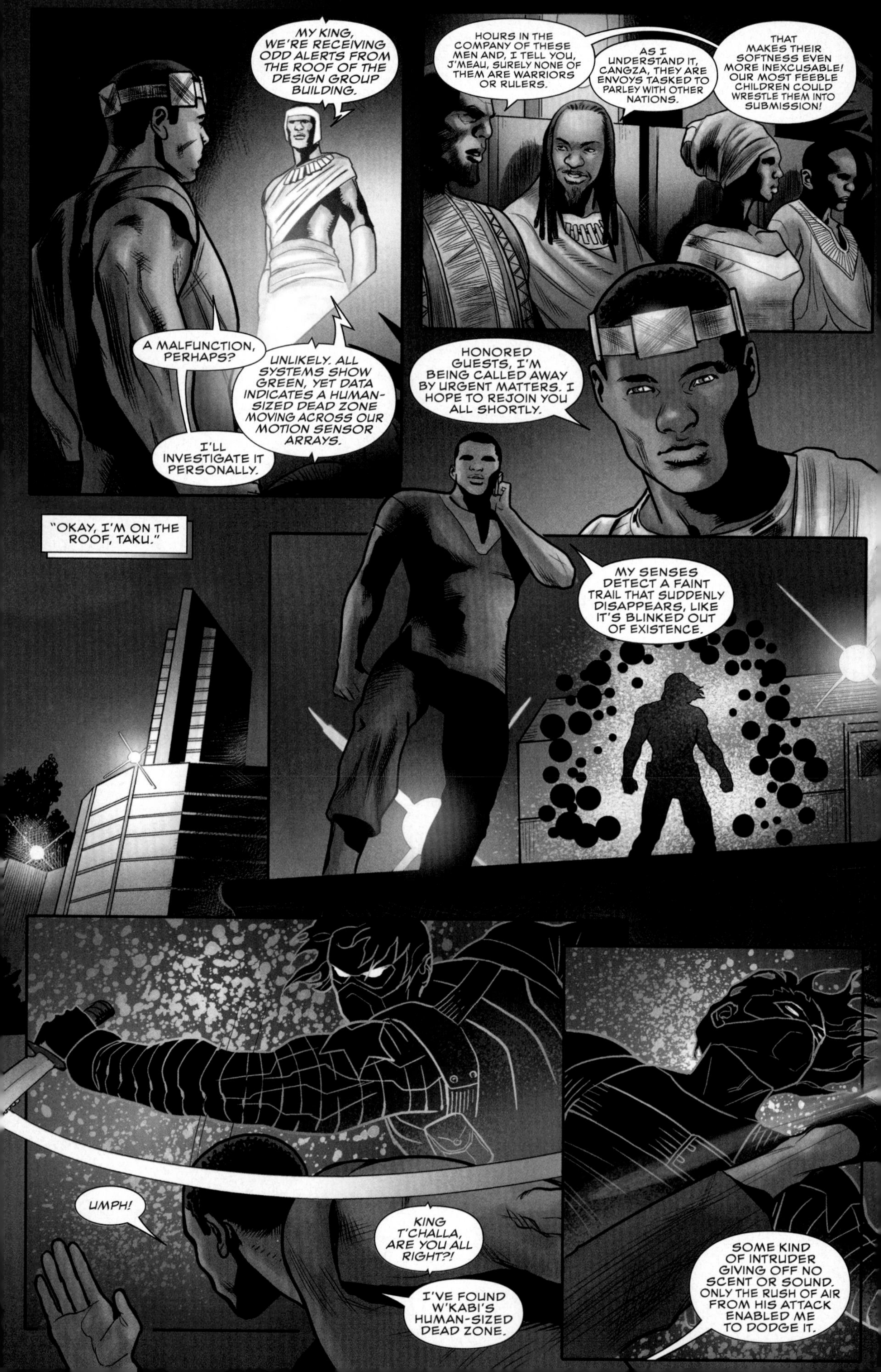
MY KING, WE'RE RECEIVING ODD ALERTS FROM THE ROOF OF THE DESIGN GROUP BUILDING.
A MALFUNCTION, PERHAPS?
UNLIKELY. ALL SYSTEMS SHOW GREEN, YET DATA INDICATES A HUMAN-SIZED DEAD ZONE MOVING ACROSS OUR MOTION SENSOR ARRAYS.
I'LL INVESTIGATE IT PERSONALLY.
HOURS IN THE COMPANY OF THESE MEN AND, I TELL YOU, J'MEAU, SURELY NONE OF THEM ARE WARRIORS OR RULERS.
AS I UNDERSTAND IT, CANGZA, THEY ARE ENVOYS TASKED TO PARLEY WITH OTHER NATIONS.
THAT MAKES THEIR SOFTNESS EVEN MORE INEXCUSABLE! OUR MOST FEEBLE CHILDREN COULD WRESTLE THEM INTO SUBMISSION!
HONORED GUESTS, I'M BEING CALLED AWAY BY URGENT MATTERS. I HOPE TO REJOIN YOU ALL SHORTLY.
"OKAY, I'M ON THE ROOF, TAKU."
MY SENSES DETECT A FAINT TRAIL THAT SUDDENLY DISAPPEARS, LIKE IT'S BLINKED OUT OF EXISTENCE.
UMPH!
KING T'CHALLA, ARE YOU ALL RIGHT?!
I'VE FOUND W'KABI'S HUMAN-SIZED DEAD ZONE.
SOME KIND OF INTRUDER GIVING OFF NO SCENT OR SOUND. ONLY THE RUSH OF AIR FROM HIS ATTACK ENABLED ME TO DODGE IT.

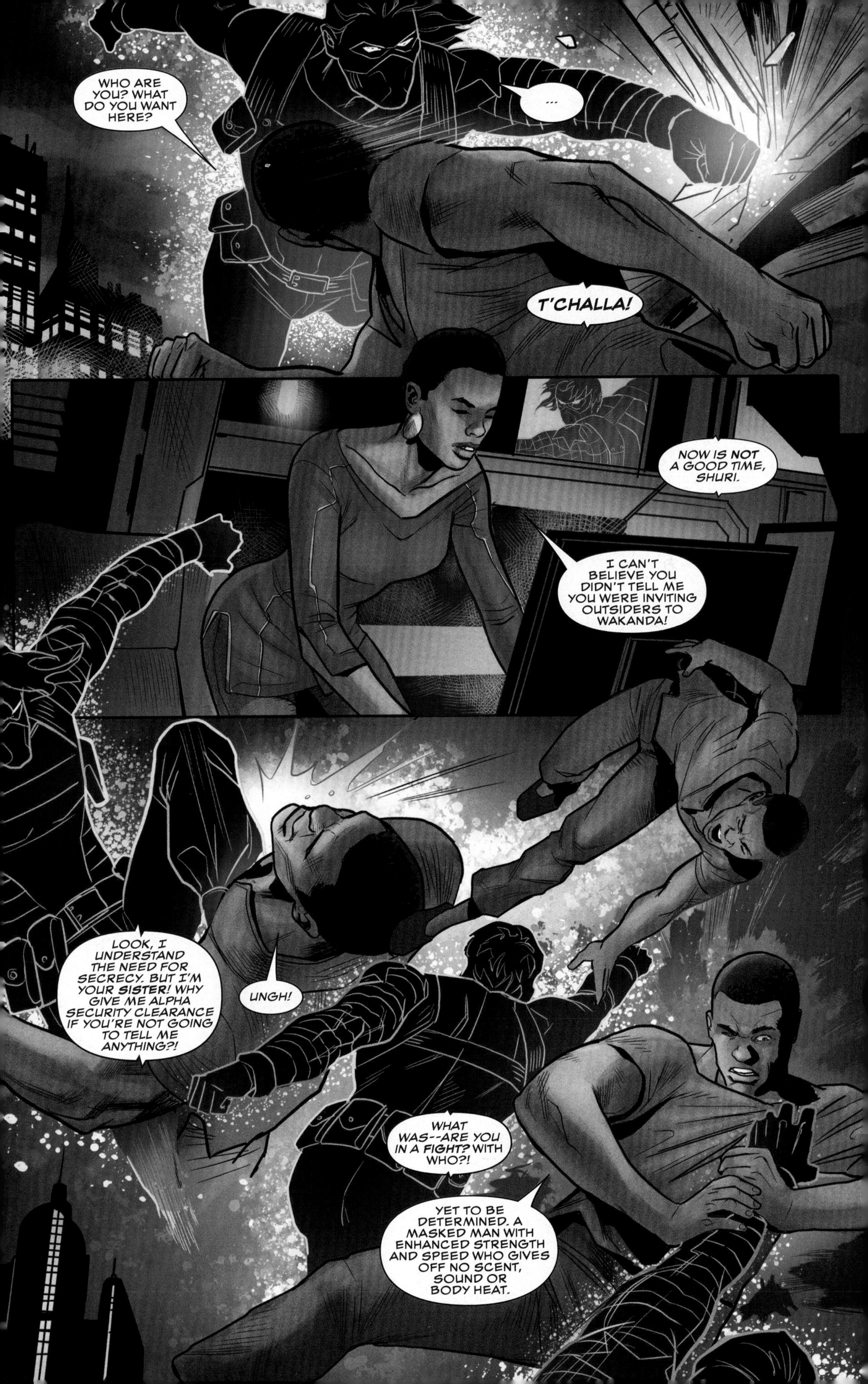
WHO ARE YOU? WHAT DO YOU WANT HERE?
...
T'CHALLA!
NOW IS NOT A GOOD TIME, SHURI.
I CAN'T BELIEVE YOU DIDN'T TELL ME YOU WERE INVITING OUTSIDERS TO WAKANDA!
LOOK, I UNDERSTAND THE NEED FOR SECRECY. BUT I'M YOUR SISTER! WHY GIVE ME ALPHA SECURITY CLEARANCE IF YOU'RE NOT GOING TO TELL ME ANYTHING?!
UNGH!
WHAT WAS--ARE YOU IN A FIGHT? WITH WHO?!
YET TO BE DETERMINED. A MASKED MAN WITH ENHANCED STRENGTH AND SPEED WHO GIVES OFF NO SCENT, SOUND OR BODY HEAT.

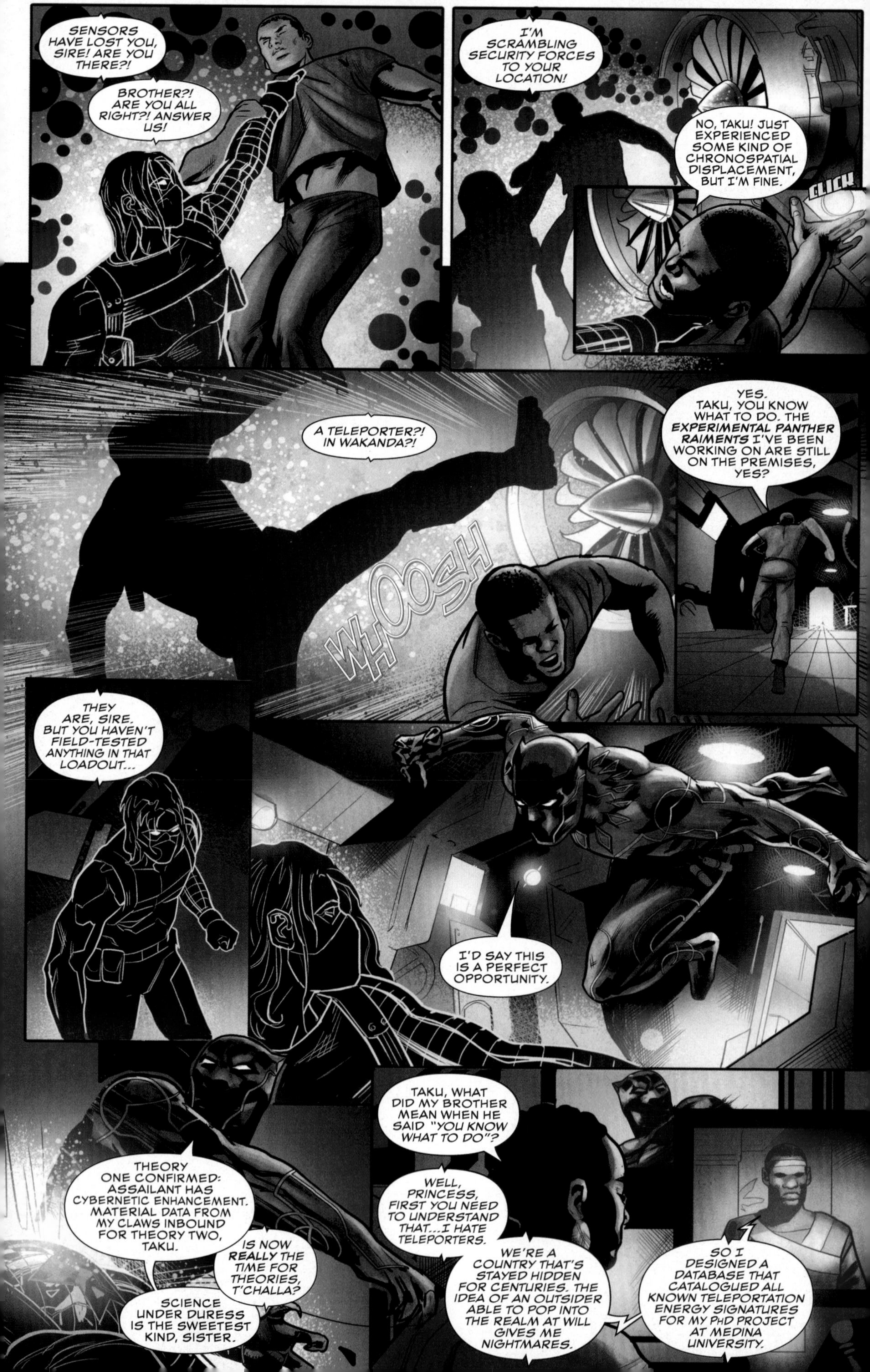
SENSORS HAVE LOST YOU, SIRE! ARE YOU THERE?!
BROTHER?! ARE YOU ALL RIGHT?! ANSWER US!
I'M SCRAMBLING SECURITY FORCES TO YOUR LOCATION!
NO, TAKU! JUST EXPERIENCED SOME KIND OF CHRONOSPATIAL DISPLACEMENT, BUT I'M FINE.
CLICK
A TELEPORTER?! IN WAKANDA?!
WHOOSH
YES. TAKU, YOU KNOW WHAT TO DO. THE EXPERIMENTAL PANTHER RAIMENTS I'VE BEEN WORKING ON ARE STILL ON THE PREMISES, YES?
THEY ARE, SIRE. BUT YOU HAVEN'T FIELD-TESTED ANYTHING IN THAT LOADOUT...
I'D SAY THIS IS A PERFECT OPPORTUNITY.
THEORY ONE CONFIRMED: ASSAILANT HAS CYBERNETIC ENHANCEMENT. MATERIAL DATA FROM MY CLAWS INBOUND FOR THEORY TWO, TAKU.
IS NOW REALLY THE TIME FOR THEORIES, T'CHALLA?
SCIENCE UNDER DURESS IS THE SWEETEST KIND, SISTER.
TAKU, WHAT DID MY BROTHER MEAN WHEN HE SAID "YOU KNOW WHAT TO DO"?
WELL, PRINCESS, FIRST YOU NEED TO UNDERSTAND THAT...I HATE TELEPORTERS.
WE'RE A COUNTRY THAT'S STAYED HIDDEN FOR CENTURIES. THE IDEA OF AN OUTSIDER ABLE TO POP INTO THE REALM AT WILL GIVES ME NIGHTMARES.
SO I DESIGNED A DATABASE THAT CATALOGUED ALL KNOWN TELEPORTATION ENERGY SIGNATURES FOR MY PHD PROJECT AT MEDINA UNIVERSITY.

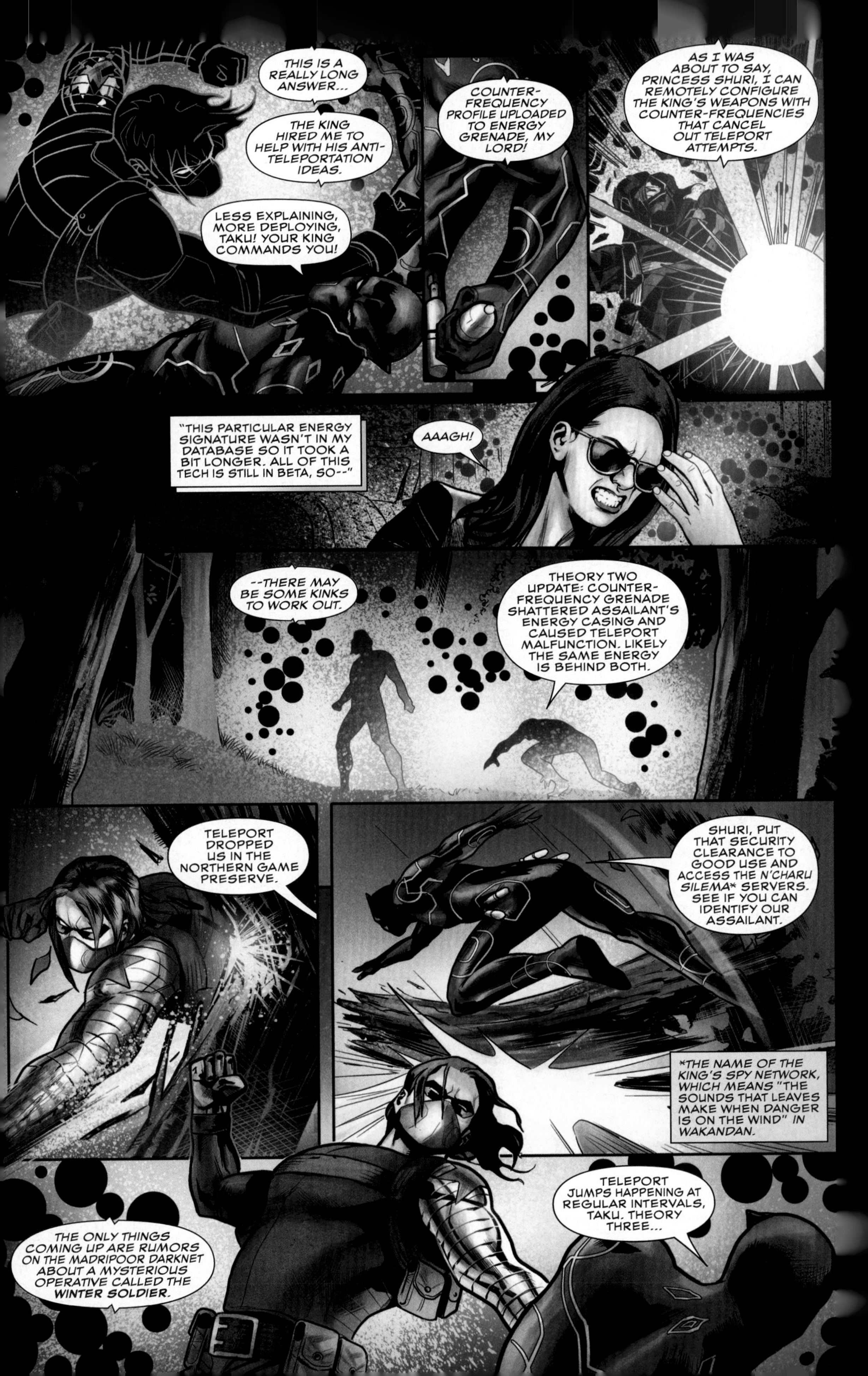
THIS IS A REALLY LONG ANSWER...
THE KING HIRED ME TO HELP WITH HIS ANTI-TELEPORTATION IDEAS.
LESS EXPLAINING, MORE DEPLOYING, TAKU! YOUR KING COMMANDS YOU!
COUNTER-FREQUENCY PROFILE UPLOADED TO ENERGY GRENADE, MY LORD!
AS I WAS ABOUT TO SAY, PRINCESS SHURI, I CAN REMOTELY CONFIGURE THE KING'S WEAPONS WITH COUNTER-FREQUENCIES THAT CANCEL OUT TELEPORT ATTEMPTS.
"THIS PARTICULAR ENERGY SIGNATURE WASN'T IN MY DATABASE SO IT TOOK A BIT LONGER. ALL OF THIS TECH IS STILL IN BETA, SO--"
AAAGH!
--THERE MAY BE SOME KINKS TO WORK OUT.
THEORY TWO UPDATE: COUNTER-FREQUENCY GRENADE SHATTERED ASSAILANT'S ENERGY CASING AND CAUSED TELEPORT MALFUNCTION. LIKELY THE SAME ENERGY IS BEHIND BOTH.
TELEPORT DROPPED US IN THE NORTHERN GAME PRESERVE.
SHURI, PUT THAT SECURITY CLEARANCE TO GOOD USE AND ACCESS THE N'CHARU SILEMA* SERVERS. SEE IF YOU CAN IDENTIFY OUR ASSAILANT.
*THE NAME OF THE KING'S SPY NETWORK, WHICH MEANS "THE SOUNDS THAT LEAVES MAKE WHEN DANGER IS ON THE WIND" IN WAKANDAN.
THE ONLY THINGS COMING UP ARE RUMORS ON THE MADRIPOOR DARKNET ABOUT A MYSTERIOUS OPERATIVE CALLED THE WINTER SOLDIER.
TELEPORT JUMPS HAPPENING AT REGULAR INTERVALS, TAKU. THEORY THREE...

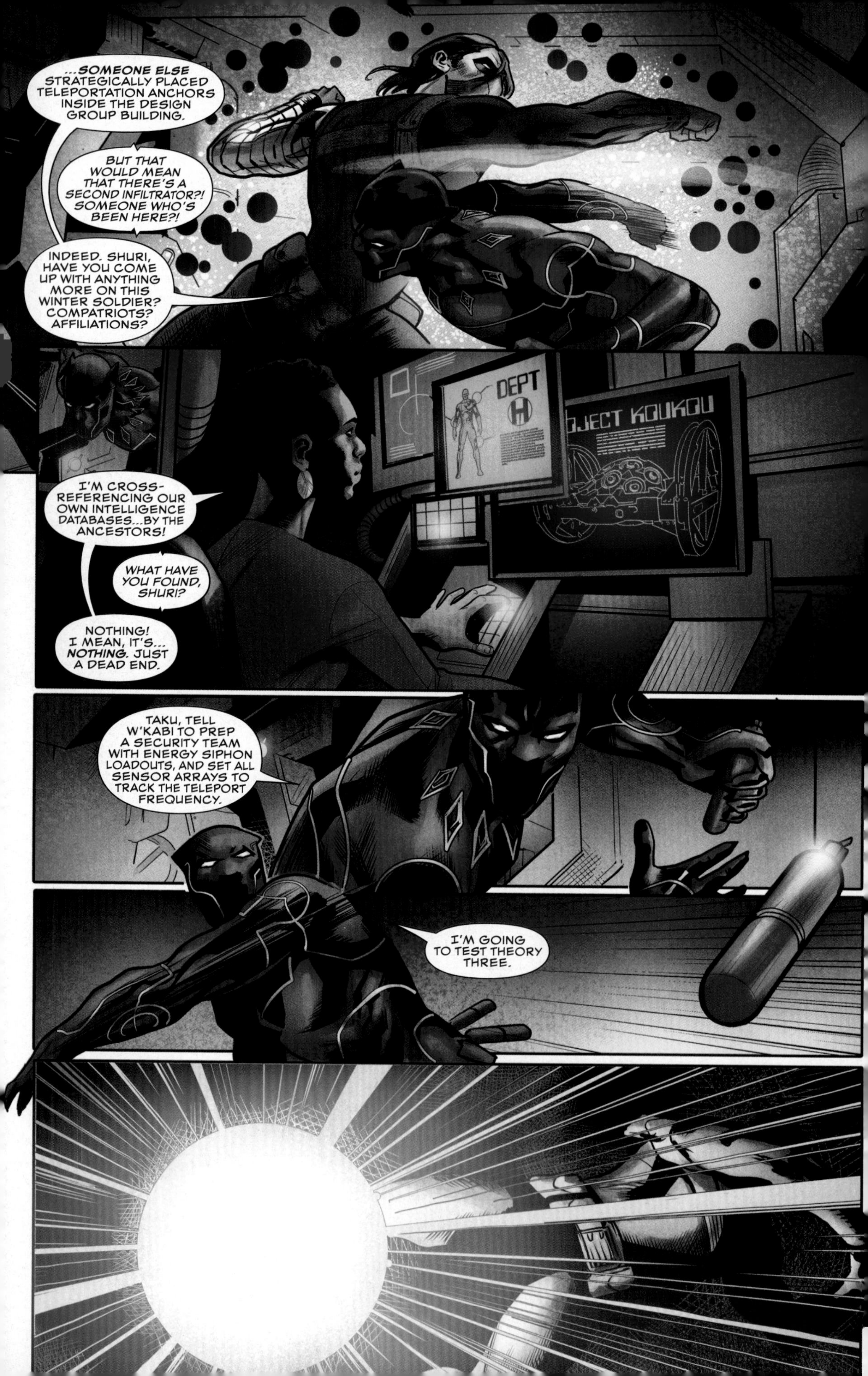
...SOMEONE ELSE STRATEGICALLY PLACED TELEPORTATION ANCHORS INSIDE THE DESIGN GROUP BUILDING.
BUT THAT WOULD MEAN THAT THERE'S A SECOND INFILTRATOR?! SOMEONE WHO'S BEEN HERE?!
INDEED. SHURI, HAVE YOU COME UP WITH ANYTHING MORE ON THIS WINTER SOLDIER? COMPATRIOTS? AFFILIATIONS?
DEPT
OJECT KOUKOU
I'M CROSS-REFERENCING OUR OWN INTELLIGENCE DATABASES...BY THE ANCESTORS!
WHAT HAVE YOU FOUND, SHURI?
NOTHING! I MEAN, IT'S... NOTHING. JUST A DEAD END.
TAKU, TELL W'KABI TO PREP A SECURITY TEAM WITH ENERGY SIPHON LOADOUTS, AND SET ALL SENSOR ARRAYS TO TRACK THE TELEPORT FREQUENCY.
I'M GOING TO TEST THEORY THREE.

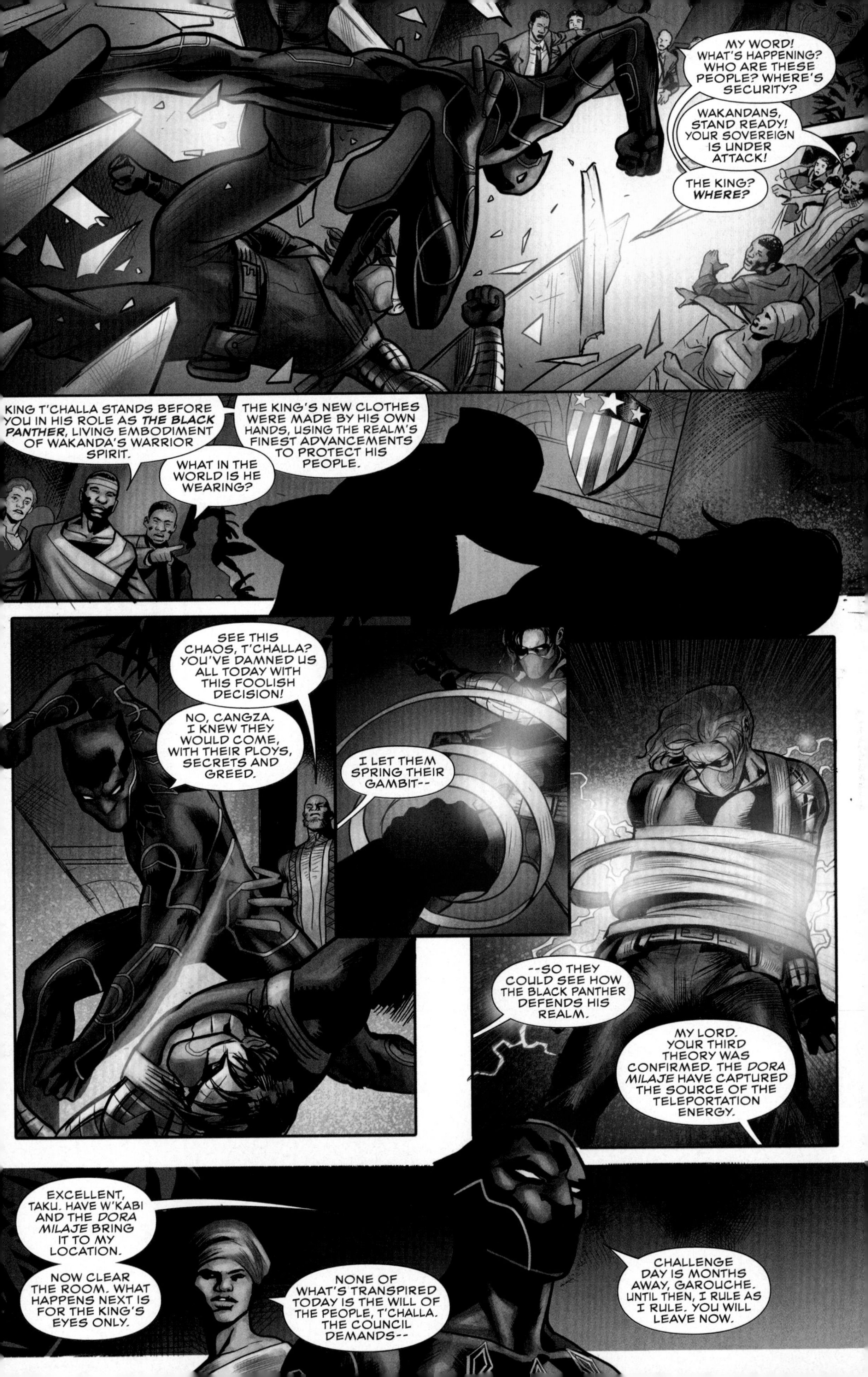
MY WORD! WHAT'S HAPPENING? WHO ARE THESE PEOPLE? WHERE'S SECURITY?
WAKANDANS, STAND READY! YOUR SOVEREIGN IS UNDER ATTACK!
THE KING? *WHERE?*
KING T'CHALLA STANDS BEFORE YOU IN HIS ROLE AS *THE BLACK PANTHER*, LIVING EMBODIMENT OF WAKANDA'S WARRIOR SPIRIT.
THE KING'S NEW CLOTHES WERE MADE BY HIS OWN HANDS, USING THE REALM'S FINEST ADVANCEMENTS TO PROTECT HIS PEOPLE.
WHAT IN THE WORLD IS HE WEARING?
SEE THIS CHAOS, T'CHALLA? YOU'VE DAMNED US ALL TODAY WITH THIS FOOLISH DECISION!
NO, CANGZA. I KNEW THEY WOULD COME, WITH THEIR PLOYS, SECRETS AND GREED.
I LET THEM SPRING THEIR GAMBIT--
--SO THEY COULD SEE HOW THE BLACK PANTHER DEFENDS HIS REALM.
MY LORD. YOUR THIRD THEORY WAS CONFIRMED. THE *DORA MILAJE* HAVE CAPTURED THE SOURCE OF THE TELEPORTATION ENERGY.
EXCELLENT, TAKU. HAVE W'KABI AND THE *DORA MILAJE* BRING IT TO MY LOCATION.
NOW CLEAR THE ROOM. WHAT HAPPENS NEXT IS FOR THE KING'S EYES ONLY.
NONE OF WHAT'S TRANSPIRED TODAY IS THE WILL OF THE PEOPLE, T'CHALLA. THE COUNCIL DEMANDS--
CHALLENGE DAY IS MONTHS AWAY, GAROUCHE. UNTIL THEN, I RULE AS I RULE. YOU WILL LEAVE NOW.

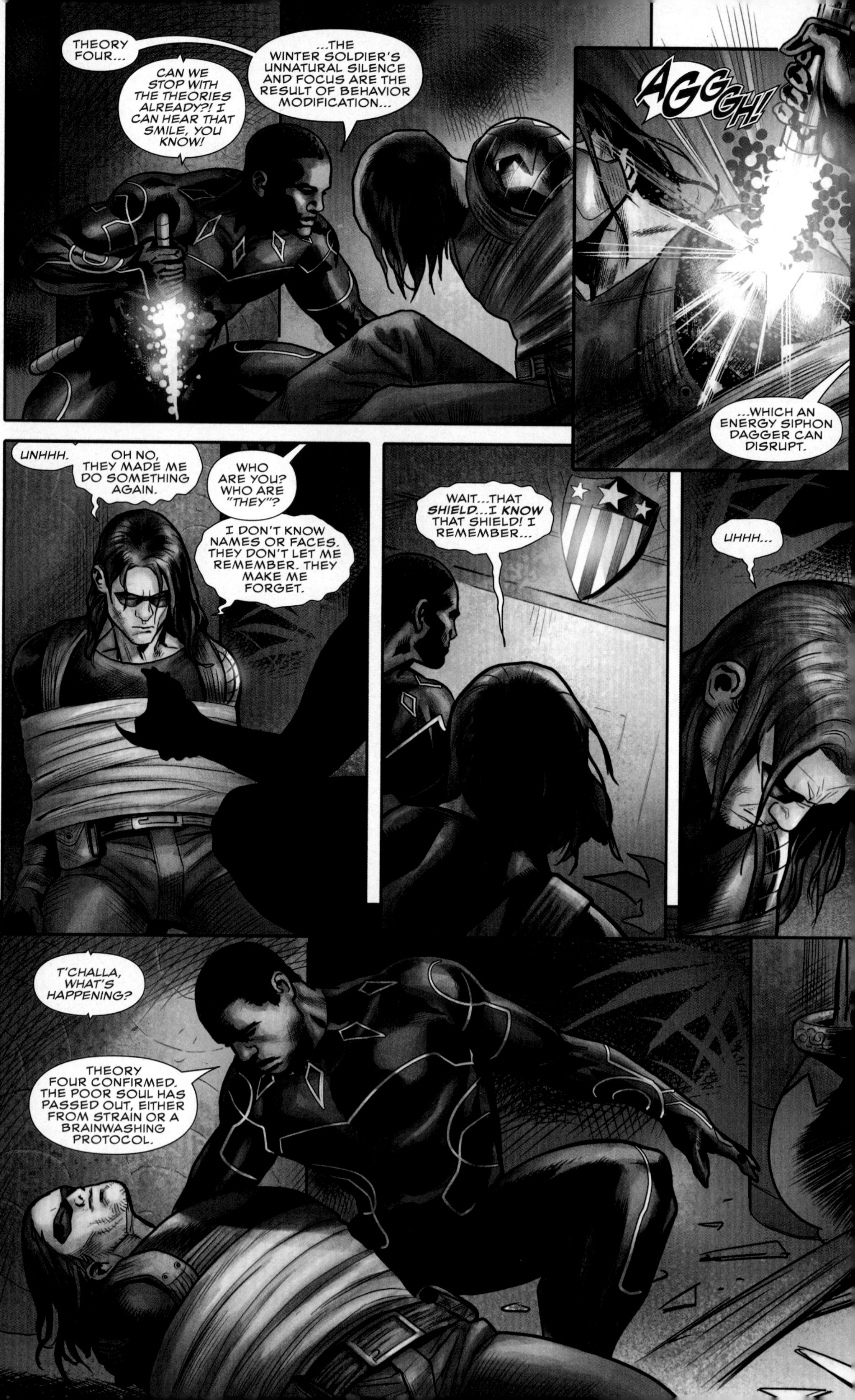
THEORY FOUR...
CAN WE STOP WITH THE THEORIES ALREADY?! I CAN HEAR THAT SMILE, YOU KNOW!
...THE WINTER SOLDIER'S UNNATURAL SILENCE AND FOCUS ARE THE RESULT OF BEHAVIOR MODIFICATION...
AGGGH!
...WHICH AN ENERGY SIPHON DAGGER CAN DISRUPT.
UNHHH.
OH NO, THEY MADE ME DO SOMETHING AGAIN.
WHO ARE YOU? WHO ARE "THEY"?
I DON'T KNOW NAMES OR FACES. THEY DON'T LET ME REMEMBER. THEY MAKE ME FORGET.
WAIT...THAT SHIELD...I KNOW THAT SHIELD! I REMEMBER...
UHHH...
T'CHALLA, WHAT'S HAPPENING?
THEORY FOUR CONFIRMED. THE POOR SOUL HAS PASSED OUT, EITHER FROM STRAIN OR A BRAINWASHING PROTOCOL.

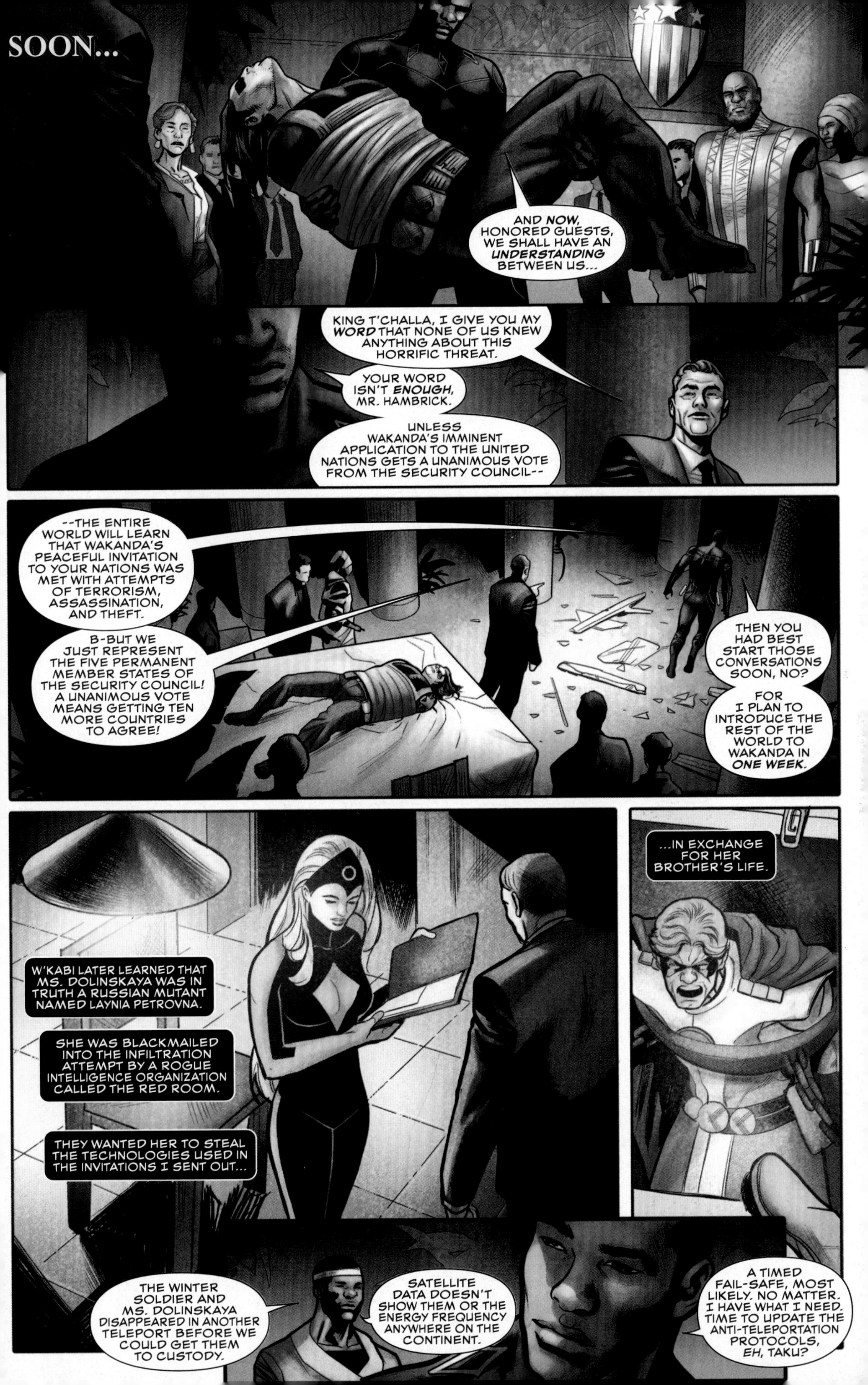
SOON...
AND NOW, HONORED GUESTS, WE SHALL HAVE AN UNDERSTANDING BETWEEN US...
KING T'CHALLA, I GIVE YOU MY WORD THAT NONE OF US KNEW ANYTHING ABOUT THIS HORRIFIC THREAT.
YOUR WORD ISN'T ENOUGH, MR. HAMBRICK.
UNLESS WAKANDA'S IMMINENT APPLICATION TO THE UNITED NATIONS GETS A UNANIMOUS VOTE FROM THE SECURITY COUNCIL--
--THE ENTIRE WORLD WILL LEARN THAT WAKANDA'S PEACEFUL INVITATION TO YOUR NATIONS WAS MET WITH ATTEMPTS OF TERRORISM, ASSASSINATION, AND THEFT.
B-BUT WE JUST REPRESENT THE FIVE PERMANENT MEMBER STATES OF THE SECURITY COUNCIL! A UNANIMOUS VOTE MEANS GETTING TEN MORE COUNTRIES TO AGREE!
THEN YOU HAD BEST START THOSE CONVERSATIONS SOON, NO?
FOR I PLAN TO INTRODUCE THE REST OF THE WORLD TO WAKANDA IN ONE WEEK.
W'KABI LATER LEARNED THAT MS. DOLINSKAYA WAS IN TRUTH A RUSSIAN MUTANT NAMED LAYNIA PETROVNA.
SHE WAS BLACKMAILED INTO THE INFILTRATION ATTEMPT BY A ROGUE INTELLIGENCE ORGANIZATION CALLED THE RED ROOM.
THEY WANTED HER TO STEAL THE TECHNOLOGIES USED IN THE INVITATIONS I SENT OUT...
...IN EXCHANGE FOR HER BROTHER'S LIFE.
THE WINTER SOLDIER AND MS. DOLINSKAYA DISAPPEARED IN ANOTHER TELEPORT BEFORE WE COULD GET THEM TO CUSTODY.
SATELLITE DATA DOESN'T SHOW THEM OR THE ENERGY FREQUENCY ANYWHERE ON THE CONTINENT.
A TIMED FAIL-SAFE, MOST LIKELY. NO MATTER. I HAVE WHAT I NEED. TIME TO UPDATE THE ANTI-TELEPORTATION PROTOCOLS, EH, TAKU?

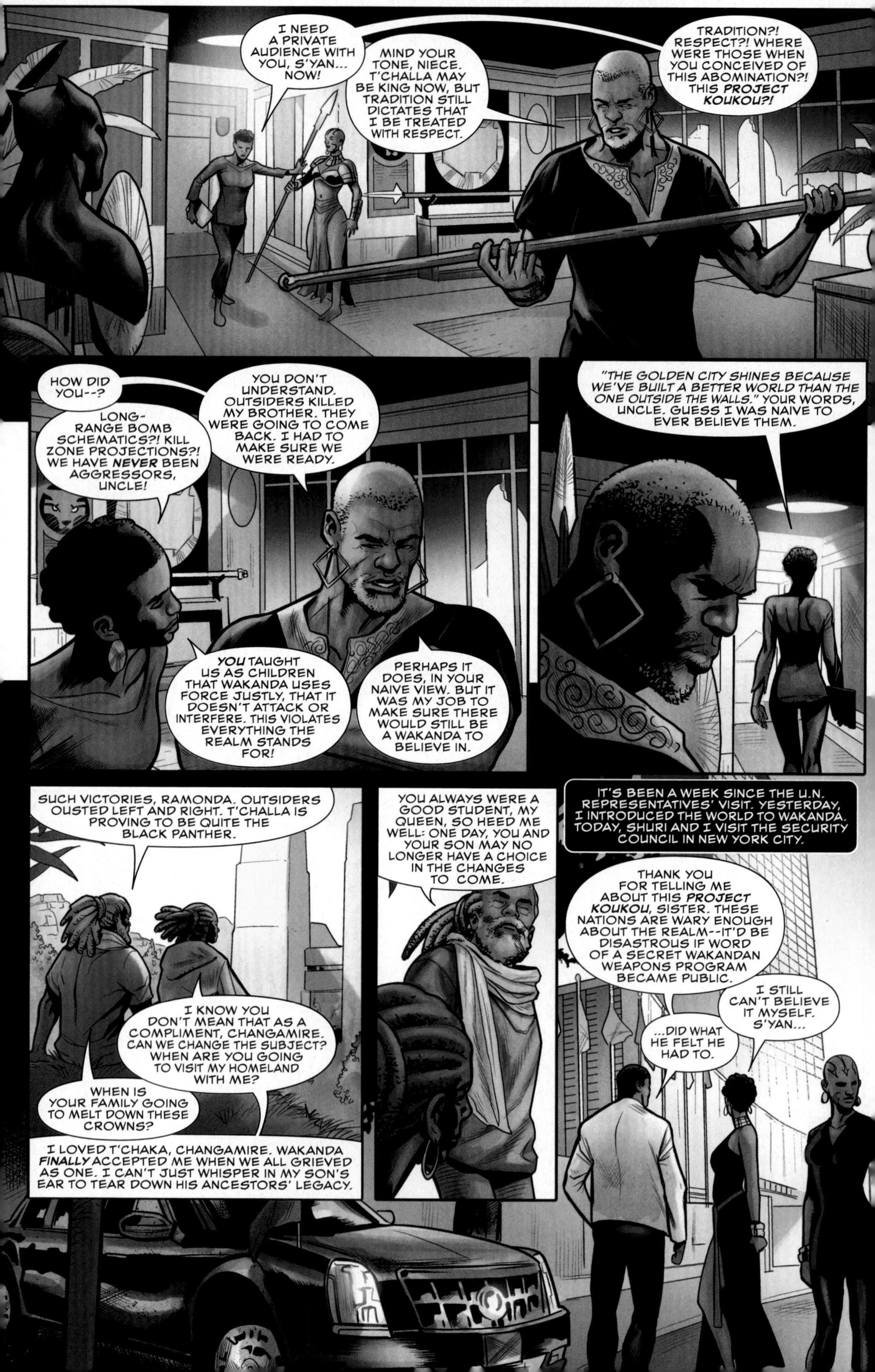
I NEED A PRIVATE AUDIENCE WITH YOU, S'YAN... NOW!
MIND YOUR TONE, NIECE. T'CHALLA MAY BE KING NOW, BUT TRADITION STILL DICTATES THAT I BE TREATED WITH RESPECT.
TRADITION?! RESPECT?! WHERE WERE THOSE WHEN YOU CONCEIVED OF THIS ABOMINATION?! THIS PROJECT KOUKOU?!
HOW DID YOU--?
LONG-RANGE BOMB SCHEMATICS?! KILL ZONE PROJECTIONS?! WE HAVE NEVER BEEN AGGRESSORS, UNCLE!
YOU DON'T UNDERSTAND. OUTSIDERS KILLED MY BROTHER. THEY WERE GOING TO COME BACK. I HAD TO MAKE SURE WE WERE READY.
YOU TAUGHT US AS CHILDREN THAT WAKANDA USES FORCE JUSTLY, THAT IT DOESN'T ATTACK OR INTERFERE. THIS VIOLATES EVERYTHING THE REALM STANDS FOR!
PERHAPS IT DOES, IN YOUR NAIVE VIEW. BUT IT WAS MY JOB TO MAKE SURE THERE WOULD STILL BE A WAKANDA TO BELIEVE IN.
"THE GOLDEN CITY SHINES BECAUSE WE'VE BUILT A BETTER WORLD THAN THE ONE OUTSIDE THE WALLS." YOUR WORDS, UNCLE. GUESS I WAS NAIVE TO EVER BELIEVE THEM.
SUCH VICTORIES, RAMONDA. OUTSIDERS OUSTED LEFT AND RIGHT. T'CHALLA IS PROVING TO BE QUITE THE BLACK PANTHER.
I KNOW YOU DON'T MEAN THAT AS A COMPLIMENT, CHANGAMIRE. CAN WE CHANGE THE SUBJECT? WHEN ARE YOU GOING TO VISIT MY HOMELAND WITH ME?
WHEN IS YOUR FAMILY GOING TO MELT DOWN THESE CROWNS?
I LOVED T'CHAKA, CHANGAMIRE. WAKANDA FINALLY ACCEPTED ME WHEN WE ALL GRIEVED AS ONE. I CAN'T JUST WHISPER IN MY SON'S EAR TO TEAR DOWN HIS ANCESTORS' LEGACY.
YOU ALWAYS WERE A GOOD STUDENT, MY QUEEN, SO HEED ME WELL: ONE DAY, YOU AND YOUR SON MAY NO LONGER HAVE A CHOICE IN THE CHANGES TO COME.
IT'S BEEN A WEEK SINCE THE U.N. REPRESENTATIVES' VISIT. YESTERDAY, I INTRODUCED THE WORLD TO WAKANDA. TODAY, SHURI AND I VISIT THE SECURITY COUNCIL IN NEW YORK CITY.
THANK YOU FOR TELLING ME ABOUT THIS PROJECT KOUKOU, SISTER. THESE NATIONS ARE WARY ENOUGH ABOUT THE REALM--IT'D BE DISASTROUS IF WORD OF A SECRET WAKANDAN WEAPONS PROGRAM BECAME PUBLIC.
I STILL CAN'T BELIEVE IT MYSELF. S'YAN...
...DID WHAT HE FELT HE HAD TO.

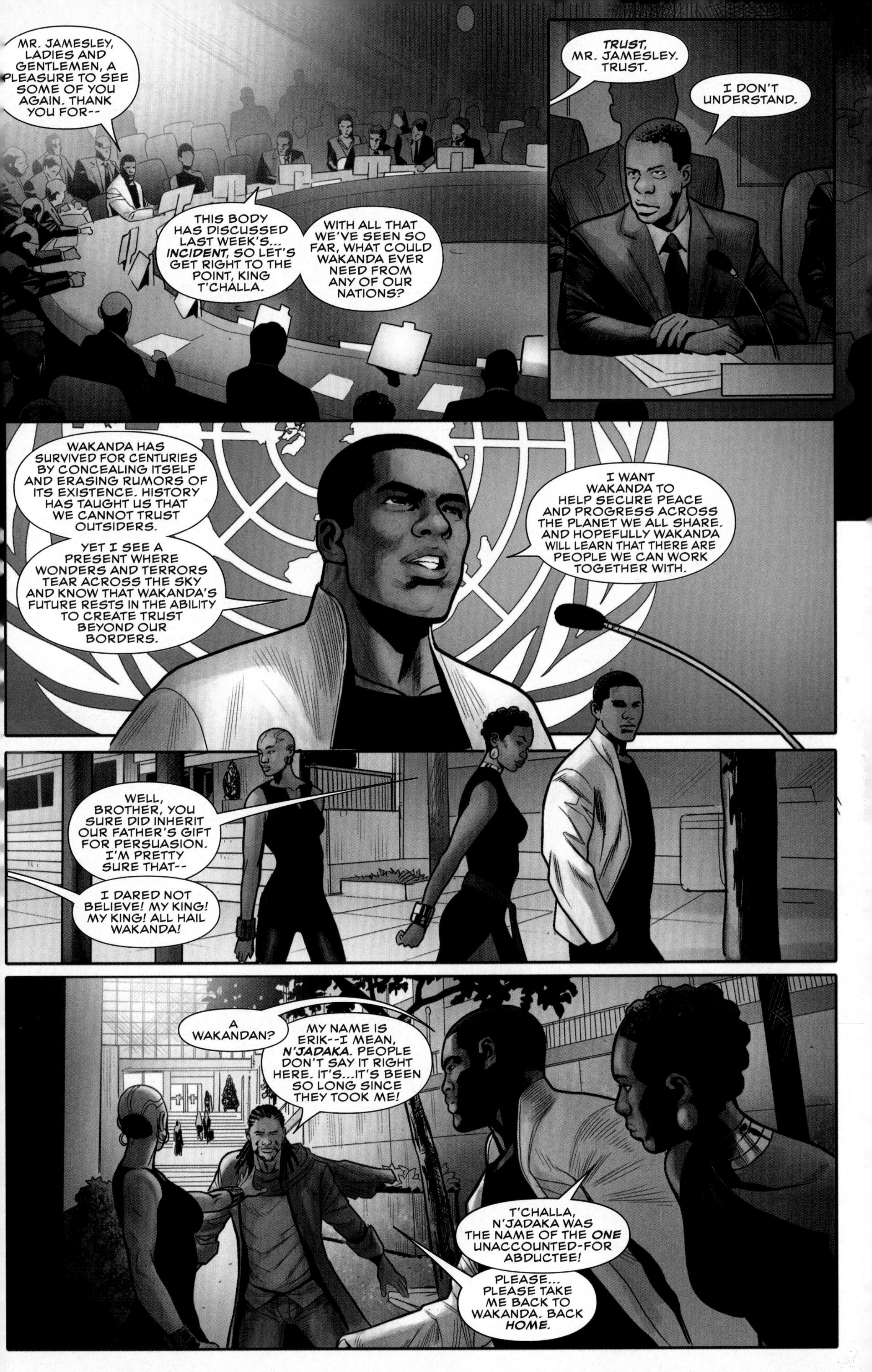
MR. JAMESLEY, LADIES AND GENTLEMEN, A PLEASURE TO SEE SOME OF YOU AGAIN. THANK YOU FOR--
THIS BODY HAS DISCUSSED LAST WEEK'S... INCIDENT, SO LET'S GET RIGHT TO THE POINT, KING T'CHALLA.
WITH ALL THAT WE'VE SEEN SO FAR, WHAT COULD WAKANDA EVER NEED FROM ANY OF OUR NATIONS?
TRUST, MR. JAMESLEY. TRUST.
I DON'T UNDERSTAND.
WAKANDA HAS SURVIVED FOR CENTURIES BY CONCEALING ITSELF AND ERASING RUMORS OF ITS EXISTENCE. HISTORY HAS TAUGHT US THAT WE CANNOT TRUST OUTSIDERS.
YET I SEE A PRESENT WHERE WONDERS AND TERRORS TEAR ACROSS THE SKY AND KNOW THAT WAKANDA'S FUTURE RESTS IN THE ABILITY TO CREATE TRUST BEYOND OUR BORDERS.
I WANT WAKANDA TO HELP SECURE PEACE AND PROGRESS ACROSS THE PLANET WE ALL SHARE. AND HOPEFULLY WAKANDA WILL LEARN THAT THERE ARE PEOPLE WE CAN WORK TOGETHER WITH.
WELL, BROTHER, YOU SURE DID INHERIT OUR FATHER'S GIFT FOR PERSUASION. I'M PRETTY SURE THAT--
I DARED NOT BELIEVE! MY KING! MY KING! ALL HAIL WAKANDA!
A WAKANDAN?
MY NAME IS ERIK--I MEAN, N'JADAKA. PEOPLE DON'T SAY IT RIGHT HERE. IT'S...IT'S BEEN SO LONG SINCE THEY TOOK ME!
T'CHALLA, N'JADAKA WAS THE NAME OF THE ONE UNACCOUNTED-FOR ABDUCTEE!
PLEASE... PLEASE TAKE ME BACK TO WAKANDA. BACK HOME.

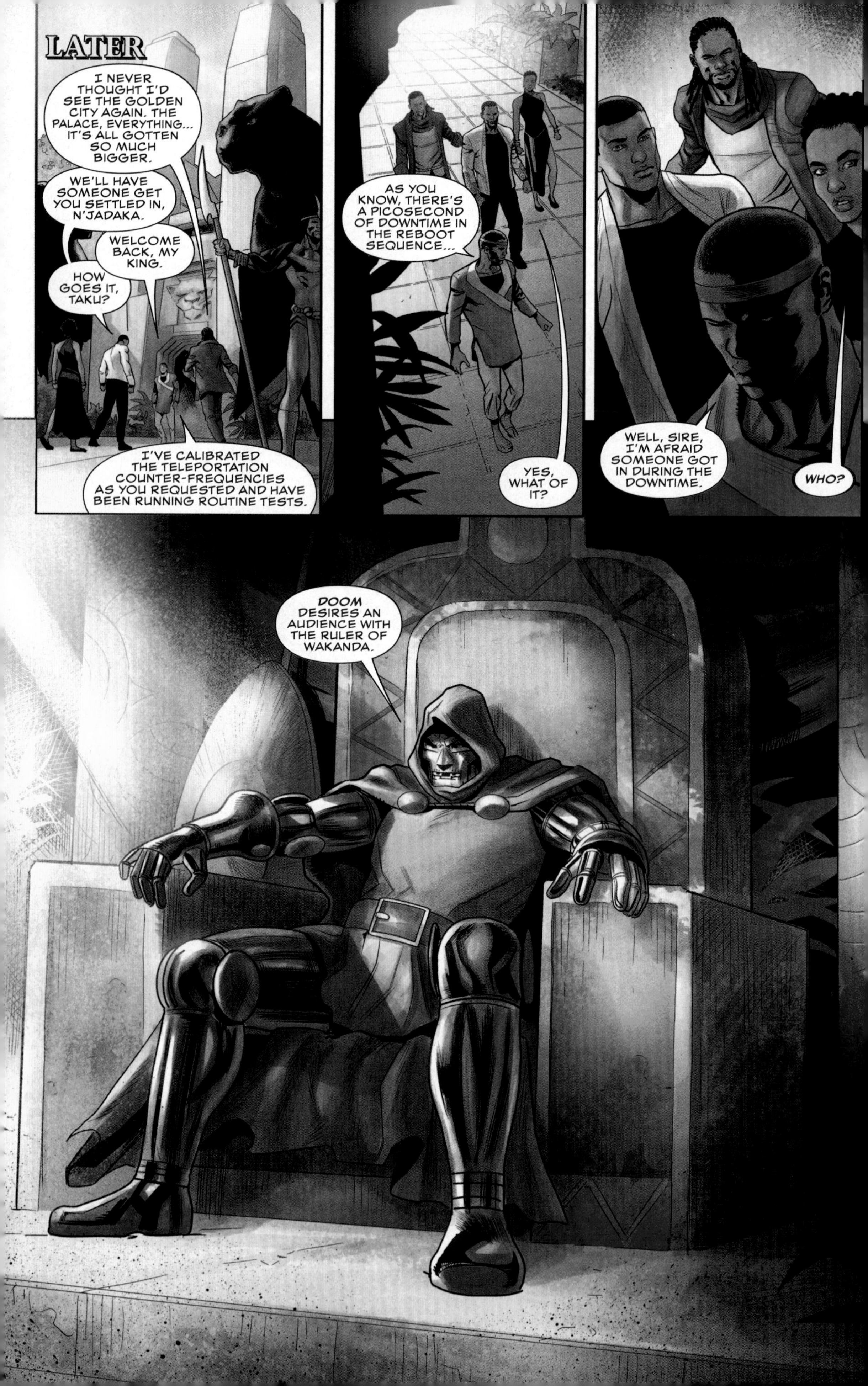
LATER
I NEVER THOUGHT I'D SEE THE GOLDEN CITY AGAIN. THE PALACE, EVERYTHING... IT'S ALL GOTTEN SO MUCH BIGGER.
WE'LL HAVE SOMEONE GET YOU SETTLED IN, N'JADAKA.
WELCOME BACK, MY KING.
HOW GOES IT, TAKU?
I'VE CALIBRATED THE TELEPORTATION COUNTER-FREQUENCIES AS YOU REQUESTED AND HAVE BEEN RUNNING ROUTINE TESTS.
AS YOU KNOW, THERE'S A PICOSECOND OF DOWNTIME IN THE REBOOT SEQUENCE...
YES, WHAT OF IT?
WELL, SIRE, I'M AFRAID SOMEONE GOT IN DURING THE DOWNTIME.
WHO?
DOOM DESIRES AN AUDIENCE WITH THE RULER OF WAKANDA.

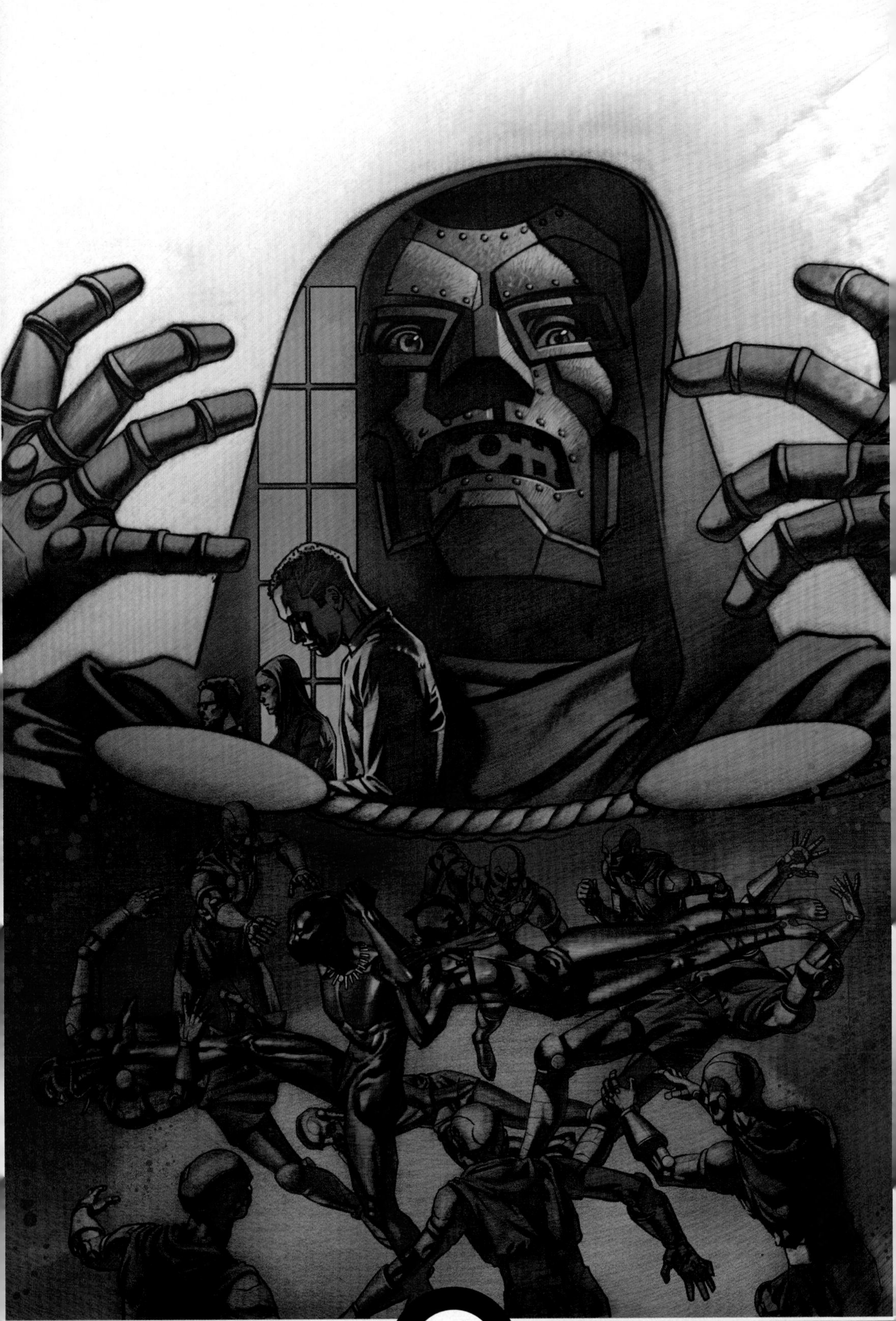

4

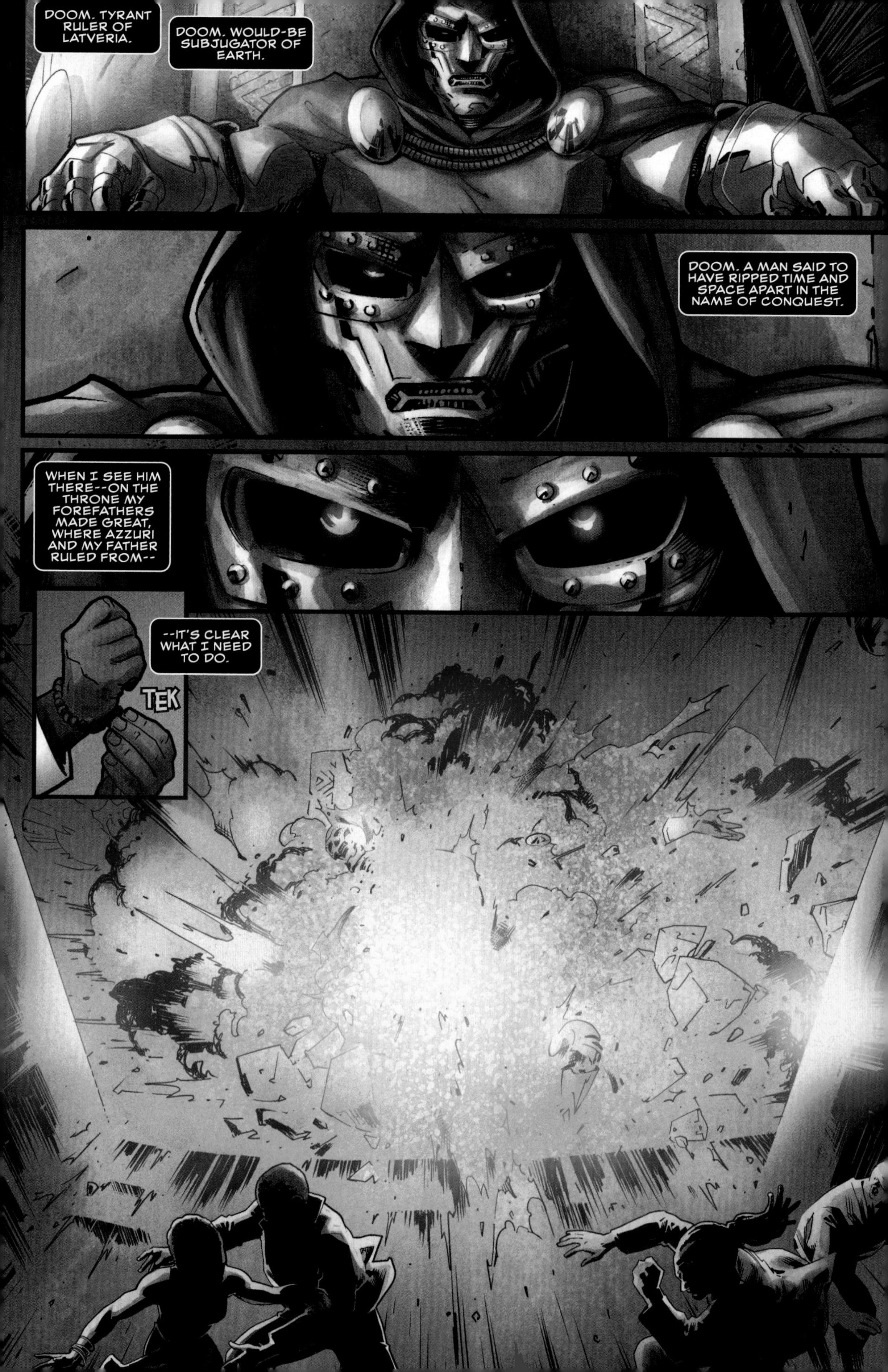
DOOM. TYRANT RULER OF LATVERIA.
DOOM. WOULD-BE SUBJUGATOR OF EARTH.
DOOM. A MAN SAID TO HAVE RIPPED TIME AND SPACE APART IN THE NAME OF CONQUEST.
WHEN I SEE HIM THERE--ON THE THRONE MY FOREFATHERS MADE GREAT, WHERE AZZURI AND MY FATHER RULED FROM--
--IT'S CLEAR WHAT I NEED TO DO.
TEK

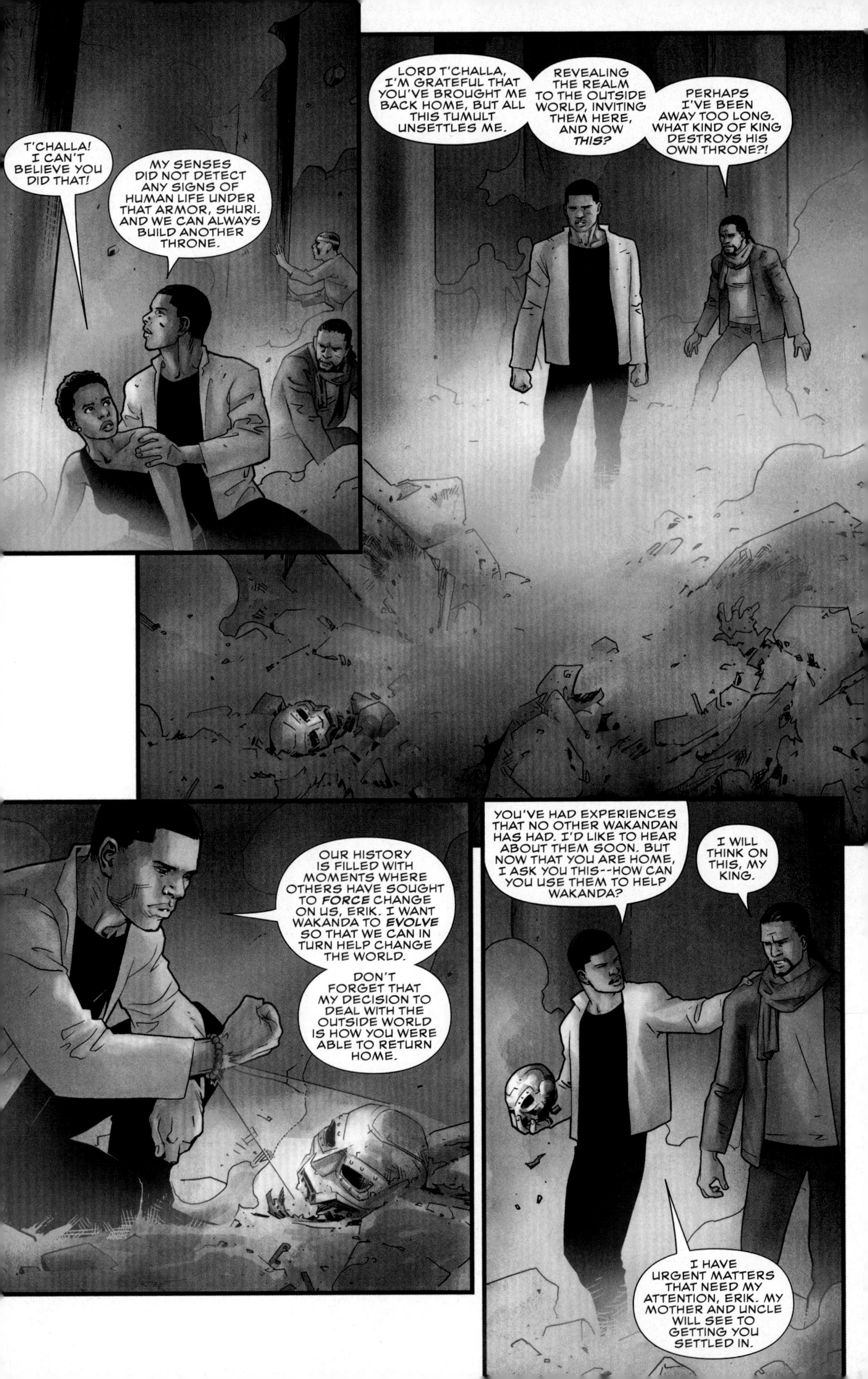
T'CHALLA! I CAN'T BELIEVE YOU DID THAT!
MY SENSES DID NOT DETECT ANY SIGNS OF HUMAN LIFE UNDER THAT ARMOR, SHURI. AND WE CAN ALWAYS BUILD ANOTHER THRONE.
LORD T'CHALLA, I'M GRATEFUL THAT YOU'VE BROUGHT ME BACK HOME, BUT ALL THIS TUMULT UNSETTLES ME.
REVEALING THE REALM TO THE OUTSIDE WORLD, INVITING THEM HERE, AND NOW *THIS?*
PERHAPS I'VE BEEN AWAY TOO LONG. WHAT KIND OF KING DESTROYS HIS OWN THRONE?!
OUR HISTORY IS FILLED WITH MOMENTS WHERE OTHERS HAVE SOUGHT TO *FORCE* CHANGE ON US, ERIK. I WANT WAKANDA TO *EVOLVE* SO THAT WE CAN IN TURN HELP CHANGE THE WORLD.
DON'T FORGET THAT MY DECISION TO DEAL WITH THE OUTSIDE WORLD IS HOW YOU WERE ABLE TO RETURN HOME.
YOU'VE HAD EXPERIENCES THAT NO OTHER WAKANDAN HAS HAD. I'D LIKE TO HEAR ABOUT THEM SOON. BUT NOW THAT YOU ARE HOME, I ASK YOU THIS--HOW CAN YOU USE THEM TO HELP WAKANDA?
I WILL THINK ON THIS, MY KING.
I HAVE URGENT MATTERS THAT NEED MY ATTENTION, ERIK. MY MOTHER AND UNCLE WILL SEE TO GETTING YOU SETTLED IN.

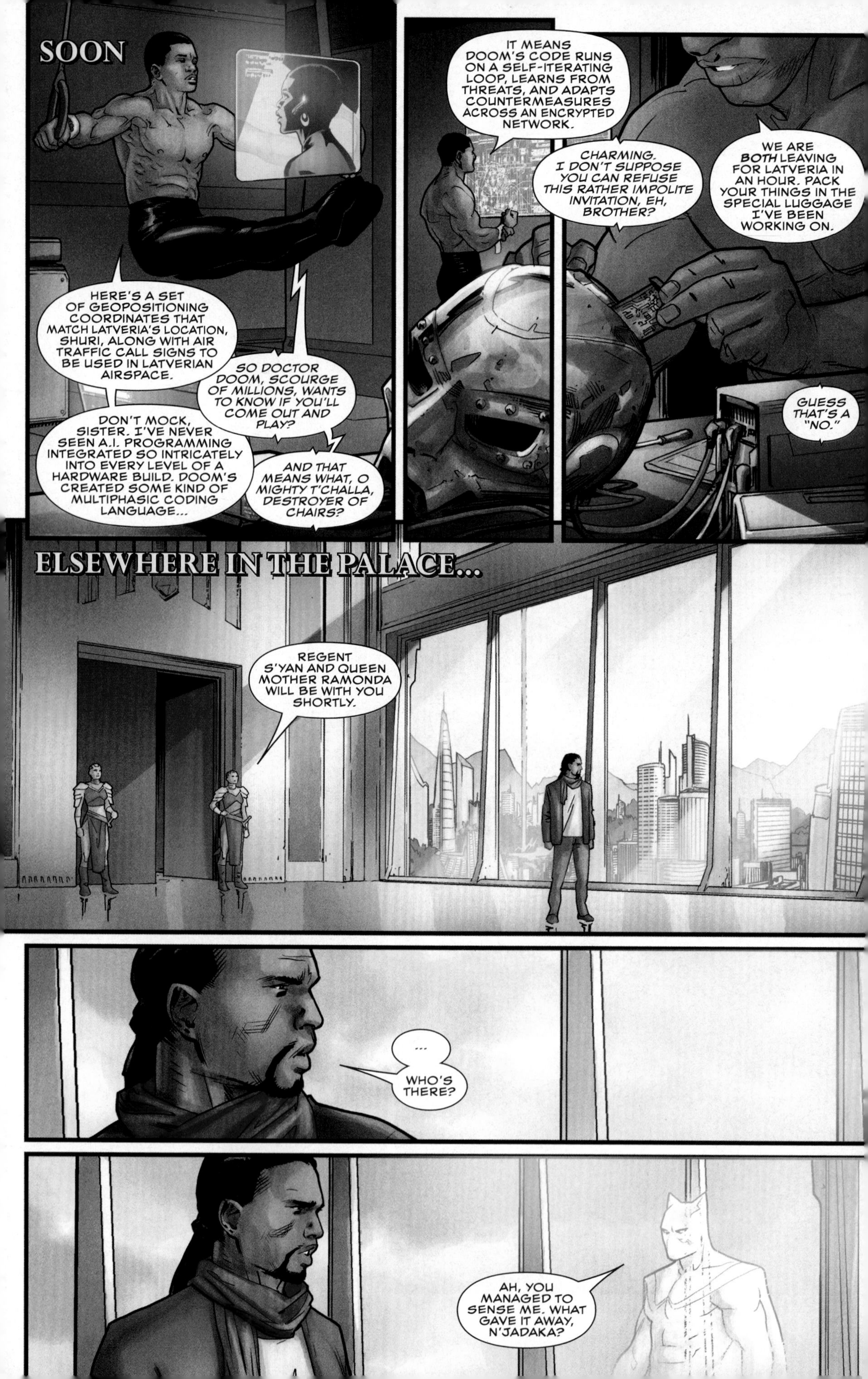
SOON
HERE'S A SET OF GEOPOSITIONING COORDINATES THAT MATCH LATVERIA'S LOCATION, SHURI, ALONG WITH AIR TRAFFIC CALL SIGNS TO BE USED IN LATVERIAN AIRSPACE.
SO DOCTOR DOOM, SCOURGE OF MILLIONS, WANTS TO KNOW IF YOU'LL COME OUT AND PLAY?
DON'T MOCK, SISTER. I'VE NEVER SEEN A.I. PROGRAMMING INTEGRATED SO INTRICATELY INTO EVERY LEVEL OF A HARDWARE BUILD. DOOM'S CREATED SOME KIND OF MULTIPHASIC CODING LANGUAGE...
AND THAT MEANS WHAT, O MIGHTY T'CHALLA, DESTROYER OF CHAIRS?
IT MEANS DOOM'S CODE RUNS ON A SELF-ITERATING LOOP, LEARNS FROM THREATS, AND ADAPTS COUNTERMEASURES ACROSS AN ENCRYPTED NETWORK.
CHARMING. I DON'T SUPPOSE YOU CAN REFUSE THIS RATHER IMPOLITE INVITATION, EH, BROTHER?
WE ARE BOTH LEAVING FOR LATVERIA IN AN HOUR. PACK YOUR THINGS IN THE SPECIAL LUGGAGE I'VE BEEN WORKING ON.
GUESS THAT'S A "NO."
ELSEWHERE IN THE PALACE...
REGENT S'YAN AND QUEEN MOTHER RAMONDA WILL BE WITH YOU SHORTLY.
...
WHO'S THERE?
AH, YOU MANAGED TO SENSE ME. WHAT GAVE IT AWAY, N'JADAKA?

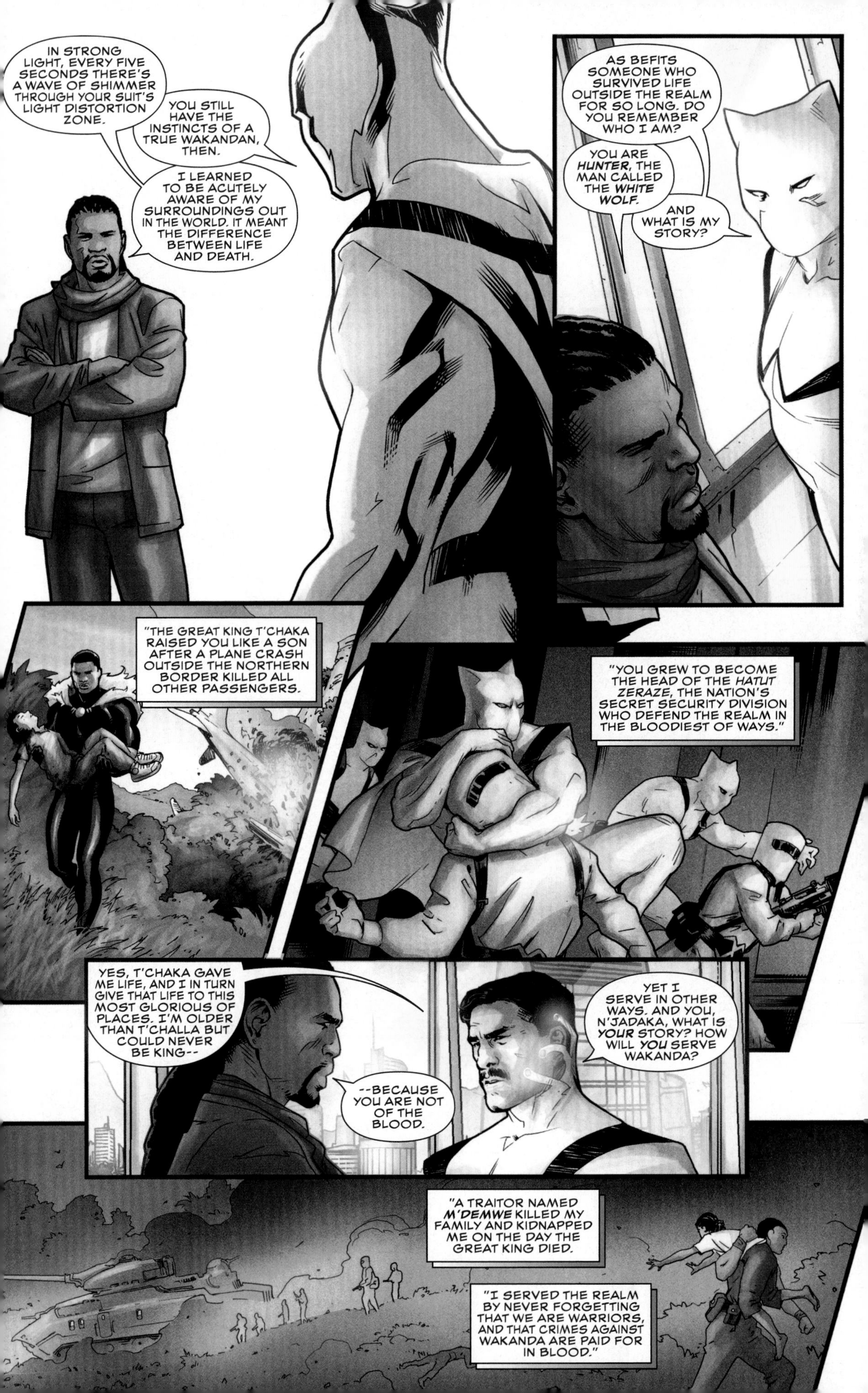
IN STRONG LIGHT, EVERY FIVE SECONDS THERE'S A WAVE OF SHIMMER THROUGH YOUR SUIT'S LIGHT DISTORTION ZONE.
YOU STILL HAVE THE INSTINCTS OF A TRUE WAKANDAN, THEN.
I LEARNED TO BE ACUTELY AWARE OF MY SURROUNDINGS OUT IN THE WORLD. IT MEANT THE DIFFERENCE BETWEEN LIFE AND DEATH.
AS BEFITS SOMEONE WHO SURVIVED LIFE OUTSIDE THE REALM FOR SO LONG. DO YOU REMEMBER WHO I AM?
YOU ARE HUNTER, THE MAN CALLED THE WHITE WOLF.
AND WHAT IS MY STORY?
"THE GREAT KING T'CHAKA RAISED YOU LIKE A SON AFTER A PLANE CRASH OUTSIDE THE NORTHERN BORDER KILLED ALL OTHER PASSENGERS.
"YOU GREW TO BECOME THE HEAD OF THE HATUT ZERAZE, THE NATION'S SECRET SECURITY DIVISION WHO DEFEND THE REALM IN THE BLOODIEST OF WAYS."
YES, T'CHAKA GAVE ME LIFE, AND I IN TURN GIVE THAT LIFE TO THIS MOST GLORIOUS OF PLACES. I'M OLDER THAN T'CHALLA BUT COULD NEVER BE KING--
--BECAUSE YOU ARE NOT OF THE BLOOD.
YET I SERVE IN OTHER WAYS. AND YOU, N'JADAKA, WHAT IS YOUR STORY? HOW WILL YOU SERVE WAKANDA?
"A TRAITOR NAMED M'DEMWE KILLED MY FAMILY AND KIDNAPPED ME ON THE DAY THE GREAT KING DIED.
"I SERVED THE REALM BY NEVER FORGETTING THAT WE ARE WARRIORS, AND THAT CRIMES AGAINST WAKANDA ARE PAID FOR IN BLOOD."

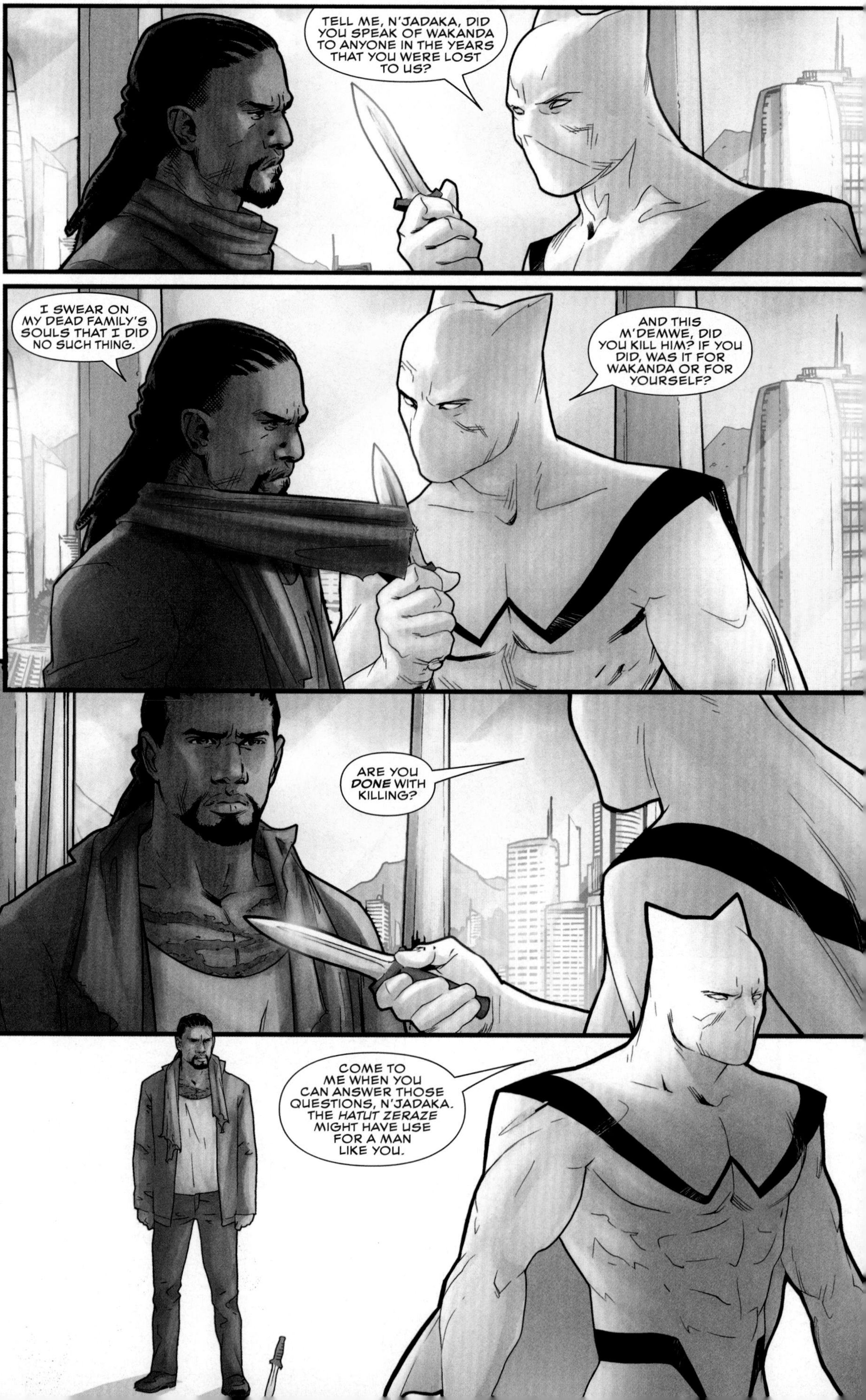
TELL ME, N'JADAKA, DID YOU SPEAK OF WAKANDA TO ANYONE IN THE YEARS THAT YOU WERE LOST TO US?
I SWEAR ON MY DEAD FAMILY'S SOULS THAT I DID NO SUCH THING.
AND THIS M'DEMWE, DID YOU KILL HIM? IF YOU DID, WAS IT FOR WAKANDA OR FOR YOURSELF?
ARE YOU DONE WITH KILLING?
COME TO ME WHEN YOU CAN ANSWER THOSE QUESTIONS, N'JADAKA. THE HATUT ZERAZE MIGHT HAVE USE FOR A MAN LIKE YOU.

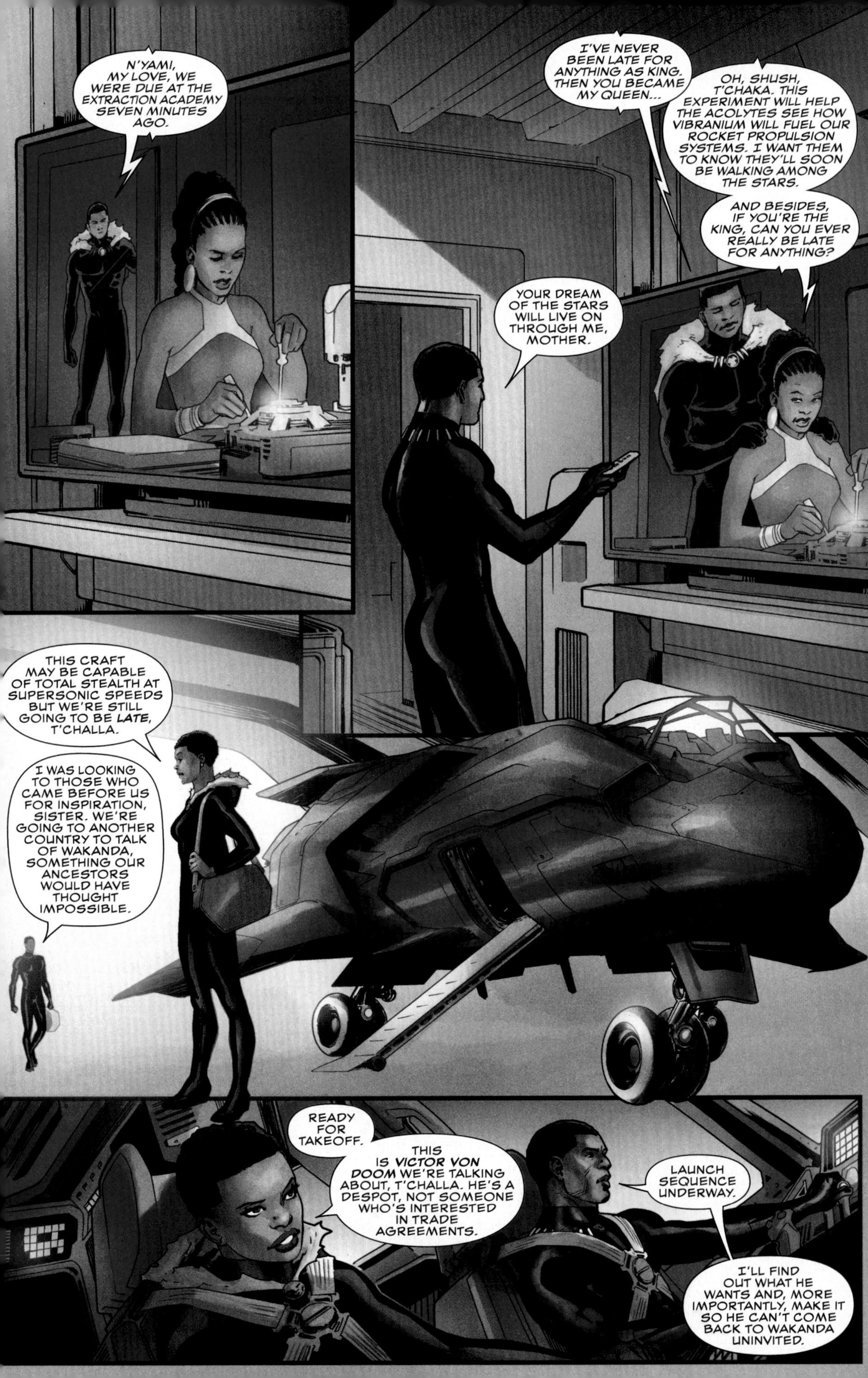
N'YAMI, MY LOVE, WE WERE DUE AT THE EXTRACTION ACADEMY SEVEN MINUTES AGO.
I'VE NEVER BEEN LATE FOR ANYTHING AS KING. THEN YOU BECAME MY QUEEN...
OH, SHUSH, T'CHAKA. THIS EXPERIMENT WILL HELP THE ACOLYTES SEE HOW VIBRANIUM WILL FUEL OUR ROCKET PROPULSION SYSTEMS. I WANT THEM TO KNOW THEY'LL SOON BE WALKING AMONG THE STARS.
AND BESIDES, IF YOU'RE THE KING, CAN YOU EVER REALLY BE LATE FOR ANYTHING?
YOUR DREAM OF THE STARS WILL LIVE ON THROUGH ME, MOTHER.
THIS CRAFT MAY BE CAPABLE OF TOTAL STEALTH AT SUPERSONIC SPEEDS BUT WE'RE STILL GOING TO BE *LATE*, T'CHALLA.
I WAS LOOKING TO THOSE WHO CAME BEFORE US FOR INSPIRATION, SISTER. WE'RE GOING TO ANOTHER COUNTRY TO TALK OF WAKANDA, SOMETHING OUR ANCESTORS WOULD HAVE THOUGHT IMPOSSIBLE.
READY FOR TAKEOFF.
THIS IS *VICTOR VON DOOM* WE'RE TALKING ABOUT, T'CHALLA. HE'S A DESPOT, NOT SOMEONE WHO'S INTERESTED IN TRADE AGREEMENTS.
LAUNCH SEQUENCE UNDERWAY.
I'LL FIND OUT WHAT HE WANTS AND, MORE IMPORTANTLY, MAKE IT SO HE CAN'T COME BACK TO WAKANDA UNINVITED.

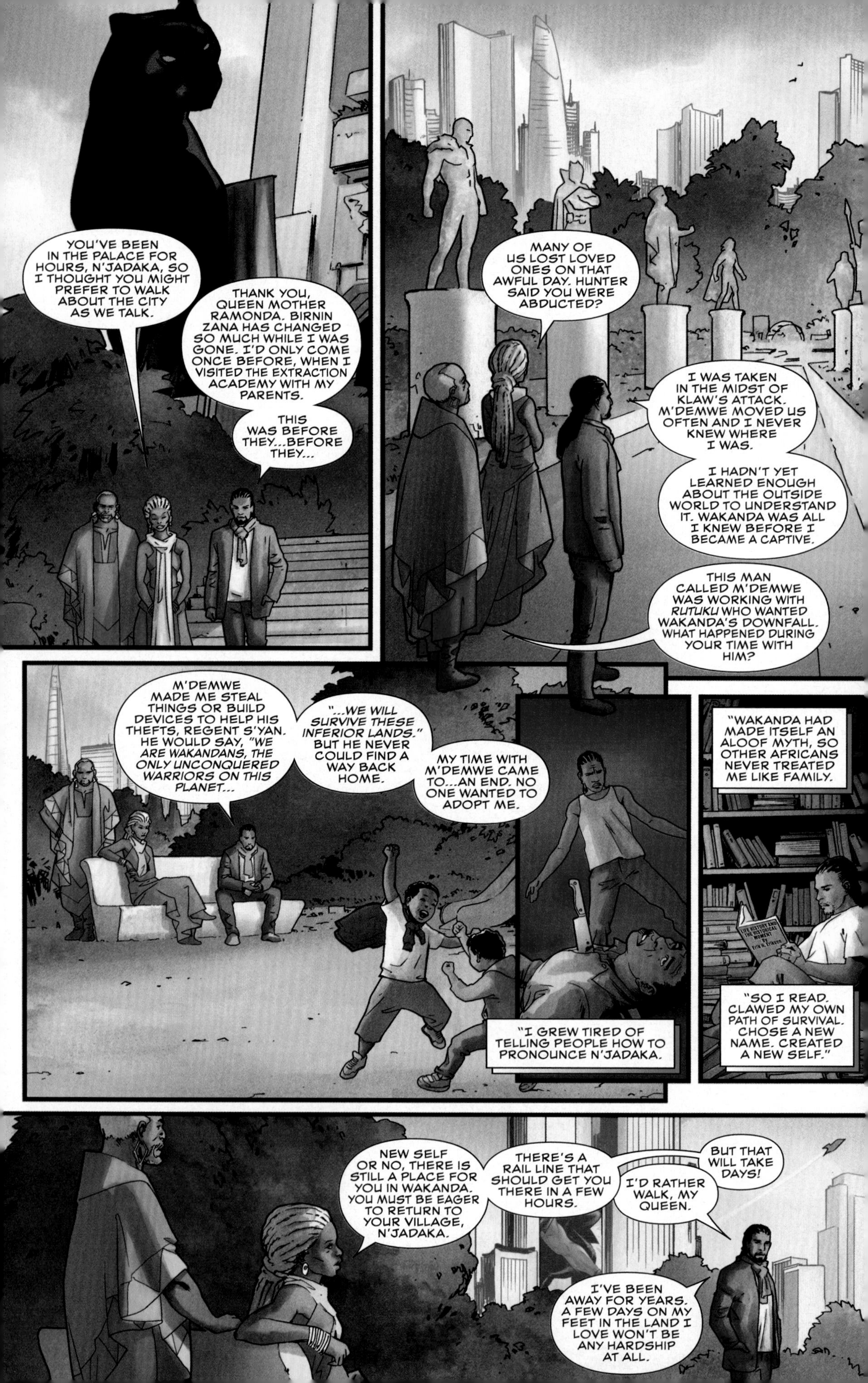
YOU'VE BEEN IN THE PALACE FOR HOURS, N'JADAKA, SO I THOUGHT YOU MIGHT PREFER TO WALK ABOUT THE CITY AS WE TALK.
THANK YOU, QUEEN MOTHER RAMONDA. BIRNIN ZANA HAS CHANGED SO MUCH WHILE I WAS GONE. I'D ONLY COME ONCE BEFORE, WHEN I VISITED THE EXTRACTION ACADEMY WITH MY PARENTS.
THIS WAS BEFORE THEY...BEFORE THEY...
MANY OF US LOST LOVED ONES ON THAT AWFUL DAY. HUNTER SAID YOU WERE ABDUCTED?
I WAS TAKEN IN THE MIDST OF KLAW'S ATTACK. M'DEMWE MOVED US OFTEN AND I NEVER KNEW WHERE I WAS.
I HADN'T YET LEARNED ENOUGH ABOUT THE OUTSIDE WORLD TO UNDERSTAND IT. WAKANDA WAS ALL I KNEW BEFORE I BECAME A CAPTIVE.
THIS MAN CALLED M'DEMWE WAS WORKING WITH *RUTUKU* WHO WANTED WAKANDA'S DOWNFALL. WHAT HAPPENED DURING YOUR TIME WITH HIM?
M'DEMWE MADE ME STEAL THINGS OR BUILD DEVICES TO HELP HIS THEFTS, REGENT S'YAN. HE WOULD SAY, *"WE ARE WAKANDANS, THE ONLY UNCONQUERED WARRIORS ON THIS PLANET...*
"...WE WILL SURVIVE THESE INFERIOR LANDS." BUT HE NEVER COULD FIND A WAY BACK HOME.
MY TIME WITH M'DEMWE CAME TO...AN END. NO ONE WANTED TO ADOPT ME.
"I GREW TIRED OF TELLING PEOPLE HOW TO PRONOUNCE N'JADAKA.
"WAKANDA HAD MADE ITSELF AN ALOOF MYTH, SO OTHER AFRICANS NEVER TREATED ME LIKE FAMILY.
"SO I READ. CLAWED MY OWN PATH OF SURVIVAL. CHOSE A NEW NAME. CREATED A NEW SELF."
NEW SELF OR NO, THERE IS STILL A PLACE FOR YOU IN WAKANDA. YOU MUST BE EAGER TO RETURN TO YOUR VILLAGE, N'JADAKA.
THERE'S A RAIL LINE THAT SHOULD GET YOU THERE IN A FEW HOURS.
BUT THAT WILL TAKE DAYS!
I'D RATHER WALK, MY QUEEN.
I'VE BEEN AWAY FOR YEARS. A FEW DAYS ON MY FEET IN THE LAND I LOVE WON'T BE ANY HARDSHIP AT ALL.

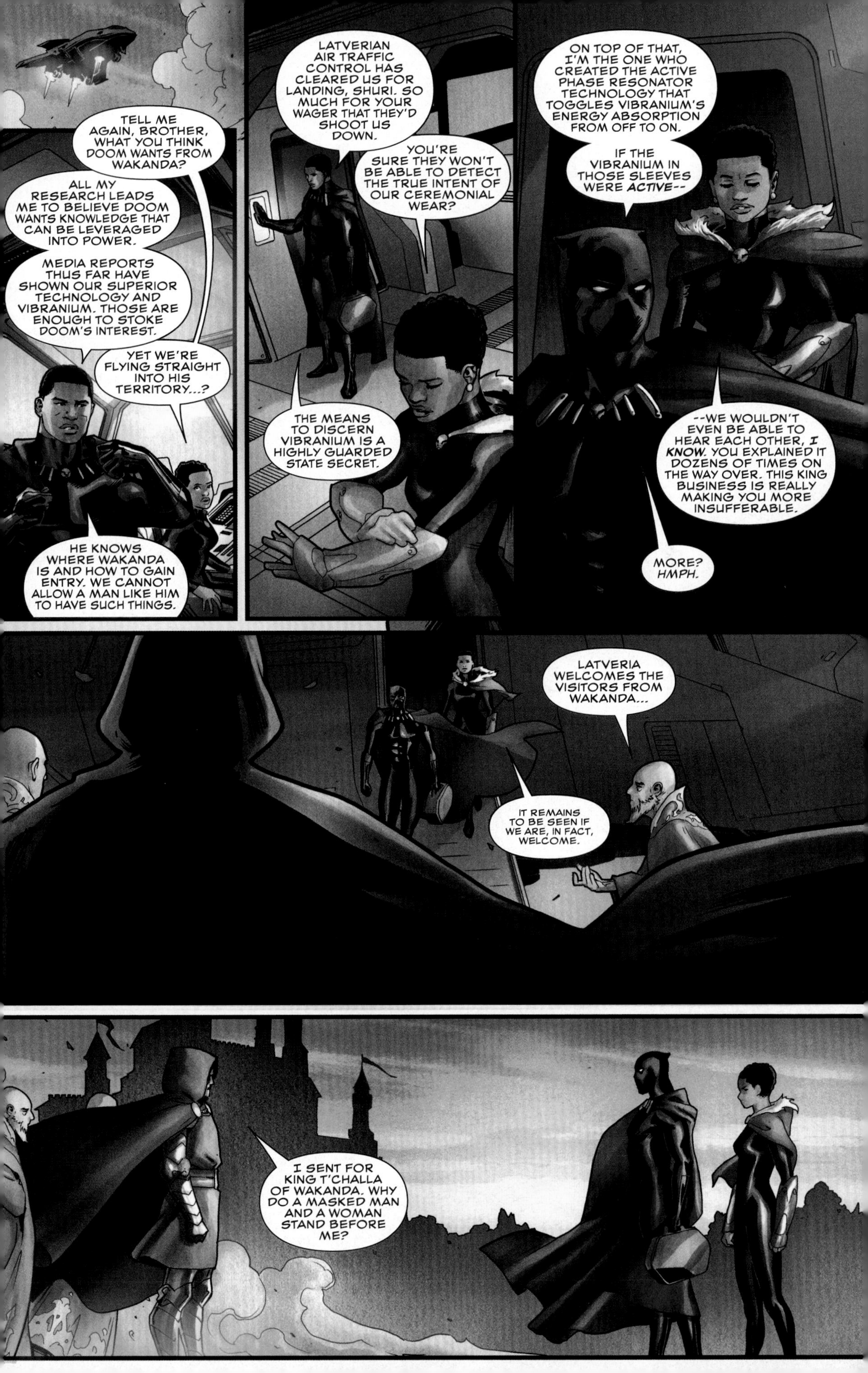
TELL ME AGAIN, BROTHER, WHAT YOU THINK DOOM WANTS FROM WAKANDA?
ALL MY RESEARCH LEADS ME TO BELIEVE DOOM WANTS KNOWLEDGE THAT CAN BE LEVERAGED INTO POWER.
MEDIA REPORTS THUS FAR HAVE SHOWN OUR SUPERIOR TECHNOLOGY AND VIBRANIUM. THOSE ARE ENOUGH TO STOKE DOOM'S INTEREST.
YET WE'RE FLYING STRAIGHT INTO HIS TERRITORY...?
HE KNOWS WHERE WAKANDA IS AND HOW TO GAIN ENTRY. WE CANNOT ALLOW A MAN LIKE HIM TO HAVE SUCH THINGS.
LATVERIAN AIR TRAFFIC CONTROL HAS CLEARED US FOR LANDING, SHURI. SO MUCH FOR YOUR WAGER THAT THEY'D SHOOT US DOWN.
YOU'RE SURE THEY WON'T BE ABLE TO DETECT THE TRUE INTENT OF OUR CEREMONIAL WEAR?
THE MEANS TO DISCERN VIBRANIUM IS A HIGHLY GUARDED STATE SECRET.
ON TOP OF THAT, I'M THE ONE WHO CREATED THE ACTIVE PHASE RESONATOR TECHNOLOGY THAT TOGGLES VIBRANIUM'S ENERGY ABSORPTION FROM OFF TO ON.
IF THE VIBRANIUM IN THOSE SLEEVES WERE *ACTIVE*--
--WE WOULDN'T EVEN BE ABLE TO HEAR EACH OTHER, ***I KNOW***. YOU EXPLAINED IT DOZENS OF TIMES ON THE WAY OVER. THIS KING BUSINESS IS REALLY MAKING YOU MORE INSUFFERABLE.
MORE? HMPH.
LATVERIA WELCOMES THE VISITORS FROM WAKANDA...
IT REMAINS TO BE SEEN IF WE ARE, IN FACT, WELCOME.
I SENT FOR KING T'CHALLA OF WAKANDA. WHY DO A MASKED MAN AND A WOMAN STAND BEFORE ME?

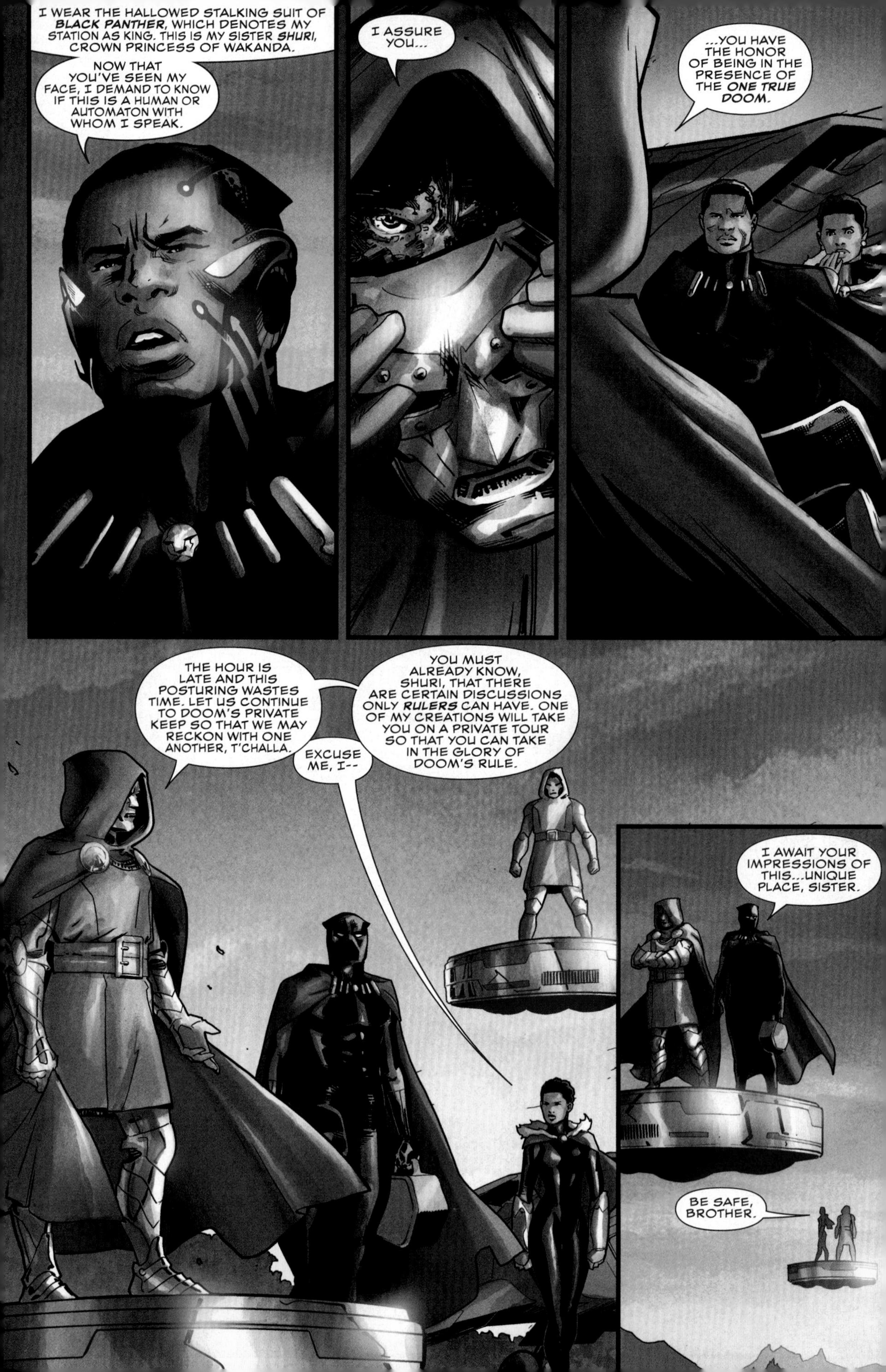
I WEAR THE HALLOWED STALKING SUIT OF BLACK PANTHER, WHICH DENOTES MY STATION AS KING. THIS IS MY SISTER SHURI, CROWN PRINCESS OF WAKANDA.
NOW THAT YOU'VE SEEN MY FACE, I DEMAND TO KNOW IF THIS IS A HUMAN OR AUTOMATON WITH WHOM I SPEAK.
I ASSURE YOU...
...YOU HAVE THE HONOR OF BEING IN THE PRESENCE OF THE ONE TRUE DOOM.
THE HOUR IS LATE AND THIS POSTURING WASTES TIME. LET US CONTINUE TO DOOM'S PRIVATE KEEP SO THAT WE MAY RECKON WITH ONE ANOTHER, T'CHALLA.
YOU MUST ALREADY KNOW, SHURI, THAT THERE ARE CERTAIN DISCUSSIONS ONLY RULERS CAN HAVE. ONE OF MY CREATIONS WILL TAKE YOU ON A PRIVATE TOUR SO THAT YOU CAN TAKE IN THE GLORY OF DOOM'S RULE.
EXCUSE ME, I--
I AWAIT YOUR IMPRESSIONS OF THIS...UNIQUE PLACE, SISTER.
BE SAFE, BROTHER.

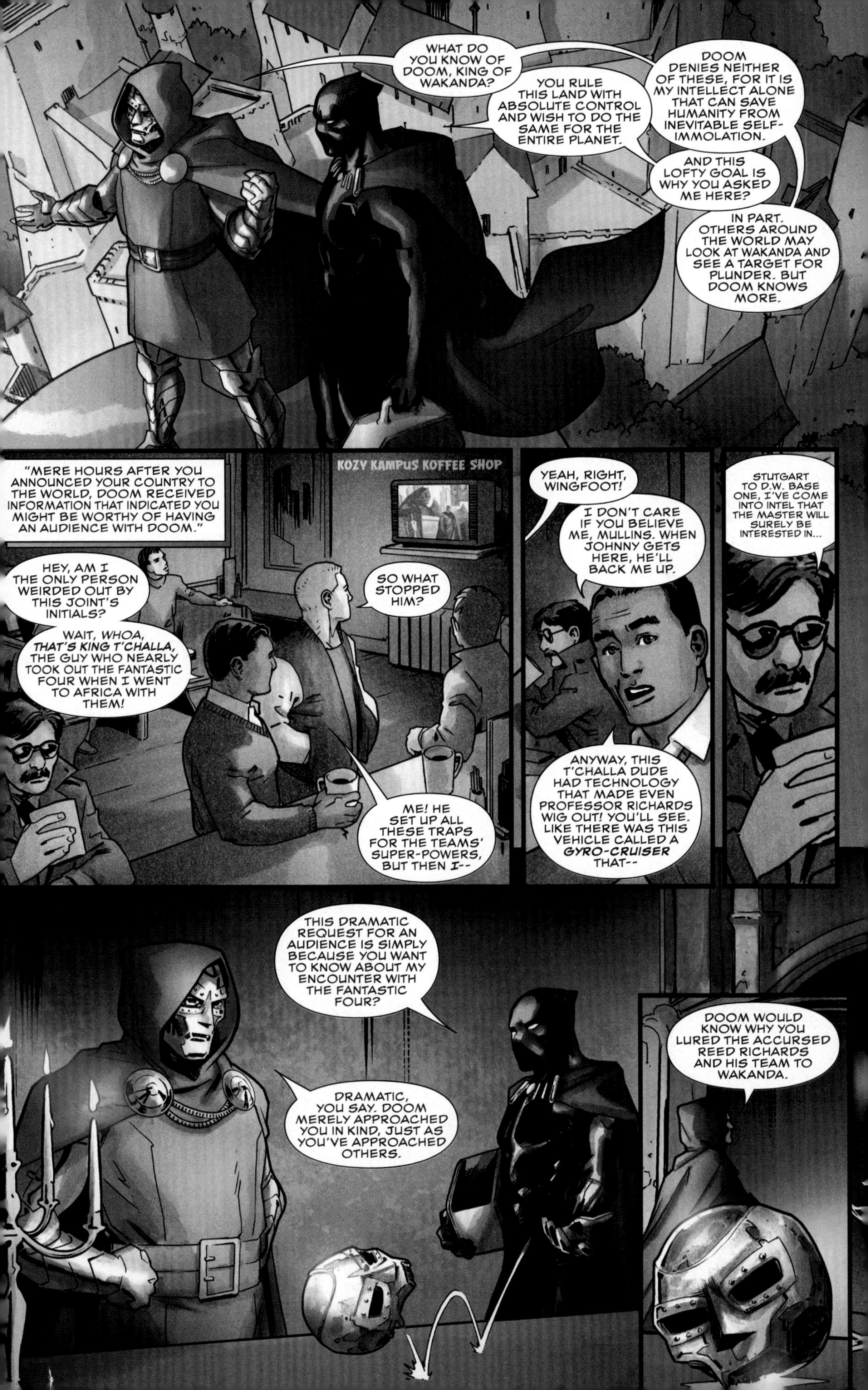
WHAT DO YOU KNOW OF DOOM, KING OF WAKANDA?
YOU RULE THIS LAND WITH ABSOLUTE CONTROL AND WISH TO DO THE SAME FOR THE ENTIRE PLANET.
DOOM DENIES NEITHER OF THESE, FOR IT IS MY INTELLECT ALONE THAT CAN SAVE HUMANITY FROM INEVITABLE SELF-IMMOLATION.
AND THIS LOFTY GOAL IS WHY YOU ASKED ME HERE?
IN PART. OTHERS AROUND THE WORLD MAY LOOK AT WAKANDA AND SEE A TARGET FOR PLUNDER. BUT DOOM KNOWS MORE.
"MERE HOURS AFTER YOU ANNOUNCED YOUR COUNTRY TO THE WORLD, DOOM RECEIVED INFORMATION THAT INDICATED YOU MIGHT BE WORTHY OF HAVING AN AUDIENCE WITH DOOM."
KOZY KAMPUS KOFFEE SHOP
HEY, AM I THE ONLY PERSON WEIRDED OUT BY THIS JOINT'S INITIALS?
WAIT, WHOA, ***THAT'S KING T'CHALLA,*** THE GUY WHO NEARLY TOOK OUT THE FANTASTIC FOUR WHEN I WENT TO AFRICA WITH THEM!
SO WHAT STOPPED HIM?
ME! HE SET UP ALL THESE TRAPS FOR THE TEAMS' SUPER-POWERS, BUT THEN ***I***--
YEAH, RIGHT, WINGFOOT!
I DON'T CARE IF YOU BELIEVE ME, MULLINS. WHEN JOHNNY GETS HERE, HE'LL BACK ME UP.
ANYWAY, THIS T'CHALLA DUDE HAD TECHNOLOGY THAT MADE EVEN PROFESSOR RICHARDS WIG OUT! YOU'LL SEE. LIKE THERE WAS THIS VEHICLE CALLED A ***GYRO-CRUISER*** THAT--
STUTGART TO D.W. BASE ONE, I'VE COME INTO INTEL THAT THE MASTER WILL SURELY BE INTERESTED IN...
THIS DRAMATIC REQUEST FOR AN AUDIENCE IS SIMPLY BECAUSE YOU WANT TO KNOW ABOUT MY ENCOUNTER WITH THE FANTASTIC FOUR?
DRAMATIC, YOU SAY. DOOM MERELY APPROACHED YOU IN KIND, JUST AS YOU'VE APPROACHED OTHERS.
DOOM WOULD KNOW WHY YOU LURED THE ACCURSED REED RICHARDS AND HIS TEAM TO WAKANDA.

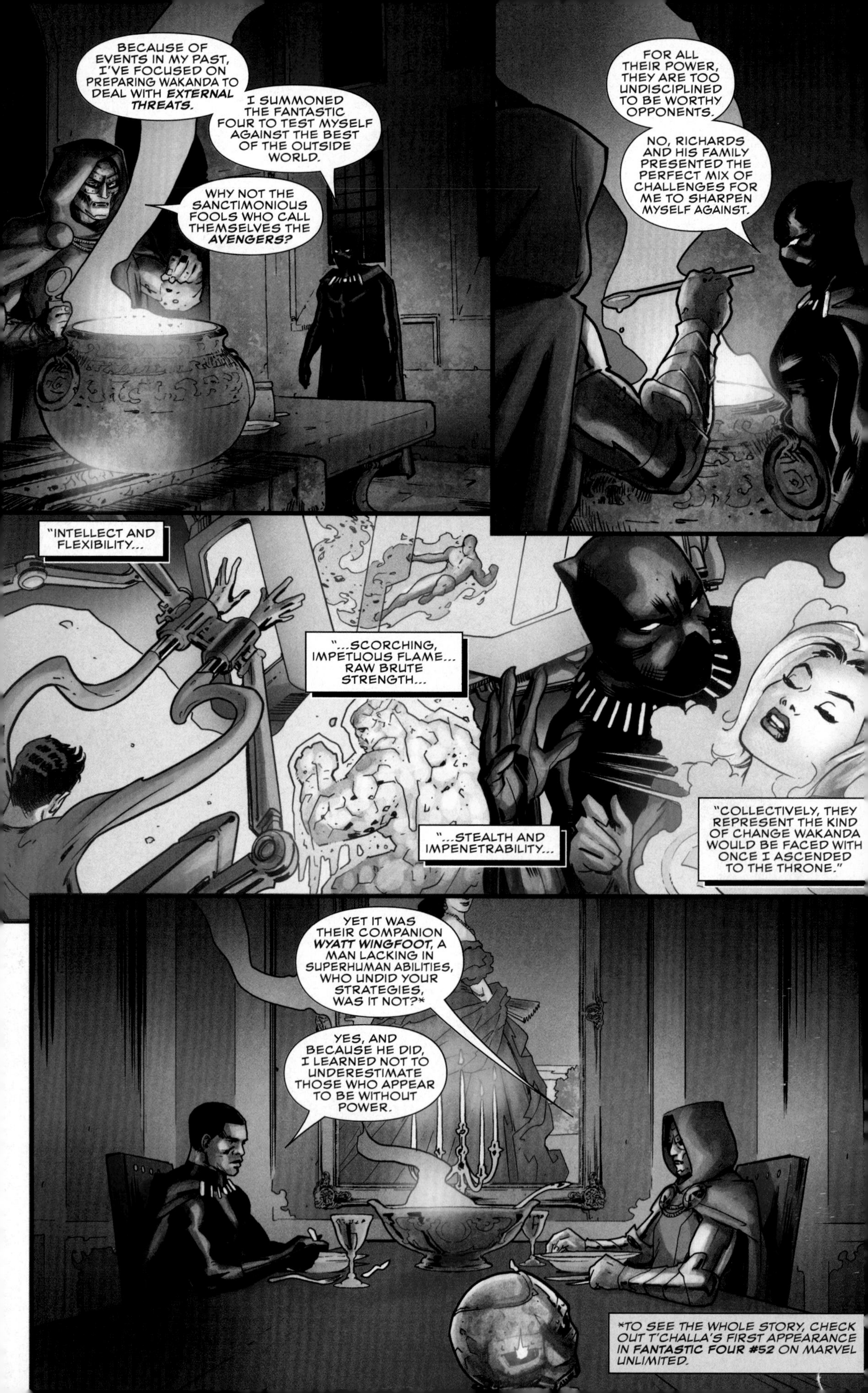
BECAUSE OF EVENTS IN MY PAST, I'VE FOCUSED ON PREPARING WAKANDA TO DEAL WITH EXTERNAL THREATS.
I SUMMONED THE FANTASTIC FOUR TO TEST MYSELF AGAINST THE BEST OF THE OUTSIDE WORLD.
WHY NOT THE SANCTIMONIOUS FOOLS WHO CALL THEMSELVES THE AVENGERS?
FOR ALL THEIR POWER, THEY ARE TOO UNDISCIPLINED TO BE WORTHY OPPONENTS.
NO, RICHARDS AND HIS FAMILY PRESENTED THE PERFECT MIX OF CHALLENGES FOR ME TO SHARPEN MYSELF AGAINST.
"INTELLECT AND FLEXIBILITY...
"...SCORCHING, IMPETUOUS FLAME... RAW BRUTE STRENGTH...
"...STEALTH AND IMPENETRABILITY...
"COLLECTIVELY, THEY REPRESENT THE KIND OF CHANGE WAKANDA WOULD BE FACED WITH ONCE I ASCENDED TO THE THRONE."
YET IT WAS THEIR COMPANION WYATT WINGFOOT, A MAN LACKING IN SUPERHUMAN ABILITIES, WHO UNDID YOUR STRATEGIES, WAS IT NOT?*
YES, AND BECAUSE HE DID, I LEARNED NOT TO UNDERESTIMATE THOSE WHO APPEAR TO BE WITHOUT POWER.
*TO SEE THE WHOLE STORY, CHECK OUT T'CHALLA'S FIRST APPEARANCE IN FANTASTIC FOUR #52 ON MARVEL UNLIMITED.

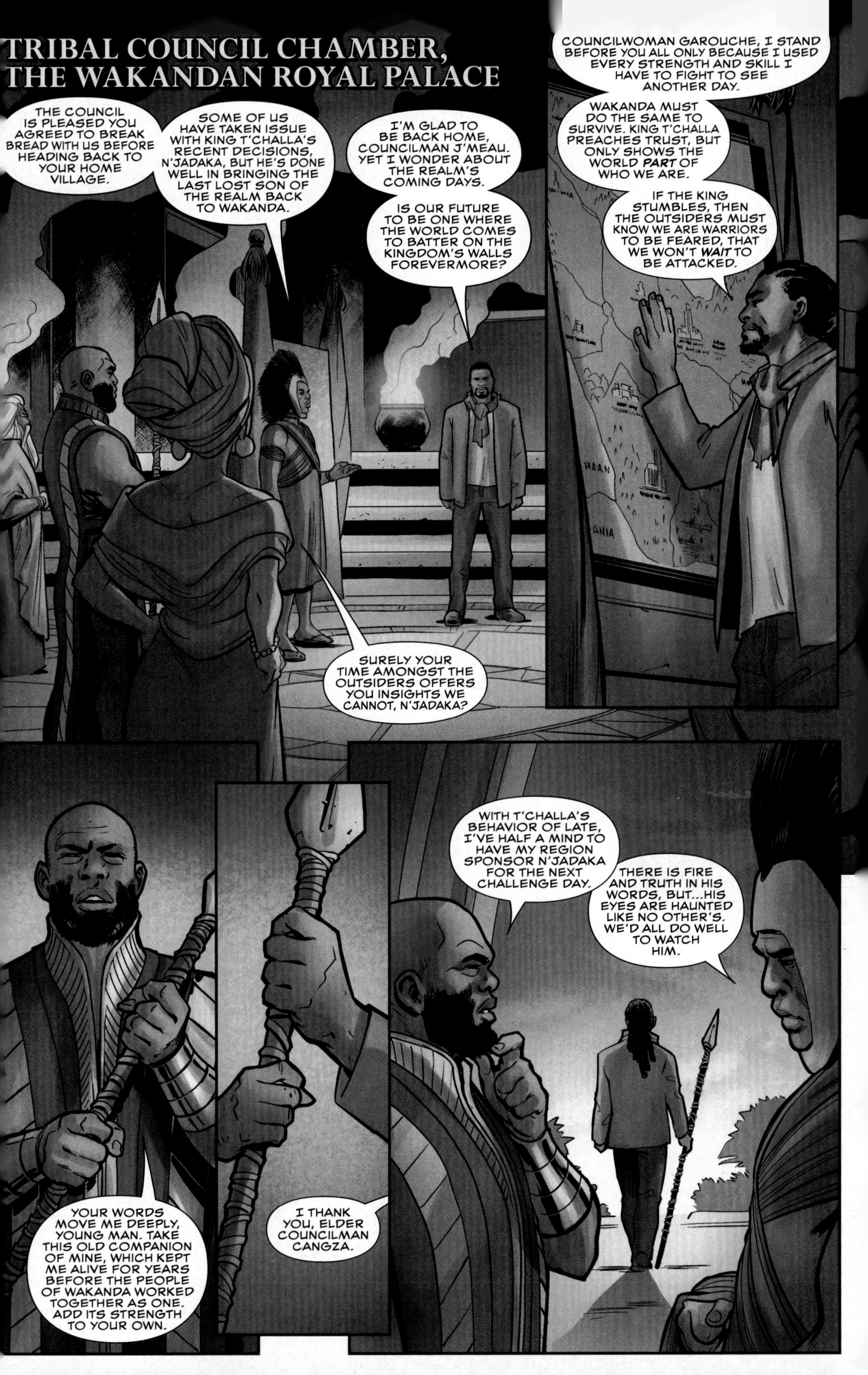
TRIBAL COUNCIL CHAMBER, THE WAKANDAN ROYAL PALACE
THE COUNCIL IS PLEASED YOU AGREED TO BREAK BREAD WITH US BEFORE HEADING BACK TO YOUR HOME VILLAGE.
SOME OF US HAVE TAKEN ISSUE WITH KING T'CHALLA'S RECENT DECISIONS, N'JADAKA, BUT HE'S DONE WELL IN BRINGING THE LAST LOST SON OF THE REALM BACK TO WAKANDA.
SURELY YOUR TIME AMONGST THE OUTSIDERS OFFERS YOU INSIGHTS WE CANNOT, N'JADAKA?
I'M GLAD TO BE BACK HOME, COUNCILMAN J'MEAU. YET I WONDER ABOUT THE REALM'S COMING DAYS.
IS OUR FUTURE TO BE ONE WHERE THE WORLD COMES TO BATTER ON THE KINGDOM'S WALLS FOREVERMORE?
COUNCILWOMAN GAROUCHE, I STAND BEFORE YOU ALL ONLY BECAUSE I USED EVERY STRENGTH AND SKILL I HAVE TO FIGHT TO SEE ANOTHER DAY.
WAKANDA MUST DO THE SAME TO SURVIVE. KING T'CHALLA PREACHES TRUST, BUT ONLY SHOWS THE WORLD ***PART*** OF WHO WE ARE.
IF THE KING STUMBLES, THEN THE OUTSIDERS MUST KNOW WE ARE WARRIORS TO BE FEARED, THAT WE WON'T ***WAIT*** TO BE ATTACKED.
YOUR WORDS MOVE ME DEEPLY, YOUNG MAN. TAKE THIS OLD COMPANION OF MINE, WHICH KEPT ME ALIVE FOR YEARS BEFORE THE PEOPLE OF WAKANDA WORKED TOGETHER AS ONE. ADD ITS STRENGTH TO YOUR OWN.
I THANK YOU, ELDER COUNCILMAN CANGZA.
WITH T'CHALLA'S BEHAVIOR OF LATE, I'VE HALF A MIND TO HAVE MY REGION SPONSOR N'JADAKA FOR THE NEXT CHALLENGE DAY.
THERE IS FIRE AND TRUTH IN HIS WORDS, BUT...HIS EYES ARE HAUNTED LIKE NO OTHER'S. WE'D ALL DO WELL TO WATCH HIM.

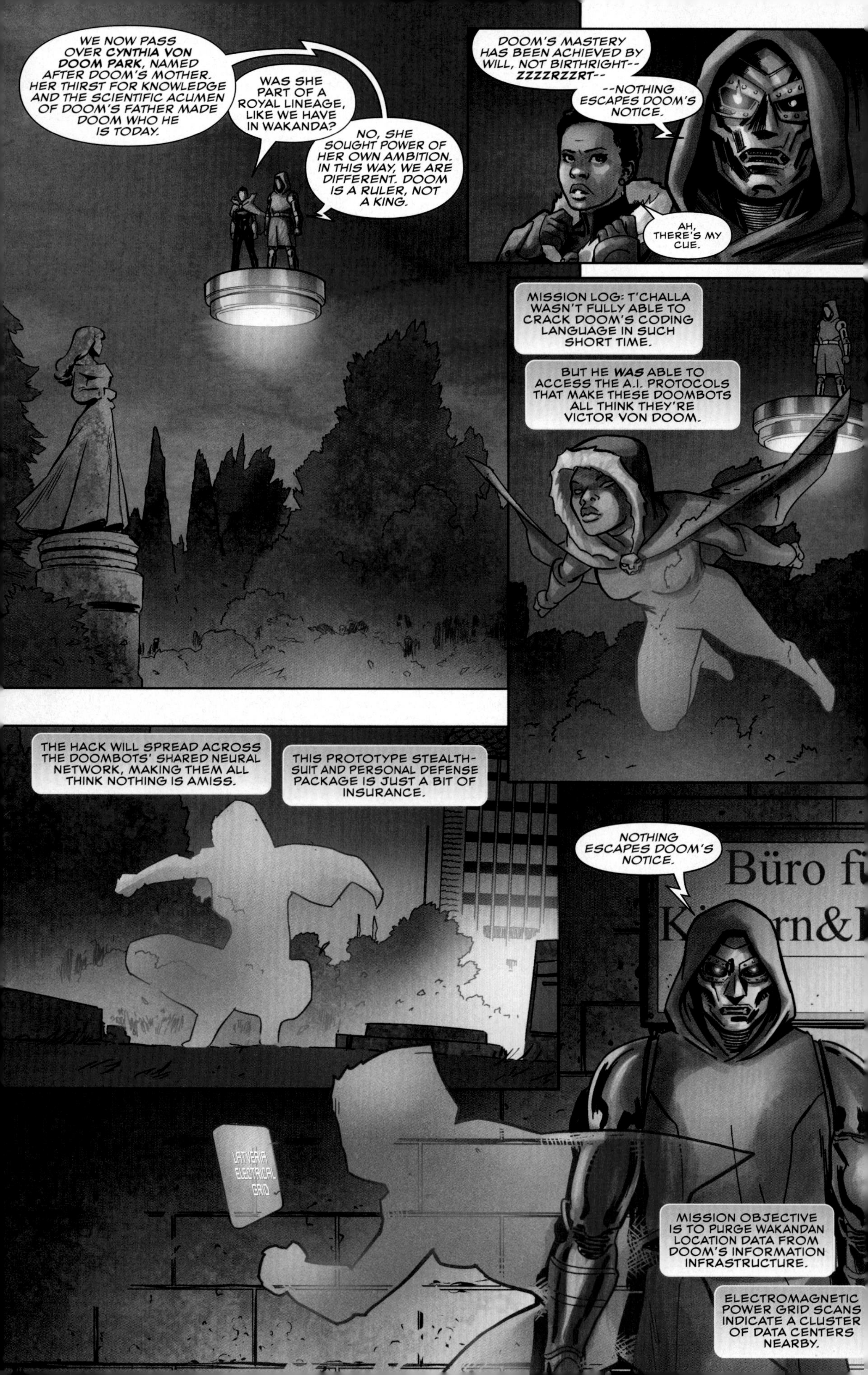
WE NOW PASS OVER CYNTHIA VON DOOM PARK, NAMED AFTER DOOM'S MOTHER. HER THIRST FOR KNOWLEDGE AND THE SCIENTIFIC ACUMEN OF DOOM'S FATHER MADE DOOM WHO HE IS TODAY.
WAS SHE PART OF A ROYAL LINEAGE, LIKE WE HAVE IN WAKANDA?
NO, SHE SOUGHT POWER OF HER OWN AMBITION. IN THIS WAY, WE ARE DIFFERENT. DOOM IS A RULER, NOT A KING.
DOOM'S MASTERY HAS BEEN ACHIEVED BY WILL, NOT BIRTHRIGHT-- ZZZZRZZRT--
--NOTHING ESCAPES DOOM'S NOTICE.
AH, THERE'S MY CUE.
MISSION LOG: T'CHALLA WASN'T FULLY ABLE TO CRACK DOOM'S CODING LANGUAGE IN SUCH SHORT TIME.
BUT HE WAS ABLE TO ACCESS THE A.I. PROTOCOLS THAT MAKE THESE DOOMBOTS ALL THINK THEY'RE VICTOR VON DOOM.
THE HACK WILL SPREAD ACROSS THE DOOMBOTS' SHARED NEURAL NETWORK, MAKING THEM ALL THINK NOTHING IS AMISS.
THIS PROTOTYPE STEALTH-SUIT AND PERSONAL DEFENSE PACKAGE IS JUST A BIT OF INSURANCE.
NOTHING ESCAPES DOOM'S NOTICE.
Büro f
K rn&
LATVERIA ELECTRICAL GRID
MISSION OBJECTIVE IS TO PURGE WAKANDAN LOCATION DATA FROM DOOM'S INFORMATION INFRASTRUCTURE.
ELECTROMAGNETIC POWER GRID SCANS INDICATE A CLUSTER OF DATA CENTERS NEARBY.

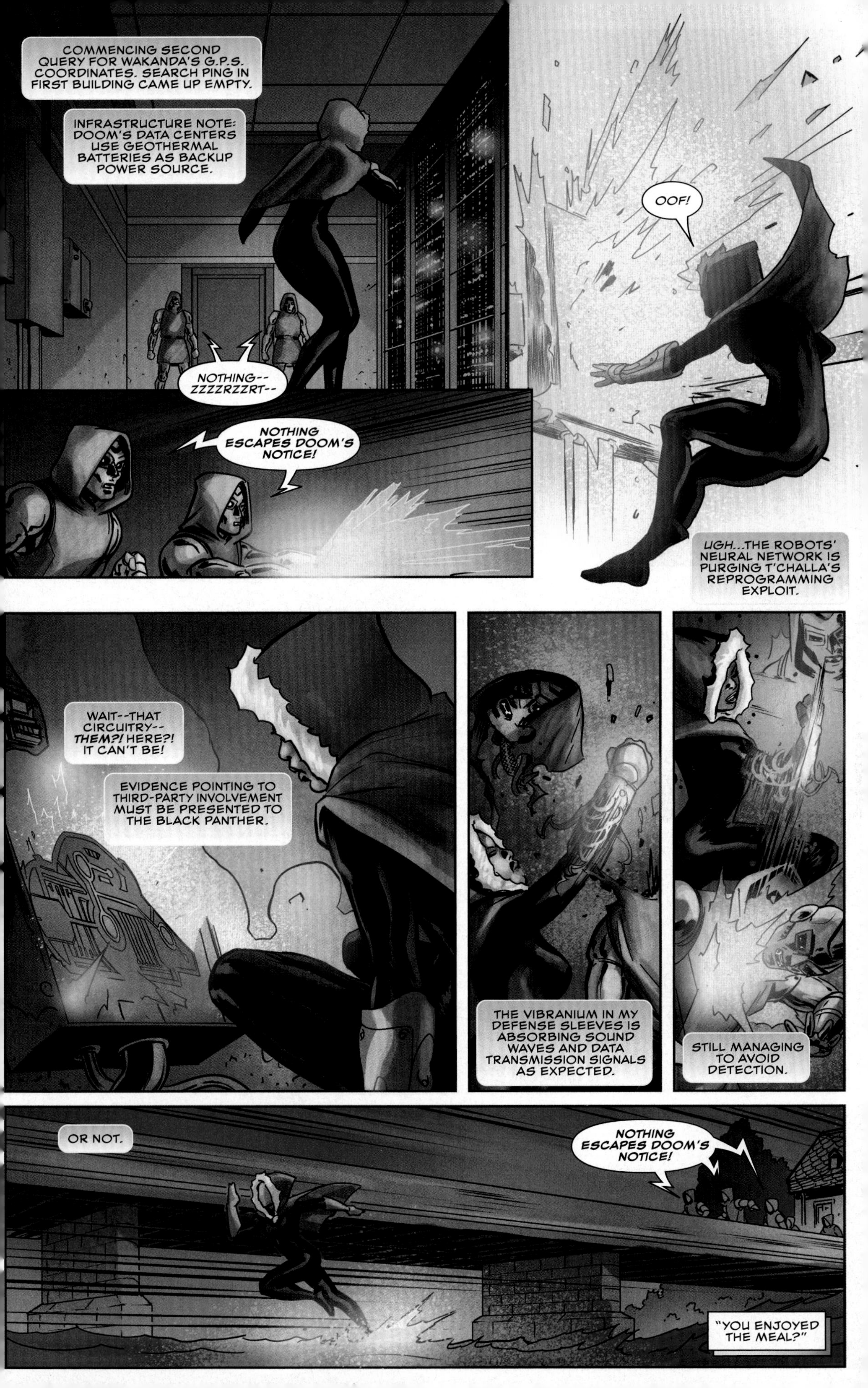
COMMENCING SECOND QUERY FOR WAKANDA'S G.P.S. COORDINATES. SEARCH PING IN FIRST BUILDING CAME UP EMPTY.
INFRASTRUCTURE NOTE: DOOM'S DATA CENTERS USE GEOTHERMAL BATTERIES AS BACKUP POWER SOURCE.
NOTHING-- ZZZZRZZRT--
NOTHING ESCAPES DOOM'S NOTICE!
OOF!
UGH...THE ROBOTS' NEURAL NETWORK IS PURGING T'CHALLA'S REPROGRAMMING EXPLOIT.
WAIT--THAT CIRCUITRY-- THEM?! HERE?! IT CAN'T BE!
EVIDENCE POINTING TO THIRD-PARTY INVOLVEMENT MUST BE PRESENTED TO THE BLACK PANTHER.
THE VIBRANIUM IN MY DEFENSE SLEEVES IS ABSORBING SOUND WAVES AND DATA TRANSMISSION SIGNALS AS EXPECTED.
STILL MANAGING TO AVOID DETECTION.
OR NOT.
NOTHING ESCAPES DOOM'S NOTICE!
"YOU ENJOYED THE MEAL?"

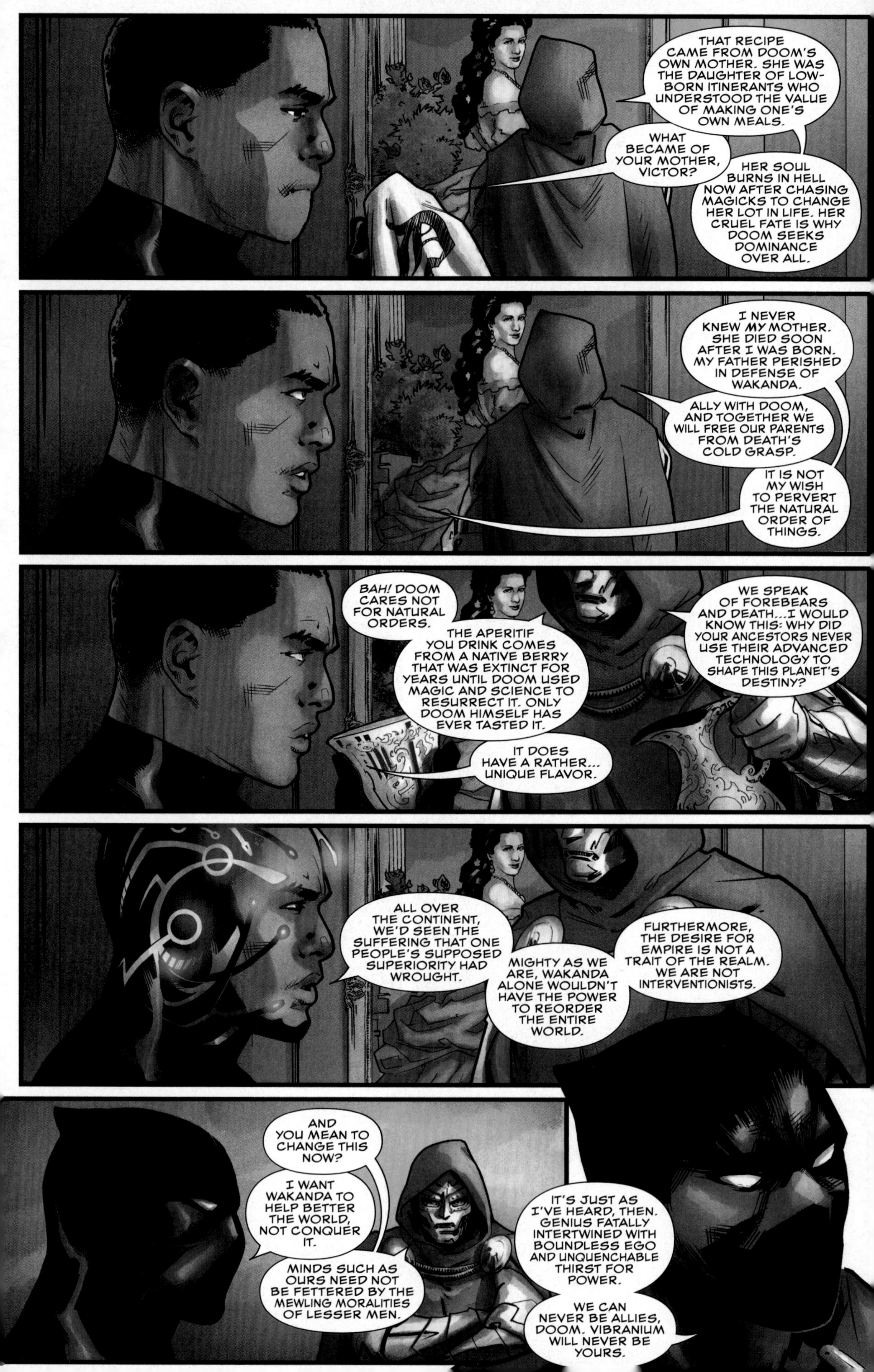
THAT RECIPE CAME FROM DOOM'S OWN MOTHER. SHE WAS THE DAUGHTER OF LOW-BORN ITINERANTS WHO UNDERSTOOD THE VALUE OF MAKING ONE'S OWN MEALS.
WHAT BECAME OF YOUR MOTHER, VICTOR?
HER SOUL BURNS IN HELL NOW AFTER CHASING MAGICKS TO CHANGE HER LOT IN LIFE. HER CRUEL FATE IS WHY DOOM SEEKS DOMINANCE OVER ALL.
I NEVER KNEW *MY* MOTHER. SHE DIED SOON AFTER I WAS BORN. MY FATHER PERISHED IN DEFENSE OF WAKANDA.
ALLY WITH DOOM, AND TOGETHER WE WILL FREE OUR PARENTS FROM DEATH'S COLD GRASP.
IT IS NOT MY WISH TO PERVERT THE NATURAL ORDER OF THINGS.
BAH! DOOM CARES NOT FOR NATURAL ORDERS.
THE APERITIF YOU DRINK COMES FROM A NATIVE BERRY THAT WAS EXTINCT FOR YEARS UNTIL DOOM USED MAGIC AND SCIENCE TO RESURRECT IT. ONLY DOOM HIMSELF HAS EVER TASTED IT.
IT DOES HAVE A RATHER... UNIQUE FLAVOR.
WE SPEAK OF FOREBEARS AND DEATH...I WOULD KNOW THIS: WHY DID YOUR ANCESTORS NEVER USE THEIR ADVANCED TECHNOLOGY TO SHAPE THIS PLANET'S DESTINY?
ALL OVER THE CONTINENT, WE'D SEEN THE SUFFERING THAT ONE PEOPLE'S SUPPOSED SUPERIORITY HAD WROUGHT.
MIGHTY AS WE ARE, WAKANDA ALONE WOULDN'T HAVE THE POWER TO REORDER THE ENTIRE WORLD.
FURTHERMORE, THE DESIRE FOR EMPIRE IS NOT A TRAIT OF THE REALM. WE ARE NOT INTERVENTIONISTS.
AND YOU MEAN TO CHANGE THIS NOW?
I WANT WAKANDA TO HELP BETTER THE WORLD, NOT CONQUER IT.
MINDS SUCH AS OURS NEED NOT BE FETTERED BY THE MEWLING MORALITIES OF LESSER MEN.
IT'S JUST AS I'VE HEARD, THEN. GENIUS FATALLY INTERTWINED WITH BOUNDLESS EGO AND UNQUENCHABLE THIRST FOR POWER.
WE CAN NEVER BE ALLIES, DOOM. VIBRANIUM WILL NEVER BE YOURS.

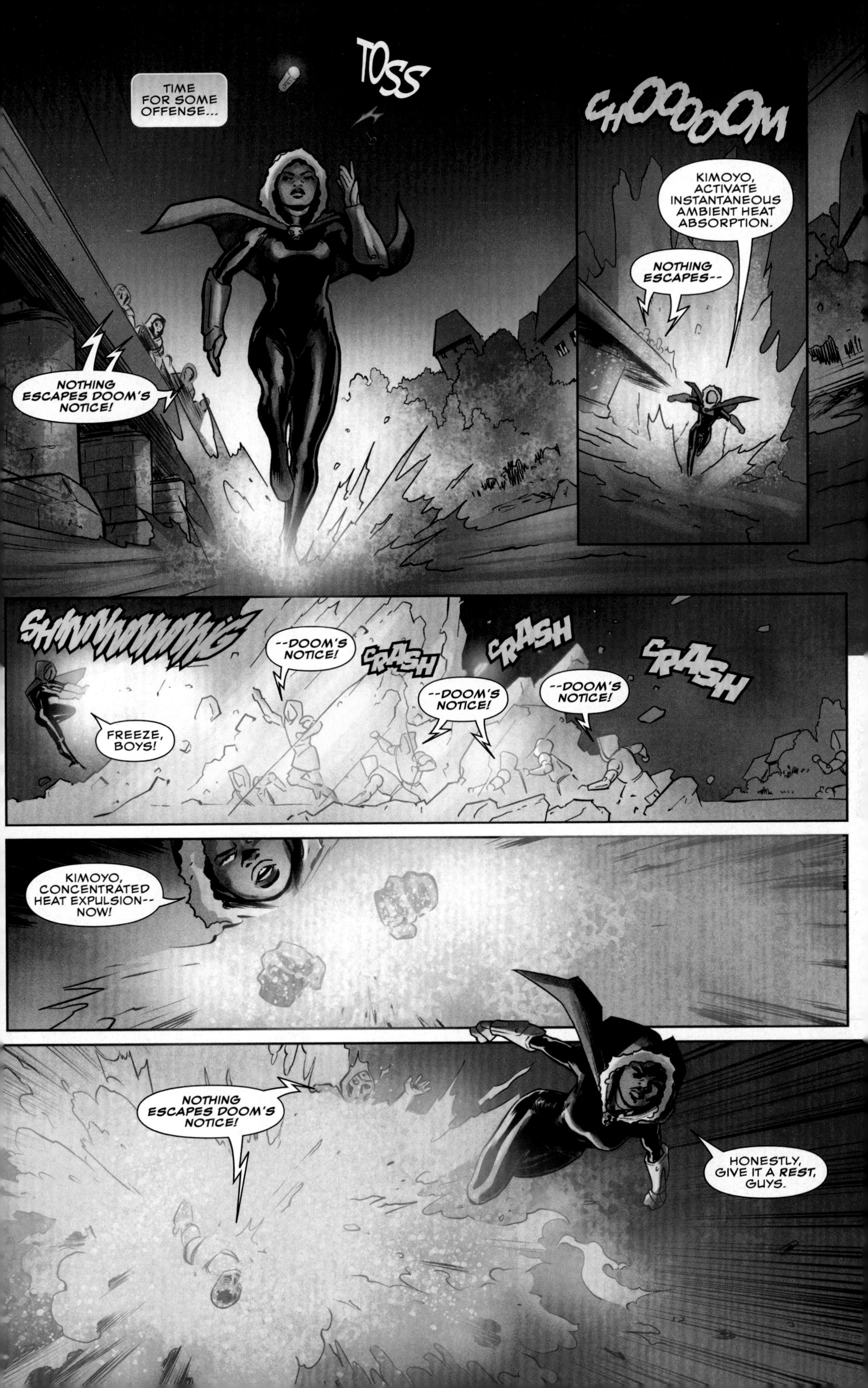
TOSS
TIME FOR SOME OFFENSE...
NOTHING ESCAPES DOOM'S NOTICE!
SHOOOOOM
KIMOYO, ACTIVATE INSTANTANEOUS AMBIENT HEAT ABSORPTION.
NOTHING ESCAPES--
SHHNNNNNNKK
FREEZE, BOYS!
--DOOM'S NOTICE!
CRASH
CRASH
--DOOM'S NOTICE!
--DOOM'S NOTICE!
CRASH
KIMOYO, CONCENTRATED HEAT EXPULSION--NOW!
NOTHING ESCAPES DOOM'S NOTICE!
HONESTLY, GIVE IT A REST, GUYS.

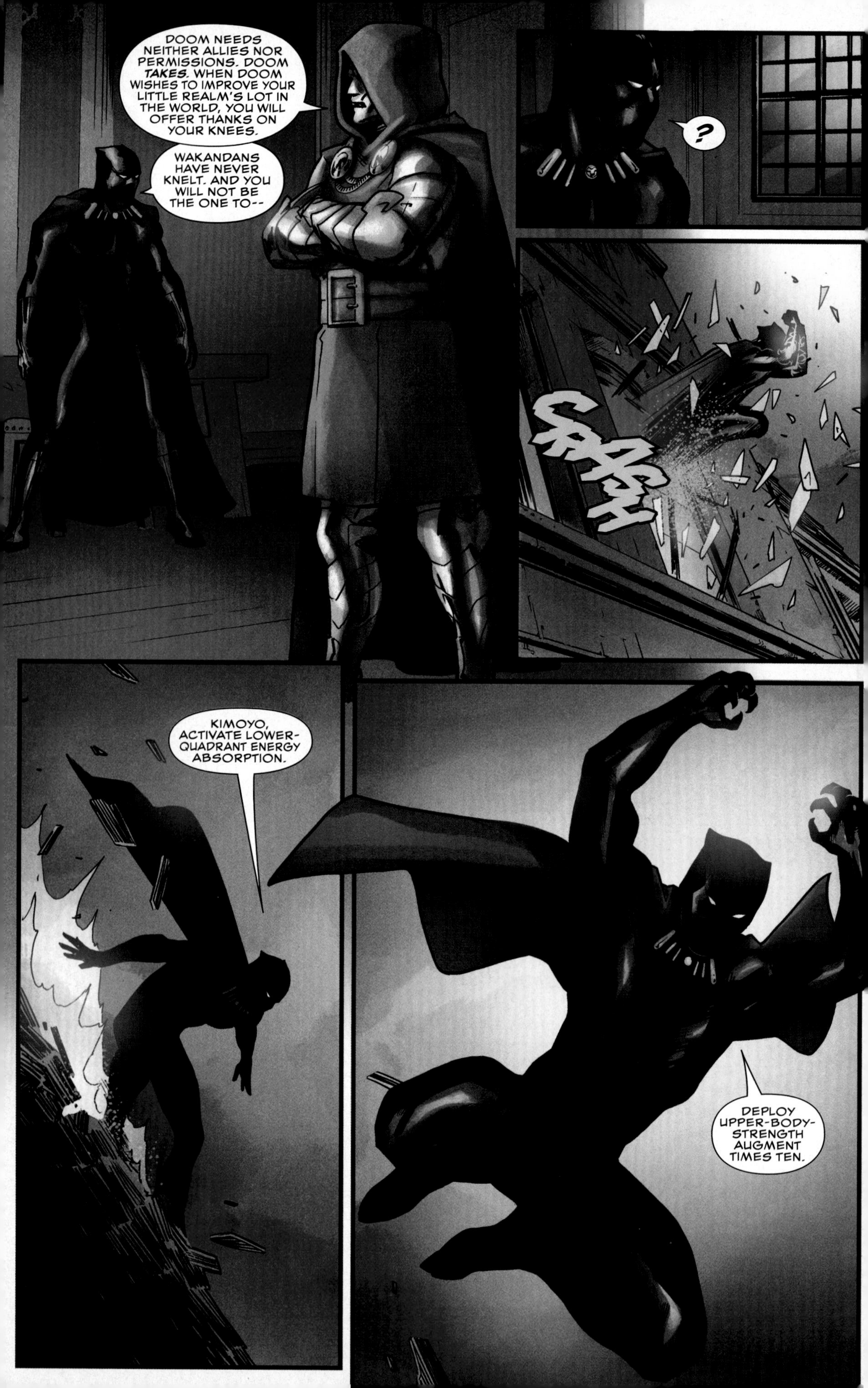
DOOM NEEDS NEITHER ALLIES NOR PERMISSIONS. DOOM *TAKES*. WHEN DOOM WISHES TO IMPROVE YOUR LITTLE REALM'S LOT IN THE WORLD, YOU WILL OFFER THANKS ON YOUR KNEES.
WAKANDANS HAVE NEVER KNELT. AND YOU WILL NOT BE THE ONE TO--
?
CRASH
KIMOYO, ACTIVATE LOWER-QUADRANT ENERGY ABSORPTION.
DEPLOY UPPER-BODY-STRENGTH AUGMENT TIMES TEN.

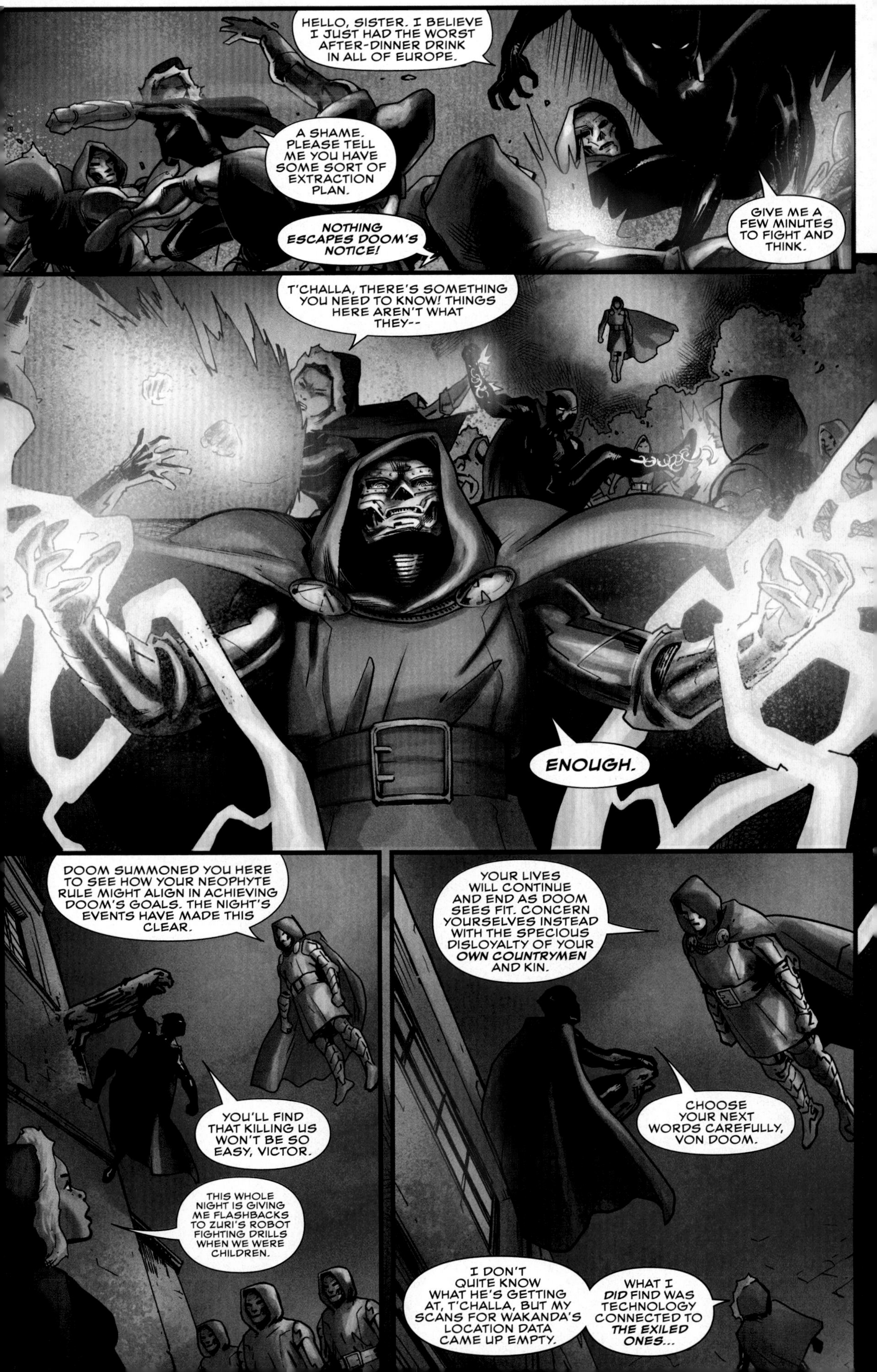

HELLO, SISTER. I BELIEVE I JUST HAD THE WORST AFTER-DINNER DRINK IN ALL OF EUROPE.
A SHAME. PLEASE TELL ME YOU HAVE SOME SORT OF EXTRACTION PLAN.
NOTHING ESCAPES DOOM'S NOTICE!
GIVE ME A FEW MINUTES TO FIGHT AND THINK.
T'CHALLA, THERE'S SOMETHING YOU NEED TO KNOW! THINGS HERE AREN'T WHAT THEY--
ENOUGH.
DOOM SUMMONED YOU HERE TO SEE HOW YOUR NEOPHYTE RULE MIGHT ALIGN IN ACHIEVING DOOM'S GOALS. THE NIGHT'S EVENTS HAVE MADE THIS CLEAR.
YOU'LL FIND THAT KILLING US WON'T BE SO EASY, VICTOR.
THIS WHOLE NIGHT IS GIVING ME FLASHBACKS TO ZURI'S ROBOT FIGHTING DRILLS WHEN WE WERE CHILDREN.
YOUR LIVES WILL CONTINUE AND END AS DOOM SEES FIT. CONCERN YOURSELVES INSTEAD WITH THE SPECIOUS DISLOYALTY OF YOUR OWN COUNTRYMEN AND KIN.
CHOOSE YOUR NEXT WORDS CAREFULLY, VON DOOM.
I DON'T QUITE KNOW WHAT HE'S GETTING AT, T'CHALLA, BUT MY SCANS FOR WAKANDA'S LOCATION DATA CAME UP EMPTY.
WHAT I DID FIND WAS TECHNOLOGY CONNECTED TO THE EXILED ONES...

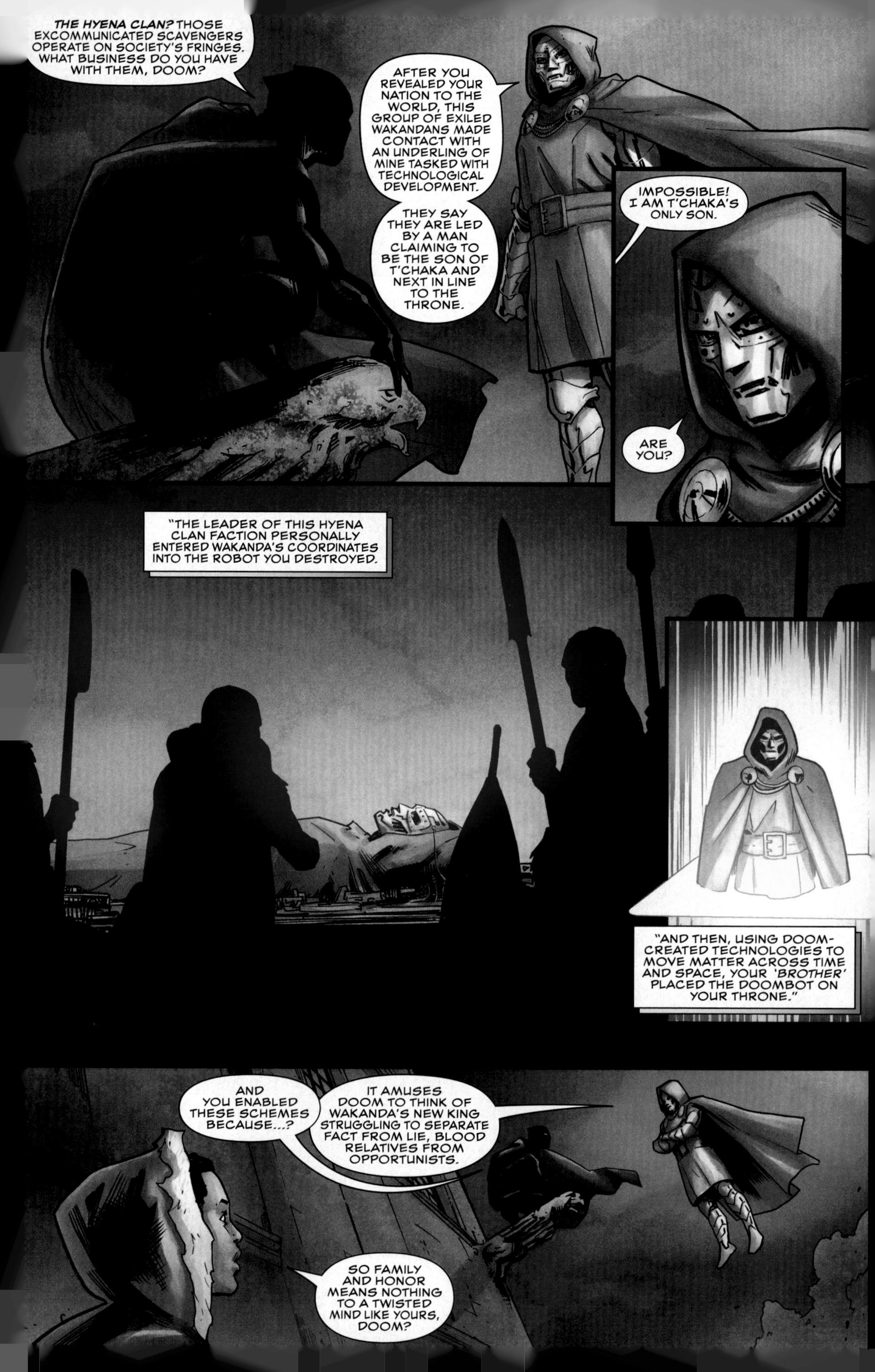
THE HYENA CLAN? THOSE EXCOMMUNICATED SCAVENGERS OPERATE ON SOCIETY'S FRINGES. WHAT BUSINESS DO YOU HAVE WITH THEM, DOOM?
AFTER YOU REVEALED YOUR NATION TO THE WORLD, THIS GROUP OF EXILED WAKANDANS MADE CONTACT WITH AN UNDERLING OF MINE TASKED WITH TECHNOLOGICAL DEVELOPMENT.
THEY SAY THEY ARE LED BY A MAN CLAIMING TO BE THE SON OF T'CHAKA AND NEXT IN LINE TO THE THRONE.
IMPOSSIBLE! I AM T'CHAKA'S ONLY SON.
ARE YOU?
"THE LEADER OF THIS HYENA CLAN FACTION PERSONALLY ENTERED WAKANDA'S COORDINATES INTO THE ROBOT YOU DESTROYED.
"AND THEN, USING DOOM-CREATED TECHNOLOGIES TO MOVE MATTER ACROSS TIME AND SPACE, YOUR 'BROTHER' PLACED THE DOOMBOT ON YOUR THRONE."
AND YOU ENABLED THESE SCHEMES BECAUSE...?
IT AMUSES DOOM TO THINK OF WAKANDA'S NEW KING STRUGGLING TO SEPARATE FACT FROM LIE, BLOOD RELATIVES FROM OPPORTUNISTS.
SO FAMILY AND HONOR MEANS NOTHING TO A TWISTED MIND LIKE YOURS, DOOM?

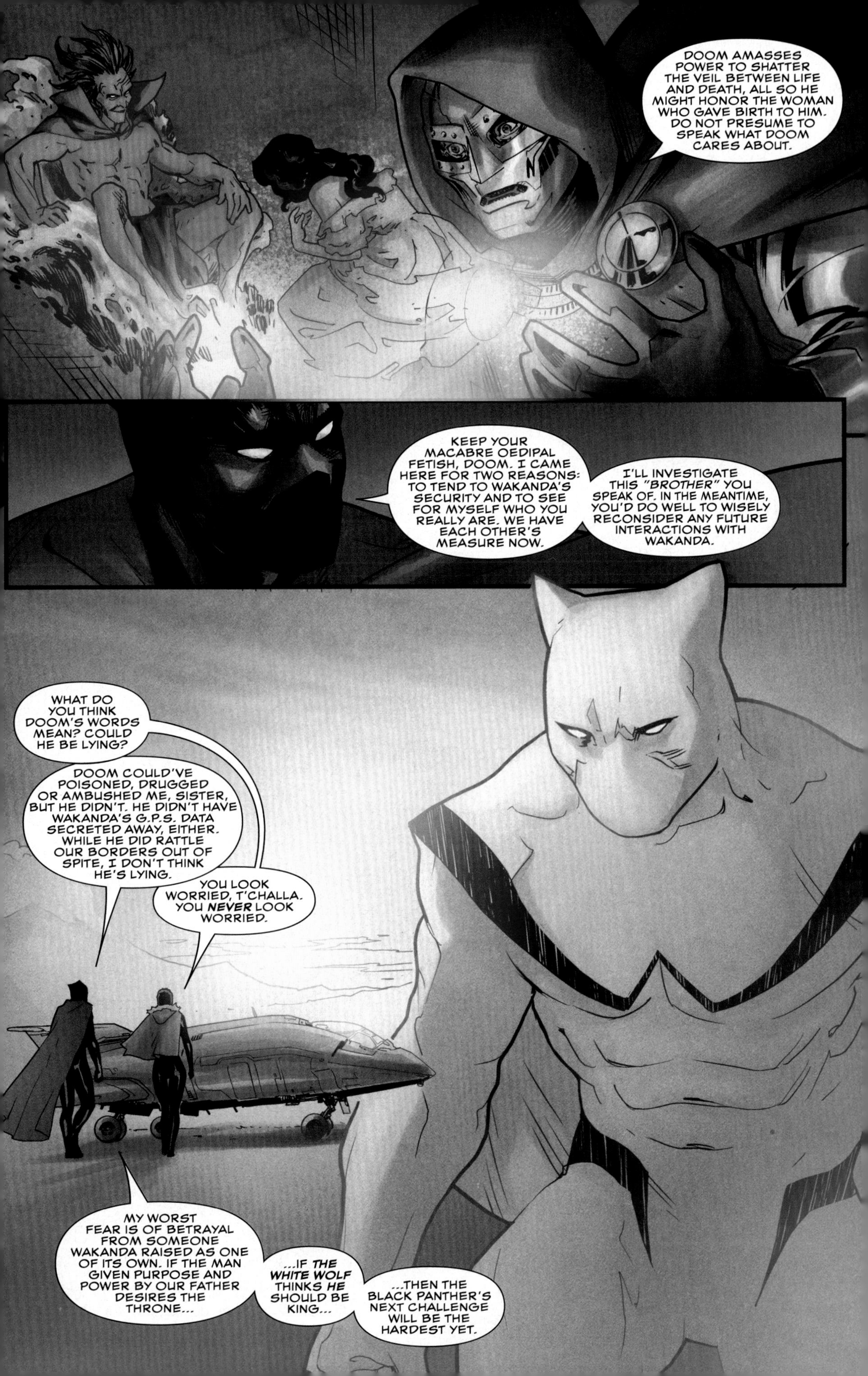
DOOM AMASSES POWER TO SHATTER THE VEIL BETWEEN LIFE AND DEATH, ALL SO HE MIGHT HONOR THE WOMAN WHO GAVE BIRTH TO HIM. DO NOT PRESUME TO SPEAK WHAT DOOM CARES ABOUT.
KEEP YOUR MACABRE OEDIPAL FETISH, DOOM. I CAME HERE FOR TWO REASONS: TO TEND TO WAKANDA'S SECURITY AND TO SEE FOR MYSELF WHO YOU REALLY ARE. WE HAVE EACH OTHER'S MEASURE NOW.
I'LL INVESTIGATE THIS "BROTHER" YOU SPEAK OF. IN THE MEANTIME, YOU'D DO WELL TO WISELY RECONSIDER ANY FUTURE INTERACTIONS WITH WAKANDA.
WHAT DO YOU THINK DOOM'S WORDS MEAN? COULD HE BE LYING?
DOOM COULD'VE POISONED, DRUGGED OR AMBUSHED ME, SISTER, BUT HE DIDN'T. HE DIDN'T HAVE WAKANDA'S G.P.S. DATA SECRETED AWAY, EITHER. WHILE HE DID RATTLE OUR BORDERS OUT OF SPITE, I DON'T THINK HE'S LYING.
YOU LOOK WORRIED, T'CHALLA. YOU NEVER LOOK WORRIED.
MY WORST FEAR IS OF BETRAYAL FROM SOMEONE WAKANDA RAISED AS ONE OF ITS OWN. IF THE MAN GIVEN PURPOSE AND POWER BY OUR FATHER DESIRES THE THRONE...
...IF THE WHITE WOLF THINKS HE SHOULD BE KING...
...THEN THE BLACK PANTHER'S NEXT CHALLENGE WILL BE THE HARDEST YET.

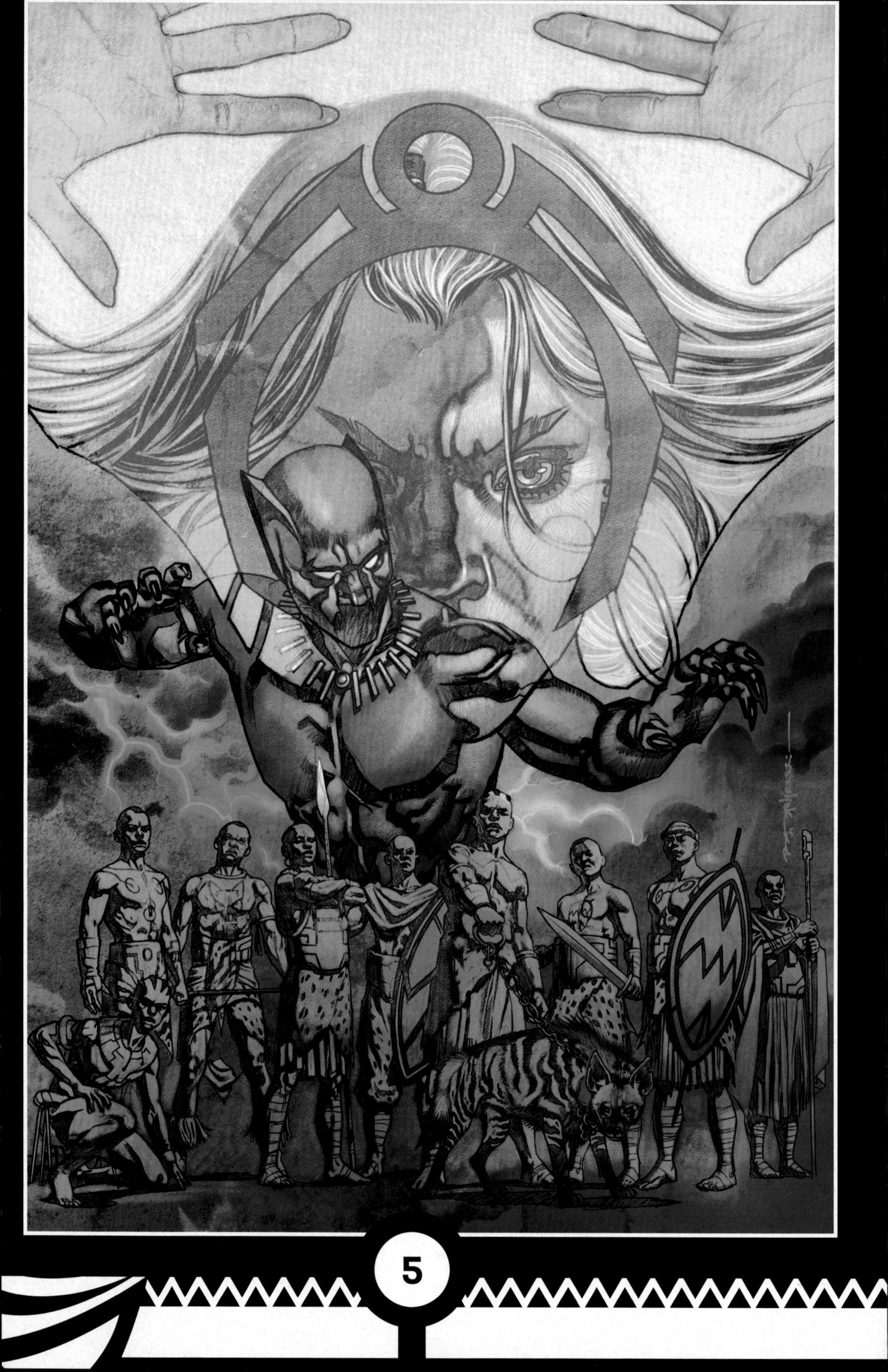

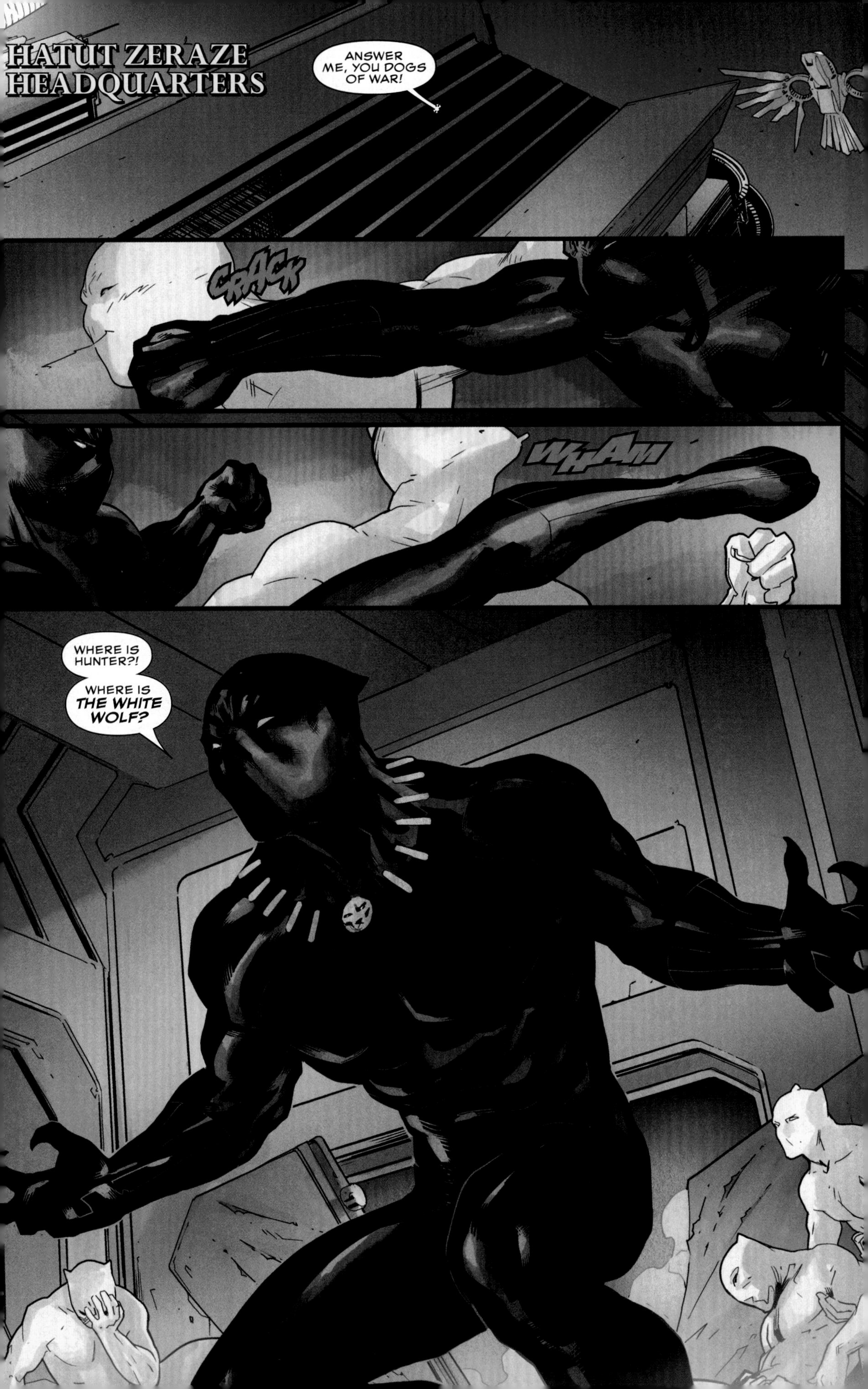
HATUT ZERAZE HEADQUARTERS
ANSWER ME, YOU DOGS OF WAR!
CRACK
WHAM
WHERE IS HUNTER?!
WHERE IS THE WHITE WOLF?

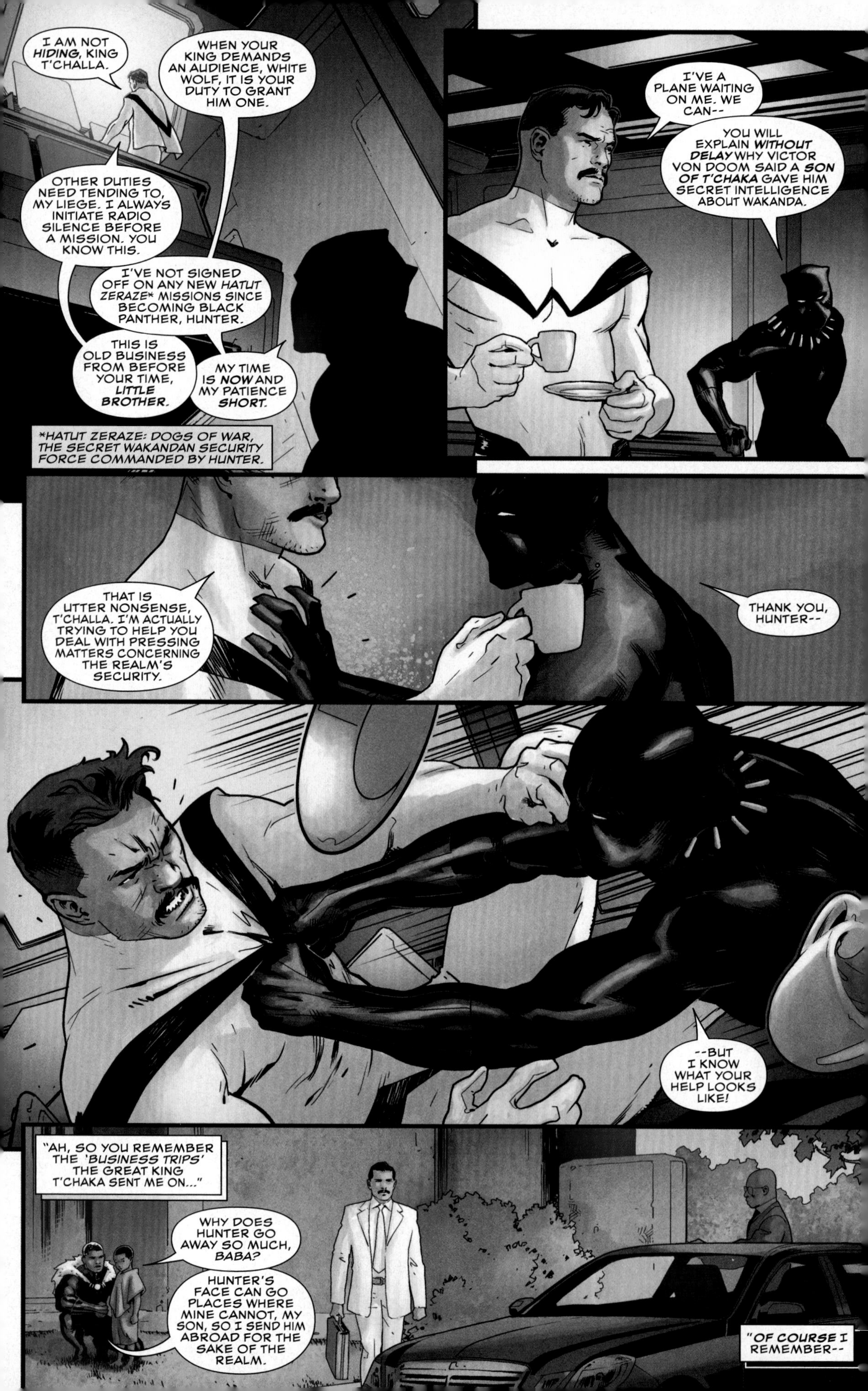
I AM NOT *HIDING*, KING T'CHALLA.
WHEN YOUR KING DEMANDS AN AUDIENCE, WHITE WOLF, IT IS YOUR DUTY TO GRANT HIM ONE.
OTHER DUTIES NEED TENDING TO, MY LIEGE. I ALWAYS INITIATE RADIO SILENCE BEFORE A MISSION. YOU KNOW THIS.
I'VE NOT SIGNED OFF ON ANY NEW *HATUT ZERAZE** MISSIONS SINCE BECOMING BLACK PANTHER, HUNTER.
THIS IS OLD BUSINESS FROM BEFORE YOUR TIME, ***LITTLE BROTHER***.
MY TIME IS ***NOW*** AND MY PATIENCE ***SHORT***.
**HATUT ZERAZE: DOGS OF WAR, THE SECRET WAKANDAN SECURITY FORCE COMMANDED BY HUNTER.*
I'VE A PLANE WAITING ON ME. WE CAN--
YOU WILL EXPLAIN ***WITHOUT DELAY*** WHY VICTOR VON DOOM SAID A ***SON OF T'CHAKA*** GAVE HIM SECRET INTELLIGENCE ABOUT WAKANDA.
THAT IS UTTER NONSENSE, T'CHALLA. I'M ACTUALLY TRYING TO HELP YOU DEAL WITH PRESSING MATTERS CONCERNING THE REALM'S SECURITY.
THANK YOU, HUNTER--
--BUT I KNOW WHAT YOUR HELP LOOKS LIKE!
"AH, SO YOU REMEMBER THE *'BUSINESS TRIPS'* THE GREAT KING T'CHAKA SENT ME ON..."
WHY DOES HUNTER GO AWAY SO MUCH, *BABA*?
HUNTER'S FACE CAN GO PLACES WHERE MINE CANNOT, MY SON, SO I SEND HIM ABROAD FOR THE SAKE OF THE REALM.
"***OF COURSE*** I REMEMBER--

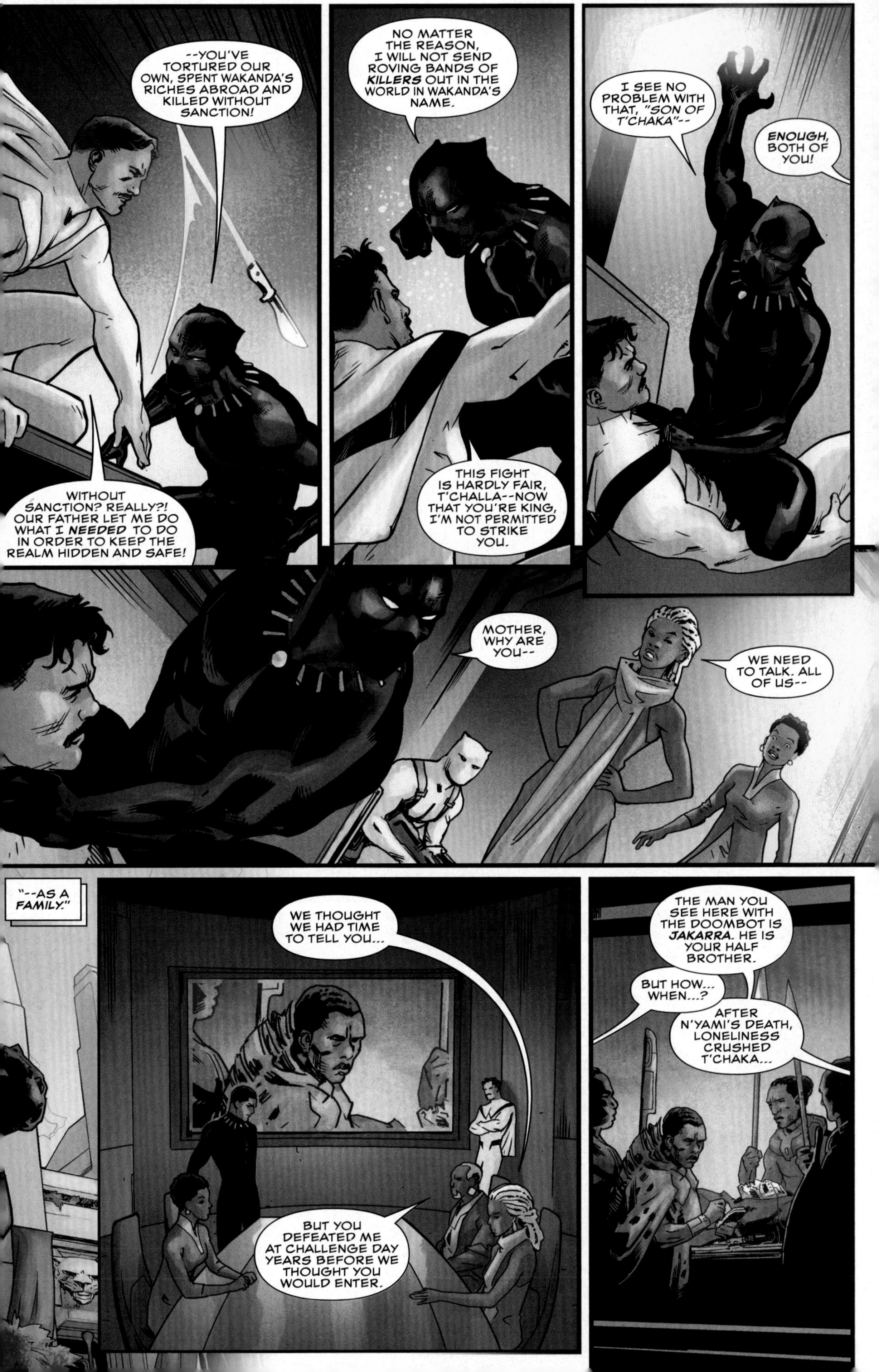
--YOU'VE TORTURED OUR OWN, SPENT WAKANDA'S RICHES ABROAD AND KILLED WITHOUT SANCTION!
WITHOUT SANCTION? REALLY?! OUR FATHER LET ME DO WHAT I NEEDED TO DO IN ORDER TO KEEP THE REALM HIDDEN AND SAFE!
NO MATTER THE REASON, I WILL NOT SEND ROVING BANDS OF KILLERS OUT IN THE WORLD IN WAKANDA'S NAME.
THIS FIGHT IS HARDLY FAIR, T'CHALLA--NOW THAT YOU'RE KING, I'M NOT PERMITTED TO STRIKE YOU.
I SEE NO PROBLEM WITH THAT, "SON OF T'CHAKA"--
ENOUGH, BOTH OF YOU!
MOTHER, WHY ARE YOU--
WE NEED TO TALK. ALL OF US--
"--AS A FAMILY."
WE THOUGHT WE HAD TIME TO TELL YOU...
BUT YOU DEFEATED ME AT CHALLENGE DAY YEARS BEFORE WE THOUGHT YOU WOULD ENTER.
THE MAN YOU SEE HERE WITH THE DOOMBOT IS JAKARRA. HE IS YOUR HALF BROTHER.
BUT HOW... WHEN...?
AFTER N'YAMI'S DEATH, LONELINESS CRUSHED T'CHAKA...

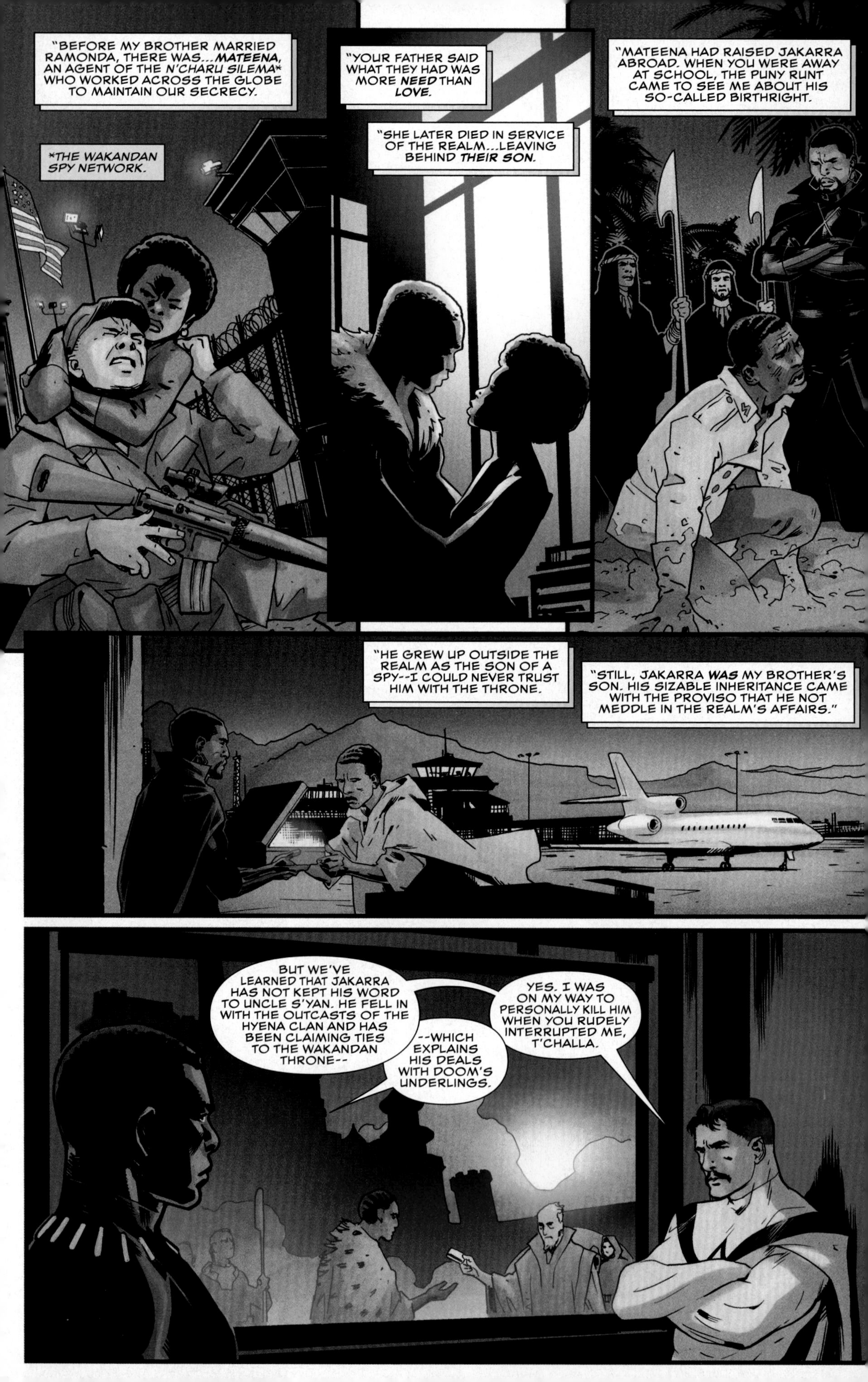
"BEFORE MY BROTHER MARRIED RAMONDA, THERE WAS... MATEENA, AN AGENT OF THE N'CHARU SILEMA* WHO WORKED ACROSS THE GLOBE TO MAINTAIN OUR SECRECY.
*THE WAKANDAN SPY NETWORK.
"YOUR FATHER SAID WHAT THEY HAD WAS MORE NEED THAN LOVE.
"SHE LATER DIED IN SERVICE OF THE REALM... LEAVING BEHIND THEIR SON.
"MATEENA HAD RAISED JAKARRA ABROAD. WHEN YOU WERE AWAY AT SCHOOL, THE PUNY RUNT CAME TO SEE ME ABOUT HIS SO-CALLED BIRTHRIGHT.
"HE GREW UP OUTSIDE THE REALM AS THE SON OF A SPY--I COULD NEVER TRUST HIM WITH THE THRONE.
"STILL, JAKARRA WAS MY BROTHER'S SON. HIS SIZABLE INHERITANCE CAME WITH THE PROVISO THAT HE NOT MEDDLE IN THE REALM'S AFFAIRS."
BUT WE'VE LEARNED THAT JAKARRA HAS NOT KEPT HIS WORD TO UNCLE S'YAN. HE FELL IN WITH THE OUTCASTS OF THE HYENA CLAN AND HAS BEEN CLAIMING TIES TO THE WAKANDAN THRONE--
--WHICH EXPLAINS HIS DEALS WITH DOOM'S UNDERLINGS.
YES. I WAS ON MY WAY TO PERSONALLY KILL HIM WHEN YOU RUDELY INTERRUPTED ME, T'CHALLA.

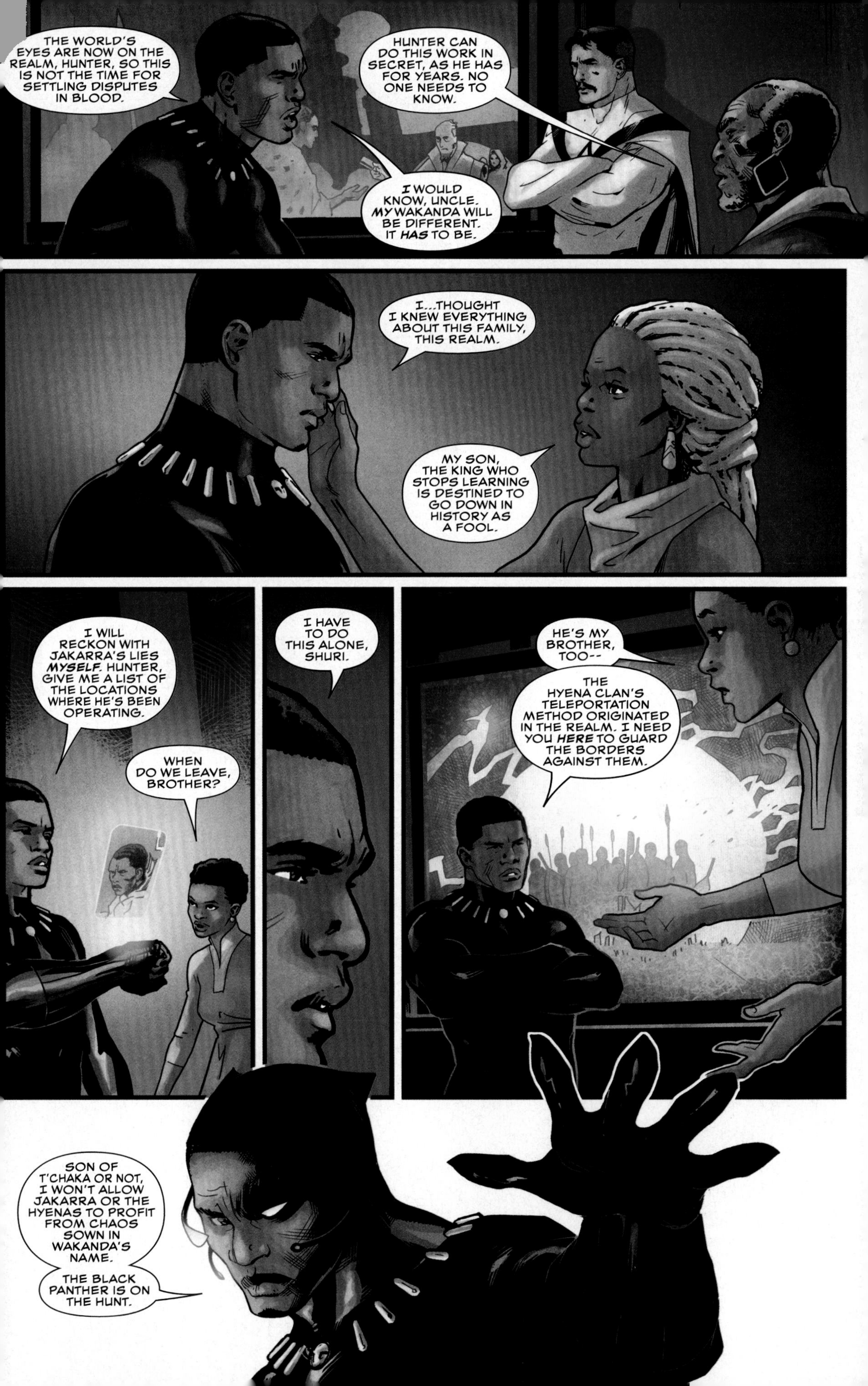

THE WORLD'S EYES ARE NOW ON THE REALM, HUNTER, SO THIS IS NOT THE TIME FOR SETTLING DISPUTES IN BLOOD.
HUNTER CAN DO THIS WORK IN SECRET, AS HE HAS FOR YEARS. NO ONE NEEDS TO KNOW.
I WOULD KNOW, UNCLE. *MY* WAKANDA WILL BE DIFFERENT. IT *HAS* TO BE.
I...THOUGHT I KNEW EVERYTHING ABOUT THIS FAMILY, THIS REALM.
MY SON, THE KING WHO STOPS LEARNING IS DESTINED TO GO DOWN IN HISTORY AS A FOOL.
I WILL RECKON WITH JAKARRA'S LIES *MYSELF*. HUNTER, GIVE ME A LIST OF THE LOCATIONS WHERE HE'S BEEN OPERATING.
WHEN DO WE LEAVE, BROTHER?
I HAVE TO DO THIS ALONE, SHURI.
HE'S MY BROTHER, TOO--
THE HYENA CLAN'S TELEPORTATION METHOD ORIGINATED IN THE REALM. I NEED YOU *HERE* TO GUARD THE BORDERS AGAINST THEM.
SON OF T'CHAKA OR NOT, I WON'T ALLOW JAKARRA OR THE HYENAS TO PROFIT FROM CHAOS SOWN IN WAKANDA'S NAME.
THE BLACK PANTHER IS ON THE HUNT.

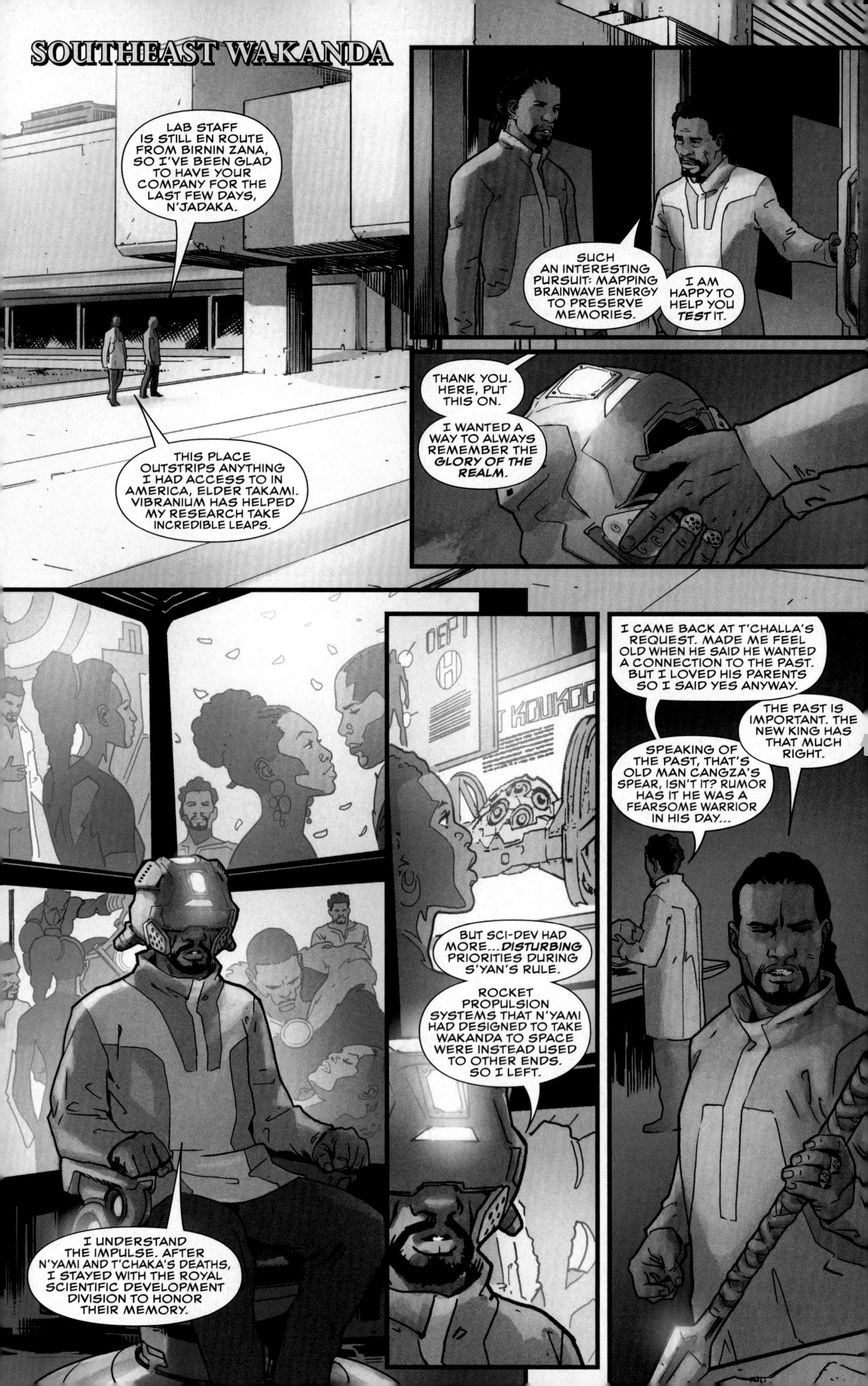
SOUTHEAST WAKANDA
LAB STAFF IS STILL EN ROUTE FROM BIRNIN ZANA, SO I'VE BEEN GLAD TO HAVE YOUR COMPANY FOR THE LAST FEW DAYS, N'JADAKA.
THIS PLACE OUTSTRIPS ANYTHING I HAD ACCESS TO IN AMERICA, ELDER TAKAMI. VIBRANIUM HAS HELPED MY RESEARCH TAKE INCREDIBLE LEAPS.
SUCH AN INTERESTING PURSUIT: MAPPING BRAINWAVE ENERGY TO PRESERVE MEMORIES.
I AM HAPPY TO HELP YOU TEST IT.
THANK YOU. HERE, PUT THIS ON.
I WANTED A WAY TO ALWAYS REMEMBER THE GLORY OF THE REALM.
I UNDERSTAND THE IMPULSE. AFTER N'YAMI AND T'CHAKA'S DEATHS, I STAYED WITH THE ROYAL SCIENTIFIC DEVELOPMENT DIVISION TO HONOR THEIR MEMORY.
BUT SCI-DEV HAD MORE... DISTURBING PRIORITIES DURING S'YAN'S RULE.
ROCKET PROPULSION SYSTEMS THAT N'YAMI HAD DESIGNED TO TAKE WAKANDA TO SPACE WERE INSTEAD USED TO OTHER ENDS. SO I LEFT.
I CAME BACK AT T'CHALLA'S REQUEST. MADE ME FEEL OLD WHEN HE SAID HE WANTED A CONNECTION TO THE PAST. BUT I LOVED HIS PARENTS SO I SAID YES ANYWAY.
THE PAST IS IMPORTANT. THE NEW KING HAS THAT MUCH RIGHT.
SPEAKING OF THE PAST, THAT'S OLD MAN CANGZA'S SPEAR, ISN'T IT? RUMOR HAS IT HE WAS A FEARSOME WARRIOR IN HIS DAY...

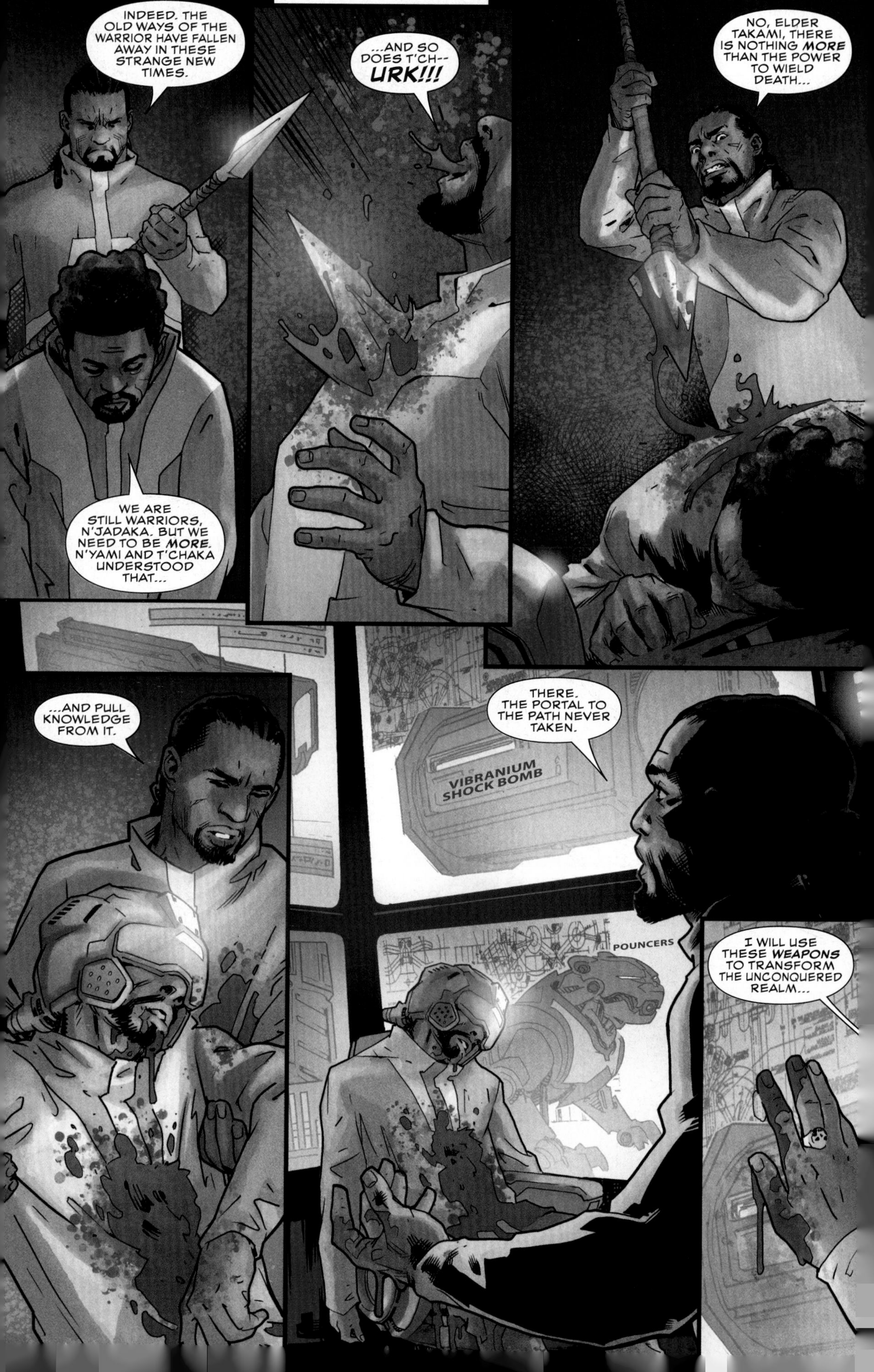
INDEED. THE OLD WAYS OF THE WARRIOR HAVE FALLEN AWAY IN THESE STRANGE NEW TIMES.
WE ARE STILL WARRIORS, N'JADAKA. BUT WE NEED TO BE MORE. N'YAMI AND T'CHAKA UNDERSTOOD THAT...
...AND SO DOES T'CH-- URK!!!
NO, ELDER TAKAMI, THERE IS NOTHING MORE THAN THE POWER TO WIELD DEATH...
...AND PULL KNOWLEDGE FROM IT.
THERE. THE PORTAL TO THE PATH NEVER TAKEN.
VIBRANIUM SHOCK BOMB
POUNCERS
I WILL USE THESE WEAPONS TO TRANSFORM THE UNCONQUERED REALM...

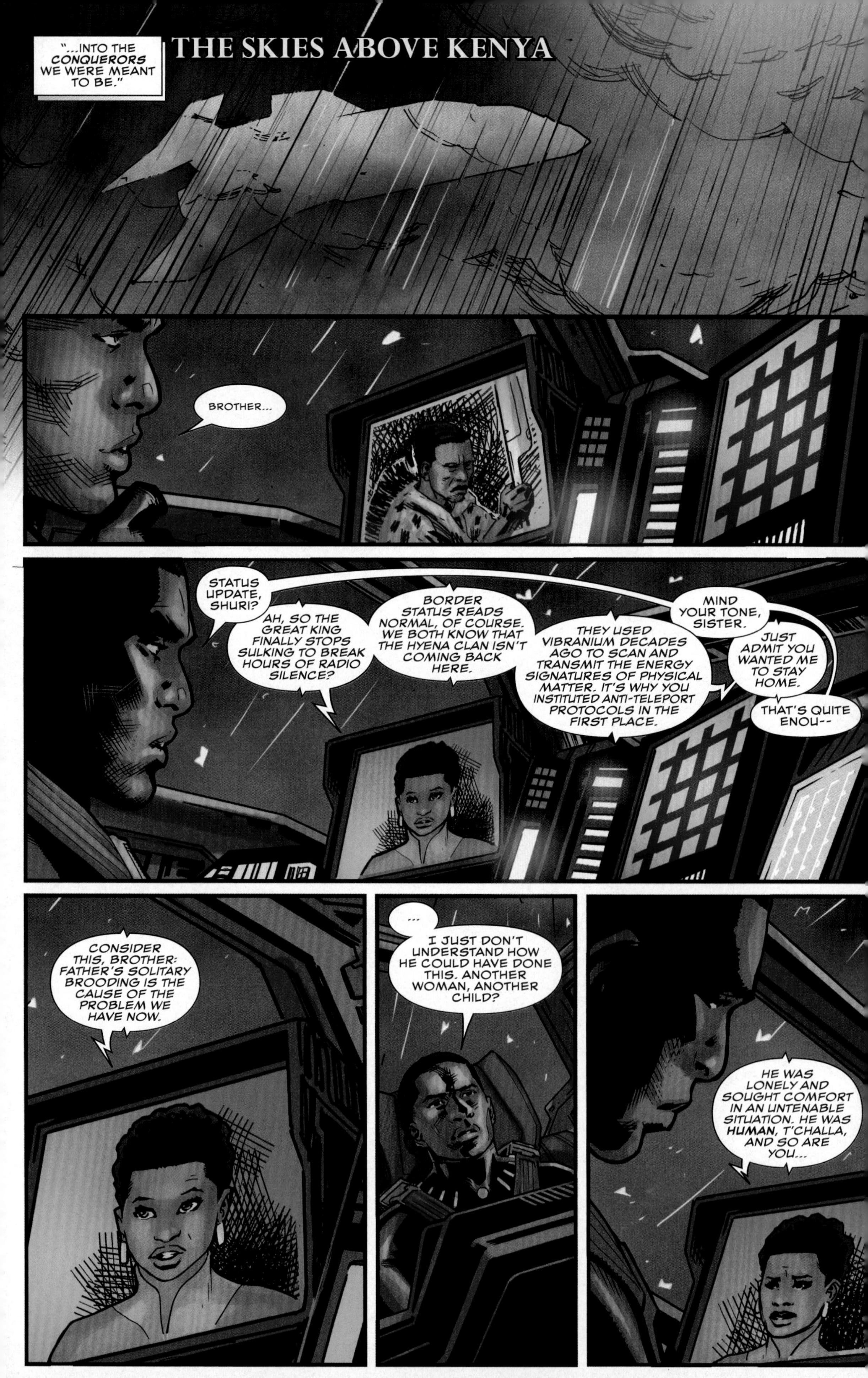
"...INTO THE CONQUERORS WE WERE MEANT TO BE."
THE SKIES ABOVE KENYA
BROTHER...
STATUS UPDATE, SHURI?
AH, SO THE GREAT KING FINALLY STOPS SULKING TO BREAK HOURS OF RADIO SILENCE?
BORDER STATUS READS NORMAL, OF COURSE. WE BOTH KNOW THAT THE HYENA CLAN ISN'T COMING BACK HERE.
THEY USED VIBRANIUM DECADES AGO TO SCAN AND TRANSMIT THE ENERGY SIGNATURES OF PHYSICAL MATTER. IT'S WHY YOU INSTITUTED ANTI-TELEPORT PROTOCOLS IN THE FIRST PLACE.
MIND YOUR TONE, SISTER.
JUST ADMIT YOU WANTED ME TO STAY HOME.
THAT'S QUITE ENOU--
CONSIDER THIS, BROTHER: FATHER'S SOLITARY BROODING IS THE CAUSE OF THE PROBLEM WE HAVE NOW.
...
I JUST DON'T UNDERSTAND HOW HE COULD HAVE DONE THIS. ANOTHER WOMAN, ANOTHER CHILD?
HE WAS LONELY AND SOUGHT COMFORT IN AN UNTENABLE SITUATION. HE WAS HUMAN, T'CHALLA, AND SO ARE YOU...

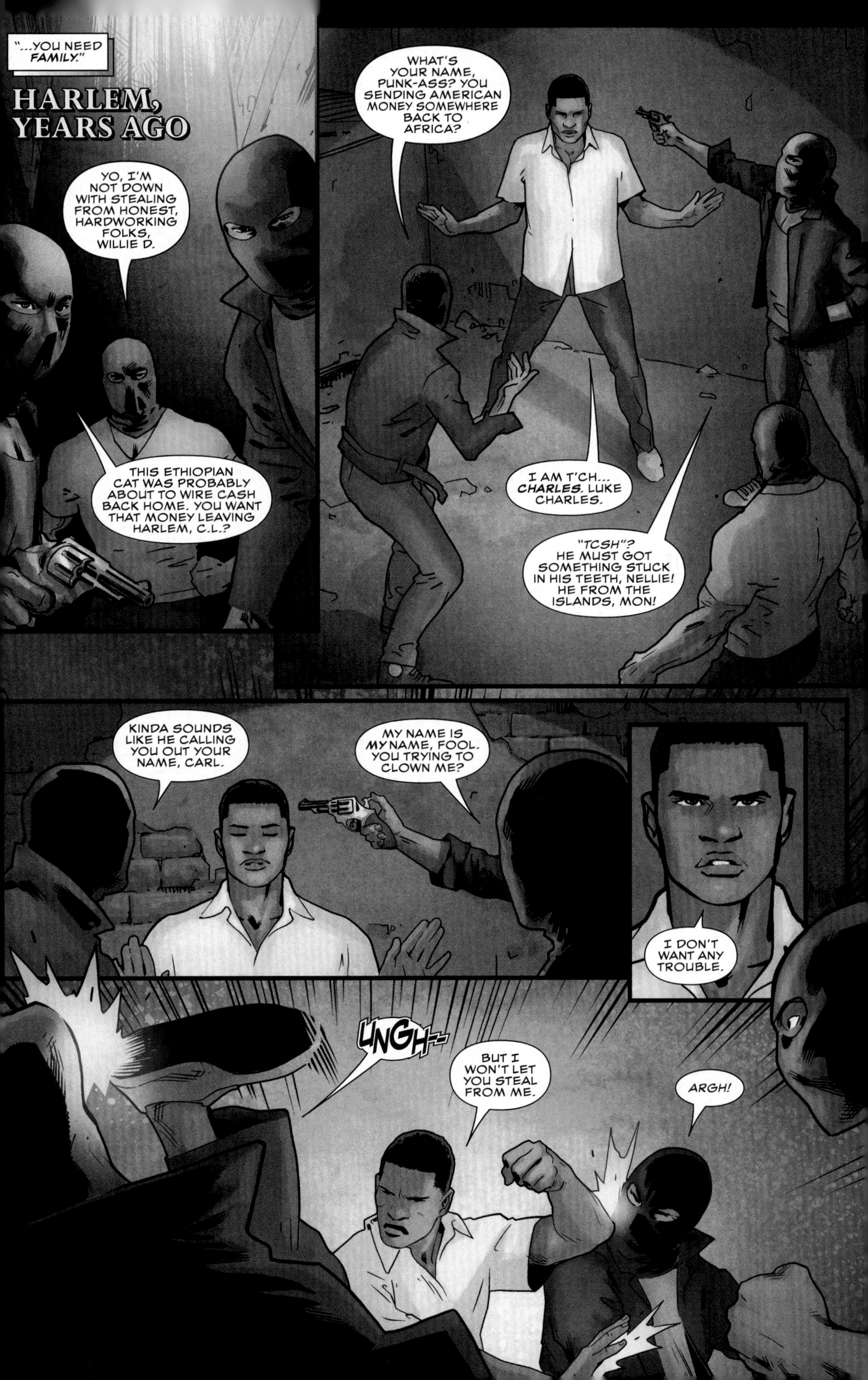
"...YOU NEED FAMILY."
HARLEM, YEARS AGO
YO, I'M NOT DOWN WITH STEALING FROM HONEST, HARDWORKING FOLKS, WILLIE D.
THIS ETHIOPIAN CAT WAS PROBABLY ABOUT TO WIRE CASH BACK HOME. YOU WANT THAT MONEY LEAVING HARLEM, C.L.?
WHAT'S YOUR NAME, PUNK-ASS? YOU SENDING AMERICAN MONEY SOMEWHERE BACK TO AFRICA?
I AM T'CH... CHARLES. LUKE CHARLES.
"TCSH"? HE MUST GOT SOMETHING STUCK IN HIS TEETH, NELLIE! HE FROM THE ISLANDS, MON!
KINDA SOUNDS LIKE HE CALLING YOU OUT YOUR NAME, CARL.
MY NAME IS MY NAME, FOOL. YOU TRYING TO CLOWN ME?
I DON'T WANT ANY TROUBLE.
UNGH--
BUT I WON'T LET YOU STEAL FROM ME.
ARGH!

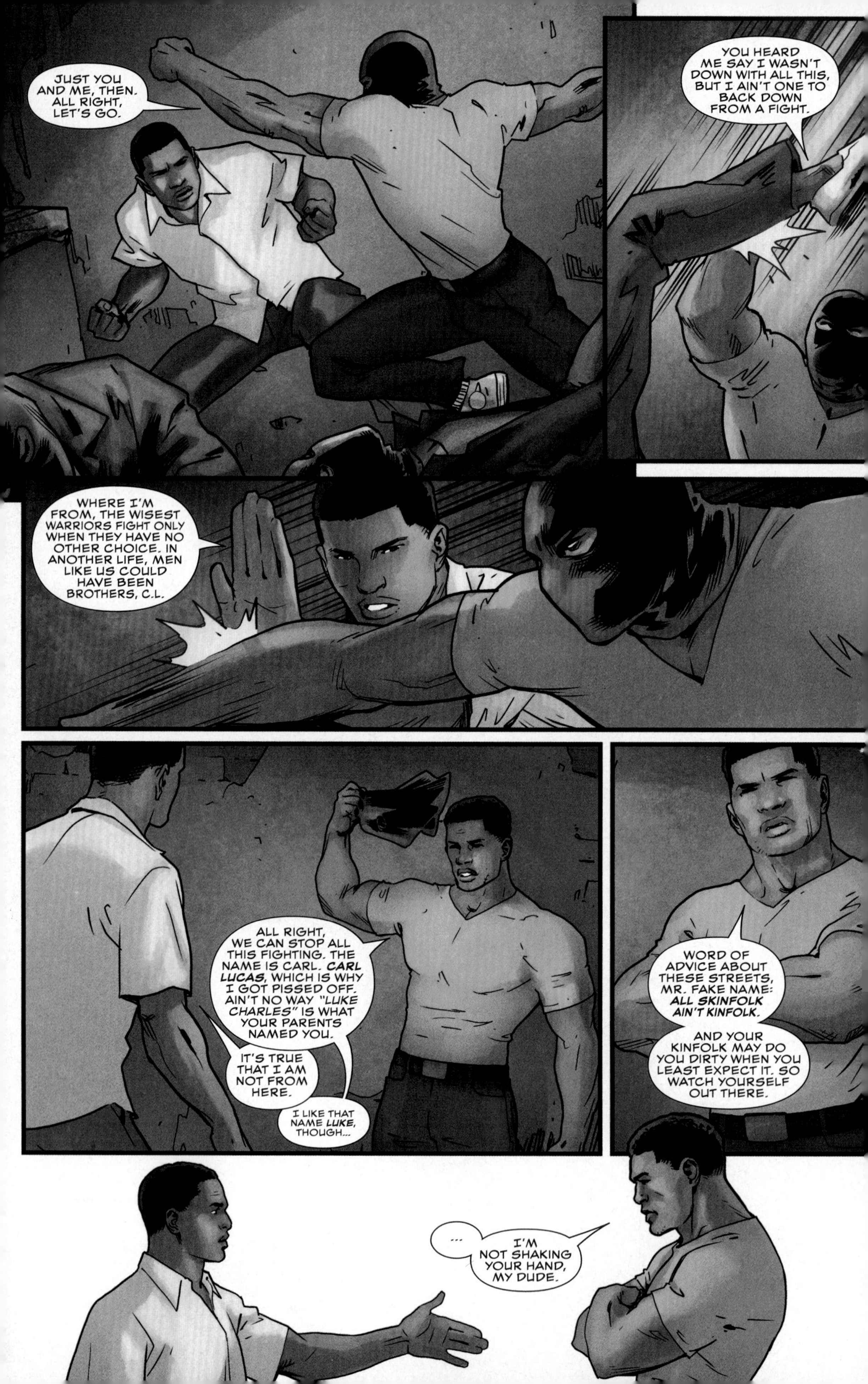
JUST YOU AND ME, THEN. ALL RIGHT, LET'S GO.
YOU HEARD ME SAY I WASN'T DOWN WITH ALL THIS, BUT I AIN'T ONE TO BACK DOWN FROM A FIGHT.
WHERE I'M FROM, THE WISEST WARRIORS FIGHT ONLY WHEN THEY HAVE NO OTHER CHOICE. IN ANOTHER LIFE, MEN LIKE US COULD HAVE BEEN BROTHERS, C.L.
ALL RIGHT, WE CAN STOP ALL THIS FIGHTING. THE NAME IS CARL. CARL LUCAS, WHICH IS WHY I GOT PISSED OFF. AIN'T NO WAY "LUKE CHARLES" IS WHAT YOUR PARENTS NAMED YOU.
IT'S TRUE THAT I AM NOT FROM HERE.
I LIKE THAT NAME LUKE, THOUGH...
WORD OF ADVICE ABOUT THESE STREETS, MR. FAKE NAME: ALL SKINFOLK AIN'T KINFOLK.
AND YOUR KINFOLK MAY DO YOU DIRTY WHEN YOU LEAST EXPECT IT. SO WATCH YOURSELF OUT THERE.
...
I'M NOT SHAKING YOUR HAND, MY DUDE.

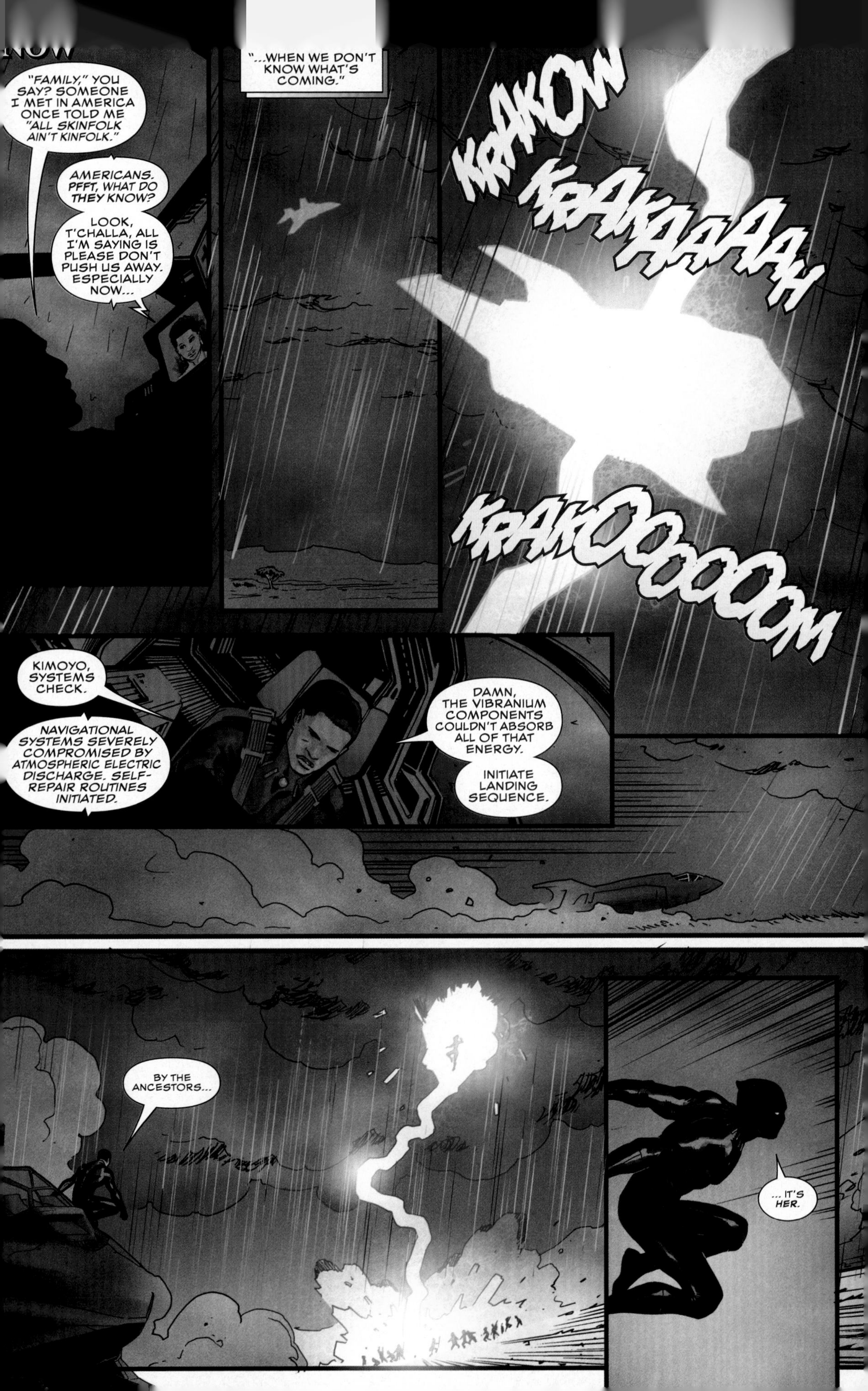
NOW
"FAMILY," YOU SAY? SOMEONE I MET IN AMERICA ONCE TOLD ME "ALL SKINFOLK AIN'T KINFOLK."
AMERICANS. PFFT, WHAT DO THEY KNOW?
LOOK, T'CHALLA, ALL I'M SAYING IS PLEASE DON'T PUSH US AWAY. ESPECIALLY NOW...
"...WHEN WE DON'T KNOW WHAT'S COMING."
KRAKOW
KRAKAAAAAH
KRAKOOOOOOM
KIMOYO, SYSTEMS CHECK.
NAVIGATIONAL SYSTEMS SEVERELY COMPROMISED BY ATMOSPHERIC ELECTRIC DISCHARGE. SELF-REPAIR ROUTINES INITIATED.
DAMN, THE VIBRANIUM COMPONENTS COULDN'T ABSORB ALL OF THAT ENERGY.
INITIATE LANDING SEQUENCE.
BY THE ANCESTORS...
...IT'S HER.

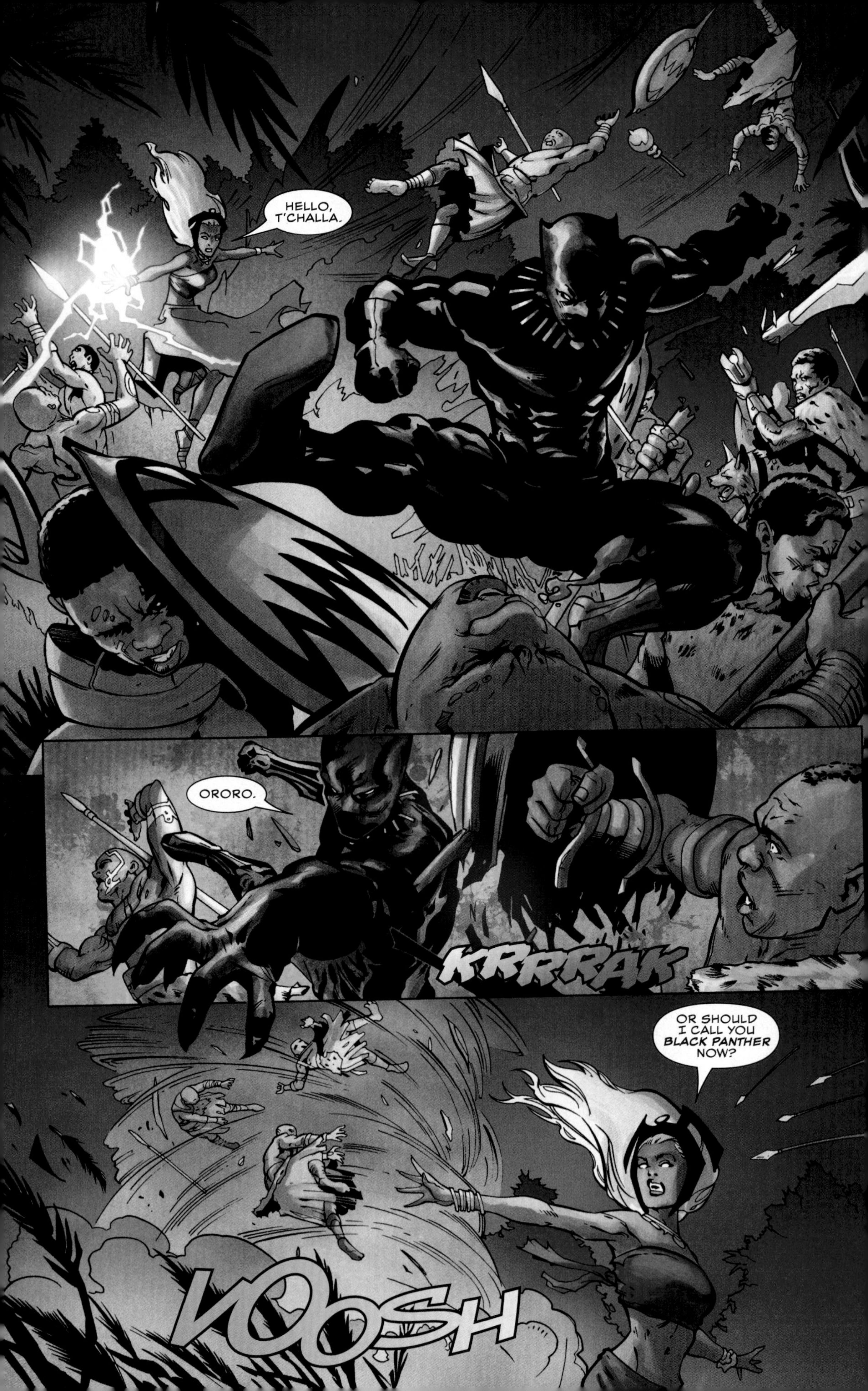
HELLO, T'CHALLA.
ORORO.
KRRRAK
OR SHOULD I CALL YOU BLACK PANTHER NOW?
VOOSH

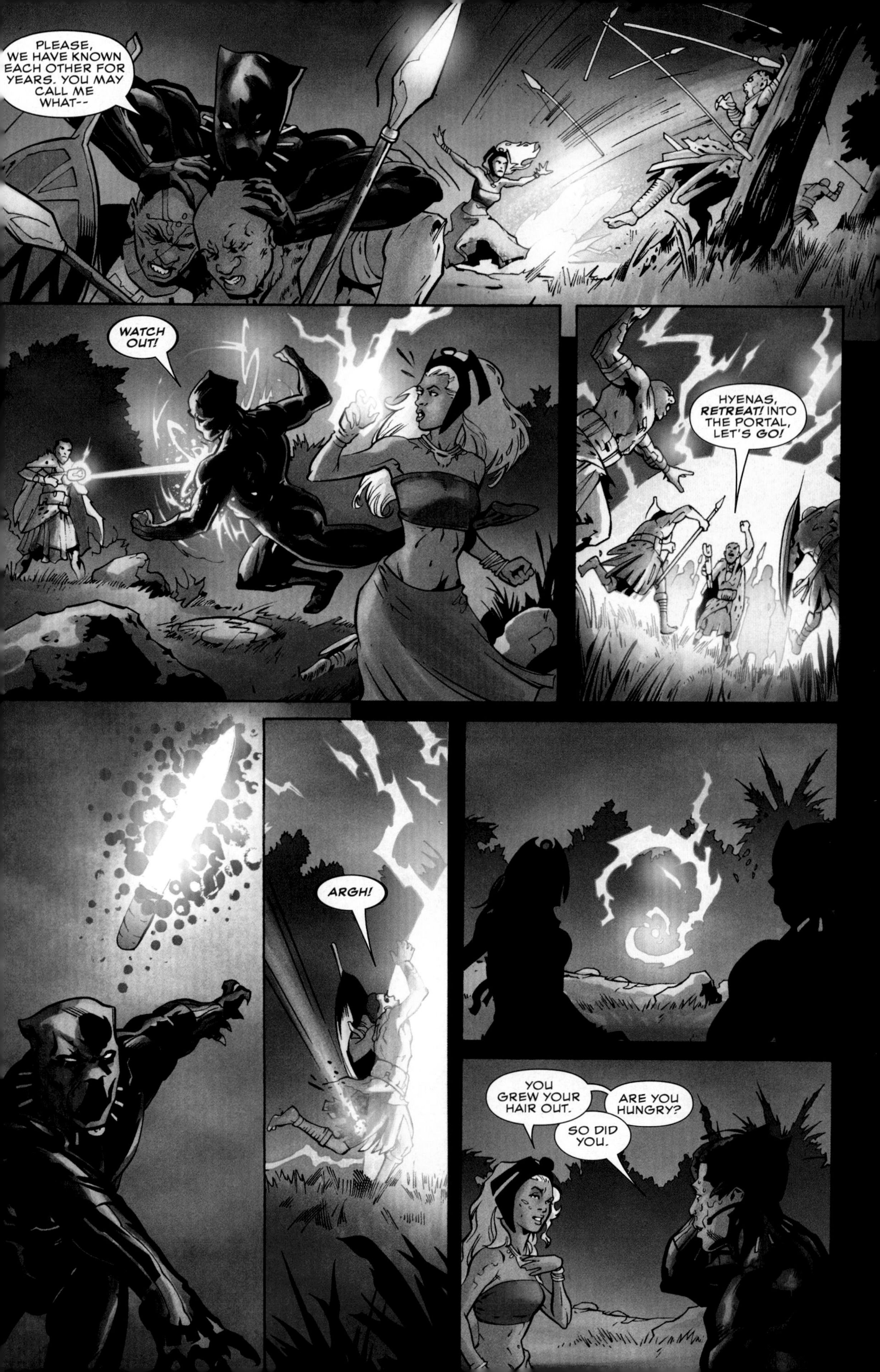
PLEASE, WE HAVE KNOWN EACH OTHER FOR YEARS. YOU MAY CALL ME WHAT--
WATCH OUT!
HYENAS, RETREAT! INTO THE PORTAL, LET'S GO!
ARGH!
YOU GREW YOUR HAIR OUT.
SO DID YOU.
ARE YOU HUNGRY?

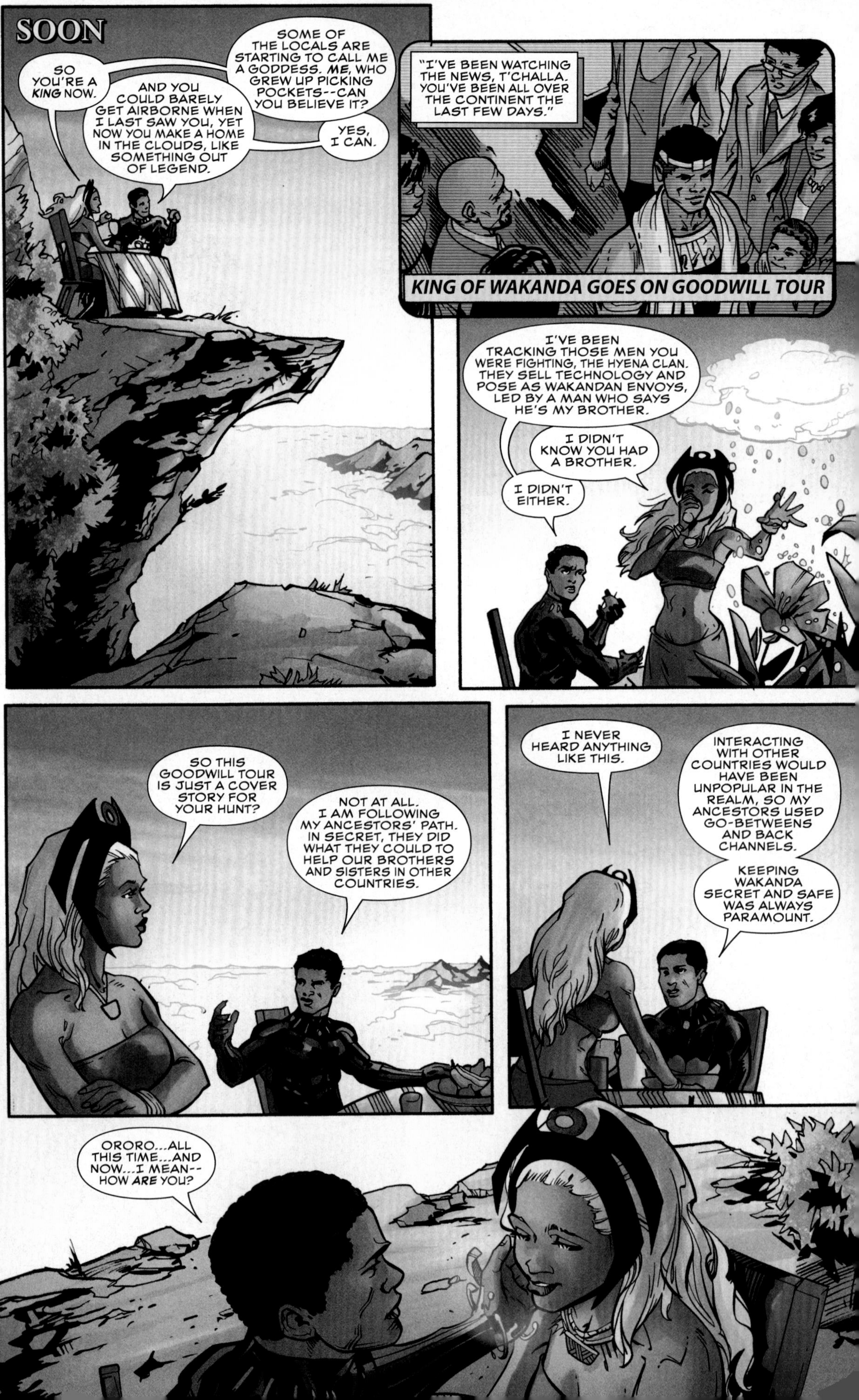
SOON
SO YOU'RE A KING NOW.
AND YOU COULD BARELY GET AIRBORNE WHEN I LAST SAW YOU, YET NOW YOU MAKE A HOME IN THE CLOUDS, LIKE SOMETHING OUT OF LEGEND.
SOME OF THE LOCALS ARE STARTING TO CALL ME A GODDESS. ME, WHO GREW UP PICKING POCKETS--CAN YOU BELIEVE IT?
YES, I CAN.
"I'VE BEEN WATCHING THE NEWS, T'CHALLA. YOU'VE BEEN ALL OVER THE CONTINENT THE LAST FEW DAYS."
KING OF WAKANDA GOES ON GOODWILL TOUR
I'VE BEEN TRACKING THOSE MEN YOU WERE FIGHTING, THE HYENA CLAN. THEY SELL TECHNOLOGY AND POSE AS WAKANDAN ENVOYS, LED BY A MAN WHO SAYS HE'S MY BROTHER.
I DIDN'T KNOW YOU HAD A BROTHER.
I DIDN'T EITHER.
SO THIS GOODWILL TOUR IS JUST A COVER STORY FOR YOUR HUNT?
NOT AT ALL. I AM FOLLOWING MY ANCESTORS' PATH. IN SECRET, THEY DID WHAT THEY COULD TO HELP OUR BROTHERS AND SISTERS IN OTHER COUNTRIES.
I NEVER HEARD ANYTHING LIKE THIS.
INTERACTING WITH OTHER COUNTRIES WOULD HAVE BEEN UNPOPULAR IN THE REALM, SO MY ANCESTORS USED GO-BETWEENS AND BACK CHANNELS.
KEEPING WAKANDA SECRET AND SAFE WAS ALWAYS PARAMOUNT.
ORORO...ALL THIS TIME...AND NOW...I MEAN--HOW ARE YOU?

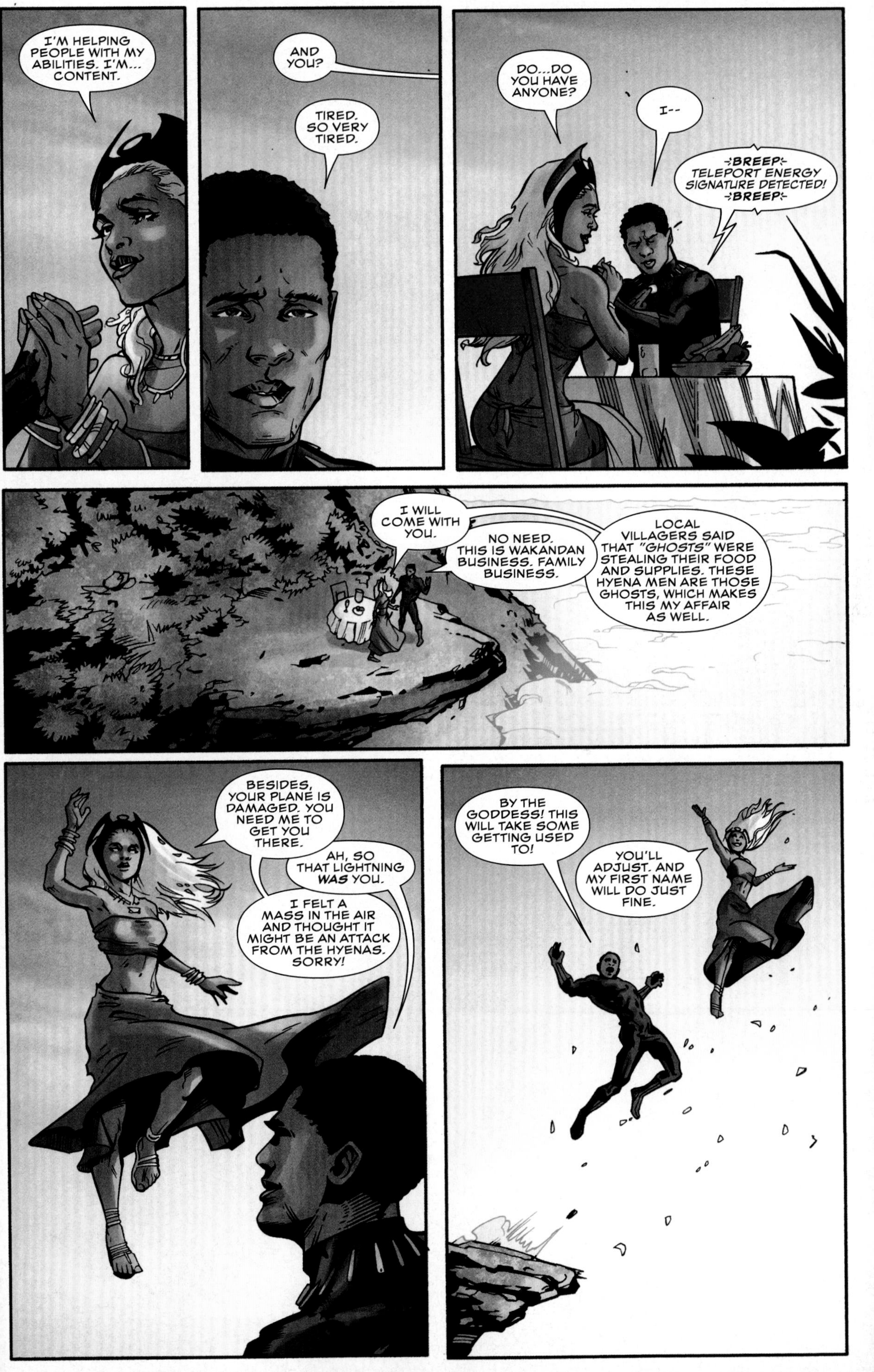

I'M HELPING PEOPLE WITH MY ABILITIES. I'M... CONTENT.
AND YOU?
TIRED. SO VERY TIRED.
DO...DO YOU HAVE ANYONE?
I--
BREEP TELEPORT ENERGY SIGNATURE DETECTED! BREEP
I WILL COME WITH YOU.
NO NEED. THIS IS WAKANDAN BUSINESS. FAMILY BUSINESS.
LOCAL VILLAGERS SAID THAT "GHOSTS" WERE STEALING THEIR FOOD AND SUPPLIES. THESE HYENA MEN ARE THOSE GHOSTS, WHICH MAKES THIS MY AFFAIR AS WELL.
BESIDES, YOUR PLANE IS DAMAGED. YOU NEED ME TO GET YOU THERE.
AH, SO THAT LIGHTNING WAS YOU.
I FELT A MASS IN THE AIR AND THOUGHT IT MIGHT BE AN ATTACK FROM THE HYENAS. SORRY!
BY THE GODDESS! THIS WILL TAKE SOME GETTING USED TO!
YOU'LL ADJUST. AND MY FIRST NAME WILL DO JUST FINE.

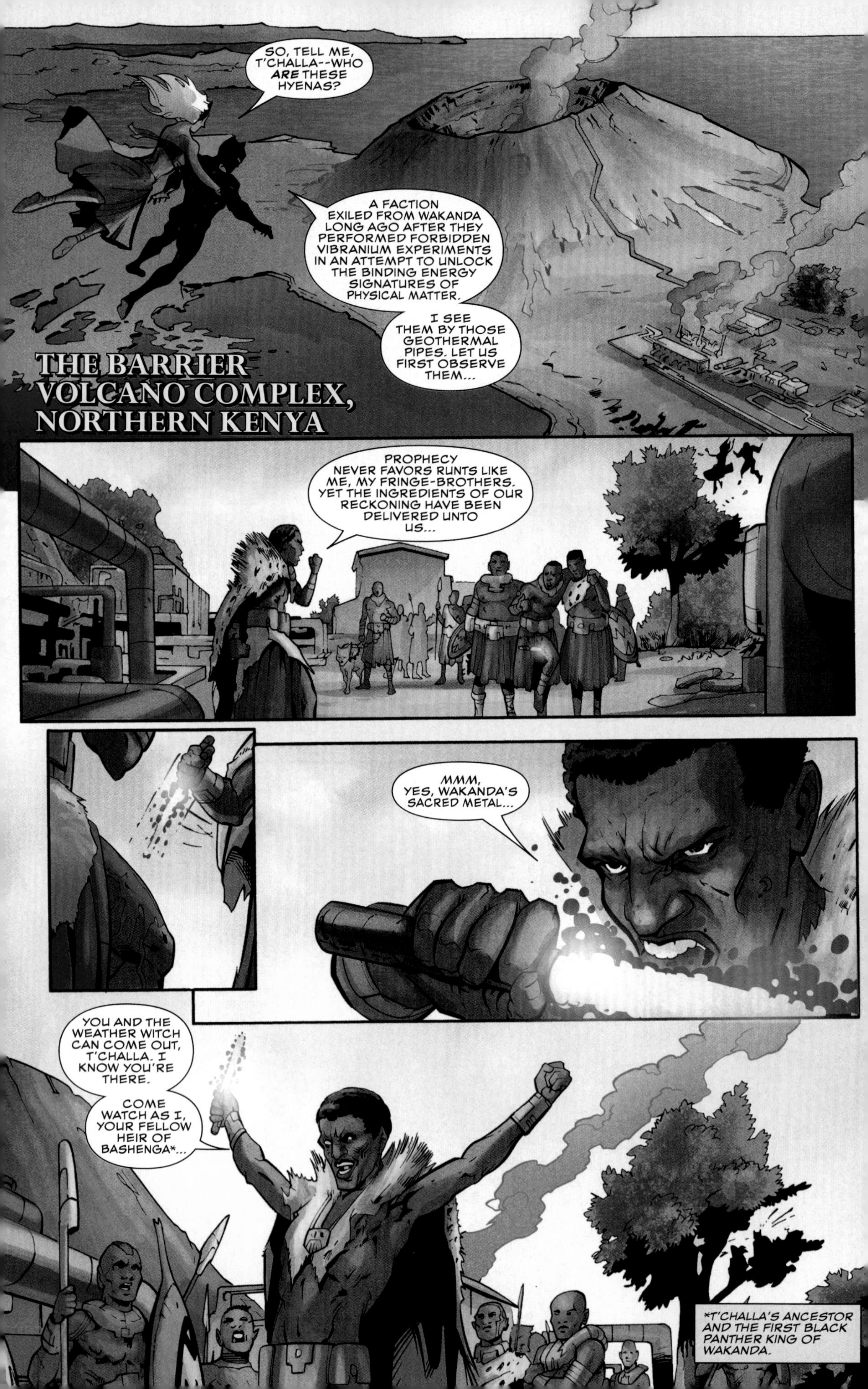
SO, TELL ME, T'CHALLA--WHO ARE THESE HYENAS?
A FACTION EXILED FROM WAKANDA LONG AGO AFTER THEY PERFORMED FORBIDDEN VIBRANIUM EXPERIMENTS IN AN ATTEMPT TO UNLOCK THE BINDING ENERGY SIGNATURES OF PHYSICAL MATTER.
I SEE THEM BY THOSE GEOTHERMAL PIPES. LET US FIRST OBSERVE THEM...
THE BARRIER VOLCANO COMPLEX, NORTHERN KENYA
PROPHECY NEVER FAVORS RUNTS LIKE ME, MY FRINGE-BROTHERS. YET THE INGREDIENTS OF OUR RECKONING HAVE BEEN DELIVERED UNTO US...
MMM, YES, WAKANDA'S SACRED METAL...
YOU AND THE WEATHER WITCH CAN COME OUT, T'CHALLA. I KNOW YOU'RE THERE.
COME WATCH AS I, YOUR FELLOW HEIR OF BASHENGA*...
*T'CHALLA'S ANCESTOR AND THE FIRST BLACK PANTHER KING OF WAKANDA.

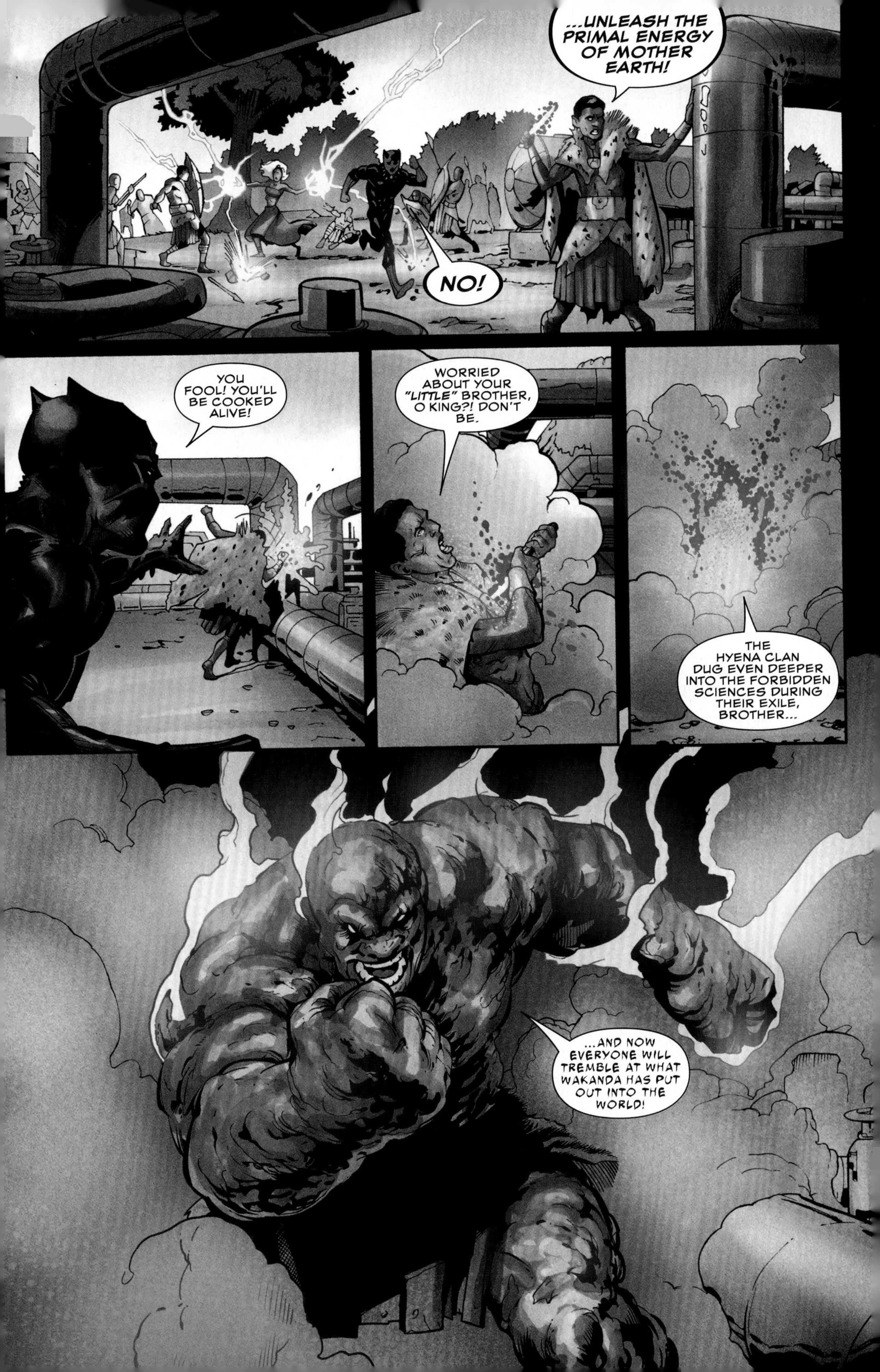
...UNLEASH THE PRIMAL ENERGY OF MOTHER EARTH!
NO!
YOU FOOL! YOU'LL BE COOKED ALIVE!
WORRIED ABOUT YOUR "LITTLE" BROTHER, O KING?! DON'T BE.
THE HYENA CLAN DUG EVEN DEEPER INTO THE FORBIDDEN SCIENCES DURING THEIR EXILE, BROTHER...
...AND NOW EVERYONE WILL TREMBLE AT WHAT WAKANDA HAS PUT OUT INTO THE WORLD!

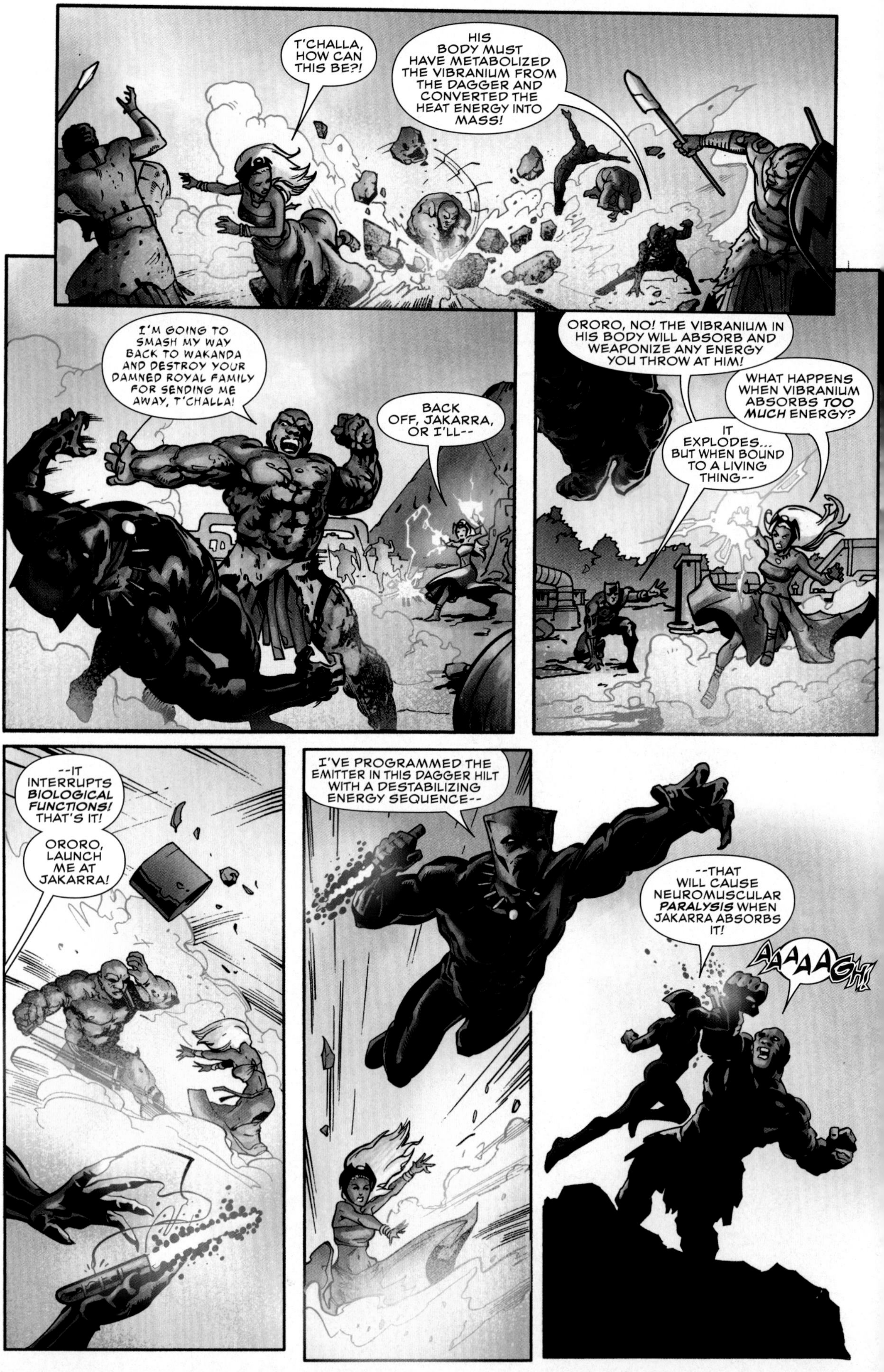
T'CHALLA, HOW CAN THIS BE?!
HIS BODY MUST HAVE METABOLIZED THE VIBRANIUM FROM THE DAGGER AND CONVERTED THE HEAT ENERGY INTO MASS!
I'M GOING TO SMASH MY WAY BACK TO WAKANDA AND DESTROY YOUR DAMNED ROYAL FAMILY FOR SENDING ME AWAY, T'CHALLA!
BACK OFF, JAKARRA, OR I'LL--
ORORO, NO! THE VIBRANIUM IN HIS BODY WILL ABSORB AND WEAPONIZE ANY ENERGY YOU THROW AT HIM!
WHAT HAPPENS WHEN VIBRANIUM ABSORBS *TOO MUCH* ENERGY?
IT EXPLODES... BUT WHEN BOUND TO A LIVING THING--
--IT INTERRUPTS *BIOLOGICAL FUNCTIONS!* THAT'S IT!
ORORO, LAUNCH ME AT JAKARRA!
I'VE PROGRAMMED THE EMITTER IN THIS DAGGER HILT WITH A DESTABILIZING ENERGY SEQUENCE--
--THAT WILL CAUSE NEUROMUSCULAR *PARALYSIS* WHEN JAKARRA ABSORBS IT!
AAAAAGH!

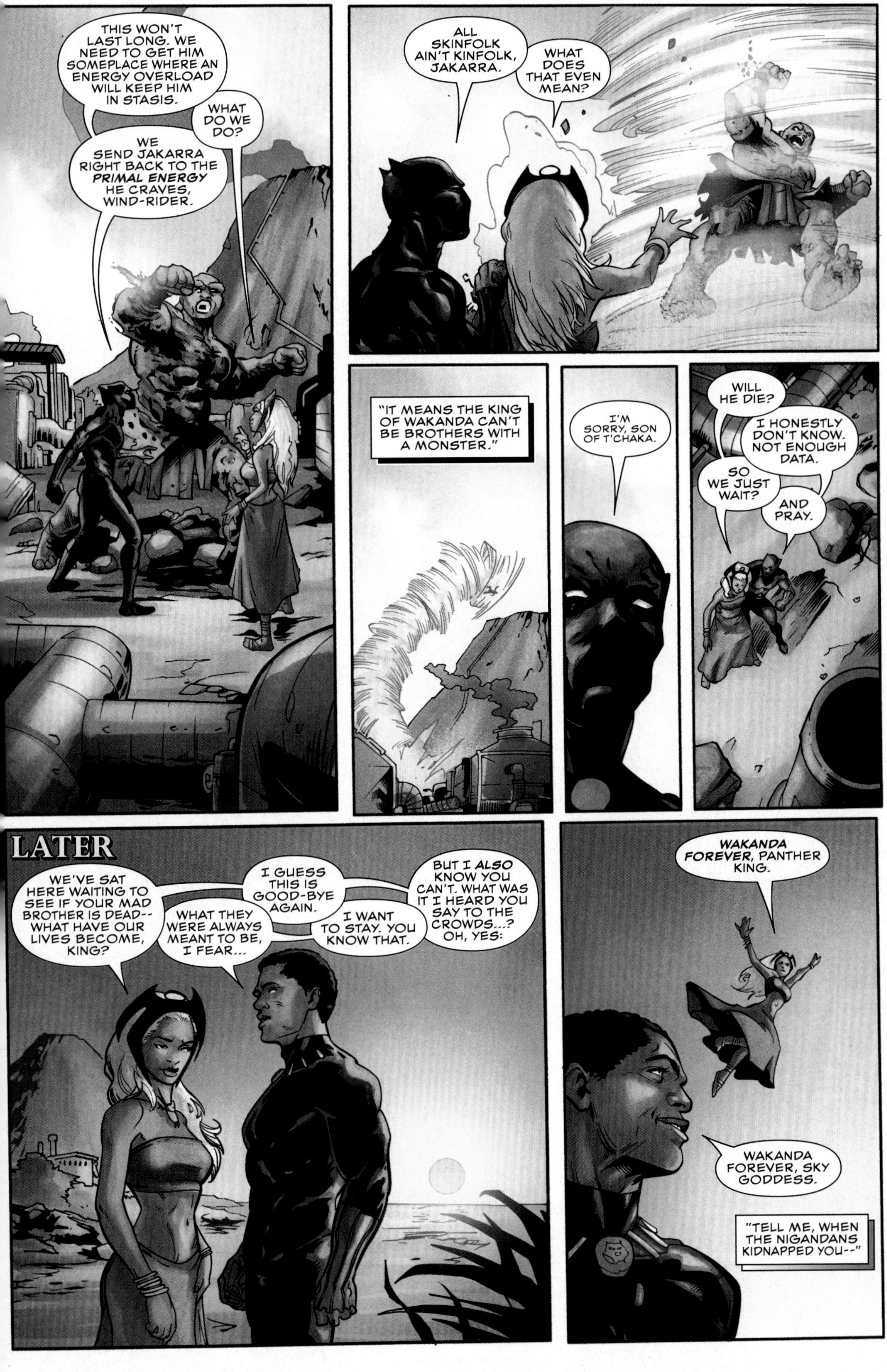
THIS WON'T LAST LONG. WE NEED TO GET HIM SOMEPLACE WHERE AN ENERGY OVERLOAD WILL KEEP HIM IN STASIS.
WHAT DO WE DO?
WE SEND JAKARRA RIGHT BACK TO THE PRIMAL ENERGY HE CRAVES, WIND-RIDER.
ALL SKINFOLK AIN'T KINFOLK, JAKARRA.
WHAT DOES THAT EVEN MEAN?
"IT MEANS THE KING OF WAKANDA CAN'T BE BROTHERS WITH A MONSTER."
I'M SORRY, SON OF T'CHAKA.
WILL HE DIE?
I HONESTLY DON'T KNOW. NOT ENOUGH DATA.
SO WE JUST WAIT?
AND PRAY.
LATER
WE'VE SAT HERE WAITING TO SEE IF YOUR MAD BROTHER IS DEAD-- WHAT HAVE OUR LIVES BECOME, KING?
WHAT THEY WERE ALWAYS MEANT TO BE, I FEAR...
I GUESS THIS IS GOOD-BYE AGAIN.
I WANT TO STAY. YOU KNOW THAT.
BUT I ALSO KNOW YOU CAN'T. WHAT WAS IT I HEARD YOU SAY TO THE CROWDS...? OH, YES:
WAKANDA FOREVER, PANTHER KING.
WAKANDA FOREVER, SKY GODDESS.
"TELL ME, WHEN THE NIGANDANS KIDNAPPED YOU--"

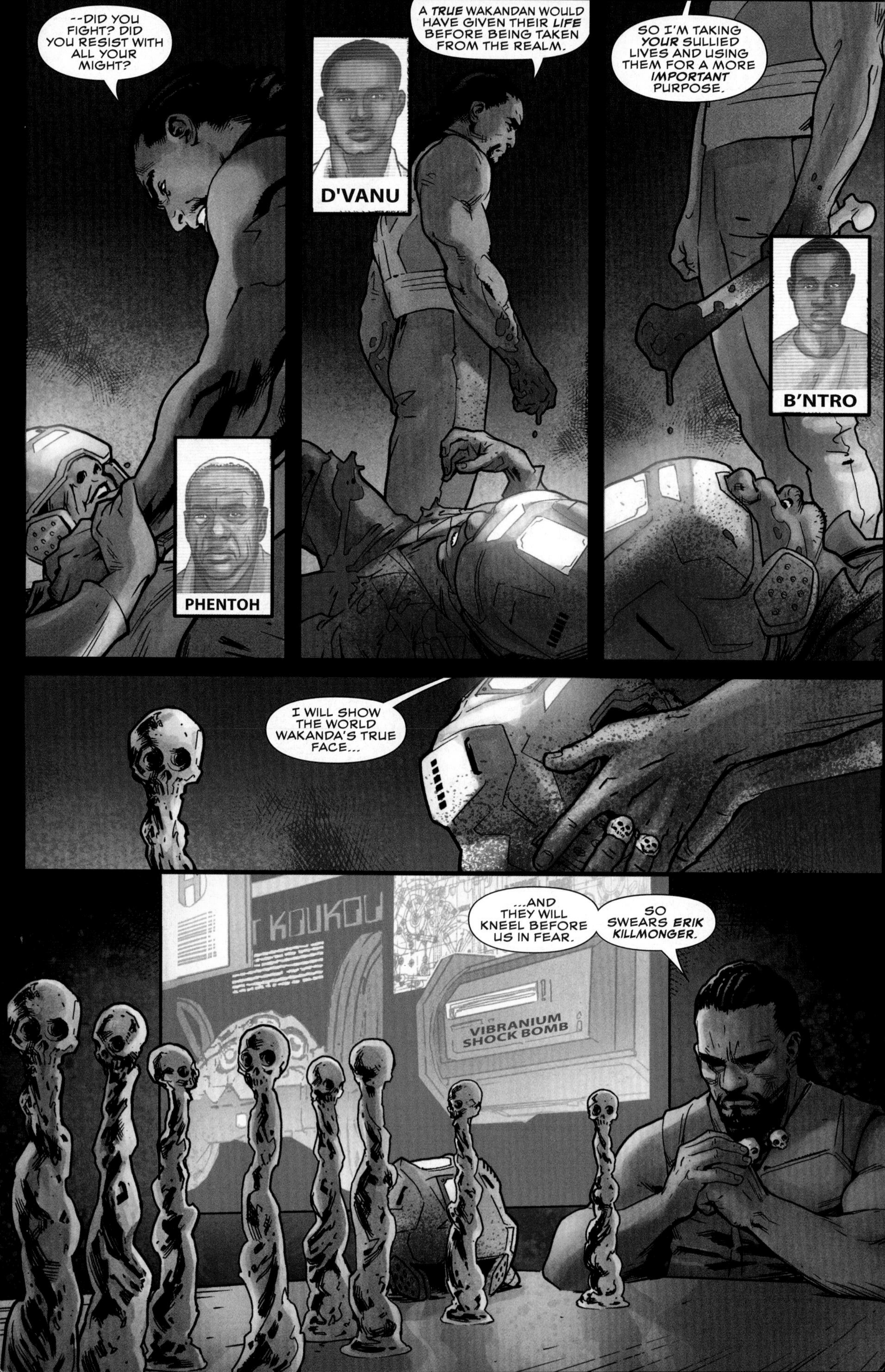
--DID YOU FIGHT? DID YOU RESIST WITH ALL YOUR MIGHT?
PHENTOH
A TRUE WAKANDAN WOULD HAVE GIVEN THEIR LIFE BEFORE BEING TAKEN FROM THE REALM.
D'VANU
SO I'M TAKING YOUR SULLIED LIVES AND USING THEM FOR A MORE IMPORTANT PURPOSE.
B'NTRO
I WILL SHOW THE WORLD WAKANDA'S TRUE FACE...
...AND THEY WILL KNEEL BEFORE US IN FEAR.
SO SWEARS ERIK KILLMONGER.
VIBRANIUM SHOCK BOMB

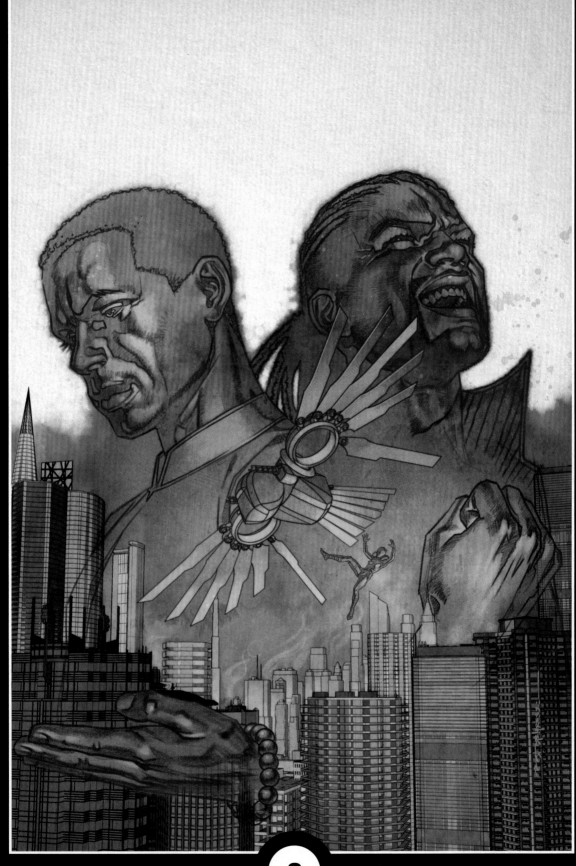

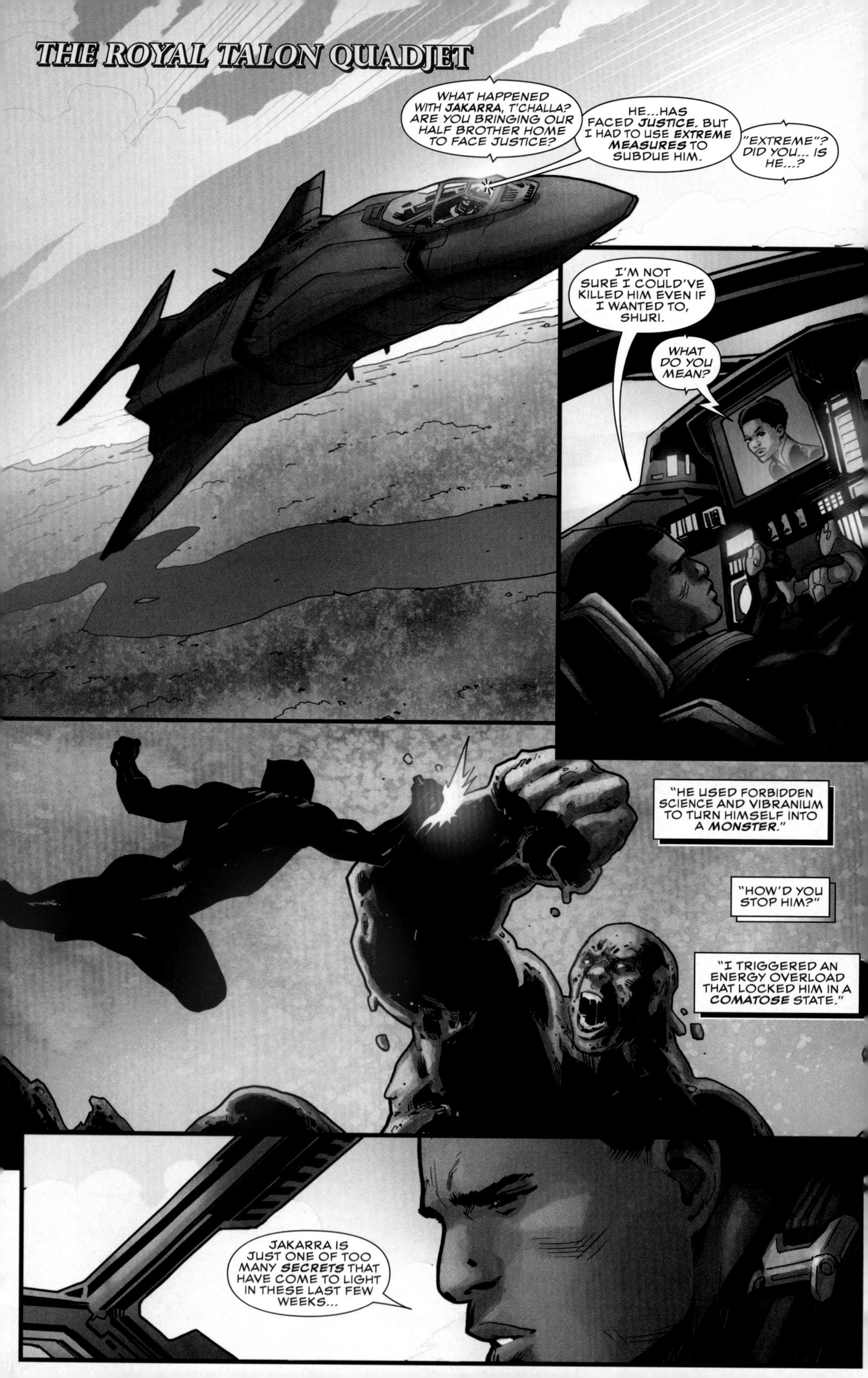
THE ROYAL TALON QUADJET
WHAT HAPPENED WITH JAKARRA, T'CHALLA? ARE YOU BRINGING OUR HALF BROTHER HOME TO FACE JUSTICE?
HE...HAS FACED JUSTICE. BUT I HAD TO USE EXTREME MEASURES TO SUBDUE HIM.
"EXTREME"? DID YOU... IS HE...?
I'M NOT SURE I COULD'VE KILLED HIM EVEN IF I WANTED TO, SHURI.
WHAT DO YOU MEAN?
"HE USED FORBIDDEN SCIENCE AND VIBRANIUM TO TURN HIMSELF INTO A MONSTER."
"HOW'D YOU STOP HIM?"
"I TRIGGERED AN ENERGY OVERLOAD THAT LOCKED HIM IN A COMATOSE STATE."
JAKARRA IS JUST ONE OF TOO MANY SECRETS THAT HAVE COME TO LIGHT IN THESE LAST FEW WEEKS...

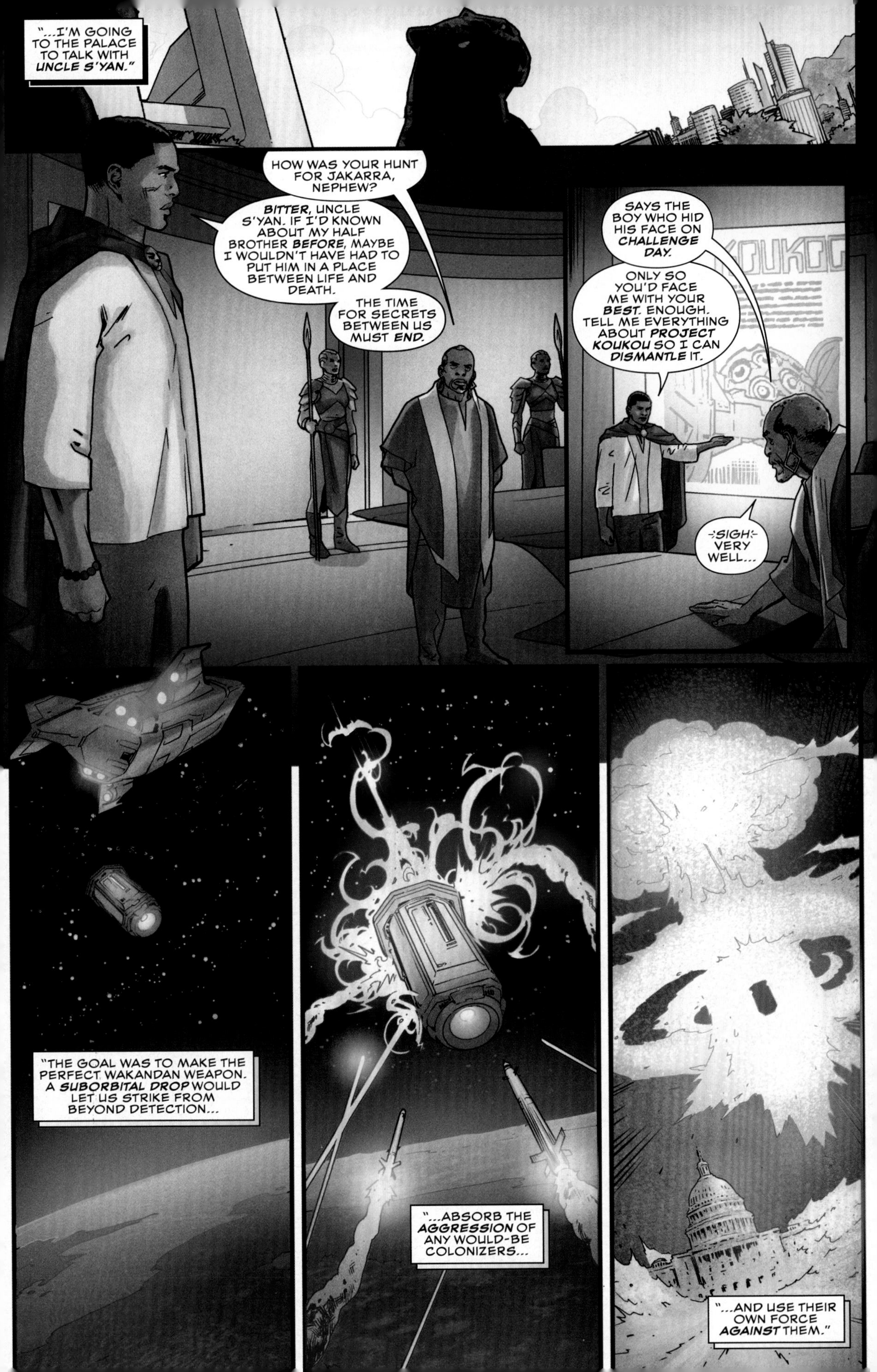
"...I'M GOING TO THE PALACE TO TALK WITH UNCLE S'YAN."
HOW WAS YOUR HUNT FOR JAKARRA, NEPHEW?
BITTER, UNCLE S'YAN. IF I'D KNOWN ABOUT MY HALF BROTHER BEFORE, MAYBE I WOULDN'T HAVE HAD TO PUT HIM IN A PLACE BETWEEN LIFE AND DEATH.
THE TIME FOR SECRETS BETWEEN US MUST END.
SAYS THE BOY WHO HID HIS FACE ON CHALLENGE DAY.
ONLY SO YOU'D FACE ME WITH YOUR BEST. ENOUGH. TELL ME EVERYTHING ABOUT PROJECT KOUKOU SO I CAN DISMANTLE IT.
-SIGH- VERY WELL...
"THE GOAL WAS TO MAKE THE PERFECT WAKANDAN WEAPON. A SUBORBITAL DROP WOULD LET US STRIKE FROM BEYOND DETECTION...
"...ABSORB THE AGGRESSION OF ANY WOULD-BE COLONIZERS...
"...AND USE THEIR OWN FORCE AGAINST THEM."

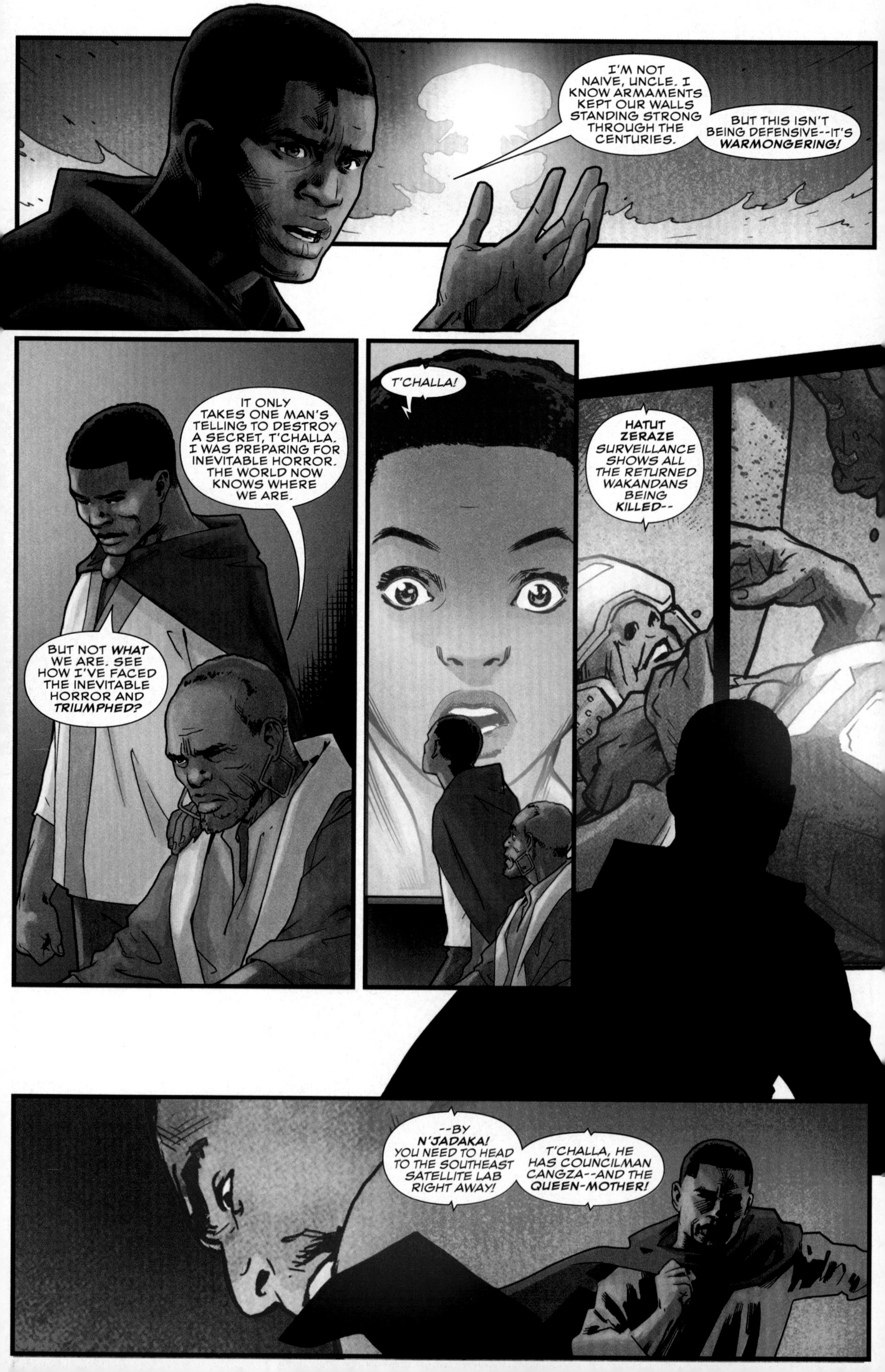
I'M NOT NAIVE, UNCLE. I KNOW ARMAMENTS KEPT OUR WALLS STANDING STRONG THROUGH THE CENTURIES.
BUT THIS ISN'T BEING DEFENSIVE--IT'S *WARMONGERING!*
IT ONLY TAKES ONE MAN'S TELLING TO DESTROY A SECRET, T'CHALLA. I WAS PREPARING FOR INEVITABLE HORROR. THE WORLD NOW KNOWS WHERE WE ARE.
BUT NOT *WHAT* WE ARE. SEE HOW I'VE FACED THE INEVITABLE HORROR AND *TRIUMPHED?*
T'CHALLA!
HATUT ZERAZE SURVEILLANCE SHOWS ALL THE RETURNED WAKANDANS BEING *KILLED--*
--BY *N'JADAKA!* YOU NEED TO HEAD TO THE SOUTHEAST SATELLITE LAB RIGHT AWAY!
T'CHALLA, HE HAS COUNCILMAN CANGZA--AND THE *QUEEN-MOTHER!*

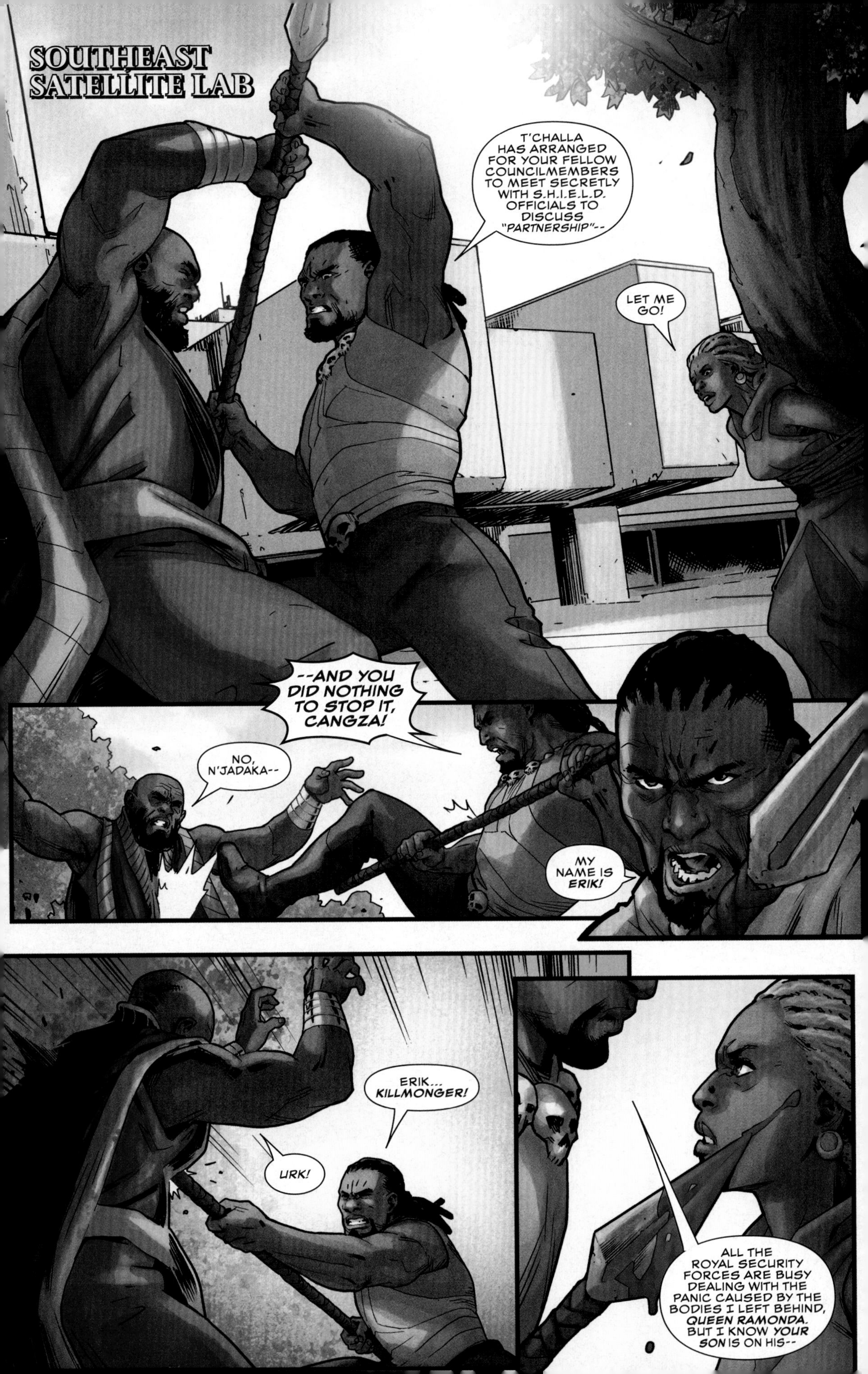
SOUTHEAST SATELLITE LAB
T'CHALLA HAS ARRANGED FOR YOUR FELLOW COUNCILMEMBERS TO MEET SECRETLY WITH S.H.I.E.L.D. OFFICIALS TO DISCUSS "PARTNERSHIP"--
LET ME GO!
--AND YOU DID NOTHING TO STOP IT, CANGZA!
NO, N'JADAKA--
MY NAME IS ERIK!
ERIK... KILLMONGER!
URK!
ALL THE ROYAL SECURITY FORCES ARE BUSY DEALING WITH THE PANIC CAUSED BY THE BODIES I LEFT BEHIND, QUEEN RAMONDA. BUT I KNOW YOUR SON IS ON HIS--

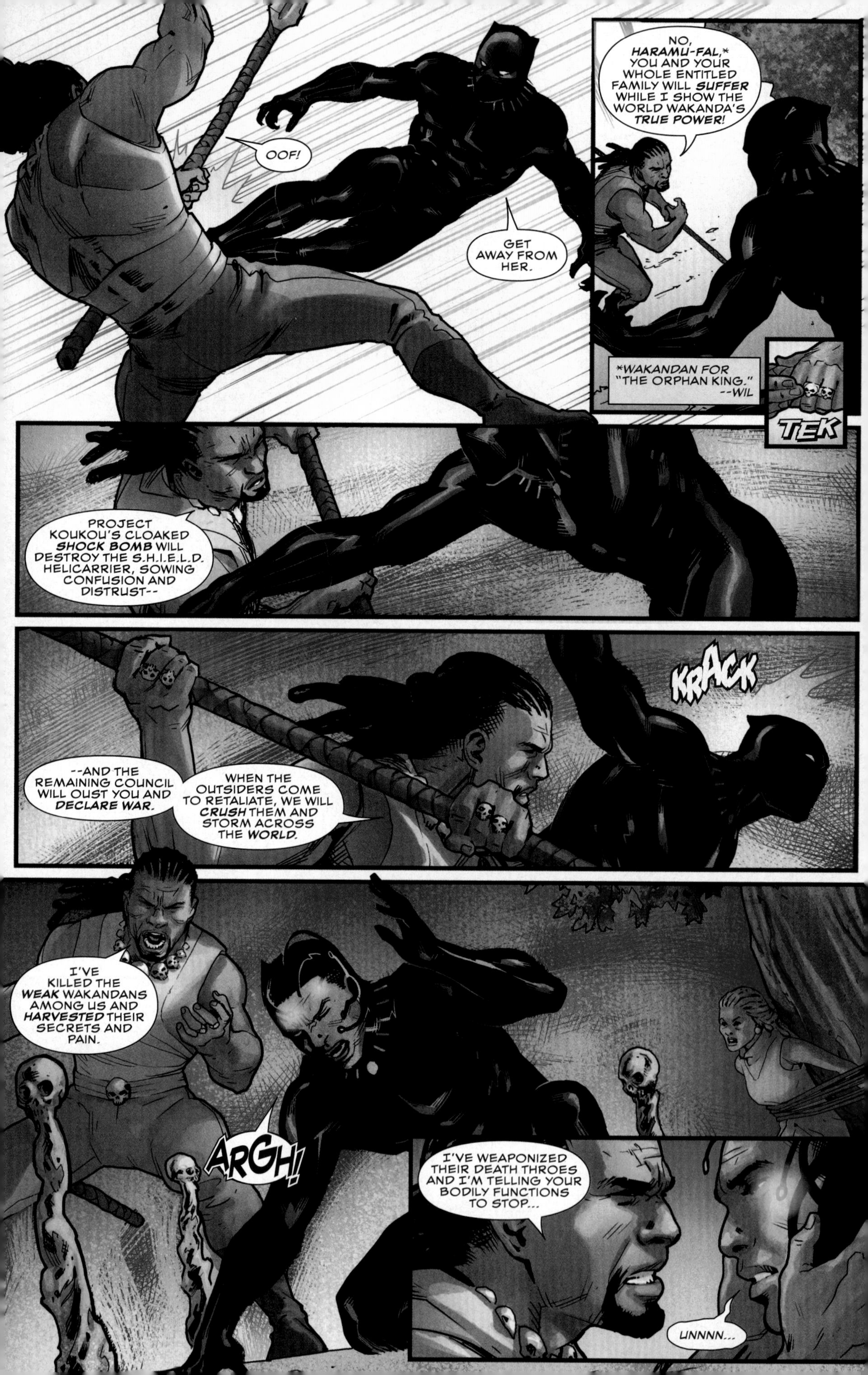
OOF!
GET AWAY FROM HER.
NO, HARAMU-FAL,* YOU AND YOUR WHOLE ENTITLED FAMILY WILL SUFFER WHILE I SHOW THE WORLD WAKANDA'S TRUE POWER!
*WAKANDAN FOR "THE ORPHAN KING." --WIL
TEK
PROJECT KOUKOU'S CLOAKED SHOCK BOMB WILL DESTROY THE S.H.I.E.L.D. HELICARRIER, SOWING CONFUSION AND DISTRUST--
KRACK
--AND THE REMAINING COUNCIL WILL OUST YOU AND DECLARE WAR.
WHEN THE OUTSIDERS COME TO RETALIATE, WE WILL CRUSH THEM AND STORM ACROSS THE WORLD.
I'VE KILLED THE WEAK WAKANDANS AMONG US AND HARVESTED THEIR SECRETS AND PAIN.
ARGH!
I'VE WEAPONIZED THEIR DEATH THROES AND I'M TELLING YOUR BODILY FUNCTIONS TO STOP...
UNNNN...

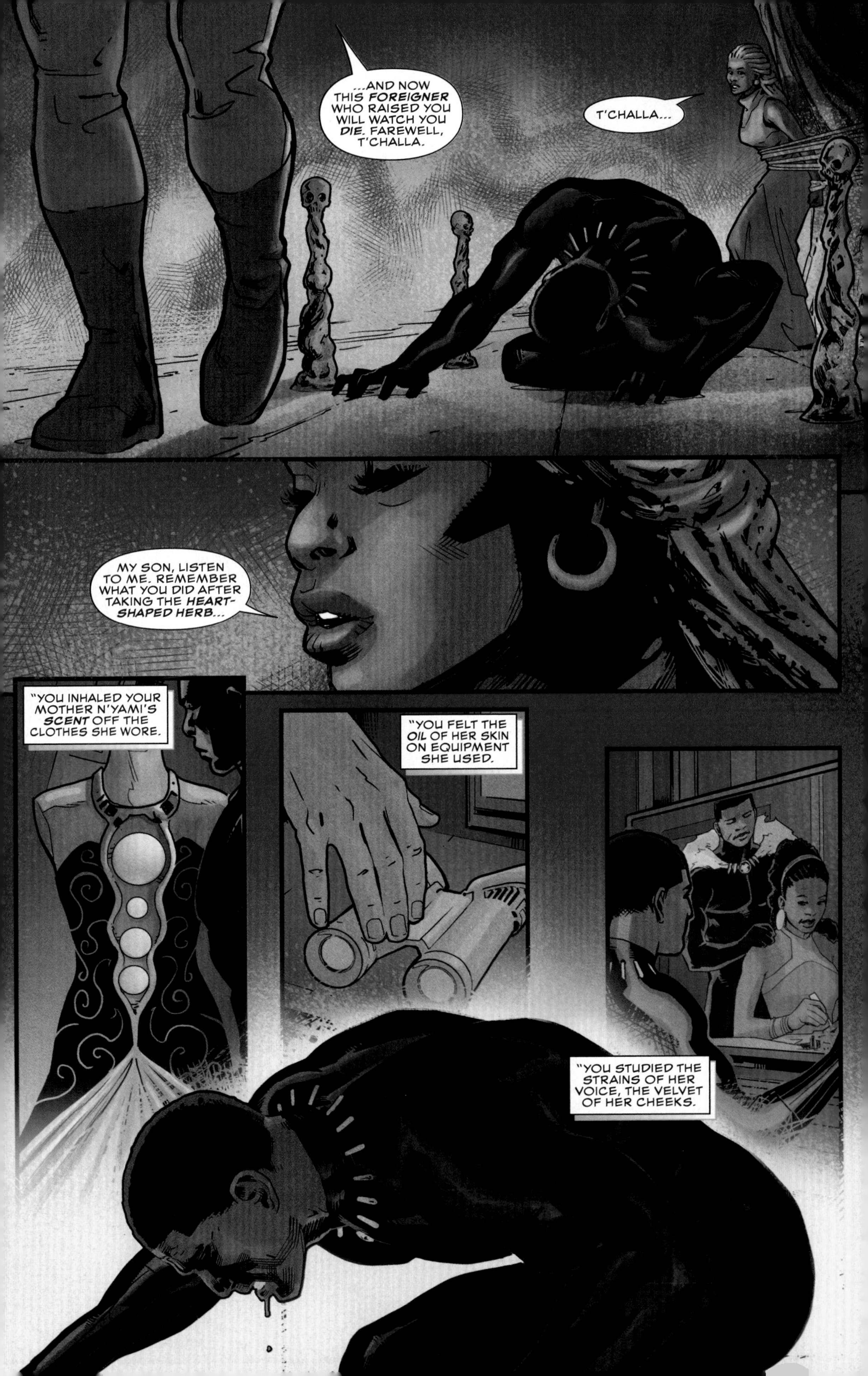
...AND NOW THIS FOREIGNER WHO RAISED YOU WILL WATCH YOU DIE. FAREWELL, T'CHALLA.
T'CHALLA...
MY SON, LISTEN TO ME. REMEMBER WHAT YOU DID AFTER TAKING THE HEART-SHAPED HERB...
"YOU INHALED YOUR MOTHER N'YAMI'S SCENT OFF THE CLOTHES SHE WORE.
"YOU FELT THE OIL OF HER SKIN ON EQUIPMENT SHE USED.
"YOU STUDIED THE STRAINS OF HER VOICE, THE VELVET OF HER CHEEKS.

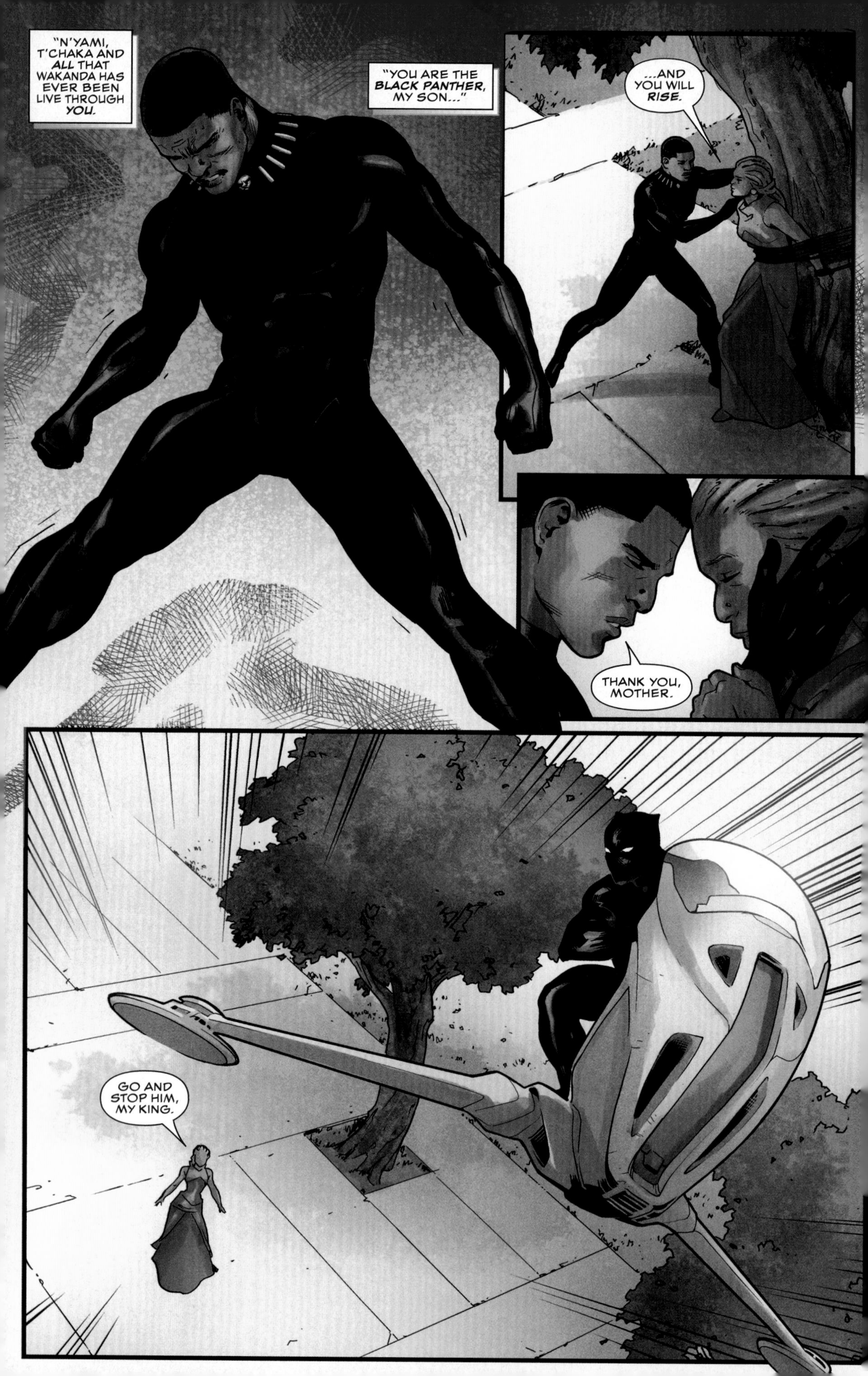
"N'YAMI, T'CHAKA AND ALL THAT WAKANDA HAS EVER BEEN LIVE THROUGH YOU.
"YOU ARE THE BLACK PANTHER, MY SON..."
...AND YOU WILL RISE.
THANK YOU, MOTHER.
GO AND STOP HIM, MY KING.

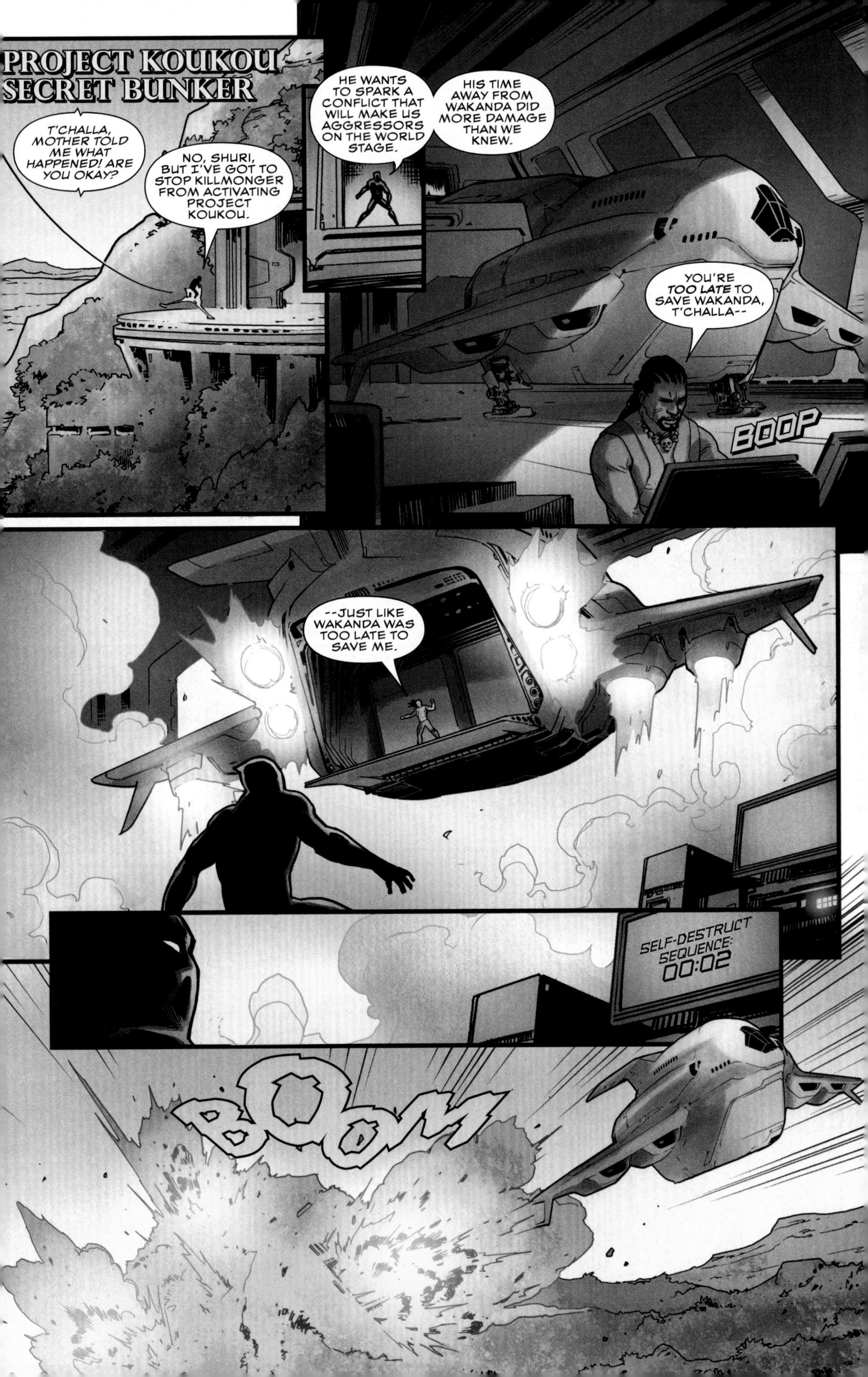
PROJECT KOUKOU SECRET BUNKER
T'CHALLA, MOTHER TOLD ME WHAT HAPPENED! ARE YOU OKAY?
NO, SHURI, BUT I'VE GOT TO STOP KILLMONGER FROM ACTIVATING PROJECT KOUKOU.
HE WANTS TO SPARK A CONFLICT THAT WILL MAKE US AGGRESSORS ON THE WORLD STAGE.
HIS TIME AWAY FROM WAKANDA DID MORE DAMAGE THAN WE KNEW.
YOU'RE TOO LATE TO SAVE WAKANDA, T'CHALLA--
BOOP
--JUST LIKE WAKANDA WAS TOO LATE TO SAVE ME.
SELF-DESTRUCT SEQUENCE: 00:02
BOOM

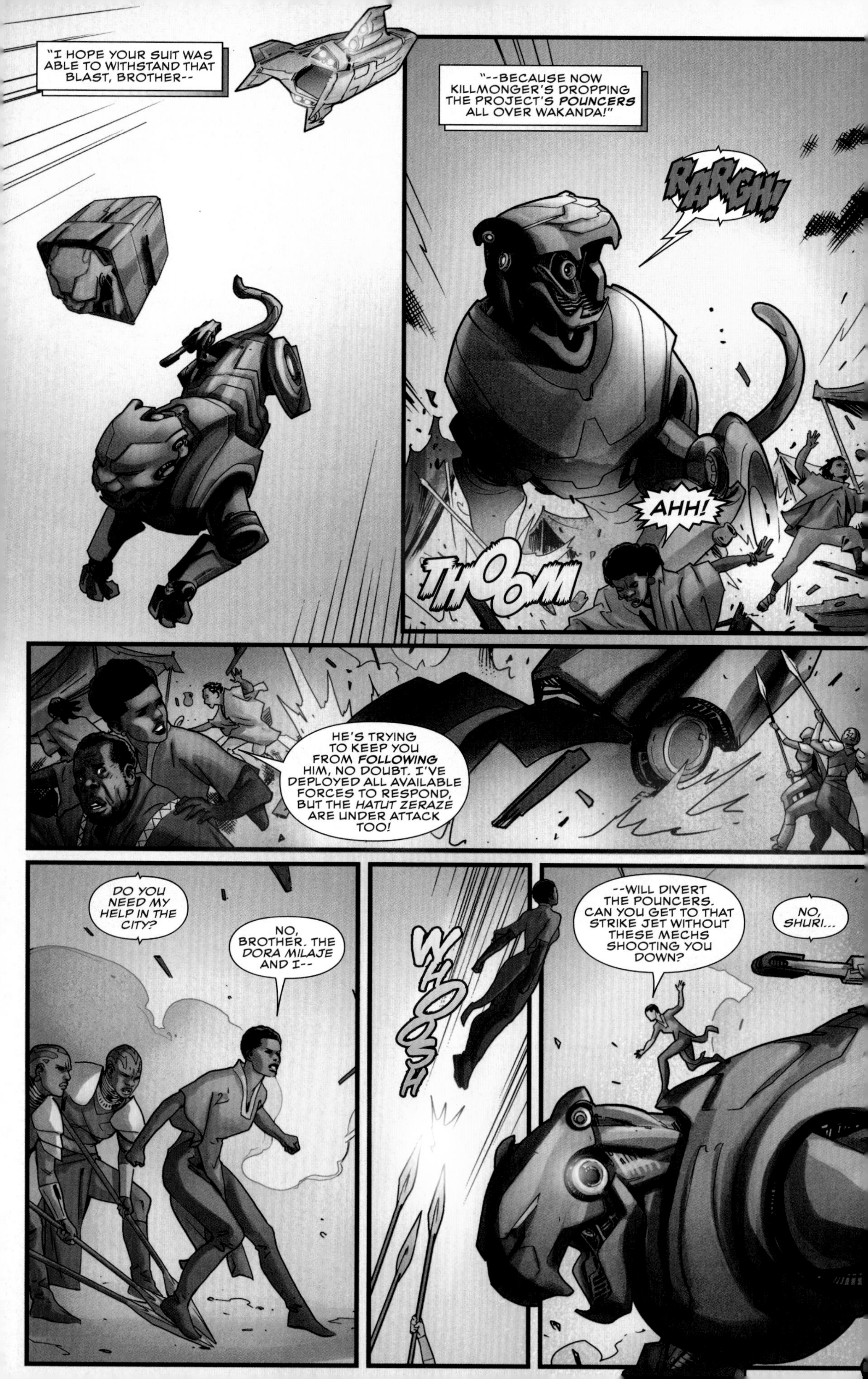
"I HOPE YOUR SUIT WAS ABLE TO WITHSTAND THAT BLAST, BROTHER--
"--BECAUSE NOW KILLMONGER'S DROPPING THE PROJECT'S POUNCERS ALL OVER WAKANDA!"
RARGH!
AHH!
THOOOM
HE'S TRYING TO KEEP YOU FROM FOLLOWING HIM, NO DOUBT. I'VE DEPLOYED ALL AVAILABLE FORCES TO RESPOND, BUT THE HATUT ZERAZE ARE UNDER ATTACK TOO!
DO YOU NEED MY HELP IN THE CITY?
NO, BROTHER. THE DORA MILAJE AND I--
WHOOSH
--WILL DIVERT THE POUNCERS. CAN YOU GET TO THAT STRIKE JET WITHOUT THESE MECHS SHOOTING YOU DOWN?
NO, SHURI...

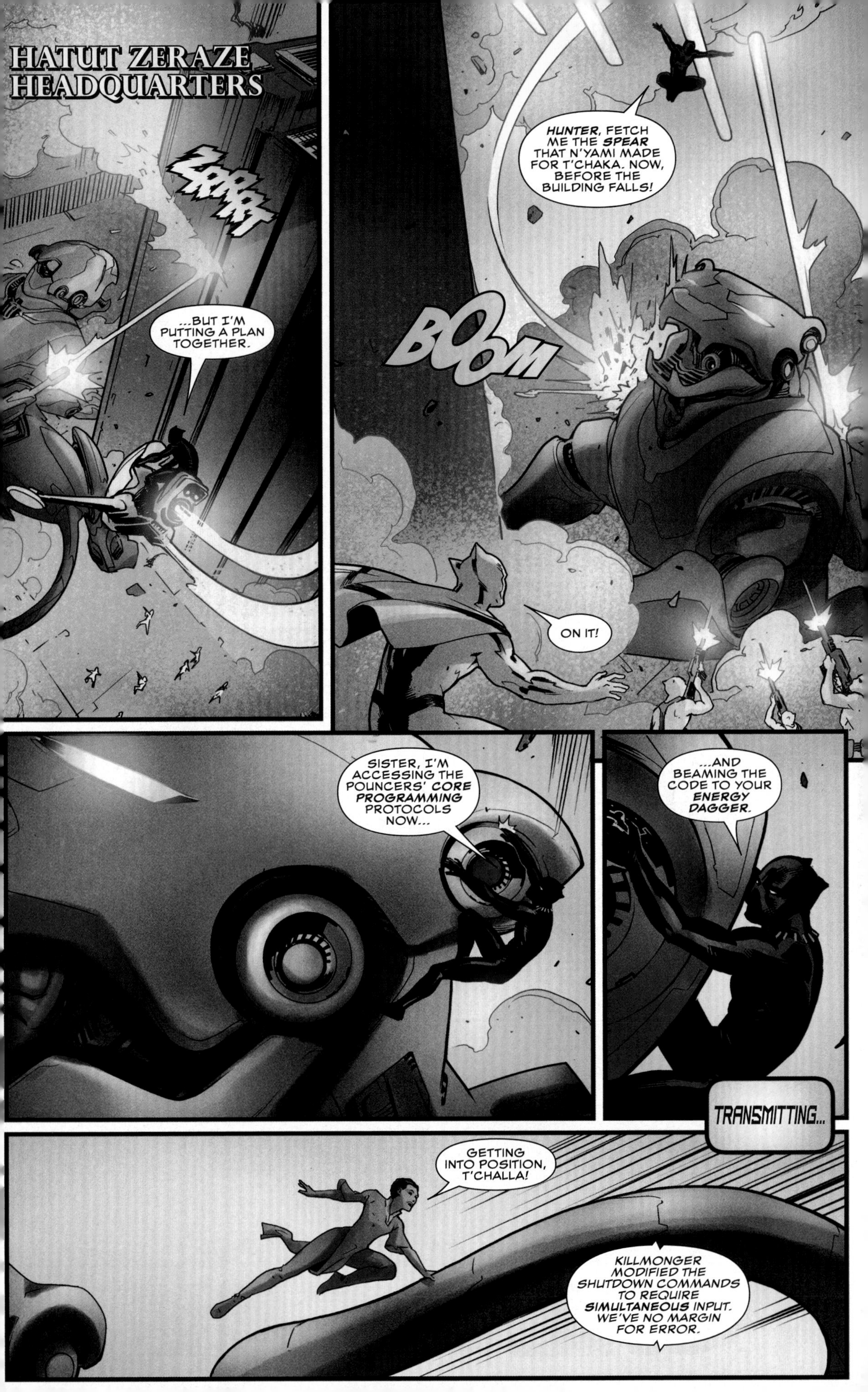
HATUT ZERAZE HEADQUARTERS
ZZRRRT
...BUT I'M PUTTING A PLAN TOGETHER.
HUNTER, FETCH ME THE SPEAR THAT N'YAMI MADE FOR T'CHAKA. NOW, BEFORE THE BUILDING FALLS!
BOOM
ON IT!
SISTER, I'M ACCESSING THE POUNCERS' CORE PROGRAMMING PROTOCOLS NOW...
...AND BEAMING THE CODE TO YOUR ENERGY DAGGER.
TRANSMITTING...
GETTING INTO POSITION, T'CHALLA!
KILLMONGER MODIFIED THE SHUTDOWN COMMANDS TO REQUIRE SIMULTANEOUS INPUT. WE'VE NO MARGIN FOR ERROR.

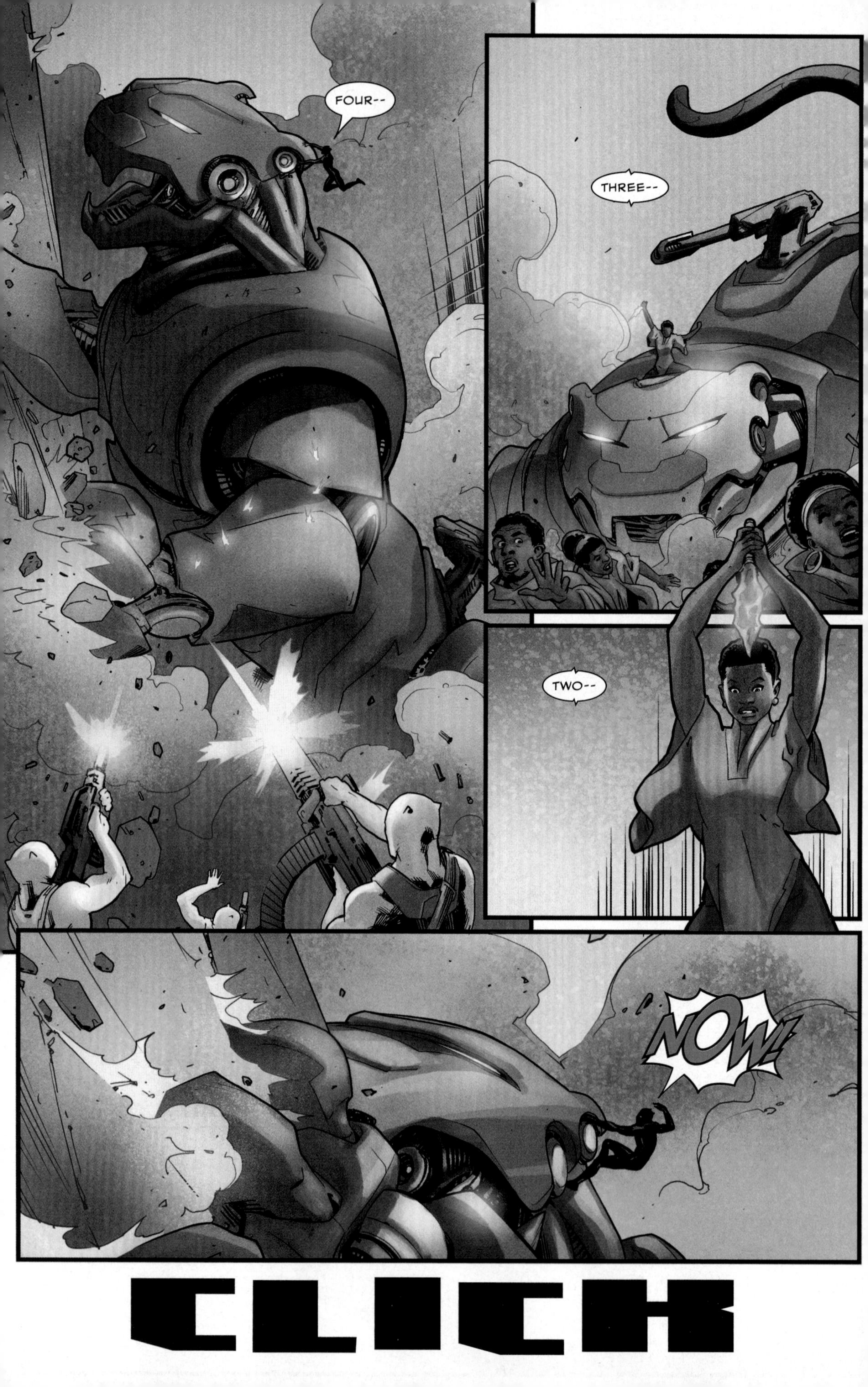
FOUR--
THREE--
TWO--
NOW!
CLICK

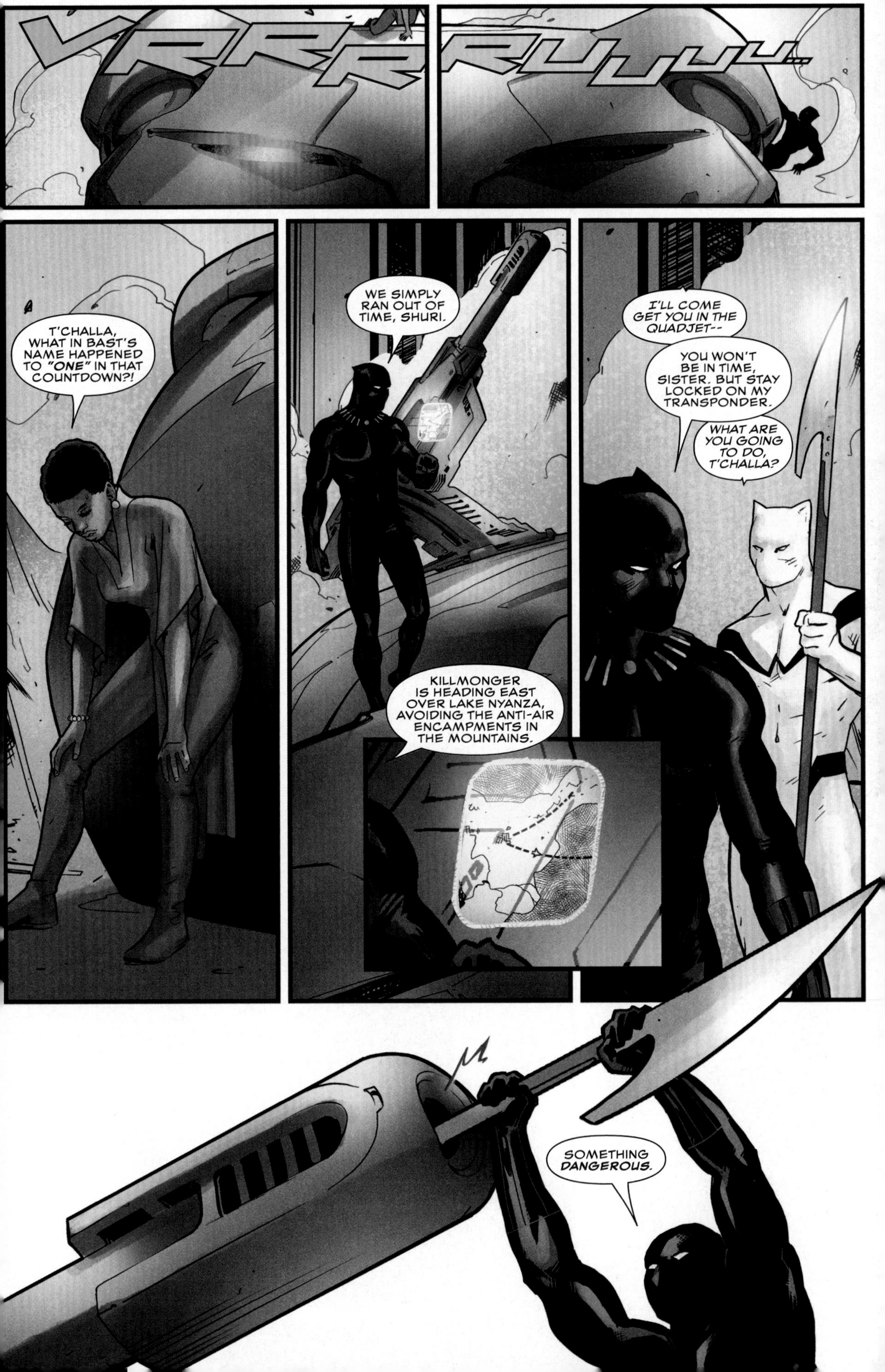
VRRRRUUUU...
T'CHALLA, WHAT IN BAST'S NAME HAPPENED TO "ONE" IN THAT COUNTDOWN?!
WE SIMPLY RAN OUT OF TIME, SHURI.
KILLMONGER IS HEADING EAST OVER LAKE NYANZA, AVOIDING THE ANTI-AIR ENCAMPMENTS IN THE MOUNTAINS.
I'LL COME GET YOU IN THE QUADJET--
YOU WON'T BE IN TIME, SISTER. BUT STAY LOCKED ON MY TRANSPONDER.
WHAT ARE YOU GOING TO DO, T'CHALLA?
SOMETHING DANGEROUS.

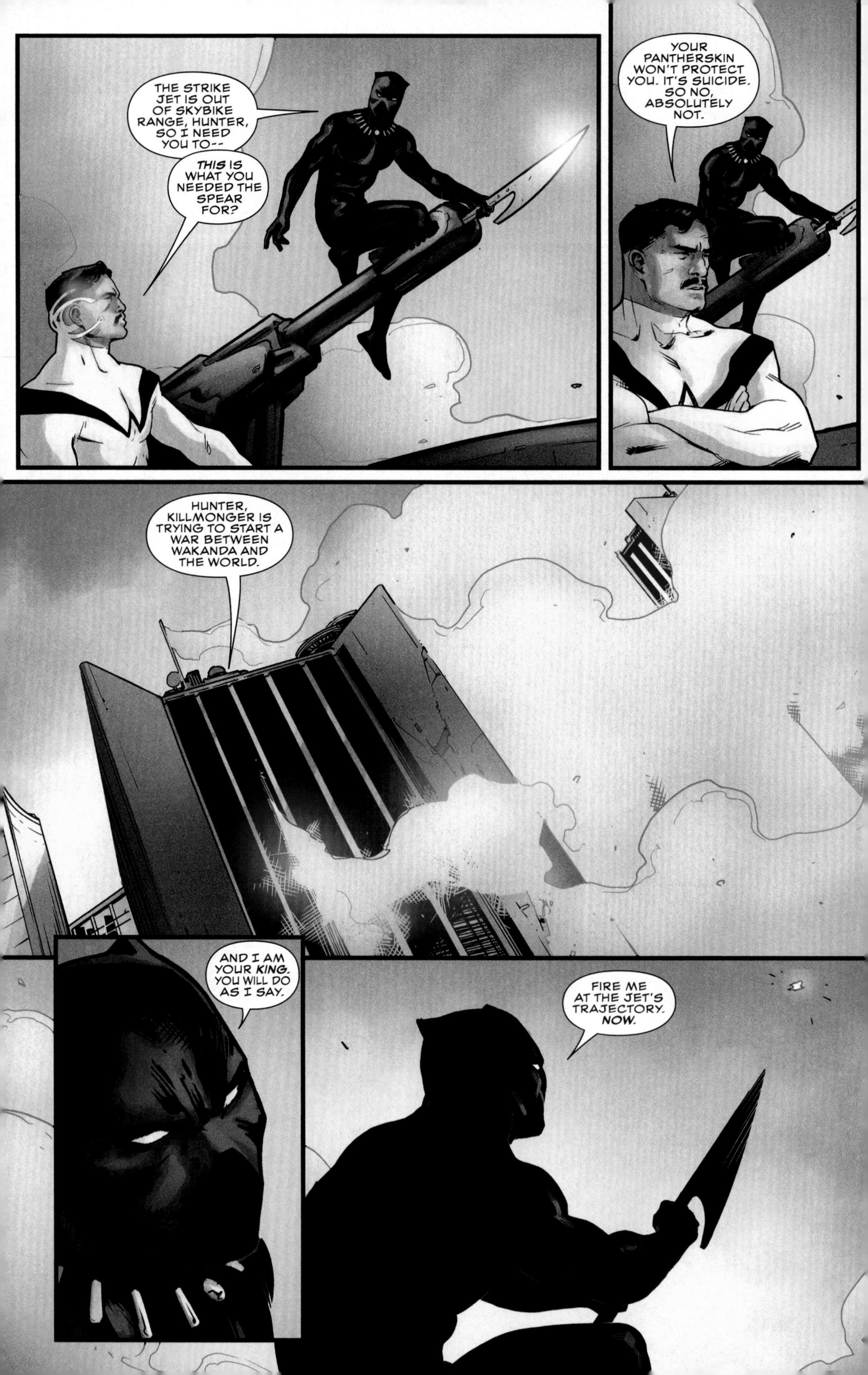
THE STRIKE JET IS OUT OF SKYBIKE RANGE, HUNTER, SO I NEED YOU TO--
THIS IS WHAT YOU NEEDED THE SPEAR FOR?
YOUR PANTHERSKIN WON'T PROTECT YOU. IT'S SUICIDE. SO NO, ABSOLUTELY NOT.
HUNTER, KILLMONGER IS TRYING TO START A WAR BETWEEN WAKANDA AND THE WORLD.
AND I AM YOUR KING. YOU WILL DO AS I SAY.
FIRE ME AT THE JET'S TRAJECTORY. NOW.

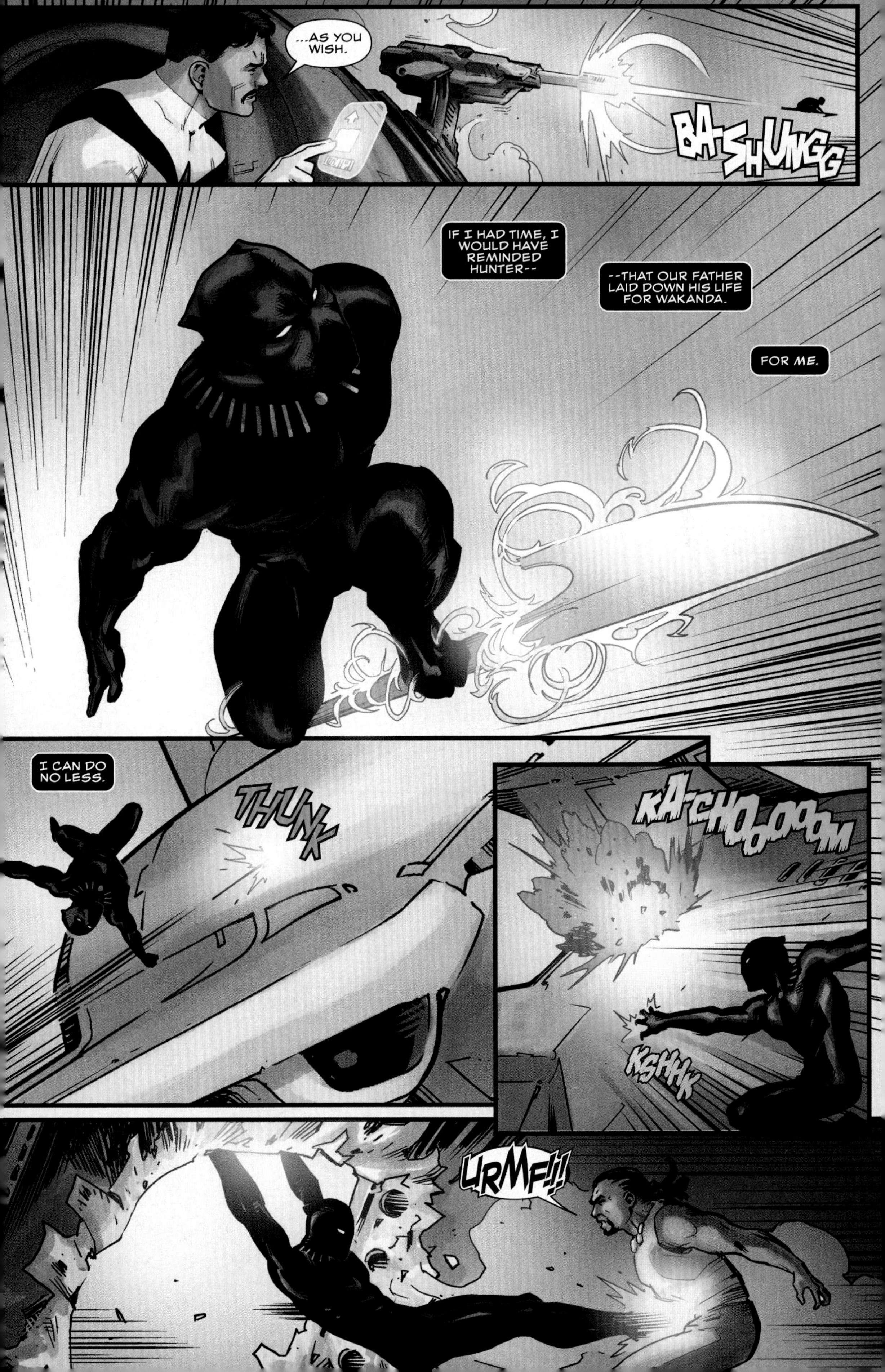
...AS YOU WISH.
BA-SHUNGG
IF I HAD TIME, I WOULD HAVE REMINDED HUNTER--
--THAT OUR FATHER LAID DOWN HIS LIFE FOR WAKANDA.
FOR ME.
I CAN DO NO LESS.
THUNK
KA-CHOOOOOM
KSHHK
URMF!!!

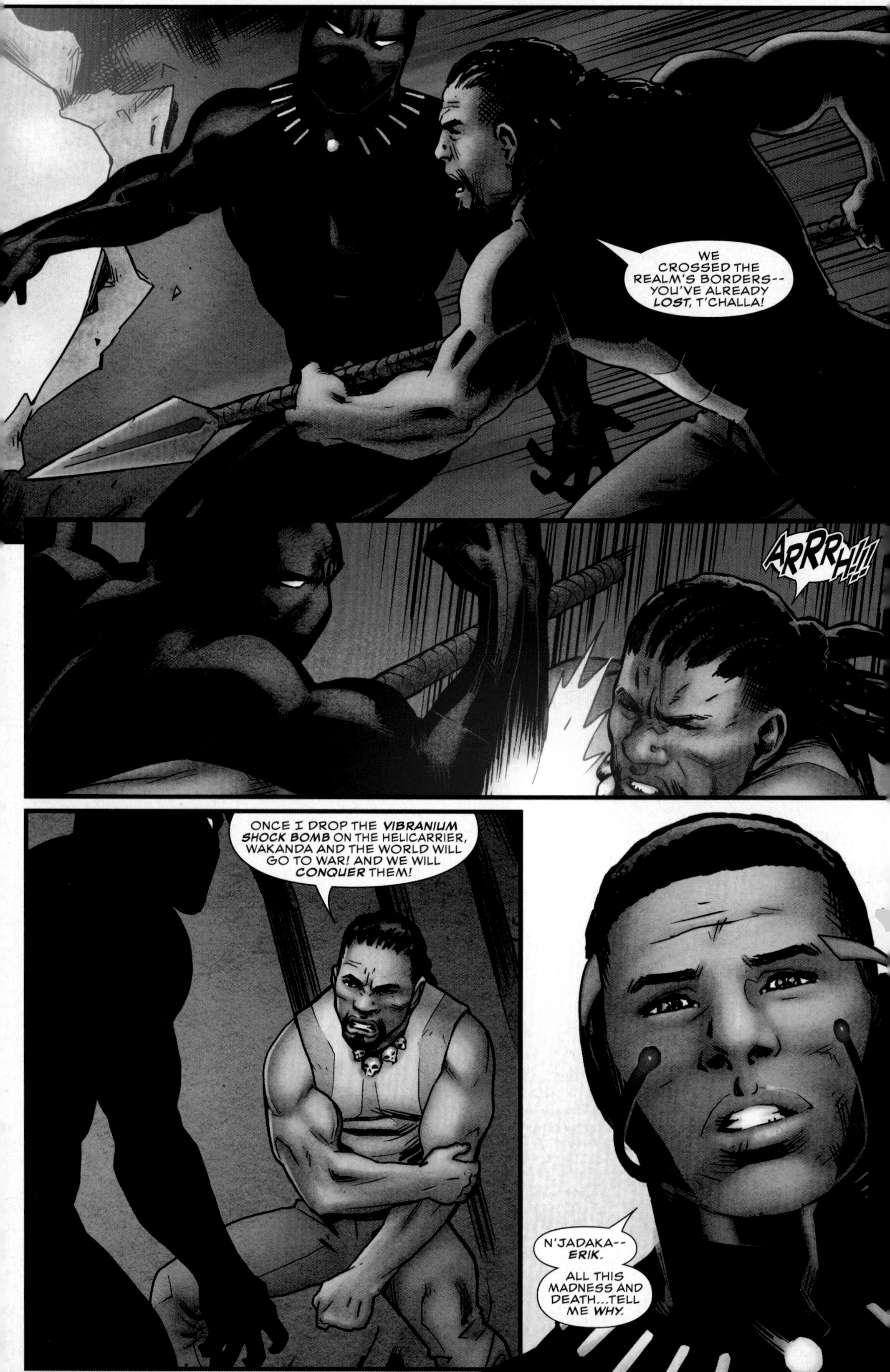
WE CROSSED THE REALM'S BORDERS--YOU'VE ALREADY LOST, T'CHALLA!
ARRRH!!!
ONCE I DROP THE VIBRANIUM SHOCK BOMB ON THE HELICARRIER, WAKANDA AND THE WORLD WILL GO TO WAR! AND WE WILL CONQUER THEM!
N'JADAKA--ERIK.
ALL THIS MADNESS AND DEATH...TELL ME WHY.

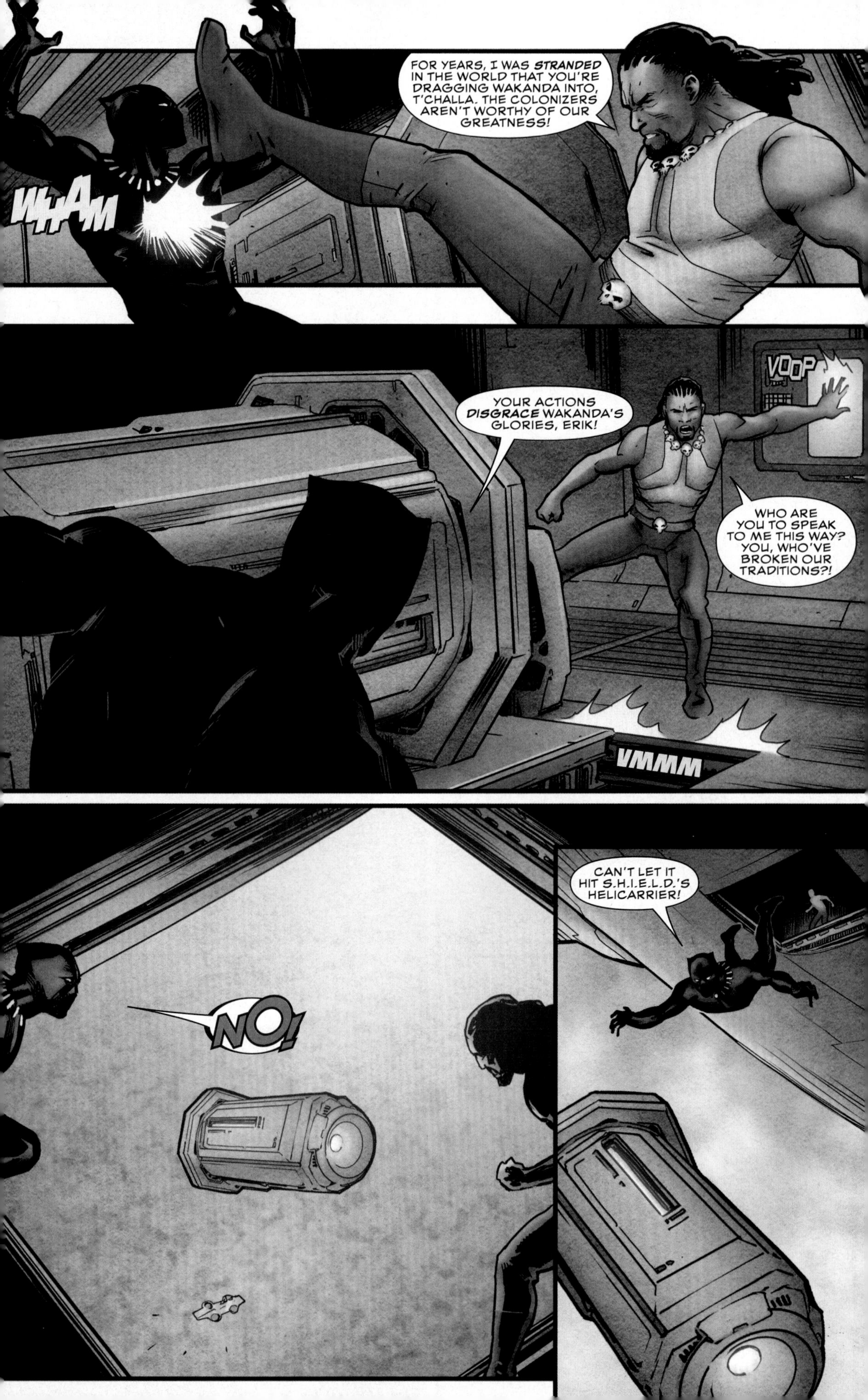
FOR YEARS, I WAS STRANDED IN THE WORLD THAT YOU'RE DRAGGING WAKANDA INTO, T'CHALLA. THE COLONIZERS AREN'T WORTHY OF OUR GREATNESS!
WHAM
VOOP
YOUR ACTIONS DISGRACE WAKANDA'S GLORIES, ERIK!
WHO ARE YOU TO SPEAK TO ME THIS WAY? YOU, WHO'VE BROKEN OUR TRADITIONS?!
VMMM
NO!
CAN'T LET IT HIT S.H.I.E.L.D.'S HELICARRIER!

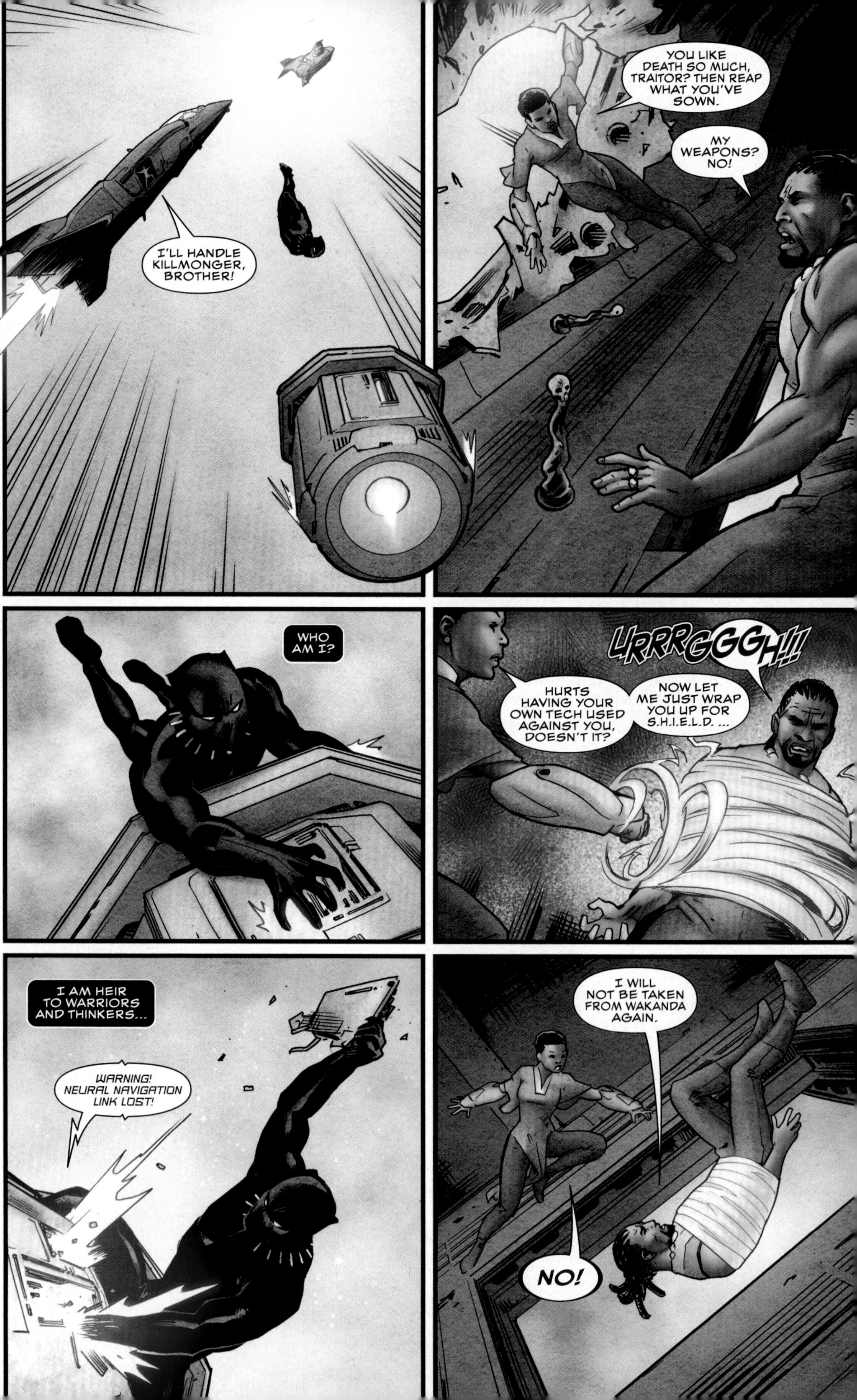
I'LL HANDLE KILLMONGER, BROTHER!
YOU LIKE DEATH SO MUCH, TRAITOR? THEN REAP WHAT YOU'VE SOWN.
MY WEAPONS? NO!
WHO AM I?
URRRGGGH!!!
HURTS HAVING YOUR OWN TECH USED AGAINST YOU, DOESN'T IT?
NOW LET ME JUST WRAP YOU UP FOR S.H.I.E.L.D. ...
I AM HEIR TO WARRIORS AND THINKERS...
WARNING! NEURAL NAVIGATION LINK LOST!
I WILL NOT BE TAKEN FROM WAKANDA AGAIN.
NO!

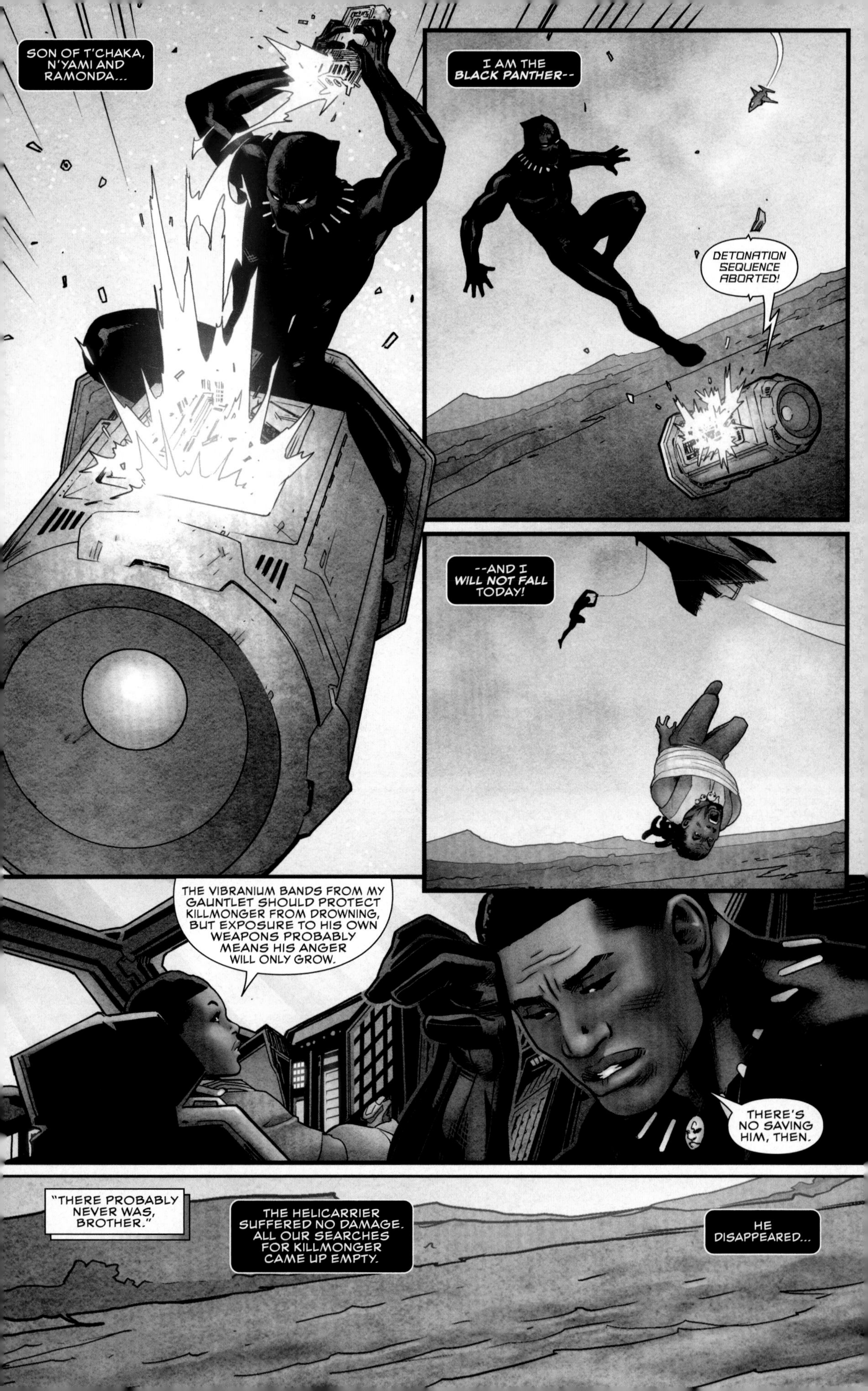
SON OF T'CHAKA, N'YAMI AND RAMONDA...
I AM THE BLACK PANTHER--
DETONATION SEQUENCE ABORTED!
--AND I WILL NOT FALL TODAY!
THE VIBRANIUM BANDS FROM MY GAUNTLET SHOULD PROTECT KILLMONGER FROM DROWNING, BUT EXPOSURE TO HIS OWN WEAPONS PROBABLY MEANS HIS ANGER WILL ONLY GROW.
THERE'S NO SAVING HIM, THEN.
"THERE PROBABLY NEVER WAS, BROTHER."
THE HELICARRIER SUFFERED NO DAMAGE. ALL OUR SEARCHES FOR KILLMONGER CAME UP EMPTY.
HE DISAPPEARED...

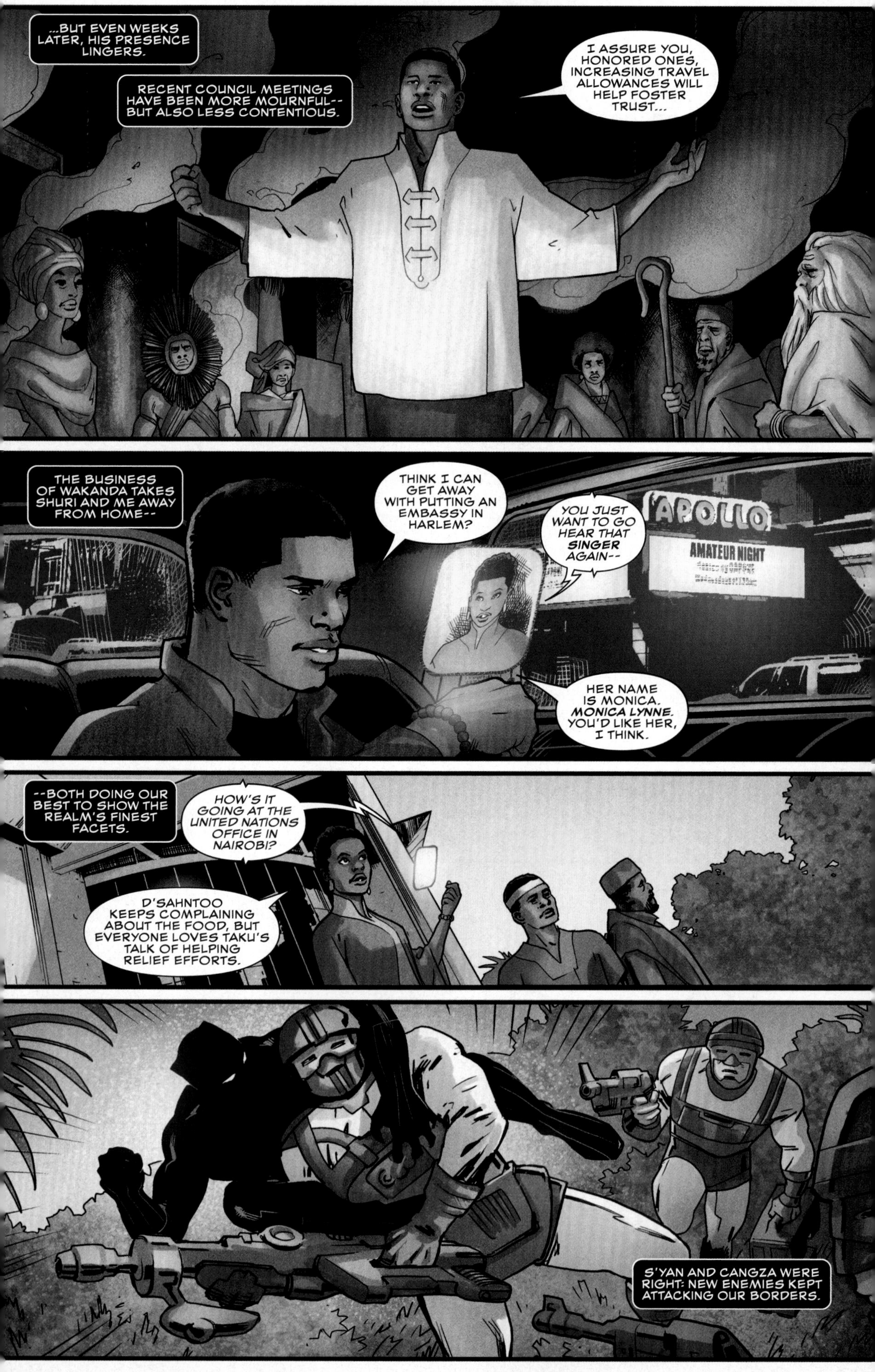
...BUT EVEN WEEKS LATER, HIS PRESENCE LINGERS.
RECENT COUNCIL MEETINGS HAVE BEEN MORE MOURNFUL-- BUT ALSO LESS CONTENTIOUS.
I ASSURE YOU, HONORED ONES, INCREASING TRAVEL ALLOWANCES WILL HELP FOSTER TRUST...
THE BUSINESS OF WAKANDA TAKES SHURI AND ME AWAY FROM HOME--
THINK I CAN GET AWAY WITH PUTTING AN EMBASSY IN HARLEM?
YOU JUST WANT TO GO HEAR THAT **SINGER** AGAIN--
APOLLO
AMATEUR NIGHT
HER NAME IS MONICA. ***MONICA LYNNE.*** YOU'D LIKE HER, I THINK.
--BOTH DOING OUR BEST TO SHOW THE REALM'S FINEST FACETS.
HOW'S IT GOING AT THE UNITED NATIONS OFFICE IN NAIROBI?
D'SAHNTOO KEEPS COMPLAINING ABOUT THE FOOD, BUT EVERYONE LOVES TAKU'S TALK OF HELPING RELIEF EFFORTS.
S'YAN AND CANGZA WERE RIGHT: NEW ENEMIES KEPT ATTACKING OUR BORDERS.

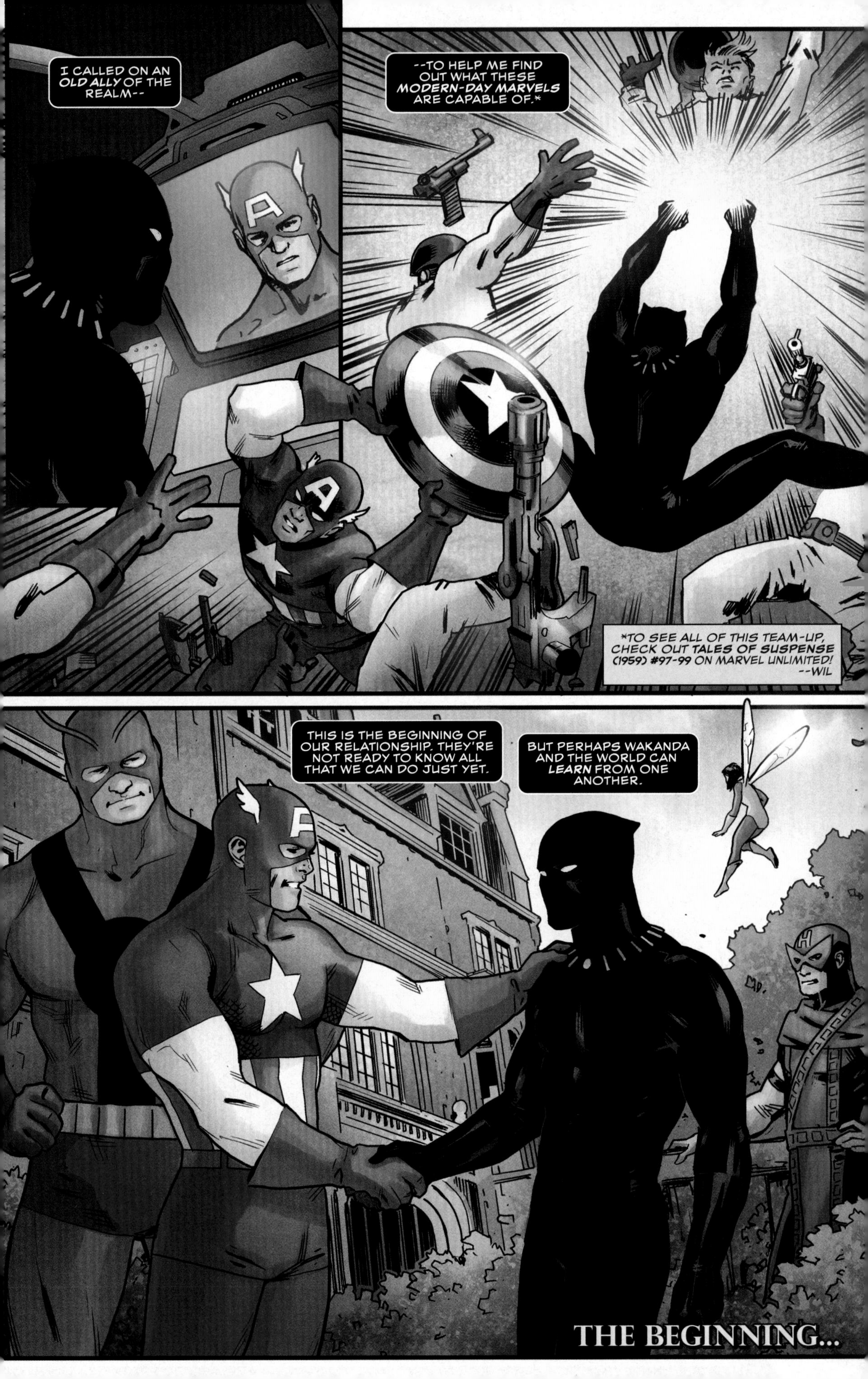
I CALLED ON AN OLD ALLY OF THE REALM--
--TO HELP ME FIND OUT WHAT THESE MODERN-DAY MARVELS ARE CAPABLE OF.*
*TO SEE ALL OF THIS TEAM-UP, CHECK OUT TALES OF SUSPENSE (1959) #97-99 ON MARVEL UNLIMITED! --WIL
THIS IS THE BEGINNING OF OUR RELATIONSHIP. THEY'RE NOT READY TO KNOW ALL THAT WE CAN DO JUST YET.
BUT PERHAPS WAKANDA AND THE WORLD CAN LEARN FROM ONE ANOTHER.
THE BEGINNING...

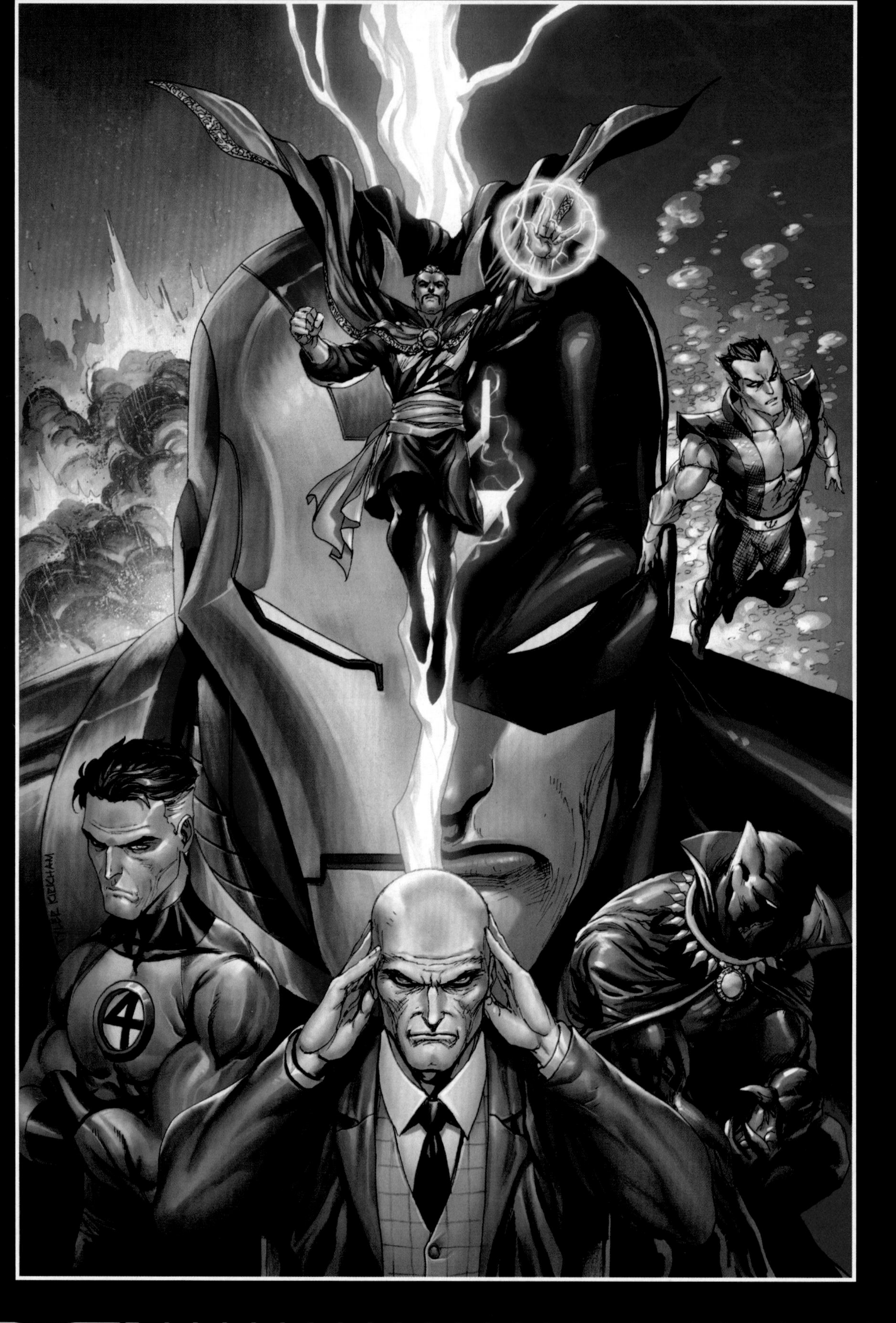
TYLER KIRKHAM

#1 ILLUMINATI VARIANT BY **TYLER KIRKHAM** & **ARIF PRIANTO**

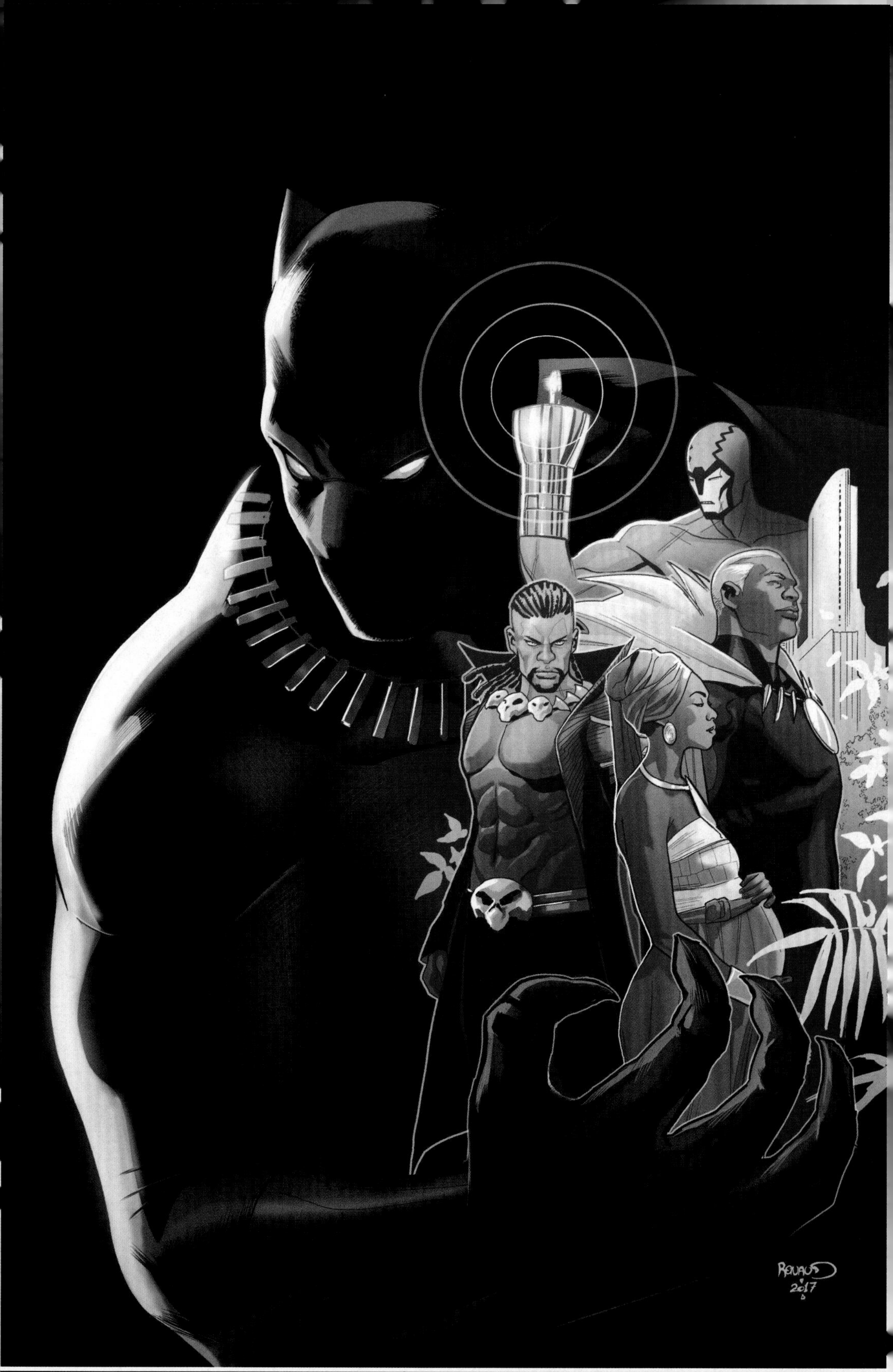
RENAUD
2017

#1 VARIANT BY **PAUL RENAUD**

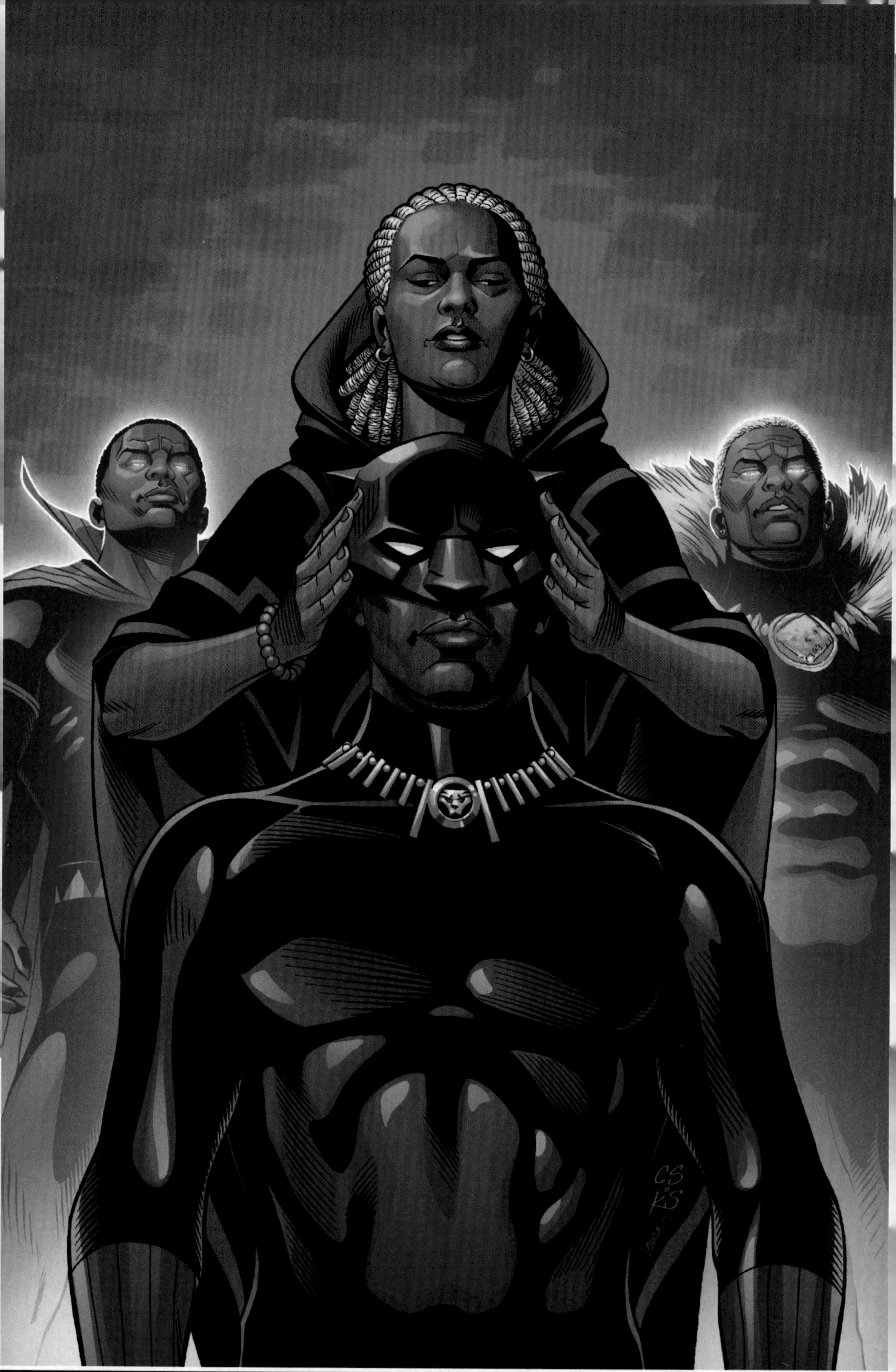

#1 VARIANT BY **CHRIS SPROUSE**

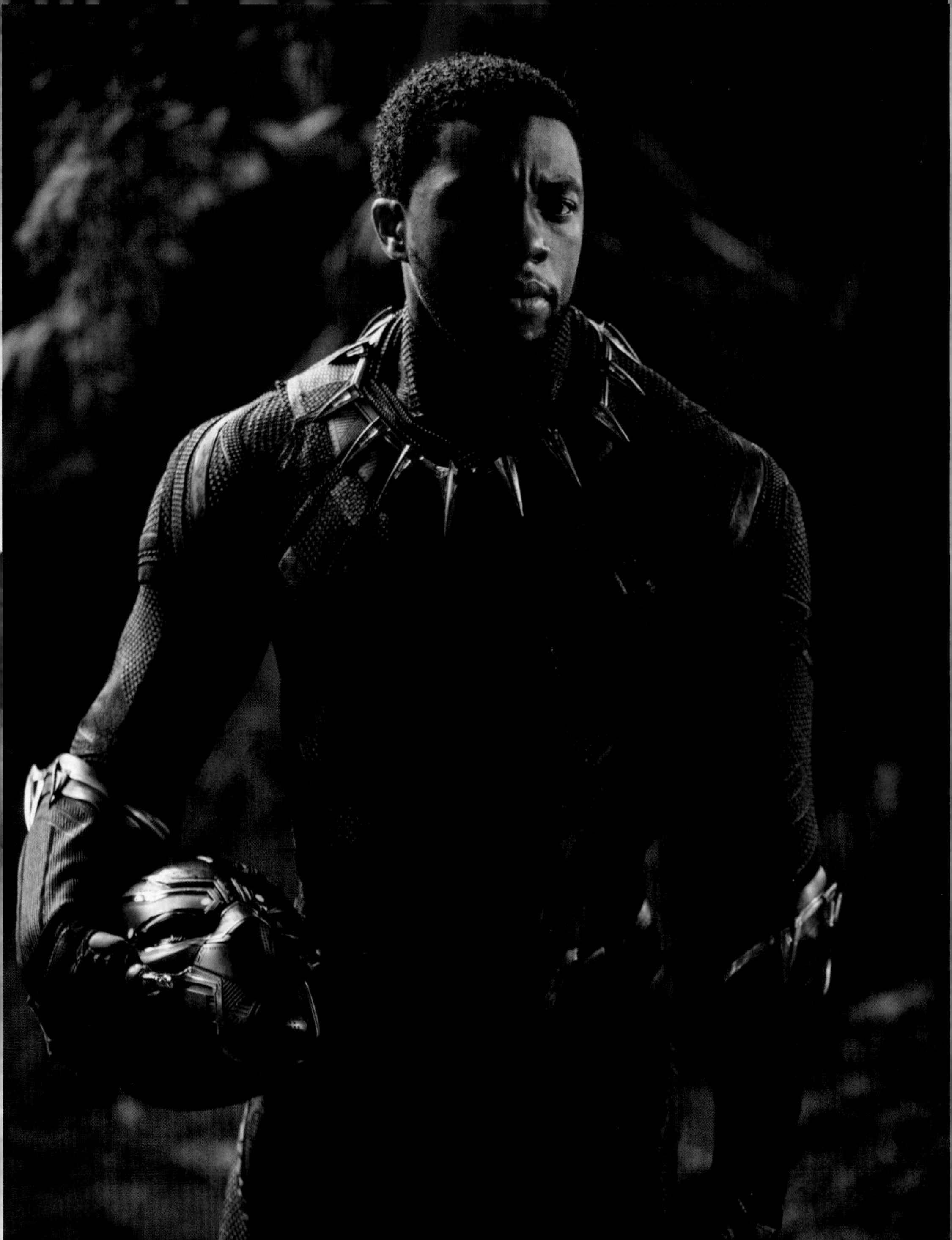

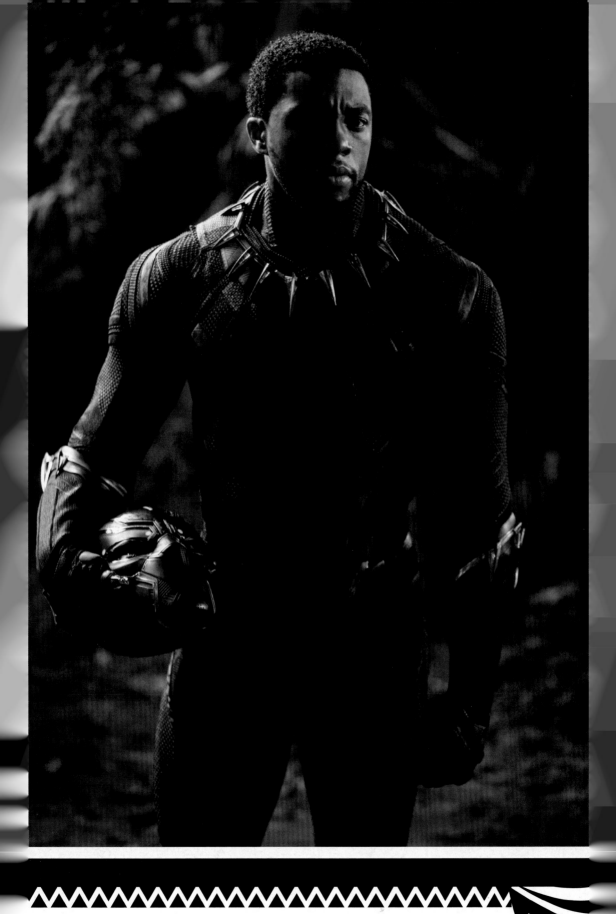

#1 MOVIE VARIANT

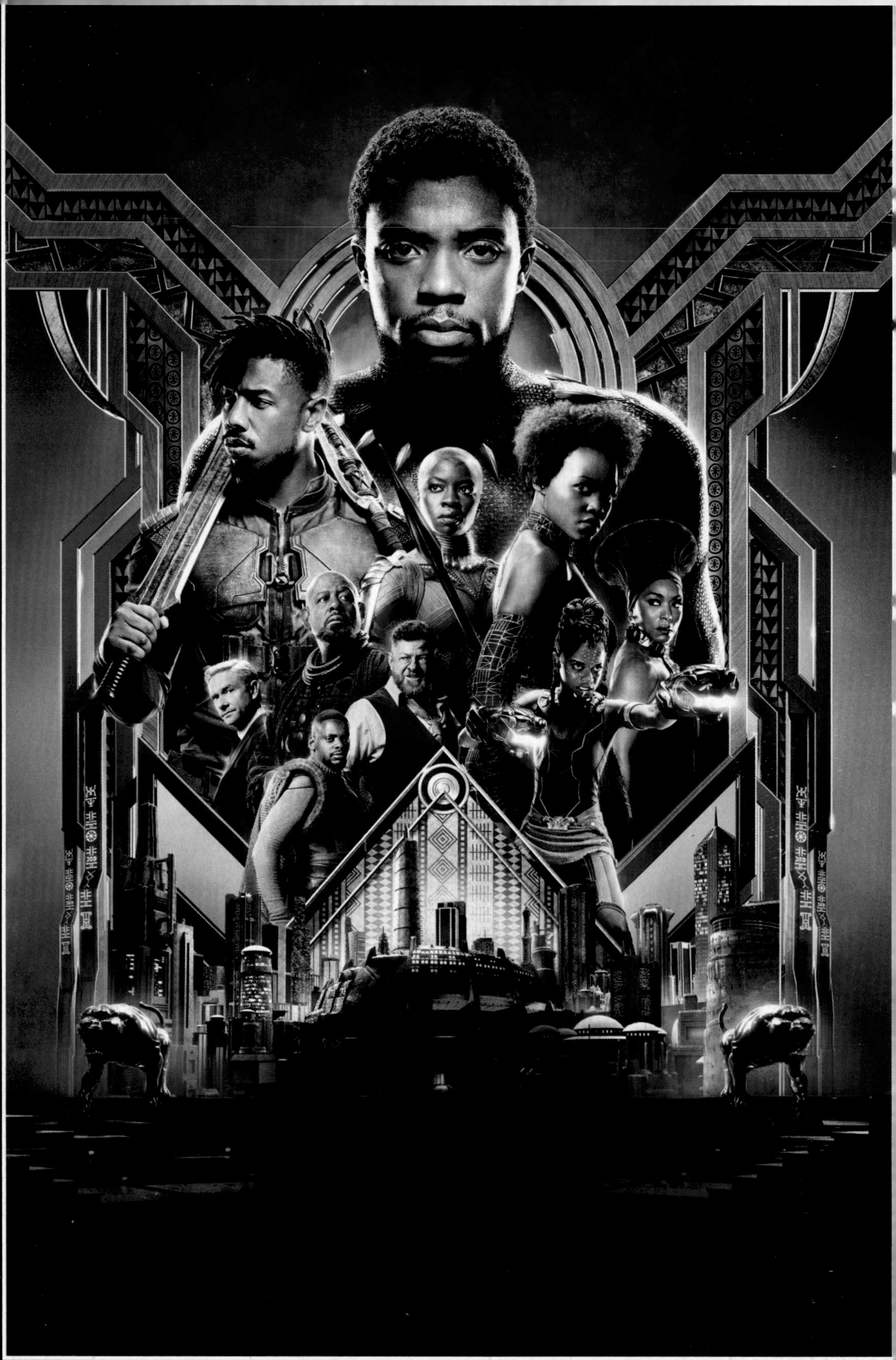

#2 MOVIE VARIANT